Poisons

Poisons

An Introduction for Forensic Investigators

by

David J. George, PhD

CRC Press
Taylor & Francis Group
Boca Raton London New York

CRC Press is an imprint of the
Taylor & Francis Group, an **informa** business

Cover: The flowers of the Monkshood plant (*Aconitum napellus*) resemble the hood of a monk's robe. It is extremely toxic due to its content of aconitine which has an estimated human lethal dose of about 2 mg.

CRC Press
Taylor & Francis Group
6000 Broken Sound Parkway NW, Suite 300
Boca Raton, FL 33487-2742

© 2018 by Taylor & Francis Group, LLC
CRC Press is an imprint of Taylor & Francis Group, an Informa business

No claim to original U.S. Government works

Printed on acid-free paper

International Standard Book Number-13: 978-1-4987-0382-6 (Hardback)

Library of Congress Cataloging-in-Publication Data

Names: George, David J., author.
Title: Poisons : an introduction for forensic investigators / by David J. George.
Description: Boca Raton : CRC Press, [2018] | Includes bibliographical references and index.
Identifiers: LCCN 2017020197| ISBN 9781498703826 (hardback : alk. paper) | ISBN 9781315371757 (ebook)
Subjects: LCSH: Poisons. | Poisoning. | Accidental poisoning.
Classification: LCC RA1211 .G465 2018 | DDC 615.9--dc23
LC record available at https://lccn.loc.gov/2017020197

**Visit the Taylor & Francis Web site at
http://www.taylorandfrancis.com**

**and the CRC Press Web site at
http://www.crcpress.com**

Printed and bound in the United States of America by
Edwards Brothers Malloy on sustainably sourced paper

To:
Ashleigh
Betsy
Cary
Catherine
Chase
Lauren
Macy
Nolan
Quentin
Rachel
Skylar
Tucker
Zachary

Contents

Section II

POTENTIAL POISONS

Preface

The subject of poisons and poisoning is usually included in the training of medical professionals and forensic toxicologists. The focus for medical professionals is on the diagnosis and treatment of poisoned patients; the focus for forensic toxicologists is on the detection and quantitation of poisons in both living and deceased individuals. Forensic investigators are involved in the process of gathering various kinds of evidence and information to support or refute theories, and providing fact-based explanations for incidents with possible forensic significance. Investigative efforts are directed toward the description and documentation of crimes, identification and arrest of the perpetrators, and the collection of evidence to support any legal action indicated. Investigations are typically group efforts involving law enforcement agencies, medical examiners and coroners offices, and legal teams. The material in this book is intended to supplement established investigative functions and procedures.

The primary goal of this book is to raise awareness of the expansive scope of poisoning possibilities for forensic investigators. A wide range of poisoning situations are presented, which could be encountered by investigators.

Excessive exposure to any chemical substance can be harmful to health and ultimately may lead to death. Essentially any chemical can be poisonous. This includes drugs, medicines, food constituents, pesticides, and all other chemicals, whether natural or man-made. The array of poisons and the circumstances of their use can have far-reaching forensic implications. Poisoning, whether intentional or accidental, can occur in a wide variety of situations and circumstances. Death can result from exposure to toxicants such as arsenic, strychnine, or cyanide as well as excessive amounts of common items such as drinking water, table salt, and other substances found in homes and workplaces not typically thought of as poisons or potentially toxic.

Poisoning possibilities are illustrated with real cases. Cases contain information on the toxicant involved, aspects of the investigative approaches, and outcomes, but it is the situations and circumstances that are of most importance. Similar cases could involve different toxicants and have different outcomes.

This book is an introduction. It is intended to assist investigators with recognizing the possibility of poisoning and provide general guidance for investigative direction. Hopefully, it will be useful to individuals with diverse educational backgrounds and experiences, and serve as a stepping stone to more detailed information on specific aspects of poisoning cases.

Author

Dr. David J. George is a clinical toxicologist and general pharmacologist with broad interests and extensive experience in both academia and the pharmaceutical industry. He was senior director of Regulatory Toxicology and senior director of Technical Affairs at Wyeth Consumer Healthcare in Madison, New Jersey. Prior to joining the pharmaceutical industry, he was an associate clinical professor (Pharmacology–Toxicology), director of the Center for Human Toxicology, and associate director of the Intermountain Regional Poison Control Center at the University of Utah, Salt Lake City, Utah. More recently, Dr. George was an adjunct professor (Clinical Toxicology) in the Division of Criminal Forensic Studies at Florida Gulf Coast University, Fort Myers, Florida. He participates in continuing education programs and lectures on poisoning, emergency toxicology, and chemical terrorism for crime scene investigators and emergency medical responders. He has a BS (Pharmacy) and an MS (Pharmacology) from the Ohio State University, Columbus, Ohio, and a PhD (Pharmacology) from the University of Utah. He has been honored by the Ohio State University with a Distinguished Alumni Award. He has served on various committees in trade organizations and professional societies including the International Life Sciences Institute, the Council for Responsible Nutrition, the Consumer Healthcare Product Association, and the United States Pharmacopeia Division of Information Development. He is a fellow of the American Academy of Clinical Toxicology, and a member of the American Society of Addiction Medicine, the American College of Medical Toxicology, the American Association of Poison Control Centers, the European Association of Poisons Centers and Clinical Toxicologists, the International Association for Forensic Toxicologists, the International Association for Identification, the Roundtable of Toxicology Consultants, and the Society of Toxicology. He lives in Boulder, Colorado.

Poison

I

Poisons are probably best defined by what they do rather than what they are. When aspirin is stored in a medicine cabinet, one might be reluctant to call or label aspirin as a poison. However, when consumed in large quantities resulting in salicylate poisoning, aspirin is clearly a poison. This type of ambiguity does not pose problems when discussing substances such as cyanide. Accordingly, the terms *poison, toxicant,* and *poisoning* should not be considered as limiting descriptors. All chemical substances can be considered potential toxicants, and poison and poisoning can be viewed from a perspective of cause and effect.

The material reviewed in this section provides a conceptual framework for thinking about poisons and poisoning from an investigative point of view. Poisons are considered very broadly as virtually any chemical that produces toxic results. This approach is intended to create a heightened awareness of poisoning potential while providing guidance for targeting investigative approaches to practical and realistic possibilities in given situations.

There are many portals for chemical substances to enter the body, each having characteristics that can influence the effects produced by the substance. Following absorption, drugs and other potential toxicants circulate within the body to reach susceptible organ sites where they alter physiological functions. The duration of the life cycle of a toxicant within the body is governed by its rate of metabolism and elimination through excretory paths such as the urinary system. General features of the absorption, distribution, metabolism, and excretion of toxicants are reviewed in this introductory section.

An overview of the analytic detection of toxicants is provided. The utility and capabilities of laboratory analyses are reviewed without any technical description of instrumentation and procedures to acquaint investigators with sufficient information to facilitate interaction with analytical laboratories both in providing material for analysis and in interpreting testing results.

Poison and Poisoning

1

1.1 Introduction

Poisons are chemical substances that are capable of causing illness or death. Excessive amounts of almost any substance can be poisonous. This would include therapeutic agents, drugs of abuse, industrial chemicals, botanical substances, venoms, and pesticides in addition to notorious poisons such as arsenic, strychnine, and cyanide. It is the amount (dose) of a substance that makes it a poison. Most often, the term *poison* is applied to substances that can be lethal to humans in relatively small doses. In forensics, poisons are considered in an expanded context that includes chemicals that can be used to modify behavior to achieve criminal goals. More formal definitions for a poison can be found in various statutes and regulations that deal with the use, labeling, and other issues relative to the availability of potentially toxic substances and public health.

The intrinsic toxicity of chemical substances as well as the circumstances and consequences of their use are important features of comprehensive forensic poisoning investigations. The focus of this chapter is on the potency of poisons, the mechanisms involved in toxic effects, and the recognition of a poisoning. Information is also provided on the incidence of mortality and morbidity due to poisoning viewed within the context of other health problems. Case studies illustrate various aspects of poisoning and provide examples in which poisoning may be involved. These cases are brief summaries of real cases that have occurred. The first consideration in these cases should be on the circumstances of the poisoning. These circumstances may very well apply to similar cases involving different poisons and have different outcomes.

1.2 Poisons

1.2.1 Potency

Potency is an extremely important characteristic of poisons. It reflects the quantity of a toxicant that produces toxicity or death. The smaller the toxic

Table 1.1 Lethal Dose of Some Poisons in One Gram

Poison	Human Lethal Dose[a]	Lethal Doses per Gram[b]
Thallium	1000 mg	1
Sodium fluoroacetate	500 mg	2
Cyanide	200 mg	5
Arsenic	200 mg	5
Strychnine	100 mg	10
Colchicine	60 mg	16
Nicotine	45 mg	22
Tetramine	10 mg	100
Aconite	2 mg	500
Botulinum toxin	50 ng	20,000,000

[a] Lethal doses are estimations and differ depending on the individual characteristics and exposure circumstances.

[b] 1 gram equals 1000 mg, which can be visualized as the amount of artificial sweetener contained in the familiar commercial single-use pink packets. Each of these packets contains 1000 mg of sweetener. This amount can be visualized as the size of 5 lethal doses of cyanide. Similarly, this amount would represent 500 lethal doses of aconite.

dose of a substance, the higher the potency. For example, tetramine, with an estimated human lethal dose of 10 mg, is 100 times more potent than thallium, which has an estimated lethal dose of 1000 mg. The lethal doses of several poisons are shown in Table 1.1. Small quantities of potent poisons have the potential to poison numerous individuals. In addition, high potency facilitates utilization for suicide and homicide, and presents a hazard for serious accidental exposures.

1.2.2 Mechanisms

Poisons modify or disrupt physiological functions through numerous mechanisms. Toxic manifestations occur because of the alteration of a critical step in the sequential processes necessary for organ-system function. For example, the lethal effects of some poisons are due to interference with oxygen availability or utilization within the body. In the lungs, oxygen diffuses from alveoli into pulmonary capillaries where it binds to hemoglobin in blood for transportation to cells throughout the body. Toxicants that interfere with components of this oxygen utilization pathway are provided in Table 1.2. Examples of other mechanisms involved in toxicity are listed in Table 1.3. Depending on the particular mechanisms involved, toxic effects can be localized to a particular organ system or can involve the whole body.

Table 1.2 Examples of Poisons That Interfere with Oxygen Availability and Utilization

Poison	Action
Inert gases • Helium • Nitrogen • Methane • Carbon dioxide	Displace oxygen from inspired air (asphyxiation)
Opioids	Depress respiratory center in CNS, which controls respiratory muscles (respiratory failure)
Succinylcholine	Paralyzes respiratory muscles (respiratory failure)
Strychnine	Causes sustained contraction of respiratory muscles (respiratory failure)
Carbon monoxide	Binds to hemoglobin, which blocks oxygen binding and transport
Cyanide	Prevents transfer (uptake) of oxygen from hemoglobin to cells

Table 1.3 Molecular Toxicology of Some Poisons

Aconite	Constituent of Monkshood Plant
	Interferes with sodium ions in the depolarization–repolarization of excitable tissue in cardiac and skeletal muscles.
Arsenic	Natural Chemical Element
	Binds to sulfhydryl groups on enzymes, which disrupts metabolic pathways for mitochondrial energy production and storage. Replaces phosphate in ATP molecules, which interferes with cellular metabolism.
Acetaminophen	Analgesic and Antipyretic
	Toxic doses overwhelm the liver's metabolic capacity to metabolize acetaminophen to nontoxic metabolites for urinary excretion. The accumulation of a toxic metabolite destroys liver cells.
Botulinum toxin	Toxin from *Clostridium botulinum*
	Binds to nerve terminals preventing the release of acetylcholine, which is necessary for muscle contraction.
Carbon monoxide	Combustion Product
	Binds to hemoglobin molecules in blood. This prevents oxygen molecules from binding to hemoglobin and being transported to the tissues.
Cocaine	Plant Constituent
	Blocks reuptake of neurotransmitters into nerve terminals, which results in the accumulation of neurotransmitters in nerve synapses producing exaggerated stimulation. Also constricts blood vessels causing ischemia and possible myocardial infarction.

(Continued)

Table 1.3 (*Continued*) Molecular Toxicology of Some Poisons

Coniine	Constituent of Poison Hemlock Plant
	Blocks nerve receptors in skeletal muscles, which cause paralysis of respiratory muscles.
Cyanide	Chemical Compound
	Inhibits oxygen uptake by cells.
Ethylene glycol	Chemical Used as an Automotive Coolant
	Metabolizes to glycolic acid and oxalic acid, which acidifies body fluids, and forms calcium oxalate crystals that damage kidneys and other organs.
Ethanol	Beverage
	Inhibits the function of the respiratory control centers in the CNS.
Fentanyl	Opioid Analgesic
	Inhibits the function of the respiratory control center in the CNS.
Nicotine	Constituent of Tobacco Plant
	Stimulates CNS to produce seizures and coma, and stimulates skeletal muscle contractions that result in sustained respiratory muscle contraction.
Organophosphates	Insecticide and Nerve Gases
	Inactivate enzyme that metabolizes acetylcholine. This leads to the accumulation of acetylcholine in nerve synapses and intensified cholinergic stimulation.
Ricin	Constituent of Castor Beans
	Prevents cellular synthesis of structural proteins and new enzymes essential for cellular function.
Strychnine	Constituent of Strychnine Tree
	Blocks inhibitory neuronal transmission leading to continued stimulation of skeletal muscles that progress to sustained generalized seizures that prevent breathing.
Thallium	Natural Chemical Element
	Substitutes for potassium. Blocks conduction of nerve impulses and metabolic processes that require potassium.

1.3 Poisoning

Poisoning can result from accidental, suicidal, or homicidal exposure to toxicants. Following the recognition of a poisoning incident, the goal of the investigative process is to collect information and evidence to support a determination of the manner by which the poisoning occurred.

Table 1.4 Indicators of Possible Poisoning

- Sudden or unexpected death in an otherwise healthy individual
- Death with no signs of trauma
- Diseases which fail to respond to appropriate treatment
- Unexplained illnesses that recur in cycles
- Similar symptoms occurring simultaneously in others
- Disease progression deviates from the expected course
- Unexplained altered consciousness

1.3.1 Recognition

Poisoning symptoms are generally not specific, and can be difficult to distinguish from symptoms associated with common medical disorders and diseases. The history of an individual and the circumstances surrounding an illness or death are often the basis for the initial consideration of possible poisoning. Some indicators of the possibility of poisoning are listed in Table 1.4.

Deaths that are sudden or unexpected with no obvious explanation are often attributed to some type of heart disease. When an autopsy is conducted, it is not uncommon to determine that the death was related to causes other than heart disease. These other causes include poisoning. Whether intentional or unintentional, poisoning can easily be missed if there are no circumstantial reasons to suspect it.

Poisoning of any nature might be overlooked when it occurs in individuals who are known to have an increased susceptibility to various illnesses, or who are in situations in which illnesses are not common but occasionally occur. This might include elderly individuals, hospitalized patients of any age, and residents of long-term health care facilities. Not all deaths have autopsies, not all death investigations include toxicology tests, and toxicological testing does not include all poisons.

1.3.2 Morbidity and Mortality in Context

Although accidents of various kinds are one of the leading causes of death in the United States, poisoning tops the list of causes of accidental deaths. Suicide and homicide are also among the leading causes of death and poisoning and are among the most common lethal methods employed. When viewed from a local jurisdictional perspective, the high incidence and impact of poisoning may or may not be evident. A comparison of the frequency of poisoning deaths to other causes is provided in Table 1.5. When viewing this type of statistical ranking, it is important to keep in mind that the items are ranked according to incidence data, and there can be relatively small differences between individual items. The position of such a listing is not as significant as the fact that these are the leading causes of death.

Table 1.5 Poisoning Deaths in the United States[a]

Leading Causes of Death	Leading Causes of Accidental Deaths
1. Heart disease	1. *Poisoning*
2. Cancer	2. Automobile accidents
3. Stroke	3. Falls
4. Respiratory disease	4. Drowning
5. *Accidents*	5. Fires
6. Alzheimer's disease	6. Suffocation
7. Diabetes	7. Firearms
8. Influenza	8. *Poison gases*
9. Kidney Disease	9. Medical complications
10. Septicemia	10. Machinery
11. *Suicide*	
12. Liver disease	
13. Hypertension	
14. Parkinson's disease	
15. *Homicide*	

Most Common Methods for Suicide	Most Common Methods for Homicide
1. Firearms	1. Firearms
2. Suffocations/Hanging	2. Knives
3. *Poisoning*	3. Punching/Beating
4. Falls	4. Blunt objects
5. Cutting	5. Strangulation
6. Drowning	6. *Poisoning*
	7. Fire
	8. Drowning
	9. *Poison gases*
	10. Explosives

[a] Based on the latest data available (2013) from the U.S. Center for Disease Control and Prevention.

The number of poisonings that occur annually is difficult to estimate. For example, approximately 2 million poison exposures are identified each year by poison centers in the United States. These exposures are recorded because a poison center was contacted for assistance in diagnosing and managing a particular exposure, but many common types of poisoning are managed without any poison center assistance. Based on poison center contacts, hospital emergency department reports of poisoning, suicides, and attempted suicides using toxic substances, and information from death certificates, the total number of poisonings that occur annually appears to be several million.

1.4 Case Studies

Case: Water

In 2007, a 28-year-old medical secretary living in California with her husband and three children entered a water-drinking contest sponsored by a local radio station. Along with about 18 other contestants, she began drinking 8-oz bottles of water every 15 min starting at around 9 a.m. The contestant who could drink the most water without using the restroom would receive a popular video-game system. The contest lasted for about 3 h, and the secretary finished in second place. Toward the end of the contest she was feeling nauseous and developed a severe headache. She drove home to recuperate. She was found dead in her home by her mother at around 2 p.m. that same day. The cause of death was hyponatremia due to water intoxication. No criminal charges were filed, but several radio station employees lost their jobs and the secretary's family was awarded several million dollars in a wrongful death suit.

Comments

The concentration of sodium in body fluids is normally maintained in a critical range. Either an increase or a decrease in sodium levels can have serious medical consequences. When very large amounts of water are consumed, there is a drop in plasma sodium concentration (hyponatremia) because the increased volume of fluid dilutes the sodium. Hyponatremia can cause headache, nausea, dizziness, and muscle weakness that may progress to hallucinations, seizures, coma, and death. Water intoxication-related deaths caused by intentional or forced water consumption are rare. Situations in which this might occur include fraternity hazing, child abuse, water diets, endurance sports, and in some psychiatric and metabolic disorders. Individuals using stimulant drugs in prolonged rave situations can lose large amounts of fluids through perspiration and, in an effort to compensate for this fluid loss, can drink excessive amounts of water leading to hyponatremia.

Case: Potato Salad

A 41-year-old otherwise healthy man was admitted to a hospital because of an acute onset of nausea and vomiting. The only abnormalities identified with standard laboratory testing were elevated liver enzymes. His condition improved and he was discharged a few days later. About 4 months later, he was readmitted to the hospital when he again developed nausea and vomiting accompanied by profuse diarrhea and severe abdominal pain.

He felt that his symptoms were due to food poisoning from some questionable potato salad eaten the previous day. He was dehydrated and laboratory testing again revealed only elevated liver enzyme levels. Some abnormalities were noted on ECG tracings. On the second hospital day, he became short of breath and had a seizure that was followed by a cardiopulmonary arrest, which was unresponsive to resuscitation efforts. No anatomic abnormalities to account for his death were identified at autopsy, and a toxicology screen of antemortem serum was negative. His death was determined to be due to cardiac arrest from undetermined natural causes. Months later, it became known to police that the man's wife had purchased a large amount of colchicine from a chemical supply store prior to the man's hospital admissions and death. This information triggered a death investigation that included a review of autopsy slides, and toxicology testing of retained serum and tissue samples. High levels of colchicine were found in serum, kidney, and liver specimens and histological alterations consistent with colchicine toxicity were identified in the autopsy slides. Ultimately, the wife was tried and convicted of intentional homicide.

Comments

Colchicine is an extremely potent toxicant obtained from plants. It is used in clinical medicine to treat several conditions, the most common being gout. It is also used in certain types of cellular biological research. Colchicine is responsible for the toxicity of some common plants (e.g., Meadow Saffron and Glory Lilly), and it is used occasionally for both suicide and homicide. Unless there is some suspicion for possible colchicine poisoning, its detection in routine toxicology testing is unlikely.

Case: Methadone

In 2013, a previously healthy 11-month-old boy was found dead in his bed by his mother. There were no signs of trauma, and autopsy findings were indicative of death from respiratory failure. The initial impression was that the death could best be categorized as sudden infant death syndrome; however, postmortem toxicology testing identified methadone and its metabolites in all fluids and tissues analyzed. Both of the child's parents had a criminal history and both were currently enrolled in a methadone maintenance treatment program. The child had two siblings (aged 5 and 15 years). All family members underwent drug testing and only the parents were positive for methadone, heroin, and cocaine. Based on the relative concentrations of methadone and its metabolite in postmortem specimens (blood, gastric contents, urine, and bile), it was concluded that the child's death was caused by an acute oral dose of methadone. Further investigation indicated that the methadone was self-administered by the child who obtained it from an unattended liquid methadone container accessible to the child in his baby walker. For their contributory negligence, each parent received a 6-month prison sentence.

Comments

Children living in homes where active substance abuse is occurring are at a heightened risk for accidental poisoning because of the availability of toxic substances and the negligent behaviors of caregivers. However, accidental poisoning in children due to the accessibility of medications is also relatively common. This typically occurs when medications are removed from safe storage by adults for use and the adult becomes distracted, or are otherwise delayed in replacing the medication to a child-safe location. The case presented highlights the potential lethality of methadone in children, but there are a number of adult medications that are as lethal to children as methadone.

Case: Cancer

In 2000, a 30-year-old mother of two children called emergency responders after beating and stabbing her 33-year-old husband, allegedly as an act of self-defense. Paramedics found the husband dead in a pool of blood.

Two years prior to his death, the husband had been diagnosed with terminal cancer and was unable to work. This required the wife to work full time to support the family. Unhappy and discontented with the situation, the wife began frequenting local bars and having extramarital affairs. She eventually decided to kill her husband and profit from his insurance. She researched various poisons and discreet methods for attaining them. This led her to purchase sodium azide, which she purchased from a chemical supply company and began adding to her husband's food and medications. She attempted to purchase life insurance for her husband without disclosing his terminal illness. To do this, she solicited a friend to pose as her husband and undergo the physical examination required by the insurance company. However, her efforts to acquire insurance were unsuccessful, so she began to devise a scheme to bring a malpractice suit against the physicians treating her husband. She apparently became impatient with the length of time the lethal poisoning was requiring and she killed her husband in a fit of rage. The cause of death was determined to be due to the beating and stabbing injuries. Sodium azide was identified in postmortem specimens of blood and gastric contents, and in prepared food samples and containers from the home. The sodium azide container and shipping package were recovered; all contained the wife's fingerprints. Evidence from the murder scene indicated that the husband was lying down when he was beaten and stabbed and was most likely too weak from the poisoning and chemotherapy to defend himself. The wife was tried and convicted of first-degree murder and sentenced to death.

Comments

Sodium azide interferes with the cellular utilization of oxygen. It is odorless and tasteless and water soluble. Symptoms of poisoning can begin with hypotension, dizziness, and labored breathing and can progress to seizures, coma, arrhythmias, and cardiorespiratory arrest. In this case, the victim was severely ill and experiencing side effects from chemotherapy. Had he not been beaten and stabbed, it is likely that his increasing deterioration and death from sodium azide poisoning would have been attributed to his terminal illness.

Case: Muscle Liniment

In 2007, a 17-year-old female track star died in New York because of extreme use of sports creams and liniments for muscle aches and pains due to a grueling training program. Her death resulted from the regular use of these products on her legs in excessive amounts from which toxic quantities of methyl salicylate (oil of wintergreen) were absorbed over a period of days. A death investigation determined that her death was accidental and caused by salicylate poisoning.

Comments

There are many commercial creams and liniments containing methyl salicylate. When used as directed by the product label, these liniments are not likely to produce salicylate poisoning. In this case, multiple products were used excessively with respect to the amounts used, the frequency of use, and the surface areas treated. Other factors that might have increased absorption in this case would include wrapping areas with elastic bandages after application and the use of heating pads.

Case: Cherry Trees, Caterpillars, and Race Horses

In 2001, cyanide caused more than 500 stillbirths or deaths of newborn thoroughbred foals in Kentucky. The cyanide came from black cherry trees and was passed on to mares by caterpillars. Cyanide (from cyanogenic glycosides) became concentrated in dry cherry leaves due to a hot, early spring followed by a freeze and drought. Caterpillars feasted on the leaves and then contaminated (cyanide-laden caterpillars plus their toxic feces) the pastures and water tanks used by the pregnant mares. An additional component of the caterpillars' toxicity was the barbed hair-like outer skin of the caterpillars that apparently penetrated the intestinal lining of the horses and facilitated bacterial invasion of internal organs. This was a multimillion-dollar tragedy and required many scientists and veterinarians from around the world to identify the toxic mechanisms involved.

Comments

Cyanogenic glycosides are present in a number of plants. When plants containing these compounds are ingested, the digestive processes cause liberation of cyanide from these glycosides.

Case: Scorpions

In 2015, a previously healthy 12-month-old girl was taken to the emergency department of a hospital in Arizona where she became irritable, started sweating, and twitching began throughout her body. She had a rapid heart rate and was hyperventilating. There were decrements in eye-movement control, and excessive salivation. Externally, there were no signs of trauma, skin lesions, bruises, or bites. The girl's symptoms and the environment where this occurred suggested that the child had been stung by a scorpion. The child's mother indicated that scorpions had been observed multiple times in their home. The child was administered the appropriate scorpion antivenom, which resulted in noticeable improvement, but tachycardia and tremors continued and she developed a fever. Subsequently, it became known that there was a history of methamphetamine use in the child's home. This led to a urine drug screening that was positive for methamphetamine. The child was then treated symptomatically with a benzodiazepine and IV fluids until her symptoms normalized. Additional evaluations were conducted to rule out possible complications from the methamphetamine ingestion. An investigation by a social services team was also initiated. The child was discharged on hospital day 8. Confirmatory toxicology testing results became available several weeks after discharge. High blood levels of methamphetamine and amphetamine were identified.

Comments

This case illustrates the difficulty that can arise in the clinical diagnosis of toxic exposures in certain circumstances. When a diagnosed clinical condition fails to respond to conventional therapy, it may indicate that the diagnosis was inaccurate and other possibilities should be pursued.

Case: Dimethylmercury

In 1997, a 48-year-old chemistry professor began having episodes of nausea, diarrhea, and abdominal cramps. Over a 2-month period she lost approximately 15 pounds. She then noticed a progressive deterioration in her ability to walk and talk. She was subsequently admitted to a university medical center hospital for evaluation. This chemist worked in a research laboratory that was principally involved in studies of metals toxicity. She was familiar with the symptoms of metal poisoning and recalled that about 6 months prior to her hospital admission she had spilled, onto her gloved hand, a few drops of dimethylmercury when removing it from a container for use in an experiment. Blood and urine testing for mercury revealed levels that were significantly elevated. Her neurological deterioration continued until she was unresponsive to all visual, verbal, and tactile stimuli at about 6 months after exposure. She was treated with general supportive measures that included chelation therapy. She died approximately 1 year after the dimethylmercury exposure. Autopsy findings identified extensive neurologic changes consistent with mercury toxicity, and elevated levels of mercury were found in all samples tested (blood, brain, liver, bile, kidney, hair). The death resulted from a single brief exposure to a few drops of dimethylmercury that penetrated disposable latex gloves.

Comments

Dimethylmercury is an extremely toxic substance that can be absorbed dermally. After exposure, it is necessary to start treatment immediately, even though toxic symptoms may not be evident for weeks. When this incident occurred, dimethylmercury was a common standard for calibrating laboratory instruments. Following this case, safety recommendations were revised and the use of dimethylmercury for any purpose was strongly discouraged.

Mercury has significant toxic potential in all physical and chemical forms. The vapor from elemental metal mercury, inorganic mercury salts, and organic mercury compounds are all toxic and are capable of producing organ-system damage, which is usually most apparent as disturbances in kidney function and neurological degeneration.

References and Additional Reading

Blum D: *The Poisoner's Handbook: Murder and the Birth of Forensic Medicine in Jazz Age New York.* New York: Penguin Press, 2010.

Brubacher JR, Hoffman RS: Salicylism from topical salicylates: Review of the literature. *Clin Toxicol*, 34: 431–436, 1996.

Chang S, Lamm SH: Human health effects of sodium azide exposure: A literature review and analysis. *Int J Toxicol*, 22: 175–186, 2003.

Emsley J: *The Elements of Murder: A History of Poison*. New York: Oxford University Press, 2005.

Farrell DJ, Bower L: Fatal water intoxication. *J Clin Pathol*, 56: 803–804, 2003.

Ferner RE: *Forensic Pharmacology: Medicines, Mayhem, and Malpractice*. New York: Oxford University Press, 1996.

Frank P, Ottoboni MA: *The Dose Makes the Poison: A Plain-Language Guide to Toxicology*. Hoboken, NJ: John Wiley, 2011.

Levy J: *Poison: An Illustrated History*. Gulford, CT: Lyons Press, 2011.

Macinnis P: *Poisons: A History from Hemlock to Botox*. New York: MJF Books, 2004.

Mowry JB, Spyker DA, Brooks DE, Zimmerman A, Schauben JL: 2015 Annual report of the American Association of Poison Control Centers' National Poison Data System (NPDS): 33rd Annual Report. *Clin Toxicol*, 54: 924–1109, 2016.

Nierenberg DW, Nordgren RE, Chang MB, Siegler RW, Blayney MB, Hochberg F, Toribara TY, Cernichiari E, Clarkson T: Delayed cerebrellar disease and death after accidental exposure to dimethylmercury. *N Engl J Med*, 338: 1672–1676, 1998.

Palmiere C, Staub C, LaHarpe R, Mangin P: Parental substance abuse and accidental death in children. *J Forensic Sci*, 55: 819–821, 2010.

Reichl F-X, Ritter L: *Illustrated Handbook of Toxicology*. New York: Thieme, 2011.

Stone T, Darlington G: *Pills, Potions, Poisons: How Drugs Work*. New York: Oxford University Press, 2000.

Strommen J, Shirazi F: Methamphetamine ingestion misdiagnosed as *Centruroides sculpturatus* envenomation. *Case Rep Emerg Med*, #320574, 2015.

Timbrell J: *The Poison Paradox: Chemicals as Friends and Foes*. New York: Oxford University Press, 2005.

Tournel G, Pollard J, Humbert L, Wiart J-F, Hedouin V, Allorge D: Use of hair testing to determine methadone exposure in pediatric deaths. *J Forensic Sci*, 59: 1436–1440, 2014.

Weakley-Jones B, Gerger JE, Biggs G: Colchicine poisoning: Case report of two homicides. *Am J Forensic Med Pathol*, 22: 203–206, 2001.

Zhang Y, Su M, Tian DP: Tetramine poisoning: A case report and review of the literature. *Forensic Sci Int*, 204: 24–27, 2011.

Poison Exposure

2

2.1 Introduction

Poisoning starts with an exposure to a potential toxicant. The toxicant subsequently comes into contact with target sites in the body to produce toxic alterations in vital functions. The life of a toxicant in the body is divided into four different phases: (1) absorption, (2) distribution, (3) metabolism, and (4) excretion. Absorption refers to the transfer of a substance from a site of exposure into the circulatory system. Distribution includes the circulation of a toxicant throughout the body and selective partitioning into various fluids and tissues. In the metabolic phase, toxicants are biochemically altered. This can increase or decrease their toxic potential and can modify their solubility, which facilitates elimination. Parent substances as well as metabolites usually leave the body through the urine, but elimination pathways can include sweat, feces, and expiratory gases.

The degree of exposure (i.e., how much) of a potential toxicant is a key component of causality determinations. The focus of this chapter is on some general quantitative aspects of exposures to individual and multiple toxicants.

2.2 Dose

The level of toxicity produced by a toxicant is generally proportional to the dose (exposure). The greater the exposure, the greater the toxicity. Depending on the toxic effect considered, the outcome can increase in a graded fashion with increasing doses. For example, when considering CNS depression, there is a progression of effects with increasing doses that starts with mild forms of sedation and advances through stages of sleep, coma, and death. When considering lethality, there is a singular lethal dose that is unique to a particular toxicant, and a particular individual for a given set of circumstances. Unfortunately, the term *overdose* has become a common synonym for a lethal dose. This implies that the dose involved was much greater than nonlethal doses. Overdoses involving a combination of medications are similarly often assumed to be much greater than the usual nonlethal doses. For example, consider the ingestion of several different medications each of which has a sedating effect. For illustrative purposes, suppose sedative potential could be expressed on a monetary scale. Say one capsule might be a nickel, while another is a dime, another a half-dollar and two others a quarter each, and the amount required for a lethal CNS depression dose is a dollar. If one ingests all of these medications, the total sedation is $1.15, and this is a lethal overdose. Using this analogy, the behavior of many individuals utilizing these substances suggests that their mindset is often aligned with an expectation that lethal overdoses require significantly more money. The point is that lethality can result from just a small amount over the lethal dose level. Individuals who die from unintentional overdoses do not generally take huge amounts of toxicants.

In animal toxicity testing, the lethal dose for a particular species in a given set of circumstances can be determined. This dose is most commonly expressed as a LD50 value, which is the estimated lethal dose for 50% of the test species used in its determination. These values are specific for the test species and cannot be used to extrapolate lethal doses for humans. Moreover, LD50 values determined in one species cannot even be used to extrapolate the lethal dose for another animal species.

The use of human LD50 values to express the human lethality potential of toxicants is not practical or useful. The application of an estimated dose of a substance that would be lethal to half of those exposed to the substances has little utility. In evaluating the severity of poisoning in clinical situations, estimates of LD1 or LD100 values might be ideal if such information were available. Clinicians frequently are more interested in the smallest dose of a substance that has been reported to have caused death, and the highest dose that anybody has survived. Even with this information, there is still the issue of the particular circumstances of the cases in which these doses occurred.

The lethal dose of a substance cannot be standardized. It depends on many factors related to a particular individual in particular circumstances. An estimate of the possible range of a lethal dose can be made based on the available information. Some influential factors are listed in Table 2.1. The lethal dose is the dose that is found to have caused the death under consideration. There is not a *red line* dose that defines doses above which are lethal.

**Table 2.1   Factors That Can Influence
the Response Produced by Toxicants**

Adulterants
Age
Body mass index
Body weight
Concurrent drug use
Dosage form
Dose
Dosing intervals
Gender
Health status
Route of administration
Tolerance
Withdrawal effects

2.3 Blood Levels

There are extensive compilations of reported blood levels (concentrations) of substances, which are most often grouped as therapeutic, toxic, or lethal levels. Therapeutic and toxic levels represent levels determined antemortem and can be quite useful as guides to the relevance of determinations of blood levels in living individuals. However, postmortem blood levels are seldom related to antemortem blood levels determined at the time of death. There is generally a significant overlap in the levels listed in reference compilations of therapeutic, toxic, and lethal ranges. In making comparisons of measured blood levels to reference compilations or to any individually published medical case report, the comparison values should be obtained in circumstances identical or very similar to the case under review. Individual cases can differ from one another due to postmortem changes, delayed deaths, concomitant drug exposures, and other influential factors.

There is generally a correlation between antemortem concentrations of toxicants in circulating blood and the magnitude of the effects produced. The correlation can be influenced by many factors such as tolerance and the presence of other toxicants. These factors can be important components of the interpretative process. Some potential influential factors on the effects produced by toxicants are listed in Table 2.1. Many of these factors can be overshadowed by high doses of toxicants, but some might be important in particular circumstances.

Postmortem blood levels are often not a reflection of antemortem levels and therefore usually do not provide an accurate basis for predicting what effects might have been causative in deaths. Furthermore, postmortem blood levels cannot be used to estimate the amount of toxicant involved in a lethal exposure. Postmortem blood levels cannot be interpreted solely by comparison to referenced compilations of previously reported values. They must be considered in concert with the information on the circumstances of the death, medical history, medication history, autopsy findings, and toxicology testing results from other fluids and organs.

2.4 Kinetics

The kinetic behavior of medicinal drugs following absorption is generally well known. Clinical studies carried out with medications provide compound-specific information on the time period for an agent to produce its peak effect, its duration of action, and the rate of elimination. These characteristics apply to the therapeutic situations in which medications are used to achieve treatment goals with minimal adverse effects. These pharmacokinetic features apply to dose ranges employed in clinical medicine.

Medicinal drug exposures that occur at doses higher than therapeutic doses may reflect dose-dependent changes in kinetics as well as the toxic effects on organ systems involved in biodisposition. The rates of absorption and biodisposition are based on biological processes and the capacity of those processes can be exceeded. The application of kinetic concepts in poisoning situations is extremely difficult because the dose and time of exposure are not usually known, and the kinetic characteristics of most toxicants are not known. Kinetic features of substances in doses well beyond the therapeutic dose ranges are usually referred to as toxicokinetic properties.

2.5 Multiple Substance Exposures

The combined toxicity of substances used simultaneously is characterized as being additive or synergistic. Substances with similar mechanistic actions produce cumulative or additive effects. Synergistic interactions result from combining substances that act through different mechanisms. Synergistic effects are often unpredictable and to a degree that is greater than would be expected from considering the effect of substances used individually. The mechanistic basis for some commonly encountered multiple exposures in forensic toxicity cases are described in the following sections. In evaluating multiple substance exposures, it is often best to start by considering each substance individually, and then examining the possible interactions.

2.5.1 CNS Depressants

Different classes of CNS depressants act through different mechanisms within the brain to inhibit brain activity. The resultant effect from the convergence of the mechanistic pathways can depress the CNS control of respiration, cardiac function, and consciousness. This occurs most commonly with combinations of ethanol, opioids, benzodiazepines, muscle relaxants, antihistamines, and the various types of psychotherapeutic agents.

2.5.2 Serotonergic Agents

There are many drugs that can increase active serotonin levels in the CNS. These agents may act in a variety of ways to increase serotonin to toxic levels. Major mechanisms include the following: (1) the inhibition of serotonin reuptake into the nerve terminals, (2) the inhibition of the metabolism of serotonin, and (3) the stimulation of serotonin release from nerve terminals. Combinations of serotonergic agents have the potential to produce life-threatening hyperthermia, muscle rigidity, and multiple organ failures.

2.5.3 Agents That Produce QT Prolongation

Sudden cardiac deaths are most often caused by acute ventricular arrhythmias. An important cause of ventricular arrhythmias is prolongation of ventricular repolarization, which is evident on ECG tracings as a lengthening of the QT segment. Drugs that prolong the QT interval act by blocking the potassium or sodium channels in cardiac tissue. QT prolongation can occur with the therapeutic administration of medications as well as with toxic overdoses. The concomitant administration of multiple QT-prolonging drugs can act in an additive fashion to increase the possibility of a fatal arrhythmia. The number of agents implicated in QT prolongation is large and includes some antiarrhythmics, antibiotics, antifungals, antipsychotics, antiemetics, antidepressants, antihistamines, and opioids.

2.5.4 Effects on Multiple Organ Systems

The coingestion of substances having toxic effects on different organ systems can have a collective lethal effect. For example, a death might result from the combined effect of an opioid on respiration with a cardiotoxic substance that reduces heart rate causing hypoperfusion of tissues. This can lead to multiple organ failures from hypoxia.

2.5.5 Pharmacokinetic Interactions

Pharmacokinetic interactions occur when one substance affects the absorption, distribution, metabolism, or excretion of another substance.

2.6 Case Studies

Case: Pain and Depression

In 2008, an adult male arrived at a hospital emergency department about an hour after ingesting 200 mg of methadone. He had been prescribed methadone (20 mg/day) for chronic pain. His other prescribed medications included sertraline and venlafaxine. On arrival, he had no symptoms of opioid overdose and a toxicology urine screening for common drugs of abuse was negative. He was transferred to a psychiatric unit for observation. About 4 h later, he became panicked and started hallucinating. His blood pressure, heart rate, and respiration were elevated. His condition was diagnosed as serotonin syndrome. About 10 h from the estimated initial methadone overdose he lost consciousness and aspirated stomach contents. At this time, blood pressure, heart rate, and respiration were markedly depressed. He never regained consciousness and life support was discontinued 5 days later. The cause of death was judged to be acute methadone intoxication.

Comments

Methadone was not included in the toxicology screening panel utilized by the emergency facility in this case. Serotonin syndrome is a potentially life-threatening condition that is produced by serotonergic drugs, which elevate serotonin levels at the central and peripheral serotonin receptors. This results in marked changes in mental state, neuromuscular hyperactivity, and autonomic hyperactivity. Sertraline and venlafaxine are serotonergic antidepressants that block serotonin reuptake by neurons. Methadone also blocks serotonin reuptake. In this case, toxicity resulted from serotonin syndrome and an opioid overdose.

Case: Multiple Depressants and Enzyme Inhibition

In 2015, an adult woman was found dead in her home. Her recent medical history indicated that she was being treated for an acute anxiety disorder. An autopsy revealed some generalized congestion in organs but no evidence of diseases. Postmortem toxicological testing of blood and urine identified diphenhydramine, paroxetine, phenobarbital, and

diazepam with its metabolites. Levels of diphenhydramine and paroxetine were elevated. The cause of death was concluded to be from multiple drug ingestion. Based on the drug levels, the principal factor in the
multiple drug lethality was postulated to be an excessive ingestion of
diphenhydramine.

Comments

This case involved the cumulative CNS depressant effects of four drugs:
(1) antidepressant, (2) antihistamine, (3) barbiturate, and (4) benzodiazepine. The metabolism of diphenhydramine is mediated by a cytochrome
P450 enzyme (CYP2D6) that is inhibited by paraxetine. The toxic levels of
diphenhydramine may have been due to both the high dose ingested and
the inhibition of its metabolism. The levels of phenobarbital and diazepam were each consistent with the therapeutic doses. However, these
substances would contribute to CNS depression and could play a minor
role in altering the metabolic rate of the other drugs.

References and Additional Reading

Baselt RC: *Disposition of Toxic Drugs and Chemicals in Man*, 10th ed. Seal Beach,
    CA: Biomedical Publications, 2014.
Gill JR, Lin PT, Nelson L: Reliability of postmortem fentanyl concentrations in
    determining the cause of death. *J Med Toxicol*, 9: 34–41, 2013.
Goldsmith MA, Slavik M, Carter SK: Quantitative prediction of drug toxic-
    ity in humans from toxicology in small and large animals. *Cancer Res*, 35:
    1354–1364, 1975.
Gupa AK, Vema P, Praharaj SK, Roy D, Singh A: Paroxetine overdose. *Indian J
    Psychiatry*, 47: 167–168, 2005.
Isbister GK, Buckley NA, Whyte IM: Serotonin toxicity: A practical approach to
    diagnosis and treatment. *Med J Aust*, 187: 361–365, 2007.
Kinoshita H, Tanaka N, Takakura A, Kumihashi M, Jamal M, Ito A, Tsutsui K et al.:
    Multiple drug poisoning case caused by a pharmacokinetic interaction involv-
    ing paroxetine. *Rom J Leg Med*, 23: 208–210, 2015.
Klys M, Kowalski P, Rojek S, Gross A: Death of a female cocaine user due to the
    serotonin syndrome following moclobemide-venlafaxine overdose. *Forensic
    Sci Int*, 184: 16–20, 2009.
Leikin JB, Watson WA: Post-mortem toxicology: What the dead can and cannot tell us.
    Clin Toxicol, 41: 47–56, 2003.
Martinez TT, Martinez DN: A case of serotonin syndrome associated with metha-
    done overdose. *Proc West Pharmacol Sci*, 51: 42–44, 2008.
Molina DK: *Handbook of Forensic Toxicology for Medical Examiners*. Boca Raton,
    FL: CRC Press, 2010.
Roberts DM, Buckley NA: Pharmacokinetic considerations in clinical toxicology:
    Clinical application. *Clin Pharmacokinet*, 46: 897–939, 2007.
Rosenberg J, Benowitz NL, Pond S: Pharmacokinetics of drug overdose. *Clin
    Pharmacokinet*, 6: 161–192, 1981.

Rosenkranz HS, Cunningham AR: Lack of predictivity of the rat lethality (LD50) test for ecological and human health effects. *Altern Lab Anim*, 33: 9–19, 2005.

Van Noord C, Eijelsheim M, Stricker BH: Drug-and-non-drug-associated QT interval prolongation. *Br J Clin Pharmacol*, 70: 16–23, 2010.

Wisniowska B, Tylutki Z, Wyszogrodzka G, Polak S: Drug-drug interactions and QT prologation as a commonly assessed cardiac effect: Comprehensive overview of clinical trials. *BMC Pharmacol Toxicol Series*, 17: 1–23, 2016.

Poison Absorption

3

3.1 Introduction

Poisons may enter the body through several portals. Whether self-administered, administered by another individual, or otherwise exposed, toxicants must be absorbed from the site of administration or exposure, and must be transported by blood to organs and tissues within the body where they exert their toxic effects. Absorption refers specifically to the passage into the systemic circulation. For example, when a substance is swallowed, absorption occurs in the stomach or intestine. The absorption of substances administered intravenously is considered instantaneous.

This chapter presents a brief review of the usual dosage forms and routes of administration employed in clinical medicine. This is followed by an overview of additional methods of administration and absorption sites unique to substance abuse and the potential absorption of substances concealed in the body cavities for illegal transportation or to evade discovery and arrest. Finally, some aspects of the administrative methods employed by criminal poisoners are presented. Features of the absorptive processes in different situations are illustrated with case studies having forensic implications. The biodisposition of substances following absorption is reviewed in the next chapter.

3.2 Routes of Administration and Dosage Forms Utilized in Clinical Medicine

3.2.1 Oral

Following oral administration, absorption can occur from any surface within the gastrointestinal tract. This would include the oral cavity, esophagus, stomach, intestine, colon, and rectum. However, only substances formulated in specifically designed dosage forms are appreciably absorbed from the oral cavity. Swallowed capsules, tablets, and liquids pass from the mouth to the stomach through the esophagus. Absorption from the esophagus is virtually nil because of the rapid transit time. Very few substances are absorbed from the stomach. The main site of absorption for most drugs administered orally is the initial section of the small intestine. From the intestine, the absorbed drugs travel directly to the liver where some degree of metabolism usually occurs before the drugs enter the systemic circulation.

Some specially formulated tablets may be placed under the tongue (sublingual) or between the gingival and buccal mucosa. These tablets then dissolve and substances diffuse across the mucous membranes and pass into the systemic circulation. Absorption from this site is much more rapid than that which occurs in the stomach or intestines because there is no transient time involved in reaching the site of absorption. Medications administered in this way avoid gastrointestinal digestive juices, which inactivates some drugs.

Fast-dissolving tablets melt or disintegrate in the mouth within seconds but should not be confused with the aforementioned sublingual tablets. They are simply oral tablets that can be conveniently taken without liquid and are easily swallowed. They may create an illusion of a fast onset of action, but they simply disintegrate in the mouth and are then swallowed and absorbed in the intestine in the same way as conventional oral tablets taken with a liquid.

3.2.2 Rectal

Rectal suppositories are usually used to provide medication locally to the anal region for the treatment of hemorrhoids and other disorders. The rectal administration of medications for systemic action may be indicated when individuals are nauseated, comatose, or otherwise unable to tolerate oral medications. Most drugs are well absorbed by the rectal mucosa.

3.2.3 Vaginal

Dosage forms designed for vaginal drug administration include solutions, tablets, creams, suppositories, tampons, and other drug delivery devices. These dosage forms can deliver medication for local effects, and also to provide systemic effects after absorption from the vaginal lining. Locally acting hormones, antimicrobials, anesthetics, and spermicides are the most common drugs administered intravaginally.

3.2.4 Nasal

Nasal sprays administered by squeeze bottles or metered dose devices are used to deliver medications for both local and systemic effects. Decongestants and anti-inflammatory agents are examples of locally acting medication. Drugs that are administered intranasally for systemic absorption from the nasal mucosa include nicotine, fentanyl, antimigraine agents, and some hormones. Absorption from the nasal mucosa can be relatively rapid and provide a quick onset of action.

3.2.5 Transdermal

The intact skin is a barrier to the absorption of most drugs. Only a few substances (e.g., nerve gases and insecticides) are absorbed after application to the skin. However, when the skin surface is denuded by trauma, chemical or thermal burns, and some disease process, drug absorption can take place. Drugs can also be absorbed after passing through hair follicles and sebaceous gland ducts. Systemic effects and occasionally serious toxic effects can result from the application of drugs to large areas of the body because of a greater absorbing surface. For example, problems due to systemic absorption of topically applied antibacterial agents and local anesthetics used in burn therapy where the barrier qualities of skin are destroyed and medications are applied over large areas.

Several medications have been incorporated into transdermal patches that contain penetration enhancers that circumvent the barrier qualities of normal skin. Patches are a unique bandage-like therapeutic system that provides continuous, controlled release of a drug from a reservoir. The drug is slowly absorbed into the bloodstream in the area of contact. Two common examples of drug-containing patches are those that contain nicotine and those that contain fentanyl. Other examples of medicated transdermal patches are listed in Table 3.1.

Table 3.1 Examples of Drugs Commercially Available in Transdermal Patches

Drug	Common Brand Name	Indication
Buprenorphine	Butrans	Pain relief
Clonidine	Catapres-TTS	Hypertension
Diclofenac	Flector	Pain relief
Estradiol	Estraderm	Hormone replacement
Fentanyl	Duragesic	Pain relief
Methylphenidate	Daytrana	ADHD
Nicotine	Nicoderm	Smoking cessation
Nitroglycerin	Nitro-Dur	Angina prevention
Norgesterone and Ethinylestradiol	Ortho Evra	Contraception
Oxybutynin	Oxytrol	Overactive bladder
Scopolamine	Transderm Scop	Motion sickness
Testosterone	Testoderm	Hormone replacement
Rotigotine	Neupro	Parkinson's disease
Rivastigmine	Excelon	Dementia
Selegiline	EMSAM	Depression

3.2.6 Injection

The administration of drugs by injection employs intravenous, intramuscular, or subcutaneous routes. Administration by intravenous injection produces a more prompt response than does oral administration because the drug can be immediately distributed to its sites of action. Drugs that are injected into skeletal muscle (usually arm, thigh, or buttock) are usually absorbed quite rapidly. The rate of absorption varies, depending on the blood flow to the muscle, the solubility of the drug, the volume of the injection, and the solution in which the drug is dissolved. Absorption of drugs injected subcutaneously is also rapid. The rate depends mainly on the ease of penetration of the drug into blood vessels, and the blood flow through the area of the injection site.

Accidental intra-arterial injections of drugs intended for intramuscular, subcutaneous, or intravenous use can be catastrophic. The intra-arterial injection of substances can cause severe tissue ischemia and necrosis. Vascular injury results from vasoconstriction, vasospasm, or thrombosis. The direct toxic irritant effect of high concentrations of chemicals on the lining of arteries can cause occlusion of the vessel resulting in ischemia of the distal areas supplied by the artery. Arterial blood flow transports the concentrated injected substances toward vessels with diminishing diameters. Veins carry blood to vessels with increasing diameters and injected substances are quickly diluted, so that local irritation does not occur.

3.2.7 Inhalation

Lung tissues provide a large surface area through which large amounts of blood flows, allowing for easy and rapid exchange of drugs between lung surfaces and blood vessels. Drugs absorbed into pulmonary capillaries are carried by pulmonary veins to the heart and then to the arteries carrying blood to the brain. As a result, centrally acting drugs administered by inhalation can have a faster onset of action than drugs administered intravenously. The rapid onset of action can be intense. Various toxic gases and vaporized liquids are absorbed across lung membranes into the arterial circulation nearly as fast as they are inhaled, allowing for the rapid onset of toxicity.

3.3 Routes of Administration Unique to Substance Abuse

3.3.1 Snorting and Injecting Powdered Tablets

To achieve faster and more intense effects, tablets intended for oral administration are commonly ground to powder and then be either snorted or liquefied and injected. Typically, 30%–60% of snorted drugs enter the bloodstream through the nasal mucosal membranes; the remainder is swallowed and absorbed from the intestine. The insoluble excipients from the tablet formulation can cause irritation and erosion of the nasal surfaces over time, which can diminish the sense of smell and alter speech characteristics. However, many individuals engage in frequent snorting for years without noticeable adverse nasal effects.

When powdered tablet excipients are injected, particles can be entrapped in capillary beds throughout the body; they are most frequently found in the lungs. Particles can form thrombosis and foreign body granulomas. Talc (magnesium trisilicate) granulomatosis is a common finding in autopsies of IV abusers. Attempts to remove particles before injection by filtering through various materials are minimally effective. Filtering has no effect on infectious microorganisms.

Some opioids are marketed in abuse-deterrent formulations that make them resistant to crushing for snorting or dissolving for injecting. These formulations employ a variety of technologies that alter the physicochemical properties of substances when tablets are pulverized. Other formulations incorporate pharmacologically aversive or antagonistic ingredients that become active when the integrity of the product is breached prior to use.

3.3.2 Inhalation

Volatile solvents, aerosols, and gases can be inhaled through the nose or mouth. Substances can be inhaled directly from commercial products such as paint or marking pens, sprayed into the nose from aerosol products, or dispersed in bags or other containers that facilitate inhaling the fumes. Chemicals contained in numerous commercial products can produce euphoria, delusions, and hallucinations. They also have the capacity to induce significant toxic cellular effects in the liver, kidneys, and nervous system.

3.3.3 Transdermal Patches

Abusers use fentanyl patches in a variety of ways, which include intravenous injection of the fentanyl gel extracted from the patch, inhalation of the fumes from heated patches, ingestion of the gel matrix, application of patches to the oral mucosal surfaces, and drinking hot water in which the patches have been steeped, similar to tea bags. The source of fentanyl patches used by abusers includes theft of new patches, retrieval of used patches discarded carelessly, and theft of patches from the bodies of living or dead patients. The residual amount of fentanyl remaining in a patch reservoir, even 72 h after application, is significant and can exceed a lethal human dose.

3.3.4 Smoking

E-cigarettes intended for nicotine replacement can be used for smoking illegal drugs such as marijuana, methamphetamine, and other hallucinogens. Marijuana is occasionally adulterated with various substances, or intentionally mixed with other drugs for smoking in cigarettes, various types of pipes, and vaporizers. Conventional tobacco cigarettes may also be dipped in liquids containing drugs prior to smoking.

3.3.5 Fad Methods of Substance Abuse

The scope of methods of administration utilized by substance abusers is illustrated by the lengths some will go to become intoxicated with ethanol faster or in a manner that might conceal their alcohol use from parents or bystanders. Techniques are often inspired by faulty logic and generally enhance the possibility of serious toxic consequences. Ethanol, usually in the form of vodka, has been applied to the surface of the eyes, vaporized in a variety of ways for inhalation, injected intravenously, absorbed by tampons for rectal and vaginal use, and ingested using funnels connected to hoses to deliver huge volumes rapidly. Alcoholic beverages, as well as other substances, have also been incorporated into frozen dessert-type foods, injected into fruit, and added to all varieties of hot and cold beverages that are not typically mixed with alcohol.

3.4 Absorption from Body Cavities

Individuals conceal drugs in body cavities to either illegally transport them across the borders, carry them into jails and prisons, or to avoid detection and arrest. These objectives often overlap, but it is important from a toxicological viewpoint to distinguish between them. The distinctions focus on the types of drugs involved, the quantities concealed, and the sophistication of the drug packaging. The toxicological issue is the potential exposure to massive amounts of drugs. When body cavity concealment is undertaken for purposes of transportation and smuggling, it is referred to as body packing. When concealment is more or less spontaneous to avoid arrest, it is termed body stuffing. In body packing, the packaging tends to be elaborate and substantial. With body stuffing, the drugs may be unwrapped or simply enclosed in containers utilized for drug sales.

Drug units can be concealed in the stomach, intestine, rectum, colon, vagina, and even surgically implanted into tissues or abdominal spaces. Systemic absorption can take place from any of these sites. In addition, due to the amounts of drugs involved, any packaging failure can be a life-threatening situation. The amount of drugs that an individual can transport in the gastrointestinal tract can be as large as 2–3 kg. Hundreds of pills can be concealed vaginally, and bulk drug substances can be custom molded into a single unit shaped to maximally fill a vaginal cavity.

In terms of the number of smugglers transporting drugs across borders, most involve cocaine or heroin, but methamphetamine and other amphetamines are also frequently smuggled using body cavities. All varieties of drugs can be encountered when a smuggler is transporting his or her personal drug supply. Individuals utilize body cavities to transport drugs into jails and prisons for inmates who in turn can store and transport drugs in body cavities while incarcerated. Individuals sometimes show up for scheduled jail sentence with their personal drug supply concealed in body cavities.

Medical facilities located in known high drug trafficking areas usually have management protocols in place to deal with real or suspected body cavity drug concealment. The medical issues encompass not only potential toxicity, but also intestinal erosion or obstruction that might necessitate emergency surgical intervention.

3.5 Intentional Poisoning

Poisoners most commonly incorporate toxicants into foods or beverages. When injections are involved, they are often preceded by sedation produced by depressants added to meals. Substituting poisoned dosage forms into regularly used medications and dietary supplements can also be a method of exposure. In most of the methods that are employed for intentional poisoning, the properties of the specific poison dictate the method of administration. Taste, smell, and physical size of a lethal dose are the most important factors that govern administration choices. Some examples of criminal poison administration methods are provided in Table 3.2.

Table 3.2 Examples of Criminal Poisoning Administration Methods

Poisons	Administration
Ethylene glycol	Added to desserts and sweet-tasting beverages, especially Gatorade.
Arsenic	Incorporated into foods and beverages.
Cyanide	Incorporated into capsules of prescription drugs and dietary supplements, and added to intravenous fluids administered to hospitalized patients.
Poisonous plants	Extracts added to food. Plant material incorporated into salads.
Strychnine	Added to medication capsules.
Pesticides	Added to foods.
Medication overdoses	Administered with intravenous fluids in hospitalized patients.
Variety of toxicants	Blended into milkshakes and smoothies.

3.6 Case Studies

Case: Determined Individual

In 1994, a 43-year-old woman self-administered approximately 700 aspirin tablets in water as an enema. She had previously attempted suicide by oral ingestion, but was unsuccessful because of gastric irritation and vomiting. Following the enema, she had the typical symptoms of aspirin poisoning. Her symptoms intensified and her blood levels of salicylate continued to rise during the next 24 h. Hemodialysis was utilized to reduce her salicylate blood levels, but she developed hypoxic encephalopathy and remained in coma for more than a year. This patient's poor outcome was believed to be a result of retained aspirin in her rectum, which continued to release salicylate at levels that produced severe toxicity. The retained aspirin was not recognized before the irreversible damage had occurred.

Comments

The volume of fluid that contained the ground aspirin tablets was sufficiently small to permit the material to clump into masses within the rectum and lower large intestine, and these masses slowly released toxic amounts of salicylate for absorption.

Case: Dangerous Concealment

In 2004, a 20-year-old female concealed methamphetamine enclosed in plastic bags in her vagina when approached by police officers. She first indicated to the officers that she felt strange, and a short time later she had a major seizure. She was transported to an emergency medical facility where she had a second seizure. She remained unresponsive and required endotracheal intubation. Her body temperature, heart rate, and blood pressure were elevated. A neurological examination revealed many abnormalities. During treatment, she developed aspiration pneumonia and rhabdomyolysis. However, by the fourth day of hospitalization she had almost completely recovered and left the hospital against medical advice.

Comments

To avoid arrest, drug users and dealers often swallow or conceal substances in body cavities. Multiple unsealed packets contain large amounts of drugs, which invariably result in life-threatening overdoses. It is assumed that, despite this very serious and potentially lethal experience, this individual resumed participation in the world of drug abuse.

Case: Packaging Failure

In 2007, a Nigerian man attempted to smuggle packages of methamphetamine in his stomach. Packages were wrapped with plastic film and tape. The man died from acute poisoning from methamphetamine that had leaked from the packages into his stomach. Autopsy findings showed an extreme pulmonary congestion and edema as well as moderate hepatic edema. Extremely high concentrations of methamphetamine and its metabolite amphetamine were found in blood, urine, gastric contents, and in all other autopsy samples. These high concentrations confirmed that the cause of death was acute methamphetamine poisoning.

Comments

Smuggling drugs by ingesting packets that are later retrieved by rectal elimination is a highly perfected practice. Packages of illegal drugs for this form of human transport are generally impenetrable by physiological processes but, because of the massive quantities of drugs within individual units, even the smallest leak can have lethal consequences.

Case: Tampon

In 2009, a 30-year-old man was brought to a hospital emergency department by emergency medical responders after police forcibly removed him from a gas station restroom. He said he had ingested a large amount of methamphetamine with several beers. His heart and respiratory rate were elevated and he was agitated. Nothing alarming was noted in a physical examination, and laboratory testing results were mostly within normal ranges. A urine and serum toxicology screening was positive for methamphetamine and ethanol. The man became more manageable over a period of about 4 h and asked to use the restroom. Appearing improved, remorseful, and ambulatory, his request was granted. He then disappeared for an hour and was later found in another part of the hospital in a decompensated state with tachycardia, agitation, and altered mental status. At this point, he was restrained, sedated, and admitted to the hospital. Despite aggressive therapy over the next 12 h, tachycardia and agitation persisted. During this time, he had a bowel movement that produced a tampon. Following the bowel movement, the man's mental status improved significantly, and he admitted to inserting rectally a methamphetamine soaked tampon. A short time later, he signed out of the hospital against medical advice. Additional information regarding his past use of methamphetamine was not obtained.

Comments

Methamphetamine and other substances can be absorbed from the rectal mucosa. The use of a tampon might produce drug effects that are more prolonged than rectal administration of a liquid using a syringe or other device.

Case: Intra-Arterial Ambien

A 24-year-old woman was admitted to a hospital with a painful cyanotic right hand 2 days after she injected a crushed Ambien (zolpidem) tablet into her radial artery. The first four digits of her hand remained gangrenous even after intensive treatment. She left the hospital against medical advice after 1 month. She ultimately lost significant portions of the gangrenous fingers.

Comments

Distal ischemia and necrosis can occur after intra-arterial injection of virtually any drug or chemical.

References and Additional Reading

Allen LV, Popovich NG, Ansel HC: *Ansel's Pharmaceutical Dosage Forms and Drug Delivery Systems*, 9th ed. Philadelphia, PA: Lippincott, Williams & Wilkins, 2011.

Behal N, Wong A, Mantra R, Cantrell FL: Human poisoning through atypical routes of exposure. *J Community Health*, 41: 105–108, 2016.

Carson HJ, Feickert BL: Identification at autopsy of pulverized pills in lungs of a first-time methadone user. *J Forensic Leg Med*, 16: 494–496, 2009.

Chang ML, Lin JL: Irreversible ischemic hand following intra-arterial injection of zolpidem powder. *Clin Tox*, 41: 1025–1028, 2003.

Gupta M, Bailey S, Lovato LM: Bottoms up: Methamphetamine toxicity from an unusual route. *West J Emerg Med*, 10: 58–60, 2009.

Hind CR: Pulmonary complications of intravenous drug misuse. 1. Epidemiology and non-infective complications. *Thorax*, 45: 891–898, 1990.

Karishma KS, Kapila K, Praharaj AK: Shooting up: The interface of microbial infections and drug abuse. *J Med Microbio*, 60: 408–422, 2011.

Kashani J, Ruha AM: Methamphetamine toxicity secondary to intravaginal body stuffing. *Clin Tox*, 42: 987–989, 2004.

Lauerma H: Somnophilia and sexual abuse using vaginal administration of triazolam. *J Forensic Sci*, 61: 862–863, 2016.

Lounsbury DA, George DJ: The fentanyl patch at the crime scene. *J Forensic Ident*, 57: 512–521, 2007.

McLean S, Bruno R, Brandon S, deGraaff B: Effect of filtration on morphine and particle content of injections prepared from slow-release oral morphine tablets. *Harm Reduction J*, 6: 37–52, 2009.

Sen S, Chini EN, Brown MJ: Complications after unintentional intra-arterial injection of drugs: Risks, outcomes and management strategies. *Mayo Clin Proc*, 80: 783–795, 2005.

Suzuki J, Valenti ES: Intentional intra-arterial injection of heroin: A case report. *J Addict Med*, 11: 77–79, 2017.

Takekawa K, Ohmori T, Kido A, Oya M: Methamphetamine body packer: Acute poisoning death due to massive leaking of methamphetamine. *J Forensic Sci*, 52: 1219–1222, 2007.

Traub SJ, Hoffman RS, Nelson LS: Body packing: The internal concealment of illicit drugs. *N Engl J Med*, 349: 2519–2526, 2003.

Watson JE, Tagupa ET: Suicide attempt by means of aspirin enema. *Ann Pharmacother*, 28: 467–469, 1994.

Poison Biodisposition

4

4.1 Introduction

Following absorption into the bloodstream, drugs and other potential toxicants are distributed throughout the body. As the substances come into contact with the tissues and organs, they tend to be selectively partitioned and stored in various areas depending on the physicochemical characteristics of the substance. This partitioning is usually an equilibrium-based process that accumulates substances when blood concentrations are high and molecules are released into the blood as circulating concentrations fall. The location of target sites of action and storage areas is not necessarily the same. As circulating blood passes through the liver, toxicants are metabolized and resulting metabolites circulate in the blood stream, filtered by the kidneys, and excreted in urine. The disposition of toxicants involves many biological mechanisms that are dependent on the structural integrity of tissues and functioning organ systems. After death, the biological processes cease and toxicants distribute in patterns that can be substantially different from those observed during life.

Insight into the biodisposition of specific drugs and other potential toxicants is important for selecting biological samples for toxicological testing and interpreting testing results. Some general features of the metabolism and excretion of toxicants are reviewed in this chapter. The complexity of the application of these features is illustrated with relatively unique case studies.

4.2 Metabolism

Potential toxicants are metabolized by enzymatic systems located primarily in the liver. Some biotransformations can occur in other tissues, but the most important reactions from a forensic toxicology point of view take place in the liver. Metabolites can be either inactive or more active than the parent compound. The rate of metabolic transformation is different for each substance. The percentage of a compound that is metabolized with every passage through the liver is an inherent characteristic of the compound and the capacity of the metabolic pathway involved. The faster the compound is biotransformed, the shorter the exposure time of the toxicant with its target site and the duration of its toxicological effects. The slower the rate of conversion, the longer the duration of effects.

The most common practical result of metabolism is for active substances to be converted to inactive metabolites that are then eliminated in urine. These metabolites can be detected in toxicology testing and provide evidence of exposures. When parent substances are converted to active substances, the interpretation of analytical testing results can be more complex in terms of the identification of the substance involved in the exposure. For example, morphine is a metabolite of codeine and heroin. Consequently, if morphine is detected in toxicological testing, it remains to be determined whether it originated from an exposure to morphine or from heroin or codeine exposures, or perhaps a combination. This and some other examples of drug metabolites that might present challenges for interpreting analytical findings are provided in Table 4.1.

There can be a significant difference in the initial systemic blood concentration of a toxicant administered by different routes. Substances administered rectally, intravenously, intramuscularly, inhalationally, transdermally, and sublingually enter the blood stream from their site of exposure and are immediately distributed throughout the systemic circulation. When substances are administered orally, they are absorbed into the blood vessels serving the gastrointestinal system that converge into the portal vein, which carries the substance directly to the liver. Thus, orally administered substances travel through the liver before entering

Table 4.1 Metabolites

Parent Compound	Metabolite	Comment
Carisoprodol	Meprobamate	The metabolite is active and commercially marketed for therapeutic use.
Cocaine	Benzoylecgonine	Cocaine has a very short half-life and exposures are identified by the detection of the metabolite.
Codeine	Morphine	Morphine is the active metabolite of codeine.
Diazepam	Temazepam	The metabolite is active and commercially marketed for therapeutic use.
Heroin	Morphine	Morphine is the active form of heroin.
Methamphetamine	Amphetamine	The metabolite is active and commercially marketed for therapeutic use.
Tramadol	Demethyltramadol	The metabolite is the active form of tramadol.

the general systemic circulation. If the extent of metabolism is high, the concentration of parent substance emerging from the liver and entering the systemic circulatory system can be significantly less than the concentration following administration by other routes. This metabolic reduction is known as the first-pass effect. There are situations in which this phenomenon has an important influence on toxicity. In therapeutic medicine, drugs known to have a high first-pass effect are either administered in higher oral doses to compensate, or they are administered by other than oral routes to avoid this effect.

4.3 Excretion

As blood circulates through the kidneys, substances are filtered and ultimately excreted in the urine. In most cases, the urinary excretion of substances and their metabolites is the major pathway for reducing the body burden of toxicants. Substances can also be excreted in feces and fluids such as saliva, perspiration, milk, and bile. Volatile substances such as anesthetic gases, ethanol, and organic solvents can also be eliminated through the respiratory system in exhaled air.

Half-life refers to the period of time required for the amount of drug in the body to be reduced (eliminated) by one-half. For example, if one starts with 100 mg of a drug in the body and it has a half-life of 10 h, then in 10 h there will be 50 mg of the drug remaining in the body. In addition, from this point the level will decrease to 25 mg in another 10 h, and so on. Half-lives for substances are specific for each particular substance and can range from minutes to days or years. In clinical situations, approximations are often based on multiples of half-lives. This is also a measure of detection windows for antemortem drug testing. For example, after five half-lives, the amount of a substance remaining in the body is only about 3% of the initial exposure. This concept is illustrated in Table 4.2.

Table 4.2   Elimination Half-Life

Half-Lives	Cumulative Percent Eliminated	Percent Remaining
1	50	50
2	75	25
3	87.5	12.5
4	93.8	6.2
5	96.9	3.1

4.4 Postmortem Redistribution

For years, there was a workable assumption that poison concentrations in the tissues and fluids of the body remained at the levels attained at the time of death. The analysis of specimens collected after death was assumed to reflect the concentration at the actual time of death, and these levels could therefore be used to determine the cause of death. It is now known that this is not generally the case. The postmortem concentrations of toxicants can change considerably in different situations and are influenced by many factors. With respect to blood sampling, blood levels obtained from the heart can be significantly different from levels in blood from peripheral blood vessels, and these levels can change depending on the time after death when the samples are collected. This phenomenon is referred to as postmortem redistribution. The mechanisms can be complicated and are compound specific. Postmortem changes can involve diffusion of substances from tissues into blood, such that postmortem blood levels greatly exceed antemortem levels. In this instance, a high postmortem level might suggest an overdose when this has not occurred.

It is seldom possible to estimate ingested doses of substances from postmortem blood levels even when postmortem redistribution is considered. The interpretation of postmortem concentrations must be considered within the context of any other existing antemortem and perimortem laboratory testing, patient-specific clinical information, and known characteristics of the toxicant. Published tabulations of lethal drug blood values are of little help with respect to evaluating postmortem lethal levels.

4.5 Case Studies

Case: Codeine Produced Morphine Toxicity

In 2004, a 62-year-old man with pneumonia was admitted to a hospital for treatment. The only medication the man took regularly was an anticonvulsant for a seizure disorder. Following diagnostic testing, he was started on intravenous antibiotics and oral codeine (25 mg 3 times a day) to relieve his cough. Four days after admission, he was found unresponsive and his pupils were miotic. Noninvasive ventilation was started and he was transferred to the intensive care unit. He was then treated with naloxone, which produced a dramatic improvement in consciousness and respiration. He recovered completely over the following 2 days.

The opioid activity of codeine is the result of its metabolic conversion to morphine. In this case, the conversion occurred at an abnormally rapid rate, and the relatively modest doses of codeine were quickly converted to life-threatening blood levels of morphine (20 to 30 times higher than expected). The biochemical basis of this phenomenon was substantiated in this case with metabolic studies using different substrates as well as identification and quantitation of codeine and morphine metabolites.

Comments

The ultrarapid metabolic rate described in this case is believed to be due to a genetically determined feature of drug metabolizing activity that is present in a small segment of the general population. There have been toxicity cases reported with possible involvement of ultrarapid codeine–morphine conversions in young children receiving codeine and in cases of neonatal toxicity possibly linked to morphine in breast milk from mothers treated with codeine. The metabolic pathways involved in the conversion of codeine to morphine are common to those of some other substances. However, the consequences of increased metabolic rates are most often only significant in overdose situations. Codeine toxicity resulting from rapid metabolism is an important clinical manifestation of this phenomenon.

Case: Cocaine Kissing

In 2009, a 23-year-old male top-ranked tennis player tested positive for cocaine in a urine sample collected in a random testing program. He was given a penalty of 2 years of ineligibility with forfeiture of certain monetary prizes and ranking points. The player appealed the ruling and, after additional testing and expert testimony, the ruling was changed to an approximately 2.5 month suspension with no effects on ranking points or prize money from his performances.

The basis for the reconsideration of the initial suspension was the circumstances that were suggested to have resulted in his cocaine exposure. The evening prior to the day that the urine sample was collected was spent at dance clubs following a group dinner with the coaching staff and friends. During the evening, the player spent most of his time with one particular female companion that he had met that evening. They danced most of the night and exchanged kisses several times. It was purported that this woman was an active cocaine user and that he received the cocaine from her through their oral contact. However, the woman denied any cocaine use and refused to testify at review hearings. Hair collected from the tennis player about 5 weeks after the exposure tested negative for cocaine. The individuals who evaluated the case accepted the possibility of cocaine exposure from the female contact.

Comments

Cocaine was present in the oral fluids of the users. Its presence in the oral cavity fluids can result from transference from the systemic circulation, residual amounts from oral or nasal use, or from smoking. The quantitative amounts in oral fluid that might be transferred from oral contact during kissing are unlikely to be sufficient for a positive urine test. But, it is possible that actual cocaine powder residue from the facial surface areas could transfer and influence testing. It was suggested that the female dance partner used cocaine throughout the evening during conspicuous absences spent in a restroom. Frequent cocaine exposures, although unlikely, from residual cocaine in the nasal and oral surface areas was considered possible. Although cocaine (metabolite) was detected in urine, the amount was very low. This, coupled with the negative results of hair testing, supported the presumption that the exposure was likely due to contamination rather than recreational use.

Case: Sexually Transmitted Cocaine

In 1999, a female sailor approaching retirement after 20 years of service in the United States Navy tested positive for cocaine in a random military drug testing program. The testing consisted of an immunoassay screening followed by confirmation and quantitation with gas chromatography/mass spectrometry. Subsequent to the drug testing result, the woman was discharged due to drug abuse. The discharge prevented the woman from attaining 20 years of service and associated retirement benefits.

The discharge was appealed. Considerable evidence was presented during the appeal process that supported the individual's long history of untarnished and admirable military service, and also included a negative hair analysis report for cocaine conducted by a private testing facility. The woman denied using cocaine and claimed that the cocaine detected in her urine samples resulted from sexual activity with her husband on the evening prior to the collection of the urine sample. Her husband was a known regular cocaine user and the cocaine exposure was postulated to have occurred by transfer in semen and saliva. Considerable scientific literature relating to the transfer of drugs through contact with semen and saliva was also provided to the military review boards. In 2006, the Navel Discharge Review Board completed their review and upheld the original discharge.

Comments

Cocaine can be present in saliva and semen of male users, and cocaine can be absorbed from oral administration as well as from vaginal administration. The issue highlighted in the case described revolved around the cocaine concentrations and the absolute amount of cocaine that could be transferred in this manner. The cocaine concentration in semen following use is relatively low compared to blood levels. The cocaine present in the semen must then be absorbed from the vagina into the female systemic circulation, and then excreted in urine. Conservative calculation of the amounts of cocaine (and metabolites) would be below the amount that would produce a positive urine test. Similarly, the total amounts that might be transferred from all body fluids (saliva, semen, and sweat) would be below levels that would have effects or be detected in urine testing. The circumstances of each situation in which this possibility exists require individualized analysis, but the likelihood of transferred amounts of substances having an influence on urine testing results is remote.

Case: Morphine Breastfeeding Death

In 2010, a 37-year-old mother in South Carolina breast fed her 6-month-old baby around midnight and then fell asleep in the bed with the baby and her husband. Around 4 a.m., the husband woke and noticed that the baby was cold and not breathing. The mother started resuscitation and emergency medical responders were notified. On arrival at the home, paramedics found the child unresponsive to resuscitation attempts and the child was pronounced dead. Postmortem toxicology testing identified morphine when testing liver and brain, and blood levels of acetaminophen, diphenhydramine, chlorpheniramine, clonazepam, morphine, and morphine metabolites. The mother had a long history of drug use and abuse. This included the current use of morphine and clonazepam. Based on the autopsy, toxicological findings, and the mother's drug use, the death was ruled to be the result of respiratory insufficiency secondary to synergistic drug intoxication. The mother was charged with homicide by child abuse, involuntary manslaughter, and unlawful conduct toward a child. She was convicted of all charges and sentenced to 20 years in prison.

Comments

The mother in this case had been a nurse, but she lost her license years earlier for drug-related issues, and she was currently using many prescribed drugs for a chronic pain condition and other medical problems. She was clearly a substance abuser and, at the time of the death, was facing charges for illegal purchase of prescription drugs.

It is known that the amount of morphine that is transferred to babies through breast milk from mothers taking therapeutic doses of morphine is almost always clinically irrelevant. However, if there is a genetic defect or other factor that prevents the morphine from being metabolized, it is possible that lethal levels could accumulate. Additional testing to elucidate the basis for the lethal morphine levels in the baby might have included measuring morphine and its metabolites in the baby's stomach contents, in addition to the mother's blood, breast milk, and hair. It would have been helpful to know if exceedingly high levels of morphine were delivered to the baby in breast milk, and if the baby had any issues that might alter the ability to metabolize morphine.

References and Additional Reading

Cone EJ, Kato K, Hillsgrove M: Cocaine excretion in the semen of drug users. *J Analyt Toxicol*, 20: 139–140, 1996.

Cone EJ, Kato K, Hillsgrove M: Cocaine in postmortem drug redistribution. *Clin Toxicol*, 43: 235–241, 2005.

Eagerton DH, Goodbar NH, Dansby MC, Abel SN, Bell WC: Morphine overdose in a 6-1/2-week-old infant: A case report. *Austin J Phramacol Ther*, 2: 1–4, 2014.

Gasche Y, Daali Y, Fathi M, Chiappe A, Cottini S, Dayer P, Desmeules J: Codeine intoxication associated with ultrarapid CYP2D6 metabolism. *N Engl J Med*, 351: 2827–2831, 2004.

Gerostamoulos D, Beyer J, Staikos V, Tayler P, Woodford N, Drummer OH: The effect of the postmortem interval on the restribution of drugs: A comparison of mortuary admission and autopsy blood specimens. *Forensic Sci Med Pathol*, 8: 373–379, 2012.

Haufroid V, Hantson P: CYP2D6 genetic polymorphism and their relevance for poisoning due to amphetamines, opioid analgesics and antidepressants. *Clin Toxicol*, 53: 501–510, 2015.

Kennedy MC: Postmortem drug concentrations. *Inter Med J*, 40: 183–187, 2010.

Kirchheiner J, Schmidt H, Tevetkov M, Keulen JT, Lotsch J, Roots I, Brockmoller J: Pharmacokinetics of codeine and its metabolite morphine in ultra-rapid metabolizers due to CYP2D6 duplication. *Pharmacogenomics J*, 7: 257–265, 2007.

Klemmt L, Scialli AR: The transport of chemicals in semen. *Birth Defects Research*, 74: 119–131, 2005.

Madadi, P, Hildebrandt D, Gong IY, Schwartz UI, Ciszkowski C, Ross CJD, Sistonen J et al.: Fatal hydrocodone overdose in child: Pharmacogenetics and drug interactions. *Pediatrics*, 126: 986–989, 2010.

McIntyre IM: Indentification of a postmortem redistribution factor (F) for forensic toxicology. *J Analyt Sci Tech*, 5: 1–4, 2014.

Roberts DM, Buckley NA: Pharmacokinetic considerations in clinical toxicology: Clinical applications. *Clin Pharamacokinet*, 46: 897–939, 2007.

Sachs H, Kintz P: Consensus of the society of hair testing on hair testing for doping agents. *Forensic Sci Int*, 107: 1–3, 2000.

Yarema MC, Becker CE: Key concepts in postmortem drug redistribution. *Clin Toxicol*, 43: 235–241, 2005.

Poison Detection

5

5.1 Introduction

The chemical identification and quantitation of drugs and other potential toxicants in biological material are the foundation of forensic toxicology. The relevance of toxicological testing results to behaviors or lethality is determined by examining analytical findings within the context of other information collected during investigations.

Instrumentation and technology currently utilized for forensic testing is capable of detecting extremely small amounts of most substances of forensic interest. One can assume that all known toxic substances can be detected if they are present in the specimens tested, and if appropriate testing methodology and instrumentation are utilized in the testing process. Obviously, substances will not be detected if no testing is undertaken. Appropriate testing methodology is targeted in some cases to specific substances of interest. In a practical sense, it is not possible to randomly test a biological specimen for everything in every case, but the analytical technology to do this does exist. There are laboratories that can test for virtually any potential toxicant in any postmortem specimen.

Screening tests are designed to determine the presence or absence of a target set of substances. These are presumptive tests and are usually used to guide more definitive testing for identification and quantitation of substances. Screening panels are limited to a finite number of substances and can also produce false positive and false negative results. Definitive tests generally utilize coupled chromatography–mass spectrometry instrumentation to specifically identify substances, and to quantify the levels of the substances detected.

The history of exposure to a potential toxicant is an important aspect of establishing a relationship between the exposure and the circumstances under investigation, but it is not conclusive evidence that the substance was the cause. To establish a cause-and-effect relationship, analytical testing results are almost always necessary to show that the toxicant was absorbed, and that the magnitude of the exposure was sufficient to cause the effects observed. The systemic level of a toxicant necessary to produce any given effect is dependent on many factors. These factors and their potential influence on the interpretation of analytical testing results are discussed in more detail in this chapter and illustrated with case studies throughout this book.

5.2 Antemortem Toxicology

The most common reason for testing is to identify recreational drug use. The particular substances included in testing can vary depending on the purpose of the testing. Routine testing is part of the employment process or necessary for continuing employment in certain fields. Testing is also commonly used to monitor compliance with treatment programs for chronic pain or substance abuse disorders and to substantiate compliance with regulations pertaining to drug use by athletes. A list of situations that involve drug testing is shown in Table 5.1.

Antemortem drug screening tests are not all comprehensive and are developed to meet the guidelines of the agencies requiring testing, or to meet the objectives of practitioners who utilize tests for monitoring compliance or providing medical care. The scope and accessibility of testing continue to evolve to meet existing and foreseeable needs. Screening results can have false positives and therefore positive finding require confirmatory testing.

Table 5.1   Antemortem Drug Testing Situations

- Accident investigations
- Child abuse investigations
- Diagnostic evaluations
- Drug-facilitated crime investigations
- Drug treatment programs
- Emergency medical evaluations
- High-risk and safety-sensitive occupations
- Military service requirements
- Participation in competitive sports
- Preemployment and employment requirements
- Probation requirements
- Therapeutic drug use monitoring
- Workplace or environmental exposure monitoring

5.3 Postmortem Toxicology

The purpose of postmortem toxicology testing is to identify potentially toxic substances that may have caused or contributed to the death under investigation. Substances may include prescribed medications, abused substances from legal or illegal sources, and all other chemical substances that might be involved in unintentional or intentional exposures. The presence of any substance without an explanation for its presence requires evaluation. In the case of regularly used therapeutic medications, the absence of medication in postmortem samples may also contribute to the determination of the cause and manner of death.

The presence of substances can also be incidental to the death being investigated. The specimens collected and analyzed vary depending on the particular case. Most often specimens are collected from many tissues and fluids, and testing begins with blood and urine, and then proceeds to the testing of samples from other organs based on the results of the initial testing. The usual specimens utilized for toxicology testing are listed in Table 5.2. Other fluids and tissues may be used for testing when indicated. Biological specimens available for postmortem testing can be limited in some situations due to decomposition, burial, dismemberment, and fire destruction. Testing in these cases might utilize specimens from what material is available with the results being interpreted in a restrictive manner dictated by the

Table 5.2   Postmortem Samples for Testing

Specimen	Utility in Death Investigations
Blood	Toxicant levels can be related to effects. Interpretation of findings requires consideration of many influential factors.
Urine	Provides evidence of toxicant exposure but not useful for estimation of exposure levels or behavioral effects.
Liver	Toxicants and their metabolites concentrate in the liver and can be detected after blood levels decrease to undetectable levels. In some cases, high levels can be an indication of total body burden.
Vitreous humor	Toxicant levels can sometimes be related to effects. Less influenced by putrefaction and other postmortem changes.
Hair	Can provide evidence of exposure and provide information on acute and chronic exposures over extended time periods.
Gastric contents	May contain residual amounts of ingested toxicants and formulation materials.

Table 5.3   Typical Postmortem Toxicology Screen

- Alcohols
- Analgesics
- Anticonvulsants
- Antidepressants
- Antihistamines
- Antipsychotics
- Barbiturates
- Benzodiazepines
- Cannabis
- Cocaine
- Cardiovascular drugs
- Digoxin
- GHB
- LSD
- Opioids
- Pesticides, metals, cyanide, carbon monoxide
- Sedatives
- Stimulants

circumstances. The substances typically included in postmortem toxicology screening tests are listed in Table 5.3.

The concentration of substances in organs and fluids after death is the result of several factors. Interpretation differs case-by-case. To reduce the possibility of testing variables due to environmental and procedural differences, there is increasing attention to standardizing the collection, storage, and analysis of postmortem biological samples, but the individuals and the circumstances of their deaths cannot be standardized. Interpretation of the concentrations of potential toxicants in biological samples obtained after death is complex and requires much more than detection, quantitation, and comparison of numerical testing results to values provided in published compilations of analytical results from previous cases. An interpretation requires consideration of all aspects of the case, and familiarity with the pharmacology and toxicology of the toxicants involved. Factors to be considered when determining the relevance of analytical findings are listed in Table 5.4. Some limitations to keep in mind when reviewing postmortem testing results are presented in Table 5.5.

Table 5.4   Considerations When Interpreting Postmortem Toxicology Testing Results

Circumstances of Death
- Illness or symptoms preceding death
- Length of unconsciousness prior to death
- Resuscitation efforts

Medical and Psychiatric History
- Diseases involving organ systems involved in biodisposition (e.g., liver, kidneys)
- Suicidal indications or risky behaviors

History of Legal and Illegal Drug Use and Possible Occupational Exposures
- Potential toxic exposures
- Possible simultaneous exposure to multiple substances
- Possibility of tolerance and cross tolerance

Autopsy Findings
- Evidence of disease processes
- Evidence of toxic exposure

Table 5.5   Evaluating Postmortem Toxicology Testing Results

- Doses (exposures) cannot be estimated from postmortem blood concentrations.
- Substances identified in postmortem testing can be incidental to death.
- Tolerance can significantly impact the relevance of observed antemortem and postmortem testing results.
- There are no clearly defined lethal doses. A lethal dose is the dose that caused death in a particular case.
- Postmortem blood levels do not reflect levels at the time of death.
- Pharmacokinetic characteristics derived from clinical studies do not apply to postmortem kinetics.
- Postmortem blood levels can be elevated due only to postmortem redistribution.
- Values derived from whole blood, plasma, and serum are not interchangeable.

5.4 Forensic Chemical Analysis

Testing results from nonbiological specimens may provide guidance for postmortem testing as well as aid in the interpretation of the postmortem testing results. Such testing might include the analysis of foods and beverages, residue from drug-use paraphernalia, samples of potential toxicants, stains on clothing and bedding, diapers, and possibly trace material in fingerprints and dried blood. In addition to the identification of the toxic substance in a product or specimen, there may be occasions to identify impurities or other substances that might be useful for tracing the substance to a particular source.

5.5 Case Studies

Case: Marine and Party Girl

In 2002, an otherwise healthy 23-year-old Marine Sergeant unexpectedly became ill and died a few days later. He had lived with his wife and children in a home on a military base in Southern California. They had been married for 3 years. They had one child together and three from the wife's previous marriage. The sergeant had been sick for about 10 days before his death and had consulted base physicians at least twice. They felt that he was experiencing some type of food poisoning and treated him accordingly. An autopsy was performed and his death was determined to be due to a heart attack. The body was cremated. As the sergeant was on active duty at the time of his death, a military investigation was also carried out. Part of this investigation involved testing the specimens collected at autopsy for the presence of arsenic. It was found that samples from the liver and the kidneys contained extraordinarily high levels of arsenic. No arsenic was found in other tissue samples. Military investigators believed that the sergeant was poisoned by his wife to collect insurance benefits and to obtain military survivor benefits. The wife was arrested (2005) and tried for murder. At the trial, significant questions were raised about the validity of the arsenic testing results. No evidence was presented that indicated how or when the arsenic might have been obtained, and no evidence linked arsenic to the sergeant's wife. She was convicted in 2007 of first-degree murder under circumstances that carried a sentence of life imprisonment without the possibility of a parole.

The widow's lifestyle seemed to overshadow all other issues. The prosecution presented graphic details of the wife's activities immediately prior to and following the death. It was shown that she adopted a partying and drinking lifestyle that included casual sex, sometimes with more than one partner. In addition, almost immediately following the death, she had breast augmentation surgery that was financed by the death benefits. However, because of legal arguments questioning the reliability of the arsenic test results, her conviction was reversed and she was granted a new trial. In preparation for the second trial, the autopsy specimens were tested by an independent laboratory and no arsenic was found. Subsequently all charges were dismissed and the wife was released after being incarcerated for over 2 years.

Comments

Many continue to speculate on whether the widow did or did not poison her husband despite the absence of evidence indicating that he was poisoned by arsenic or any other toxicant.

This was a high-profile case from the beginning, and it continues to generate considerable interest as legal action seeking compensation for this perceived injustice moves forward. It has been featured in several prime-time news specials and the widow has appeared on prime-time TV talk shows.

In the military investigation, the analytical testing for arsenic was done in a laboratory that normally analyzed environmental samples for arsenic. There were reasons to question the methodology and validation of the assays that were used by the laboratory to identify and quantitate arsenic in biological samples. Moreover, the extraordinarily high levels of arsenic found in the liver and kidney tissue samples, with the absence of arsenic in other body tissues, are inconsistent with the well-known biodisposition of arsenic.

Case: Strawberry Jell-O Homicide

In 1990, a 35-year-old woman living in Connecticut learned that her 14-year-old daughter was being sexually abused by her 61-year-old live-in boyfriend. The couple had been together for several years. The man had a history of heart disease and had undergone coronary bypass surgery. The woman apparently reasoned that if she poisoned him with mescaline, the effects would exacerbate his heart condition causing his death and be attributed to his heart disease. The woman, along with the daughter, sought out an illegal drug dealer, purchased what they believed to be mescaline, and added it to the man's strawberry Jell-O. Soon after eating the gelatin dessert, the man died. His death was attributed to his heart condition and he was buried. About a month after the death, authorities learned of the murder plot through anonymous sources and the body was exhumed for autopsy and toxicology testing. Testing results were negative for mescaline but positive for LSD. The woman was arrested and tried for first-degree murder. At the trial, the pathologist testified that the man died as a result of a combination of heart disease and acute LSD intoxication causing increased stress on the diseased heart. This conclusion was supported by the testimony of an independent cardiologist. After about 6 h of deliberation, she was found guilty and sentenced to life in prison. The case was later appealed and, following a review, a new trial was granted in 1997. The basis of the decision was that the prosecution failed to disclose the results of toxicology testing that did not confirm the involvement of LSD in the victim's death. The defense attorney failed to challenge the questionable evidence when it was presented. Eventually the charges were reduced to manslaughter with a sentence of time served. The woman pleaded guilty and was released.

Comments

Immunoassay screening tests are not specific and are susceptible to false positives. Positive results must be confirmed with specific testing. In this case, positive immunoassay screening tests for LSD were obtained but they were not confirmed. As a result, there was insufficient evidence to demonstrate that LSD was involved in the death.

High doses of LSD can cause autonomic instability leading to hypertension, tachycardia, and cardiac arrhythmias. These effects would be especially life-threatening in individuals with preexisting cardiovascular disorders. There was considerable evidence in this case to indicate that the woman intended to kill her boyfriend and had carried out the poisoning, but there was no legally acceptable evidence to demonstrate that she succeeded.

Case: Siblings—Dead and Endangered

In 2014, a 14-month-old child was found in bed with her mother, unresponsive, and not breathing. The child was transported to a hospital by emergency responders but was pronounced dead on arrival. The child had been ill with flu-like symptoms for a few days and had received oral medication the preceding evening and on the morning of the day she was discovered not breathing. Postmortem toxicology testing of urine and blood revealed methadone and diphenhydramine. No drugs were found in the gastric contents. Only the blood methadone level was quantified. The methadone level was judged to be lethal and the estimated time between the administration and death was about 6 h. To determine whether the child had previously been exposed to methadone, testing was carried out on hair. For comparison, hair testing was also carried out on samples from a 4-year-old sibling. Both methadone and its metabolite were detected in hair, and segmental analysis indicated that methadone had been administered on more than one occasion over a period of several weeks. A similar distribution of methadone and its metabolite was found in hair samples from the sibling. The mother and her live-in partner were both receiving methadone maintenance therapy. They both initially denied administering methadone to the children. Subsequently, they pleaded guilty to repeated methadone administration to both children.

Comments

Hair testing provides a detection window of weeks or months and can be used to distinguish between chronic exposures and single-occasion accidental exposures. Hair testing results can sometimes be misleading if there is the possibility of contamination from environmental contact. However, the presence of both methadone and its metabolite demonstrates that the methadone in the hair sample in this case came from the systemic circulation.

References and Additional Reading

Bevalot F, Cartiser N, Bottinelli C, Gutton J, Fanton L: State of the art in bile analysis in forensic toxicology. *Forensic Sci Intern*, 259: 133–154, 2016.

Boumba VA, Ziavrou KS, Vougiouklakis T: Hair as a biological indicator of drug use, drug abuse or chronic exposure to environmental toxicants. *Int J Toxicol*, 25: 143–163, 2006.

Brahm NC, Yeager LL, Fox MD, Farmer KC, Palmer TA: Commonly prescribed medications and potential false-positive urine drug screens. *Am J Health-Syst Pharm*, 67: 1344–1350, 2010.

Chatterton C, Turner K, Klinger N, Etter M, Duez M, Cirimele V: Interpretation of pharmaceutical drug concentrations in young children's head hair. *J Forensic Sci*, 59: 281–286, 2014.

Cone EJ, Sampson-Cone AH, Darwin WD, Huestis MA, Oyler JM: Urine testing for cocaine abuse: Metabolic and excretion patterns following different routes of administration and methods for detection of false-negative results. *J Anal Toxicol*, 27: 386–401, 2003.

Curtis J, Greenberg M: Screening for drugs of abuse: Hair as an alternative matrix: A review for the medical toxicologist. *Clin Toxicol*, 46: 22–34, 2008.

Desrosiers NA, Watterson JH: The effects of burial on drug detection in skeletal tissues. *Drug Test Analysis*, 2: 346–356, 2010.

Dolan K, Rouen D, Kimber J: An overview of the use of urine, hair, sweat and saliva to detect drug use. *Drug Alcol Rev*, 23: 213–217, 2004.

Ferner RE: Post-mortem clinical pharmacology. *Br J Clin Pharmacol*, 66: 430–443, 2008.

Flanagan RJ, Connally G: Interpretation of analytical toxicology results in life and at postmortem. *Toxicol Rev*, 24: 51–62, 2005.

Flanagan RJ, Connally G, Evans JM: Analytical toxicology: Guidelines for sample collection postmortem. *Toxicol Rev*, 24: 63–71, 2005.

Goucher E, Kicman A, Smith N, Jickells S: The detection and quantification of lorazepam and its 3-O-glucuronide in fingerprint deposits by LC-MS/MS. *J Sep Sci*, 32: 2266–2272, 2009.

Hoffmann WD, Jackson GP: Forensic mass spectrometry. *Ann Rev Anal Chem*, 8: 419–440, 2015.

Ingels AME, Lambert WE, Stove CP: Determination of gamma-hydroxybutyric acid in dried blood spots using a simple GC-MS method with direct "on spot" derivatization. *Anal Bioanal Chem*, 398: 2173–2182, 2010.

Jaffee WB, Trucco E, Levy S, Weiss RD: Is this urine really negative? A systematic review of tampering methods in urine drug screening and testing. *J Sub Abuse Treat*, 33: 33–42, 2007.

Karch SB, (Ed.): *Postmortem Toxicology of Abused Drugs*. Boca Raton, FL: CRC Press, 2008.

Kenney MC: Post-mortem drug concentrations. *Int Med J*, 40: 183–187, 2010.

Kinz P: When kissing can result in an adverse analytical finding during doping control: Case report where hair testing was determinant for the athlete. *TIAFT Bulletin*, 46: 18–19, 2016.

Kintz P, Salomone A, Vincenti M: *Hair Analysis in Clinical and Forensic Toxicology*. Cambridge, MA: Academic Press, 2015.

Levine B, (Ed.): *Principles of Forensic Toxicology*, 4th ed. Washington, DC: AACC Press, 2013.

Magnani B, Bissell MG, Kwong TC, Wu AHB, (Eds.): *Clinical Toxicology Testing: A Guide for Laboratory Professionals*. Northfield, IL: CAP Press, 2012.

McIntyre LM, King CV, Boratto M, Drummer OH: Post-mortem drug analyses in bone and bone marrow. *Ther Drug Monit*, 22: 79–83, 2000.

Milone MC: Laboratory testing for prescription opioids. *J Med Toxicol*, 8: 408–416, 2012.

Negrusz A, Cooper G: *Clarke's Analytical Forensic Toxicology*, 2nd ed. London, UK: Pharmaceutical Press, 2013.

Ropero-Miller JD, Goldberger BA, (Eds.): *Handbook of Workplace Drug Testing*, 2nd ed. Washington, DC: AACC Press, 2009.

Sadones N, Capiau S, De Kesel PM, Lambert WE, Stove CP: Spot them in the spot: Analysis of abused substances using dried blood spots. *Bioanalysis*, 6: 2211–2227, 2014.

Schulz M, Iwersen-Bergmann S, Andresen H, Schmoldt A: Therapeutic and toxic blood concentrations of nearly 1,000 drugs and other xenobiotics. *Crit Care*, 16: R136, 2012.

Stove CP, Ingels AS, De Kesel PM, Lambert WE: Dried blood spots in toxicology: From the cradle to the grave. *Crit Rev Toxicol*, 42: 230–243, 2012.

Unger KA, Watterson JH: Analysis of dextromethorphan and dextromorphan in skeletal remains following decomposition in different microclimate conditions. *J Anal Toxicol*, 40: 669–676, 2016.

Verstraete AG: Detection times of drugs of abuse in blood, urine, and oral fluid. *Ther Drug Monit*, 26: 200–205, 2004.

Wyman JF: Principles and procedures in forensic toxicology. *Clin Lab Med*, 32: 493–507, 2012.

Poisoning Treatment

6

6.1 Introduction

The outcome of poisoning treatment depends on numerous factors, such as the type of substance involved, the degree of exposure, the previous health of the individual exposed, and the time between exposure and initiation of treatment. The treatment of poisoning might begin with asymptomatic individuals with known or likely toxic exposures, or later when toxicity is more evident and life-threatening.

The material presented in this chapter is a broad overview for investigators to assist in reviewing medical information, and facilitate communicating with health care providers.

6.2 Assessment

6.2.1 Patient History

Information from any source that relates to a poisoning situation is collected. Specifically, information is sought on the identity of the toxicant, the amount involved, and approximately when the exposure occurred. The circumstances of the poisoning event that may be particularly important for selecting and initiating treatment include the following: (1) the reason for the exposure (accidental, suicidal, and abuse), (2) the environment where the exposure occurred, (3) the general medical and psychiatric state of health of the patient, and (4) the toxicants that were accessible.

Poisoned patients may be unable to provide a reliable history or be elusive because of suicidal intentions or legal issues. These issues may also compromise the information obtained from family, friends, or bystanders. In clinical poisoning situations, the relevant history of the incident is often an ongoing and evolving process of collecting and correcting information throughout the course of medical care.

When symptomatology correlates with an exposure to a toxicant, they are usually related. However, symptomatology might be a reflection of an unrelated disease process, or the result of both toxicity and a medical disorder. Assessment and diagnosis of toxic exposures require maintaining a high index of suspicion.

6.2.2 Clinical and Medical Laboratory Evaluation

Laboratory testing for metabolic disturbances and electrolyte imbalances are important features of patient management, and can provide important diagnostic clues for the identity and substantiation of toxicants involved. Other standard evaluation and monitoring practices utilized in emergency management of patients with serious medical issues also provide diagnostic clues for implementation of targeted treatment. ECG monitoring can identify or exclude cardiotoxicity. Cardiotoxic medications can have distinct ECG patterns.

6.2.3 Toxidromes

Toxidromes are a constellation of signs and symptoms suggestive of a particular class of toxicants. They can narrow the range of diagnostic possibilities, suggest management approaches, and provide guidance for targeting additional clinical and laboratory testing. There are many exceptions to toxidromes, and multiple exposures can produce a confusing variety of symptoms because of overlapping toxidromes. Moreover, the poisonings may be superimposed on preexisting illness. Toxidromes are analogous to the characteristic symptoms associated with a particular medical condition or disease such as diabetes or myocardial infarction. Symptom patterns point to possible disorders but are not diagnostic or exclusive. Examples of toxidromes are provided in Table 6.1.

6.2.4 Toxicology Testing

Urine drug screens are rarely helpful in emergency treatment, and can be misleading due to the limited scope of the screening panels employed. There can be false positives or negatives and drugs that are identified may be unrelated to the toxicity observed. Screening immunoassays have limitations in scope, sensitivity, and specificity. Quantitative testing is required for emergency management of only a relatively small number of toxicants. Examples of these are acetaminophen, aspirin, digoxin, iron, lithium, methanol, and ethylene glycol.

Table 6.1   Common Toxidromes

Syndrome	Symptoms	Toxicants
Anticholinergic	Delirium Dry mucous membranes Hallucinations Hyperthermia Mydriasis Picking gestures Seizures Tachycardia Urinary retention	Tricyclic antidepressants Antihistamines Scopolamine Angel's trumpet Jimson weed Many psychotropic drugs
Cholinergic	Bradycardia Diarrhea Miosis Muscle fasciculations Muscle weakness Salivation Sweating	Organophosphate pesticides Nicotine Some mushrooms
Opioid	Bradycardia CNS depression Hypotension Hypothermia Hypoventilation Miosis	Opioids Clonidine Dextromethorphan Tramadol
Sympathomimetic	Agitation Diaphoresis Hyperactivity Hypertension Hyperthermia Mydriasis Seizures Tachycardia	Amphetamines Cocaine Methylphenidate MDMA

6.3   Treatment

6.3.1   Life Support

The first consideration in the management of critically poisoned individuals is resuscitation and life-support measures to establish and stabilize respiration and circulation. This may include mechanical ventilation and circulatory support with fluids and medications. Focus is then shifted to a more specific therapy.

6.3.2 Symptomatic and Supportive Care

Treatment of acute poisoning is based on the symptomatic management of life-threatening symptoms such as seizures, cardiovascular collapse, hyperthermia, and electrolyte imbalances. There are guidelines in medicine for dealing with most severe symptoms of poisoning. These can be used more judiciously and effectively when the etiology of the symptoms is known. In most cases of poisoning, effective treatment with favorable outcomes is achieved with general symptomatic and supportive care without specific knowledge regarding the likely identity of the toxicants involved.

6.3.3 Antidotes

There are specific antidotes for a relatively small number of toxicants. Antidotes in most cases have potential adverse effects, and they are usually used only when clearly indicated. The antidotes that are generally available in emergency treatment facilities are listed in Table 6.2.

6.3.4 Evidence-Based Treatment Guidelines

Based on the collected experience and expert evaluation, evidence-based treatment guidelines have been developed for many toxicants. These continue to evolve and are modified to reflect relevant new information as it becomes available. Guidelines originate and are published by many authoritative organizations. These are most easily accessible in emergency situations

Table 6.2   Antidotes

Toxic Agent	Antidote
Acetaminophen	Acetylcysteine
Anticholinergics	Physostigmine
Arsenic, lead, mercury	Selective chelating agents
Benzodiazepines	Flumazenil
Botulism	Botulinum antitoxin
Cardiac glycosides	Specific Fab fragments
Cyanide	Hydroxocobalamin
Ethylene glycol	Fomepizole
Iron	Deferoxamine
Methanol	Fomepizole
Opioids	Naloxone
Organophosphate pesticides	Atropine and pralidoxime
Snake venom	Specific antivenin
Thallium	Prussian blue

by contacting a regional poison control center. Poison centers in the United States can be contacted at any time through a single national toll-free phone number (1-800-222-1222).

6.4 Removing Ingested Substances and Hastening Their Elimination

6.4.1 Gastric Removal

Decontamination of patients following oral ingestion of toxic substances is rarely effective in improving the outcome of poisoning. The use of emetic agents, gastric lavage, or irrigation of the gastrointestinal tract to reduce the absorption of substances is not a routine practice in poisoning treatment. These procedures carry risks and can also delay or complicate appropriate treatment. Gastric decontamination is indicated in only a few specific situations. Similarly, administering activated charcoal to bind to toxicants for prevention of absorption is indicated only for certain toxicants with particular dosage forms and exposure patterns.

6.4.2 Hemodialysis

Hemodialysis is used in some emergency situations unrelated to toxic exposures. These include acute kidney failure and life-threatening changes in fluids, electrolytes, or acid–base imbalances that are resistant to other forms of medical management. In poisoning situations, hemodialysis may also be employed in selected cases to increase the elimination of toxicants from the body. Hemodialysis requires specialized equipment and expertise and is amenable to use with toxicants with low molecular weight, high solubility, minimal plasma protein binding, and limited tissue distribution. The most common poisonings in which dialysis might be considered are those involving ethylene glycol, methanol, salicylates, and lithium.

6.4.3 Intravenous Lipid Administration

Lipid emulsions are used to reduce the systemic availability of certain lipid-soluble toxicants. The emulsions are administered intravenously to provide a lipid reservoir or sink for partitioning of substances in plasma with high lipid stability. This can reduce active plasma concentrations of substances and facilitate their elimination through lipid metabolic pathways. The effectiveness of lipid emulsion administration in the treatment of poisoning continues to be evaluated, and its applicability is currently limited.

6.5 Case Studies

Case: Granddaughter

In 2011, a 20-month-old girl was taken to the emergency department of a hospital in Northern Ireland 1 h after ingesting a lethal dose of her grandmother's dothiepin (tricyclic antidepressant). Shortly after her arrival, she developed seizures that were treated with IV thiopental. She required intubation. ECG changes observed were consistent with tricyclic antidepressant toxicity. She developed life-threatening cardiac arrhythmias and severe hypotension that did not respond to standard therapeutic measures. At this point, an intravenous infusion of a lipid emulsion was initiated, followed by defibrillation. This resulted in the normalization of cardiac function and a return to baseline blood pressure. After close monitoring, she was discharged on hospital day 3 with no evidence of neurological or cardiovascular complications.

Comments

Lipid emulsions have been used for parenteral nutrition for many years. Only recently have these emulsions become utilized for treating overdoses of lipid-soluble drugs. The emulsion apparently acts as a reservoir for the drugs, making them unavailable for contact with target sites.

Case: Whole Bowel Irrigation and Hemodialysis

In 2011, a 42-year-old woman with a bipolar disorder arrived at a hospital emergency department about 90 min after ingesting 40 sustained-release potassium chloride tablets, each containing 600 mg of potassium. She was alert and hemodynamically stable. Serum potassium was elevated and ECG patterns were consistent with hyperkalemia. At least 30 radio-opaque tablets in the stomach were identified on an abdominal X-ray. Insulin was administered to lower the extracellular potassium and then whole bowel irrigation with polyethylene glycol was initiated. Over the following 24 h, 27 tablets were recovered from stool effluent, and serum potassium decreased to normal levels. The following day, the woman was stabilized and transferred to a psychiatric unit.

Six months after the incident, the woman again arrived at the hospital emergency department 5 h after ingesting 100 sustained-release potassium tablets. She was alert, tachycardic, and hypertensive. Serum potassium was significantly elevated. Only three tablets were visualized in her stomach. Insulin and other medications to shift potassium intracellulary were administered and hemodialysis was initiated. Potassium levels decreased; she was clinically stabilized and was again discharged for psychiatric care.

Comments

Potassium tablets are among the few medications that are radio-opaque and therefore visible with radiography. Whole bowel irrigation is generally applicable to poisoning treatment when dosage forms are resistant to disintegration and treatment is initiated soon after ingestion.

High blood levels of potassium can cause fatal cardiac arrhythmias. Normally, most of the potassium resides in cells, not in the bloodstream. Part of the treatment for hyperkalemia is to lower blood levels by shifting potassium into cells. Insulin stimulates cellular uptake of potassium.

Information on the psychiatric history of the suicidal individual in this case, and the circumstances of the continuing availability of potassium tablets was not available.

Case: Concurrent Toxicity and Illness

In 2014, a 60-year-old woman with chronic obstruction pulmonary disease was taken to a hospital emergency department because of increasing shortness of breath due to bronchial obstruction from mucus accumulation. She had been seen about a month earlier at the same hospital with similar symptoms. At that time, she required intubation and mechanical ventilation and was discharged 2 days later with an uncomplicated recovery. On this recent occasion, she was hemodynamically stable and alert with normal pupil size. Her respiratory rate was elevated. Physical signs, metabolic tests, and chest radiographs were consistent with a diagnosis of an acute exacerbation of obstruction pulmonary disease, and appropriate medical therapy was initiated. An hour later, her respiratory rate dropped; respiratory failure continued to worsen, and she became less alert. She was then transferred to the critical care unit for monitoring and continuing care. Although symptoms of her pulmonary illness improved, she became increasingly drowsy and respiration dropped to two breaths per minute; she now had pinpoint pupils. These symptoms were treated with naloxone, which produced an immediate improvement in her condition. On recovery, the patient indicated that she had been taking prescribed extended-release dihydrocodeine tablets for back pain (120 mg twice a day), and had doubled the dose (240 mg twice a day) without medical consultation 4 days prior to admission. Moreover, she had taken an additional dose about 8 h immediately before the current emergency visit. Following recovery, she was referred for follow-up by a pain management unit.

Comments

This case provides an example of an overdose in an individual with a concurrent illness, which complicated the diagnosis of poisoning. The failure of treatment of the illness led to the consideration of a possible medication overdose. The toxicity of the opioid dihydrocodeine is reversed by naloxone. The use of opioids in individuals with respiratory diseases presents an elevated risk of a toxic overdose. In this case, the life-threatening overdose occurred in an individual who doubled the prescribed therapeutic dose because of inadequate pain relief. It is somewhat understandable that an individual might not appreciate the toxic potential of taking two tablets instead of the single tablet dose prescribed.

Case: Antidote and Hemodialysis

In 2016, a 78-year-old man was brought to a hospital emergency department by his daughter because he was having difficulty in standing or sitting upright, his speech was garbled, and his vision was distorted. These symptoms started about 6 h prior to his arrival at the hospital. He had a history of hypertension, dementia, and transient ischemic attacks. On arrival, he was tachycardic, tachypneic, lethargic, and disoriented. Laboratory testing indicated acute kidney injury, acidosis, and electrolyte imbalances. There were no indications of possible infections and a head CT scan was negative for stroke. The metabolic disturbances and osmolality changes identified in laboratory serum samples were consistent with ethylene glycol poisoning; this was confirmed with serum testing. Subsequently, the man was transferred to the intensive care unit where fomepizole was administered and hemodialysis was initiated. Over the following 3 days, the acidosis and electrolyte imbalances were normalized, ethylene glycol levels were significantly reduced, and the man's mental status improved. However, his renal function did not improve and, following discharge from the hospital, he required long-term intermittent hemodialysis. The circumstances surrounding the ethylene glycol exposure remained vague and uncertain, and the case was referred by hospital staff to adult protective services for follow-up and investigation for the possibility of malicious activity by the man's caregivers.

Comments

Due to the general availability of ethylene glycol in the form of antifreeze products, and its unusually sweet taste, accidental ingestions can occur, especially when the antifreeze is stored in containers that originally contained familiar beverages. Suicidal and homicidal exposures also occur with ethylene glycol.

Ethylene glycol toxicity results from its metabolic conversion to toxic metabolites. Fomepizole blocks this metabolic conversion, and the unchanged ethylene glycol can be cleared from the body by hemodialysis.

Case: Scratching below the Surface

In 2015, a 27-year-old woman in Colorado was brought to a hospital emergency department by her husband. She was agitated, having visual and auditory hallucinations, intermittent muscle rigidity, and jerking movements of her arms and legs. Her symptoms started a few days earlier with nausea and heart palpitations, and then she developed signs of short-term memory loss and anxiety with intermittent fever. This previously healthy woman had no history of ethanol or illicit drug use. At admission, her heart rate, blood pressure, and respiratory rate were elevated; her body temperature and pupils were normal. Results of urine and serum toxicological screenings were negative for opioids, methamphetamine, cocaine, and ethanol. Intravenous fluids were started, physical and laboratory examinations were initiated. A CT scan of the head was normal. Antimicrobial therapy for possible meningitis was initiated. Her extreme agitation was treated with benzodiazepines and haloperidol. To facilitate deep sedation, she was intubated and placed on mechanical ventilation. Initial diagnostic considerations included a possible drug overdose or withdrawal, CNS infections, encephalitis, and metabolic disturbances. Cerebrospinal fluid test results were consistent with an inflammatory process. The woman's condition deteriorated despite an antimicrobial therapy. Autonomic hyperactivity and prominent psychiatric manifestations with movement disorders are known to occur with certain types of autoimmune encephalitis mediated by antibody interactions with glutamate receptors in central neuronal synapses. Due to these factors, transvaginal ultrasonography was performed, which revealed an ovarian tumor (teratoma). The encephalitis in this case was due to an ovarian tumor. Aggressive therapy, which included surgical removal of the tumor, was initiated. She remained hospitalized for 6 weeks and ultimately made a full recovery.

Comments

The rapid onset of illness with serious alterations in mental status and neurologic functions is not necessarily drug related. This case illustrates the potential diagnostic complexity of emergency evaluations of individuals with altered mental status.

References and Additional Reading

Archer JRH, Wood DM, Dargan PI: How to use toxicology screening tests. *Arch Dis Child Educ Pract Ed*, 97: 194–199, 2012.

Boyle JS, Bechtel LK, Holstege CP: Management of the critically poisoned patient. *Scand J Trauma Resuss Emerg Med*, 17: 1–11, 2009.

Buller GK, Moskowitz CB, Eckardt K: The role of hemodialysis and fomepizole in ethylene glycol intoxication. *J Nephrol Therapeut*, 310: 1–3, 2012.

Daly FF, Little M, Murray L: A risk assessment based approach to the management of acute poisoning. *Emerg Med J*, 23: 396–399, 2006.

Dart RC: Expert consensus guidelines for stocking of antidotes in hospitals that provide emergency care. *Am Emerg Med*, 54: 386–394, 2009.

Erikson TB, Thompson TM, Lu JJ: The approach to the patient with an unknown overdose. *Emerg Med Clin N Am*, 25: 249–281, 2007.

Frithsen IL, Simpson WM: Recognition and management of acute medication poisoning. *Am Fam Physician*, 81: 316–323, 2010.

Greene S, Harris C, Singer J: Gastrointestinal decontamination of the poisoned patient. *Pediat Emerg Care*, 24: 176–186, 2008.

Gunja N: Decontamination and enhanced elimination in sustained-release potassium chloride poisoning. *Emerg Med Aust*, 23: 769–772, 2011.

Hendron D, Menagh G, Sandilands EA, Scullion D: Tricyclic antidepressant overdose in a toddler treated with intravenous lipid emulsion. *Pediatrics*, 128: 1628–1632, 2011.

Hoffman RS, Howland MA, Lewin NA, Nelson LS, Goldfrank LR, (Eds.): *Goldfrank's Toxicologic Emergencies*, 10th ed. New York: McGraw-Hill, 2015.

Holstege CP, Dobmeier SG, Bechtel LK: Critical care toxicology. *Emerg Med Clin N Am*, 25: 715–739, 2008.

Holubek WJ, Hoffman RS, Goldfarb DS, Nelson LS: Use of hemodialysis and hemoperfusion in poisoned patients. *Kid Int*, 74: 1327–1334, 2008.

Kayser MS, Dalmau J: Anti-NMDA receptor encephalitis in psychiatry. *Curr Psychiatry Rev*, 7: 189–193, 2011.

Lam SW, Engebretsen KM, Bauer SR: Toxicology today: What you need to know now. *J Pharm Pract*, 24: 174–188, 2011.

Levine M, Brooks DE, Truitt CA, Wolk BJ, Boyer EW, Ruha A: Toxicology in the ICU Part 1: General overview and approach to treatment. *Chest*, 140: 795–806, 2011.

Levine M, Hoffman RS, Lavergne V, Stork M, Graudins A, Chuang R, Stellpflug SJ et al.: Systematic review of the effect of intravenous lipid emulsion therapy for non-local anesthetics toxicity. *Clin Toxicol*, 54: 194–221, 2016.

Marraffa JM, Cohen V, Howland MA: Antidotes for toxicological emergencies. *Am J Health Syst Pharm*, 69: 199–212, 2012.

Mathai SK, Josephson SA, Badlam J, Saint S, Janssen WJ: Scratching below the surface. *N Engl J Med*, 375: 2188–2193, 2016.

Olson KR, (Ed.): *Poisoning & Drug Overdose*, 6th ed. New York: McGraw-Hill, 2012.

Singh R, Arain E, Buth A, Kado J, Soubani A, Imran N: Ethylene glycol poisoning: An unusual case of altered mental status and the lessons learned from management of the disease in the acute setting. *Case Rep in Crit Care*, #9157393, 2016.

Steynor M, MacDuff A: Always consider the possibility of opioid induced respiratory depression in patients presenting with hypercapnic respiratory failure who fail to improve as expected with appropriate therapy. *Case Rep in Crit Care*, #562319, 2015.

Yates C, Manini A: Utility of the electrocardiogram in drug overdose and poisoning: Theoretical considerations and clinical implications. *Curr Cardiol Rev*, 8: 137–151, 2012.

Potential Poisons II

The chemicals that are included in this section are substances that forensic investigators would likely encounter. These also serve as prototypes for other possible toxicants. These natural and man-made chemicals include medications, recreational substances, plant constituents, industrial chemicals, elements, and pesticides.

Each chapter provides a background on the substances discussed with emphasis on well-known features that receive widespread attention, and provides insight into the substance's accessibility. Situations and circumstances that might be involved in exposures to the substances are highlighted along with symptoms of poisoning that might be useful for the recognition of poisoning by a particular substance. Case studies involving the toxicants are used to demonstrate the utility of the information provided. References for more specific information and in-depth reviews of various aspects of the toxicants are listed at the end of each chapter.

Arsenic

7

7.1 Introduction

Arsenic is probably the most well-known poison in the world. It has been used as a murder weapon for centuries, and remains a favorite poison for authors of murder mysteries. The mere mention of the word arsenic evokes an immediate association with poisoning. Arsenic is a naturally occurring element that everyone is exposed to in nontoxic concentrations every day. It can be found in soil, water, plants, and animals. Almost all foods, whether fresh or processed, contain arsenic. Arsenic has commercial uses and even some applications in current medical therapy. From a forensic standpoint, one should expect to find arsenic in biological as well as inert materials. The mere presence of arsenic is not generally concerning; it is the concentration or the amount of arsenic present in samples that is the prime consideration.

Arsenic has an affinity for sulfur-containing chemical structures that are involved in many important biochemical processes throughout the body. When arsenic binds to these structures, it blocks these processes and leads to toxicity.

7.2 Exposure Situations and Circumstances

Similar to most poisons, availability depends on an individual's resources and sometimes their occupation. Arsenic is very toxic in doses that are easily mixed with food and beverages without altering their flavor or texture. It produces symptoms that are easily mistaken for natural diseases.

7.3 Symptoms of Poisoning

Initial symptoms of arsenic poisoning generally relate to the gastrointestinal system manifesting as nausea, vomiting, abdominal pain, and profuse diarrhea. These symptoms may be closely followed by psychosis, toxic cardiomyopathy, and seizures. Ultimately, arsenic affects all body systems: kidneys, liver, heart, lungs, muscles, and nervous system. The most frequent neurological manifestations of poisoning are muscle weakness, tingling sensations, and intense pain starting in the lower limbs and moving upward. This can be misdiagnosed as Guillain–Barré syndrome, which is an autoimmune disorder that alters peripheral nerves and produces similar symptoms. Suspected cases of Guillain–Barré syndrome with significant gastrointestinal symptoms might be indicative of arsenic poisoning and this possibility should be considered in the differential diagnosis of these patients.

7.4 Case Studies

Case: Bitter Coffee at Church Breakfast

In 2003, 16 members of a small church in Maine became extremely ill after consuming pastries and coffee after the morning service. They were hospitalized and one church member died. It was soon determined that the congregation had been poisoned with arsenic, and that the source of the arsenic was the coffee. Biological samples from all victims were found to contain high levels of arsenic. Some of the 15 survivors had permanent neurological damage. About a week after the poisoning, a church member committed suicide, leaving a note that expressed his intense guilt for the poisoning and described how it was done. He had gone to the church kitchen during that Sunday morning service and poured a solution containing arsenic into the coffee maker. His motives appeared to involve a long-held grudge with the church members about policies and ideas for change. The most recent incident had involved the selection of a communion table for the church. The poison was obtained from an old pesticide container stored in his barn. It is not clear whether he realized that the pesticide was an arsenic compound. His stated intention was to make the other church members ill. When he realized that he had killed one member and others were likely to die, he killed himself out of shame and remorse. The man had been a respected citizen and a contributing member of the church and the community. He had worked as a substitute teacher and nurse, and he was a member of the church's historical committee. He was also an avid skier and runner. He lived alone on a farm that had been in his family for generations.

Comments

The initial focus of the authorities was on the possibility of food poisoning, or an act of terrorism. The rural town where the poisoning took place had a population of about 650. The simultaneous poisoning of over a dozen people posed major logistic problems for medical care and investigative efforts.

Case: Toxic Potato Salad at Church Picnic

In 2015, 25 members of a small church in Ohio became extremely ill after eating at a potluck luncheon following the Sunday service. They were all hospitalized and one member died. It was soon determined that they had been poisoned with botulinum toxin, and the source of the toxin was home-canned potatoes used in potato salad served at the church luncheon. All of the poisoned individuals were treated with antitoxin. Some of the individuals required endotracheal intubation and mechanical ventilation. Except for the single fatality, all individuals recovered and were discharged from area hospitals within a period of about a week. The source of the botulism toxin was identified from questioning victims about the items they consumed and testing food samples found in trash bags. The potluck meal was a regular church event, which occurred every few months. More than 70 people ate at the meal with 25 developing symptoms of poisoning within days. The potato salad had been prepared with improperly home-canned potatoes. A boiling water canner was used rather than a pressure canner, which is necessary to kill *Clostridium botulinum*, which produces the toxin. This case was the largest botulism outbreak in the United States in 40 years.

Comments

This case is presented to provide a contrast to the previous arsenic case, which involved a church meal intentionally contaminated. Most exposures to toxic substances present difficult challenges for investigators due to the need for identifying the causative agent as quickly as possible to prevent additional poisoning and to properly treat symptomatic individuals. From these very similar circumstances in the two cases, one can appreciate the prospect for many potential toxicants that might result in group poisoning in similar situations.

Botulinum toxin is a neurotoxin that blocks transmission of nerve signals to skeletal muscles. Symptoms of poisoning include paralysis of eye muscles, difficulty swallowing, muscles weakness, and paralysis of respiratory muscles.

Case: Chemistry Classmates

Eric, 30, was a research scientist who lived in North Carolina with his wife, Ann, 30, and their 10-month-old daughter. They had met in a chemistry class while in college. Ann was working as a chemist with a pharmaceutical company and Eric worked in a university laboratory. In 2000, Eric became violently ill one evening while bowling with friends. His illness started shortly after eating a hot dog and drinking a beer.

He was sick through the night, and the following morning his wife took him to a hospital. He gradually improved and left the hospital after several days. One week later, the illness returned and he was again taken to the hospital where he died a short time later. Testing of urine samples taken during his final days revealed that Eric had died from arsenic poisoning. The analytical results and circumstances of the death resulted in a homicide investigation. Early in the investigation police discovered that Ann had a relationship with a coworker, and they both had access to arsenic where they worked. The coworker was one of the individuals at the bowling event that preceded the first episode of the husband's illness. About 4 months after Eric's death, Ann's coworker committed suicide. Prior to the suicide he had spoken to an attorney and provided details about his relationship with Ann and the poisoning. He indicated that Ann had poisoned her husband before his death and even injected arsenic into her husband's IV bag while he was hospitalized. The progress of the case was initially hampered by the legal issues involved with attorney–client privileges and the availability of the confession to authorities. While the investigation was ongoing, Ann moved out of state and remarried. She was finally arrested in 2005 and charged with first-degree murder. She pled guilty to second-degree murder and conspiracy to commit first-degree murder, and she was sentenced to 25–31 years in prison. She admitted that she and her former coworker poisoned her husband by adding arsenic to his food and drinks.

Comments

This case illustrates how arsenic might be used in repeated poisonings, and that an individual with severe arsenic poisoning can be hospitalized and the poisoning not be recognized. The victim received an amount of arsenic in his food at the bowling event that caused severe toxicity but was not lethal. He was poisoned a second time with an amount that was again not lethal. The wife then administered more arsenic in his IV line while he was hospitalized. This pattern of experimentation with escalating doses of poisons is not unusual among reported poison murder cases that include spouses or others having daily access to the victims.

Case: Arsenic Suicide by Substance Abuser

In 2007, a 30-year-old woman living with her parents intentionally injected an arsenic compound intravenously. She had a 10-year history of using cocaine and heroin, and was frequently intoxicated with ethanol and other substances. Her initial symptoms of abdominal pain and vomiting were at first attributed by her parents to ethanol as they had often seen her markedly intoxicated. When the symptoms intensified over several hours, she was admitted to an intensive care unit of a hospital. Approximately 14 h after the injection, she had a sudden cardiac arrest that was unresponsive to resuscitation. At autopsy, organ examination, histopathological findings, and the presence of a high concentration of arsenic were consistent with arsenic poisoning. A few days after her death, a suicide note was discovered in her room.

Comments

The arsenic compound injected in this case was disodium hydrogen arsenic, which is a component of a fungicide used in gardening. The liquid fungicide product was regularly used by the woman's parents. These arsenic-containing products are no longer popular and have been largely replaced by more effective and less toxic products.

Case: Tragic Accident

In 2003, two children became ill while attending a cook-out hosted by a business client of the father. The father was a financial planner, and the host was a retired 72-year-old dentist who lived in an upscale seaside home in Massachusetts with his wife. The illness began shortly after the children drank bottled spring water supplied by the host. The water was used to make baby formula for the 4-month-old infant and added to a drinking cup for the 2-year-old toddler. Within minutes after drinking the liquids, the children became seriously ill and the parents rushed them to a nearby hospital for treatment. It was soon discovered that the bottle containing the spring water had a folded label from another product taped to its carrying handle. The label was from an arsenic-containing weed killer. The plastic bottle was of the type that might be used for a product such as cranberry juice, and the handle was a plastic flip-up loop that was a component of the screw cap closure system. The bottle was one of several similar bottles containing spring water that was stored together in the same location in the home. Periodically, empty bottles were taken and refilled at a local spring.

Two days after the ingestion, the infant died; the toddler developed significant cardiovascular problems, but these were amendable to treatment and she was discharged after 13 days in the hospital. Testing results from the water container, the infant's formula, and biological samples from the children were used to estimate the probable amount of arsenic ingested by each child. The amount was 3400 mg for the infant and 200 mg for the toddler. An investigation concluded that the poisonings were most likely caused by a tragic accident. However, the host was formally charged with involuntary manslaughter. The presiding judge at his trial found him not guilty of the charge.

Comments

The retired couple had several plastic containers from juice products and used them to obtain spring water from a source near their home. At some point, someone had prepared a solution of pesticide from a more concentrated product using one of the plastic containers. Later, someone straightening up the items in the storage area likely included the pesticide container with the group of spring water containers. The precise way this happened is not known.

Case: Toxic Solution for Troubled Marriage

In 1991, a 37-year-old mother of two was taken by her 34-year-old husband to the emergency department of a hospital in Dallas. She had been ill for several days and was severely dehydrated due to protracted episodes of vomiting. On arrival, the emergency physician felt that she may be suffering from some form of food poisoning or possibly toxic shock syndrome. Her condition rapidly deteriorated and soon she was transferred to the hospital intensive care unit. Aggressive symptomatic therapy was provided but she died 6 days later. Following an autopsy and toxicological testing, her death was determined to be the result of arsenic poisoning, and ruled a homicide.

She had been married for 10 years prior to her death. She met her husband in college while studying landscape design. After graduating, they both pursued successful careers with companies that specialized in property development. They were devoted parents and participated in church and community affairs. To all, they seemed to be an ideal couple with strong family values. However, things started to change during the year preceding the wife's death. The husband had begun to pursue other women and eventually developed a rather strong relationship with one. The couple separated. Several reconciliations were attempted, but it was finally decided that they would divorce. They had arrived at an acceptable settlement and child custody terms and the finalization of the divorce was in progress when the wife died.

After the death, it became known that both the wife as well as her parents suspected that she was being poisoned by her husband. There had been occasions when she became unusually ill immediately after consuming substances provided by her husband. Most notably, this included wine, soft drinks, and dietary supplement capsules. Investigators also learned that the husband had purchased several toxic chemicals from chemical supply companies. These included barium carbonate, sodium carbonate, sodium nitroferricyanide, and arsenic trioxide. It was later found that barium carbonate was present in the wife's dietary supplement capsules, and sodium nitroferricyanide was present in some prescription antibiotic capsules that she was taking. The husband was arrested, tried for murder, convicted, and sentenced to life in prison. He testified during his trial. Jurors interviewed following the trial indicated that his testimony was compelling and strongly impacted them in considering his innocence, but the evidence of his guilt was so overwhelming that they had to find him guilty. A major portion of the damming evidence included documents allegedly written by his wife that offered explanations for the toxic ingestions. These documents were unquestionably shown to be forgeries that the husband had produced. Investigators also learned that while in college, the couple had developed the unusual skill of being able to copy each other's handwriting. It was this skill that enabled the husband to support his innocence by producing diaries and other documents allegedly from his wife.

Comments

The motive for the murder was probably the financial assets of the wife that would be lost if the couple divorced. The evidence collected during this investigation suggests that the husband experimented with several poisons administered in a variety of ways prior to the fatal dose of arsenic.

Case: Gastroenteritis

In 1985, a 32-year-old man presented at a local hospital emergency department with flu-like symptoms that included vomiting and diarrhea that began 9 days earlier. He was diagnosed as having viral gastroenteritis, treated with an antiemetic, and was discharged. He returned 4 days later severely ill and agitated. He had bruising on his body from falling. Blood studies suggested that he might have a disorder affecting blood-forming organs, possibly leukemia or aplastic anemia. Approximately 6 h after the second hospital admission, he suffered a fatal cardiac arrhythmia. Toxicology testing of samples obtained at autopsy revealed significant levels of arsenic in both blood and organ specimens. When confronted with the autopsy results, the decedent's wife confessed to the poisoning. The couple had a variety of marital problems that included infidelity by both partners. She had been regularly adding arsenic to her husband's food. She became impatient with how slow the poison was working and used a much larger amount on the day of his death. The couple had two young children (ages 2 and 3 years old) who had died previous to this incident. Their bodies were exhumed and reexamined, but no evidence of poisoning was identified.

Comments

Acute arsenic poisoning can cause severe gastroenteritis similar to that produced by bacterial or viral food poisoning. This can progress within hours to shock and cardiac arrhythmias. Individuals who survive these cardiovascular effects generally develop hematologic abnormalities and peripheral neuropathy.

References and Additional Reading

Donofrio PD, Wilbourn J, Albers JW, Rogers L, Salanga V, Greenberg HS: Acute arsenic intoxication presenting as Guillain-Barre-like syndrome. *Muscle Nerve*, 10: 114–120, 1987.

Gensheimer KF, Rea V, Mills DA, Montagna CP, Simone K: Arsenic poisoning caused by intentional contamination of coffee at a church gathering: An epidemiological approach to a forensic investigation. *J Forensic Sci*, 55: 1116–1119, 2010.

Isbister GK, Dawson AH, Whyte IM: Arsenic trioxide poisoning: A description of two acute overdoses. *Hum Exp Toxicol*, 23: 359–364, 2004.

Lai MW, Boyer EW, Kleinman ME, Rodig NM, Ewald MB: Acute arsenic poisoning in two siblings. *Pediatrics*, 116: 249–257, 2005.

Lamb A: *Deadly Dose: The Untold Story of a Homicide Investigator's Crusade for Truth and Justice.* New York: Berkley, 2008.

Mackell MA, Poklis A, Gantner GE, Graham M: An unsuspected arsenic poisoning murder disclosed by forensic autopsy. *Am J Forensic Med Path*, 6: 358–361, 1985.

McCarty CL: Large outbreak of botulism associated with a church potluck meal—Ohio, 2015. *CDC MMWR*, 64: 802–803, 2015.

Mills DA, Tommassoni AJ, Tallon LA, Kade KA, Savoia ES: Mass arsenic poisoning and the public health response in Maine. *Disaster Med Public Health Prep*, 7: 319–326, 2013.

Tournel G, Houssaye C, Humbert L, Dhorne C, Gnemmi V, Becart-Robert A, Nisse P et al.: Acute arsenic poisoning: Clinical toxicological, histopathological, and forensic features. *J Forensic Sci*, 56: 275–279, 2011.

Young CE: *A Bitter Brew: Faith, Power, and Poison in a Small New England Town.* New York: Berkley, 2005.

Carbon Monoxide

8

8.1 Introduction

Carbon monoxide is a leading cause of poisoning deaths in the United States. Hundreds die each year from carbon monoxide poisoning and many thousands are treated in medical facilities. Survivors of poisonings can suffer significant neurological damage that may be permanent. Carbon monoxide is an odorless and colorless gas. Anything that burns fuel or generates combustion gases can be a source of carbon monoxide (Table 8.1). Fuel sources include wood, charcoal, coal, oil, gasoline, diesel fuel, kerosene, propane, and natural gas. Many vehicles, heating units, appliances, tools, and other devices utilize these fuels. When carbon monoxide enters the lungs during respiration, it combines with hemoglobin in the blood and prevents the hemoglobin from transporting oxygen to vital organs.

8.2 Exposure Situations and Circumstances

Power outages during disasters result in the widespread use of portable gasoline-powered generators for lighting, refrigerators, air-conditioning, and other appliances. Generators used inside homes, in attached garages, or near ventilation intake ducts are responsible for a large number of carbon monoxide poisonings and fatalities. Small gasoline engines running in confined spaces can generate lethal levels of carbon monoxide within minutes.

Suicide utilizing engine exhaust from automobiles is well known. Sometimes this is accomplished by using a hose to direct the exhaust from a tailpipe directly into the interior of the car. The introduction of automotive catalytic converters in 1975 significantly reduced the concentration of carbon monoxide in exhaust gases, which decreased but did not eliminate engine exhaust gas suicides. Tanks of compressed carbon monoxide are commercially available and can be employed for self-poisoning using a face mask. Similarly, small charcoal grills in confined spaces such as an automobile or a bathroom can be a source of lethal exposure. Chemical generation of carbon monoxide using a mixture of formic acid and sulfuric acid has also been employed for suicide.

Table 8.1   Sources of Carbon Monoxide

Appliances

Cooking stoves
Ovens
Gas clothes dryers
Gas water heaters

Heating Units

Furnaces
Space heaters
Stoves
Fireplaces
Pool heaters

Vehicles

Automobiles, trucks, campers, buses
Industrial forklifts
Motorcycles, ATVs
Ice skating rink resurfacing machines
Boats

Portable Equipment

Generators
Stoves
Lanterns
Grills

Tools

Lawn mowers
Snow blowers
Chainsaws
Power washers
Construction equipment

Carbon monoxide is sometimes confused with carbon dioxide. The toxicity of these two gases is significantly different. When one is exposed to high levels of carbon dioxide, death results from the fact that oxygen is excluded from the breathing environment. Carbon monoxide is toxic in low concentrations even when oxygen is available. It prevents inhaled oxygen from combining with hemoglobin in blood for distribution through the body.

8.3 Symptoms of Poisoning

The toxic effects of carbon monoxide are related to its concentration in air, and the duration of exposure. Depending on concentration, fatalities can occur within minutes or after several hours. Initial symptoms include headache, nausea, and fatigue resembling flu symptoms. Increasing exposure produces more serious symptoms that could include cardiac arrhythmias, hallucinations, seizures, unconsciousness, and respiratory arrest leading to death (Table 8.2). Since symptoms of carbon monoxide poisoning are variable and nonspecific, misdiagnosis is common. Some of the more common misdiagnoses for carbon monoxide poisoning are provided in Table 8.3. Misdiagnosis

Table 8.2 Symptoms of Carbon Monoxide Poisoning

Ataxia
Cardiac arrhythmias
Chest pain
Coma
Confusion
Dizziness
Dyspnea
Fainting
Headache
Myocardial ischemia
Nausea
Seizures
Tachypnea
Visual changes
Vomiting
Weakness

Table 8.3 Common Misdiagnoses of Carbon Monoxide Poisoning

CNS depressant overdose
Cerebrovascular event (stroke)
Ethanol intoxication
Food poisoning
Gastroenteritis
Influenza (flu-like)
Myocardial infarction
Parkinsonism

can delay appropriate treatment and it can result in poisoned victims being discharged from medical facilities and returning to environmental situations that continue to poison them. Individuals who survive exposure to high levels of carbon monoxide can sustain permanent brain damage with effects on memory, cognition, and behavior. The degree of exposure to carbon monoxide can be estimated by determining the percent of hemoglobin that has been combined with carbon monoxide to form carboxyhemoglobin. Symptoms of poisoning are generally observed when carboxyhemoglobin levels exceed 15%. Effects are variable, but levels above 30% are generally considered life-threatening.

8.4 Case Studies

Case: Repeated Poisoning in Hotel

In 2013, an elderly couple died from carbon monoxide in Room 225 of a highly rated hotel in Boone, North Carolina. The hotel has three floors with 72 rooms. The hotel was built in 2000. Three weeks after the couple died, 10 girls attending a birthday celebration in Room 325 (one floor above Room 225) became violently ill. This was reported to the hotel management. A few weeks later, a mother and her 11-year-old son were staying in Room 225 of the same hotel when they were also exposed to lethal concentrations of carbon monoxide; the son died and the mother suffered permanent brain and lung damage. The mother remembers becoming nauseated and going into the bathroom. She then passed out before she could get to a phone or the door. The next morning the hotel staff discovered her unconscious on the bathroom floor and her son on the bed where he apparently had been watching television. The source of the carbon monoxide was an indoor swimming pool heater, which was not installed or maintained properly. The exhaust pipe from the heater was under Room 225. It was corroded, had several leaks, and was held in place by makeshift supporting materials. The same emergency personnel who responded to the death of the elderly couple responded to the mother and son tragedy. The responders did not test the room for carbon monoxide during the first visit. At the later incident, carbon monoxide was detected, and its source located in a relatively short period of time. The medical examiner had determined that the elderly couple's death was due to carbon monoxide but he had not notified the hotel or the police. He subsequently resigned. The president of the company that owned the hotel was indicted for involuntary manslaughter and assault. Wrongful death suits were filed for damages against the president and owners of the hotel, the hotel franchise, and other companies and individuals who worked on the pool heating system. The hotel was closed for repairs after the second incident. Room 225 was closed permanently.

Comments

There is reason to believe that the pool heater was not designed, installed, maintained, or inspected properly. The heater was originally fueled by propane, but this was converted later to natural gas. The elderly couple's initial death investigation was apparently considered to have been simultaneous heart attacks. Relatives and people within the community suspected carbon monoxide in the deaths, but officials did not investigate.

Two or more people in the same environment having simultaneous fatal heart attacks are extremely unlikely. It is not clear why further investigation was not carried out. It is noteworthy that there have been at least 200 deaths in hotel rooms throughout the country during recent years from carbon monoxide exposures.

Case: Friends in Room above the Motel Garage

In 2010, teenage boys who had gathered together in a Florida motel room to celebrate a birthday were found dead from carbon monoxide poisoning. Because of some difficulty with starting their car, they had left the engine running in a closed garage located beneath their room. Their bodies were discovered by a maid. When emergency personnel arrived, the car was still running and a door at an inside staircase leading up to the motel room was slightly open. Two boys were lying on the bed, and three were seated on the floor with bags of partially eaten fast food on their laps. They appeared to have been relaxing and watching television. No alcohol or drugs were in the room.

Comments

The location of the bodies in positions relative to the TV and the food items is an indication of simultaneous poisoning of the group. There was no indication that the boys were aware of the poisoning taking place or of any attempt to escape or seek help.

Case: Parked in a Garage

A few days after Christmas in 2014, the bodies of a young couple were found in a car parked in a family-owned storage garage. They were last seen alive 3 weeks earlier. They were reported missing when they failed to check into a bed and breakfast hotel they had reserved for a romantic weekend. They were both in their early twenties. They were fully clothed and slumped over in the car's front seats. The gas tank was empty and the battery was dead. They were a couple that participated in family activities and had plans for marriage. Nothing indicated foul play or the possibility of suicide. For unexplained reasons, the couple apparently wanted some privacy together and were overwhelmed by odorless carbon monoxide after running the engine to keep warm with the garage door shut.

Comments

The situation illustrated with this case is not uncommon. It occurs with couples of all ages. Sometimes there is evidence of sexual activity or drug use. This type of tragedy occurs more often during the winter months and is seen both in typical home garages as well as larger parking lots. Couples appear to be overcome simultaneously with no signs that they were in any way alerted to the impending danger of their situation.

Case: Houseboats

In 2000, two families vacationing on a houseboat on Lake Powell (Arizona–Utah border) started the boat generator to run the air conditioner and operate the television. About 15 min later, two brothers (aged 8 and 11 years) swam into the airspace beneath the swim platform on the back of the boat. The platform was attached just above the exit port for the exhaust gases from the generator. Within 1–2 min, one boy lost consciousness and the other began to convulse before sinking under the water. Their bodies were retrieved the next day. Autopsy results showed that the boys had been overcome by carbon monoxide and subsequently drowned; autopsy carboxyhemoglobin levels were 59% and 52%.

Comments

This incident triggered an extensive investigation of power boat drownings throughout the United States, and identified numerous carbon monoxide drowning cases. Some findings obtained during the investigation of the drownings are presented in Table 8.4.

Table 8.4   Carbon Monoxide Toxicity Symptoms and Levels Measured during Boating Investigations

Carbon Monoxide[a]	Symptoms and Investigative Results
200	Mild headache, fatigue, nausea, dizziness, and confusion
400	Serious headache, other symptoms intensify within 1–2 h; collapse after 2.5–3.5 h
1200	Considered to be immediately dangerous to life and health
3200	Death in 30 min
6400	Death in 10–15 min
>1200	Measured in open air on stern deck of several boats
As high as 10,000	Measured in open air near swim platforms of several boats
7,000–30,000	Measured in houseboat airspace under swim platforms

[a] ppm = parts of carbon monoxide per million parts of air.

Case: Heart Attacks in Elderly Couple

A 78-year-old man developed chest pain, shortness of breath, lassitude, and confusion. His examination in a hospital emergency department was indicative of acute myocardial ischemia. The physician treating the man learned later that his wife had also become a patient in the emergency department after bringing in her husband. She had developed chest pain, which radiated to her left arm and intensified with time. Initially, the wife was believed to be suffering from mental or emotional stress and anxiety due to her husband's heart problem. However, on further examination, her symptoms indicated that she also had active ischemic heart disease. The wife received the same treatment as her husband and, after 2 days, both felt much better and were discharged. Two days later, both patients were brought back to the hospital with similar symptoms. Both showed cardiac abnormalities. This was recognized as an unlikely coincidence. It was suspected that something in their surroundings initiated their symptoms. The wife recalled that a dull headache had accompanied her chest pain. She reported that she and her husband used two kerosene heaters in their unventilated apartment because their central heating system was not working. The patients' blood carboxyhemoglobin levels were checked and indicated that they were suffering from carbon monoxide poisoning. The couple was treated with oxygen, their symptoms resolved, and they returned home after their heating system had been repaired.

Comments

The circumstances of this case strongly pointed to carbon monoxide poisoning. Whenever more than one individual simultaneously develops similar symptoms of illness, poisoning should be among the first possibilities considered. In this case, it was carbon monoxide, but other cases of this nature might involve food poisoning, substance abuse, or some other common exposure situations.

References and Additional Reading

Chou C, Lai C, Liou S, Loh C: Carbon monoxide: An old poison with a new way of poisoning. *J Formos Med Assoc*, 111: 452–455, 2012.

Cuhor J, Restuccia M: Carbon monoxide poisoning during natural disasters: The Hurricane Rita experience. *J Emerg Med*, 33: 261–264, 2007.

Huston B, Froloff V, Mills K, McGee M: Carbon monoxide poisoning and death in a large enclosed ventilated area. *J Forensic Sci*, 58: 1651–1653, 2013.

Lin PT, Dunn WA: Suicidal carbon monoxide poisoning by combining formic acid and sulfuric acid within a confined space. *J Forensic Sci*, 59: 271–273, 2014.

Mevorach D, Heyman SN: Pain in the marriage. *N Engl J Med*, 332: 48–50, 1995.

Pan Y, Lee M: Charcoal burning and maternal filicide-suicide trends in Taiwan: The impact of accessibility on lethal methods. *J Formos Med Assoc*, 107: 811–815, 2008.

Sircar K, Clower J, Shin MK, Bailey C, King M, Yip F: Carbon monoxide poisoning deaths in the United States, 1999 to 2012. *Am J Emerg Med*, 33: 1440–1445, 2015.

Cyanide 9

9.1 Introduction

The public is very much aware of the toxic potential of cyanide. During World War II, the Nazis used cyanide as an agent of genocide. Starting in the early 1920s, cyanide gas chambers were used for the execution of criminals sentenced to death in the United States. There was also a widely publicized mass suicide carried out in 1978 in Jonestown, Guyana by members of a religious organization utilizing a fruit-flavored cyanide drink; more than 900 cult members died, including men, women, and children. Cyanide deaths captured the attention of the public again when it was added to Tylenol analgesic capsules sold in several drug stores in Chicago in 1982. More recently, attention to the lethality of cyanide is being dramatically illustrated by regular news reports of its use by poachers in Zimbabwe to kill large groups of elephants at watering sites to obtain their ivory tusks. These events, plus the constant flow of media reports on real or potential uses of cyanide by terrorist groups, continue to position cyanide as an effective general purpose prototypical poison.

Cyanide is a rapidly acting deadly poison. Exposures most commonly involve either hydrogen cyanide gas or potassium cyanide powder. Cyanide blocks the utilization of oxygen at the cellular level, resulting in metabolic asphyxiation. When this happens, cells die. It appears to be more harmful to the heart and brain than to other organs because they require relatively more oxygen.

9.2 Exposure Situations and Circumstances

Accidental poisoning with cyanide can occur in occupational settings involving small-scale metalwork, such as crafting jewelry, as well as in large-scale manufacturing processes such as metal plating and the synthetic production of various plastics.

Smoke inhalation is a significant cause of cyanide poisoning. Depending on the composition of burning material, smoke can include various concentrations of toxic gases. These toxic gases in combination with oxygen deprivation are responsible for more fire deaths than flames. Cyanide is a combustion product of many natural and synthetic products found in most commercial and residential structures in both the materials used for the construction of buildings as well as the composition of objects and materials stored in the buildings. The two major toxic gases associated with fires are carbon monoxide and hydrogen cyanide. These gases are chemical asphyxiates, which act to limit the availability of oxygen for vital functions. Carbon monoxide blocks the ability of blood to transport oxygen to cells, and cyanide blocks the ability of cells to utilize oxygen. However, cyanide exposure can be fatal even in the presence of normal oxygen levels, and in the presence of nontoxic levels of carbon monoxide.

There are a number of plants that contain cyanogenic constituents that produce cyanide poisoning when ingested. This can be encountered when individuals accidentally ingest these plants, or intentionally ingest the plant materials as food or dietary supplements. There is a mistaken belief that cyanogenic glycosides from plants provide a treatment or cure for some types of cancer, and there are sporadic reports of cyanide poisoning that result from using plant material or products derived from plants that contain cyanogenic constituents.

Cyanide is relatively easy to acquire and does not require advanced expertise to use. These features make it an attractive terrorism weapon for causing mass casualties that can quickly exhaust available medical resources. Terrorist training material commonly alludes to the release of cyanide by explosive devices placed in buildings and stadiums. Cyanide compounds could also be intentionally introduced into foods, medications, and other consumable items having wide distribution.

9.3 Symptoms of Poisoning

Early neurological manifestations of cyanide poisoning can include anxiety and confusion. This can rapidly progress to unconsciousness, seizures, and coma. Respiration may be initially increased. Hypotension, cardiac arrhythmias, and cardiac arrest precede death. People exposed to a small amount of cyanide by breathing it, or eating foods that contain it, may have rapid breathing, dizziness, headache, nausea, or vomiting. Exposure to large amounts of cyanide by any route may cause convulsions, hypotension, bradycardia, coma, and respiratory failure. Cyanide poisoning is treated with specific antidotes and supportive medical care in a hospital setting. Due to the rapid action, poisoned victims require medical treatment as soon as possible after exposure. Survivors of serious cyanide poisoning can develop irreversible heart and brain damage.

9.4 Case Studies

Case: Poisoning by Scientist

In 2013, a 41-year-old academic physician in Pennsylvania died of cyanide poisoning. She lived with her 64-year-old husband and their 6-year-old daughter. The husband was an accomplished research scientist and both held faculty and administrative positions at the same medical school. They had been married for about 12 years. Following a homicidal investigation, the husband was tried, convicted, and sentenced to life in prison. Evidence presented at the trial indicated that the husband had purchased cyanide and probably added it to a dietary supplement consumed by his wife immediately prior to her death. There was evidence of marital discord regarding having more children and the financial burdens associated with continuing infertility treatments and procedures. Questions were also raised about possible infidelity of the wife. There was a major disagreement among experts who testified at the trial relative to the interpretation of conflicting results of cyanide testing carried out in two different reputable laboratories. The results from one laboratory were consistent with a cyanide poisoning cause of death; whereas the other laboratory's analytical results were more consistent with high normal cyanide levels. The dilemma was how to interpret the conflicting findings. Some experts supported a view that since there was no apparent way to decide which results were correct, both must be rejected when investigating a cause of death. Other experts felt that when considered within the entire body of information available for the case, the results that supported a cyanide poisoning death were most probably correct.

Comments

Although there was disagreement among recognized experts on the validity of some toxicology testing results, the circumstantial evidence linking the murder to the scientist overshadowed the disagreement.

Case: Death of Lottery Winner

In 2012, a 46-year-old male in New Jersey died unexpectedly 2 months after winning $1 million in the state lottery. His death was attributed to heart failure and he was buried in a simple casket without being embalmed. At the time of the death, he was living in a rather modest home with his second wife, a daughter from a previous marriage, and his current wife's father. In addition to the lottery prize, the man owned several rental condominiums and was part owner of three dry cleaning stores. Suspicions by surviving relatives prompted a toxicological analysis of blood samples collected at the time of death, which revealed lethal levels of cyanide. This discovery initiated a homicide investigation that included an exhumation of the body for autopsy and further toxicological testing. Due to the degree of degradation of the body during 6 months of burial, it was not possible to determine how the cyanide entered the body. Evidence of coronary artery disease was observed, which was considered a possible contributing factor in the death. Disputes and accusations among the deceased's relatives continue with regard to the disposition of his approximately $2 million estate. The homicidal investigation remains active.

Comments

The homicide victim in this case left no will and the disposition of his estate became a contentious issue among his relatives. An agreement was reached in 2013 that divided his assets between his 18-year-old daughter and his widow. The settlement contained a stipulation that neither party would file a wrongful death lawsuit against the other unless new evidence surfaced in the ongoing criminal investigation that supported such an accusation.

Case: Teenage Love Triangle

In 2003, an 18-year-old male high school student in Maryland added potassium cyanide to a cold drink he provided to a 17-year-old male, who was a fellow student and his best friend. They had been watching movies and playing video games in the older student's home. Shortly after drinking some of the cola, the friend had seizures and parents in the home at the time called emergency responders who transported the student to a nearby hospital. He never regained consciousness and died 5 days later. In this case, the poisoner had developed a strong romantic desire for the younger student's long-time girlfriend and sought to eliminate his perceived rival. The poisoner was under the care of a physician and receiving psychotherapeutic medication at the time of the poisoning. The cyanide was purchased online from a chemical supply company and was mailed to the poisoner's home. The mailing container was conspicuously labeled as *hazardous material* and *potassium cyanide*. Copper sulfate was also ordered with the cyanide. These two chemicals are commonly used together for electroplating and their simultaneous purchase would not typically be regarded as suspicious. The poisoner ultimately confessed. He was tried and convicted of first-degree murder and sentenced to life in prison.

Comments

In 2005, the parents of the victim filed suit for damages against the company that sold the cyanide to the murderer and petitioned for additional damages from the parents and psychiatrist of the murderer. The disposition of this legal action is not known.

Case: Toxic Legal Experience

In 2009, a fire broke out in a mansion in an affluent suburb of a major city in Arizona. The 50-year-old owner, who was home at the time, narrowly escaped through a second-story window. Investigators soon determined that the fire was started intentionally and that the owner carried a sizable insurance policy for the mansion. They also learned that the owner was in significant financial difficulty, though he was quite an accomplished lawyer, an international investment banker, and the editor-in-chief of a small publishing company. He was arrested and charged with arson of an occupied building (he was the occupant), which carried a possible sentence of 10–20 years in prison. He was released on bond. At trial, he was defended by a court-appointed attorney because he lacked assets to retain legal representation. At the conclusion of the trial in 2012, the jury rendered a guilty verdict. Seconds after the verdict, the guilty owner was seen on live TV ingesting something and drinking from a sports bottle. Minutes later, he collapsed. He died from cyanide poisoning. Later, the canister from which he obtained the sodium cyanide for his suicide was found in his car. It had been purchased online a year earlier.

Comments

The individual in this case appears to have contemplated, before the actual trial took place, the possibility of spending years in prison. He was an especially accomplished individual who had even climbed Mount Everest, but the loss of his financial holdings and the contemplated prison term were things he chose not to face.

References and Additional Reading

Akhgari M, Baghdadi F, Kadkhodaei A: Cyanide poisoning related deaths: A four-year experience and review of the literature. *Aust J Forensic Sci*, 48: 186–194, 2015.

Garlich FM, Alslop JA, Anderson DL, Geller RJ, Kalugdan TT, Roberts DJ, Thomas LC: Poisoning and suicide by cyanide jewelry cleaner in the US Hmong community: A case series. *Clin Toxicol*, 50: 136–140, 2012.

Gill JR, Marker E, Stajic M: Suicide by cyanide: 17 deaths. *J Forensic Sci*, 49: 826–828, 2004.

Hamel J: A review of acute cyanide poisoning with a treatment update. *Crit Care Nurse*, 31: 72–82, 2011.

Keim ME: Terrorism involving cyanide: The prospect of improving preparedness in the prehospital setting. *Prehosp Disaster Med*, 21: 56–60, 2006.

McAllister JL, Roby RJ, Levine B, Purser D: Stability of cyanide in cadavers and in postmortem stored tissue specimens: A review. *J Anal Toxicol*, 32: 612–620, 2008.

Sahin S: Cyanide poisoning in children caused by apricot seeds. *J Health Med Informat*, 2: 1–2, 2011.

Shepherd G, Velez LI: Role of hydroxocolbalamine in acute cyanide poisoning. *Ann Pharmacother*, 42: 661–669, 2008.

Ward PR: *Death by Cyanide: The murder of Dr. Autumn Klein*. Lebanon, NH: ForeEdge University Press of New England, 2016.

Ethylene Glycol   10

10.1 Introduction

Ethylene glycol is a synthetic chemical that is the primary ingredient in most automotive antifreeze/coolant products and aircraft deicing fluids. Antifreeze products are easily accessible and, because ethylene glycol has a sweet taste, they can be surreptitiously added to sports drinks, alcoholic cocktails, and other beverages and foods. Homicides involving ethylene glycol are commonly detailed in news reports, which can provide the methodology for poisoning in various circumstances. Media coverage of antifreeze poisoning incidents has contributed to the incidences of intentional poisonings, whether suicidal or homicidal.

The lethal effects of ethylene glycol are the result of its conversion within the liver to toxic metabolites, which form crystals in urine, blood, and some organs. The oxalate crystals are especially damaging to the kidneys.

10.2 Exposure Situations and Circumstances

Antifreeze is the most common source of ethylene glycol. It is also found in some air-conditioning coolants and various other automotive products. The sweet taste of ethylene glycol clearly plays a role in its involvement in both intentional and unintentional poisoning. To discourage the ingestion of antifreeze products, several states require that these products add substances to make them taste bitter. Bittering can be a deterrent in some cases, but it has a little impact on the frequency or severity of suicidal antifreeze ingestions and accidental exposures.

One of the major factors in accidental poisoning among both children and adults is the storage of antifreeze in anything other than the original containers. Storage in liquor bottles is especially troublesome. These secondary containers are often neglected for long periods. In some cases, secondary containers wind up in places far removed from their original locations before being mistakenly consumed. Intentional poisonings with ethylene glycol are seen in a wide variety of circumstances. Poisoners may include individuals with marginal intelligence as well as those with exceptional intelligence.

Ethylene glycol is a member of a chemical family of compounds that are collectively classified as glycols. Two other glycols that are often confused with ethylene glycol are diethylene glycol and propylene glycol. In practicality, ethylene glycol and diethylene glycol can be considered identical in terms of their toxic potential. Propylene glycol does not share this toxic potential and is generally considered safe when used in a specified manner in food products and pharmaceuticals. Due to the similarity in names, products containing propylene glycol are often mistaken as objects of major consumer concern and can mislead investigators.

The minimum lethal dose of antifreeze products is on the order of 100 ml (3–4 oz).

10.3 Symptoms of Poisoning

Symptoms of ethylene glycol poisoning can start as early as 30 min following ingestion and resemble those seen with ethanol intoxication. Nausea and vomiting can progress to convulsions, stupor, and coma. Within 24 h there can be significant disturbances in body chemistry, heart failure, and pulmonary edema. Death usually results from renal failure.

10.4 Case Studies

Case: Antifreeze Black Widow

In 1995, a police officer died following a brief flu-like illness from what appeared to be heart failure. Soon after the death, the officer's wife moved to live with her boyfriend who was a fireman and part-time deputy sheriff. Five years later, her boyfriend died from what appeared to be a cardiac arrhythmia. The similarities in the circumstances surrounding the two deaths raised suspicions among the dead men's relatives who brought their concerns to the attention of authorities. Both men had flu-like symptoms prior to their deaths. They both sought medical attention and were treated symptomatically. Each died a few days later. This launched an investigation that revealed that the wife had poisoned both men with antifreeze likely added to Jell-O, teas, and soups over a period of several days. Blood tests and autopsy findings indicated that both deaths were caused by ethylene glycol poisoning. She was convicted of murdering both men and sentenced to life imprisonment. In 2010, she committed suicide in her prison cell with an overdose of a medication that she was prescribed for hypertension. The motive for both murders was life insurance.

Comments

It is interesting that the wife's early ambition was to become a police officer. She had applied to a police department and passed a rigorous physical trial but failed the psychological portion of the examination. Her first husband was a police officer and her boyfriend was a part-time sheriff's deputy, as well as a firefighter. She had been a 911 operator, an aide to a municipal judge, an assistant to a sheriff, and a secretary to a district attorney. It seems clear that she had a compelling interest in crime and police work and had accumulated knowledge that she applied to her crimes.

Case: Inconvenient Wife

In 2004, a 31-year-old registered nurse died from antifreeze poisoning. She had a progressively debilitating kidney disorder prior to death. Days before she died, she was admitted to a hospital where it was discovered that she was suffering from ethylene glycol poisoning. The diagnosis came too late to save her. No explanation for her exposure to ethylene glycol was uncovered. She was happily married and adored her husband. He was an extrovert; he dressed well, drove expensive cars, and generally impressed people. He acted and looked the part of a very successful man, but, in reality, he was in serious debt. He had lied about his education and had lost jobs because of embezzlement and other issues. After her death, he collected his wife's life insurance policy and moved to another town where he found a new job and reconnected with an old girlfriend. He suggested to friends and relatives that his wife may have intentionally ended her life with antifreeze, that she might have drunk from a Gatorade bottle that she found somewhere, and might have mistaken its contents. An investigation of the death revealed that the husband had slowly poisoned his wife over several months. He added ethylene glycol to Gatorade, which he insisted she drink regularly despite her distaste for Gatorade in general. He was tried and convicted of first-degree murder and is now serving a life sentence.

Comments

The arrogant, self-centered nature of the husband in this case elevated his position as a murder suspect. His character flaws appeared to be evident to all friends, relatives, and other associates, but not to his wife.

Case: Substance Abuse Related Suicide

In 2006, a 47-year-old man living in Massachusetts finished dinner with his family and then went outside for a short period of time to work on his car. When he came back into the home, his wife noticed that his speech was somewhat slurred and he seemed lethargic. He had some bouts of vomiting, became increasingly lethargic, and finally went to bed. A few hours later, his wife found him unconscious and called emergency medical services. He was then transported to a hospital emergency department. On arrival he was in a coma and had significant hypotension. He was intubated and started on intravenous fluids and supportive medications for cardiovascular and pulmonary stability and given antibiotics as a precaution for possible complications of aspiration of gastric fluids. He had seizures, which also required medications. Tests for ethanol were negative. Laboratory tests indicated that his symptoms could be due to ethylene glycol poisoning. This was substantiated by crystals in his urine, which are characteristic of metabolic products from ethylene glycol. Fomepizole, the antidote for ethylene glycol poisoning, was administered and hemodialysis was initiated for the removal of ethylene glycol from his blood. The man's mental status improved over the following 24 h. When he recovered consciousness, he said that he had ingested antifreeze in a suicidal effort. He also revealed that he was addicted to oxycodone, which he obtained illegally. He was unable to obtain any oxycodone during the past few days and was likely experiencing opiate withdrawal at the time of the ethylene glycol ingestion. He was discharged after 20 hospital days for medical and psychiatric outpatient care, which included treatment for his addictions.

Comments

The metabolic changes observed in this patient's laboratory test could have been produced by several poisons or by manifestations of several metabolic diseases. The crystals (calcium oxalate) found in the man's urine specimen are seen in other medical situations, but their presence in combination with the laboratory abnormalities observed were very suggestive of an ethylene glycol ingestion. At the time of admission of this patient to the hospital, he had not consumed ethanol for at least a year, and his oxycodone addiction was not suspected by his family.

Case: Regular Antifreeze Consumption

In 2014, a 41-year-old man living in Boston went to a hospital emergency department complaining of abdominal pain, nausea, and vomiting that he had been experiencing for the past 5 days. His physical examination was unremarkable and vital signs were stable. Laboratory testing revealed some abnormalities, but was not immediately suggestive in terms of explaining his illness. He had been taking medications for hypertension, migraines, and elevated cholesterol. He indicated that he did not smoke, drink, or use any illicit drugs. His urine output was low and he had signs of possible kidney failure. He was started on intravenous fluids and evaluated for renal disease, which included a kidney biopsy. The biopsy revealed large amounts of oxalate crystals, which is indicative of ethylene glycol poisoning, but the man adamantly denied any ingestion of ethylene glycol. No explanation was uncovered for the poisoning; his condition improved, and he was discharged after several days of supportive treatment. One week later, he returned to the hospital with complaints of abdominal pain and nausea. He again denied any ethylene glycol ingestion. He was seen in an outpatient renal clinic for about a month, but the source of his discomfort was not identified. Seven months after the initial hospital admission, the man was brought to the emergency department after being found unresponsive in a hotel room. On this occasion, there was clear evidence that he had overdosed on various medications and ethylene glycol. After intensive care that included hemodialysis and an ethylene glycol antidote, he recovered. He then admitted that he had been ingesting ethylene glycol over the past several months. The recent acute ingestion of medication in combination with ethylene glycol was clearly a suicide attempt, but the rationale for the continuing chronic ingestion of ethylene glycol in sublethal amounts over the preceding several months remained a mystery. The man was transferred to a psychiatric facility and was unavailable for additional follow-up.

Comments

Chronic ethylene glycol poisoning in nonlethal amounts is difficult to diagnose because metabolic abnormalities can be minimal or absent, and symptoms can be mild and resolved with supportive care. Victims of chronic intentional ethylene glycol poisoning can have repeated contact with physicians as well as hospitalizations without detection of the poisoning.

Case: Natalie and Chase

In 2010, 4-year-old Natalie and her 3-year-old brother, Chase, were murdered in Mobile, Alabama by their 27-year-old father and his 22-year-old live-in girlfriend. The children were tortured and fed antifreeze until they died and their bodies were hidden in a wooded area many miles from their home. The murders took place approximately 3 months apart. Even though the abusive behavior of the couple toward the children was observed by others, their disappearance went unreported for months. Shortly after the murders, the couple had another child and then moved to another community. The couple eventually separated and the girl-friend filed a domestic violation petition requesting a restraining order from the father. In her written complaint, she indicated that she was afraid that the father was going to harm her and their new child because of the possibility that he had murdered his previous children. This triggered an investigation into the children's disappearance. After their separation, the girlfriend was in jail for an unrelated incident and confided in another inmate how the children were killed. She told her cellmate that they had purchased gallons of antifreeze and added it regularly to the children's food. They had also experimented on the family dog to determine how long it would take to die from antifreeze poisoning. The decision was made to kill the children to reduce their responsibilities, so that they could focus on starting a new family together. They were tried separately and each received a death sentence.

Comments

This case involved cruelty and torture. The cause of death was attributed to poisoning, starvation, and strangulation.

Case: Bodybuilder—Steroid Injections

In 2013, a 42-year-old professional bodybuilder and weightlifter living in Smyrna, Delaware was found dead in the bedroom he shared with his 44-year-old wife. They had been married for 21 years and had two children. The husband worked as an environmental specialist for a large chemical company and pursued competitive bodybuilding as a hobby. His body was discovered by his wife who immediately summoned emergency medical responders. Police and investigators from the medical examiner's office also came to the scene. Among the items collected at the scene were syringes, pills, and injectable steroids. At autopsy it was revealed that the husband had kidney damage that was consistent with ethylene glycol poisoning. Subsequently, the steroid injection vials were analyzed and found to contain ethylene glycol. The medical examiner found that the death was due to ethylene glycol and ruled it a homicide. The wife was confronted with the findings of the death investigation and ultimately admitted that she had added antifreeze to the injection vials. She was charged with first-degree murder.

Comments

Information regarding the amount of ethylene glycol that may have been used in the poisoning was not made public by the authorities. It is possible that, in addition to the injected ethylene glycol, there was also poisoning by the use of sports drinks and other beverages.

Case: Therapeutic Misadventure—Rhubarb

In 2012, a 52-year-old woman sought medical care because of recurring episodes of nausea and vomiting for several days. She was diabetic and took insulin regularly, two medications for hypertension (ramipril and metoprolol), and a daily low-dose aspirin. Previously, she had severe depression that was treated with venlafaxine, but it was discontinued several months earlier when the depression abated and she appeared to be psychiatrically stable. A physical examination was unremarkable except for a slightly elevated blood pressure. Laboratory testing identified some abnormalities, the most notable of which were indications of renal failure. This prompted a more thorough evaluation of the kidney function, which included a biopsy. The biopsy showed changes consistent with diabetic nephropathy, and the presence of oxalate crystals. On the basis of further diagnostic testing, it was concluded that the woman had mild preexisting kidney disease secondary to her diabetes, and oxalate crystal deposition caused additional damage that led to acute kidney failure and the symptoms of nausea and vomiting. The source of the oxalate was investigated and led to a dietary explanation. Initially, it was suspected that the basis of her illness was ethylene glycol poisoning, which is metabolized and deposited in kidney tubules as oxalate crystals. However, oxalates are present in certain foods and can cause oxalate toxicity when consumed in excessive amounts. In this case, the culprit was rhubarb. The woman had consumed rather large amounts of fresh rhubarb leaves daily for approximately 1 month prior to the onset of her medical problems.

Comments

Rhubarb is recommended by alternative practitioners as a natural supplement for gastrointestinal problems, menopausal symptoms, allergies, and a variety of other conditions. There is little or no evidence to support these recommendations. Rhubarb leaves contain significant amounts of oxalic acid which is nephrotoxic. Rhubarb stalks are edible; the leaves are poisonous.

References and Additional Reading

Armstrong EJ, Engelhart DA, Jenkins AJ, Balraj EK: Homicidal ethylene glycol intoxication: A report of a case. *Am J Forensic Med Pathol*, 27: 151–155, 2006.

Brent J, McMartin K, Phillips S, Burkhart KK, Donovan JW, Wells M, Kulig K: Fomepizole for the treatment of ethylene glycol poisoning. *N Engl J Med*, 340: 832–838, 1999.

Bricker L: *Lie After Lie: The True Story of a Master of Deception, Betrayal, and Murder.* New York: Berkley, 2010.

Harry P, Jobard E, Briand M, Caubet A, Turcant A: Ethylene glycol poisoning in a child treated with 4-methylpyrazole. *Pediatrics*, 102: 1–3, 1998.

Kraut JA, Kurtz I: Toxic alcohol ingestions: Clinical features, diagnosis, and management. *Clin J Am Soc Nephrol*, 3: 208–225, 2008.

Morgan BW, Geller RJ, Kazzi ZN: Intentional ethylene glycol poisoning increases after media coverage of antifreeze murders. *W J Emerg Med*, 12: 296–299, 2011.

Takayesu JK, Bazari H, Linshaw M: Case 7-2006: A 47-year-old man with altered mental status and acute renal failure. *N Engl J Med*, 354: 1065–1072, 2006.

Toth-Manikowski SM, Menn-Josephy H, Bhatia J: A case of chronic ethylene glycol intoxication presenting without classic metabolic derangements. *Case Rep Nephrol*, #128145, 2014.

Wang GS, Yin S, Shear B, Heard K: Severe poisoning after accidental pediatric ingestion of glycol ethers. *Pediatrics*, 130: 1026–1029, 2012.

White NC, Litovitz T, White MK, Watson WA, Benson BE, Horowitz BZ, Marr-Lyon L: The impact of bittering agents on suicidal ingestions of antifreeze. *Clin Toxicol*, 46: 507–514, 2008.

Nicotine 11

11.1 Introduction

Nicotine is a naturally occurring component of a number of common plants and dietary vegetables such as potatoes, tomatoes, and eggplants. However, except for tobacco, the nicotine content of plants is generally insignificant in toxicological situations. After tobacco, the plant with the highest nicotine content is eggplant. In terms of nicotine content, pounds of eggplant would equate to a typical cigarette. Nicotine is an extremely toxic poison. It acts primarily on the nervous system where it stimulates certain areas while simultaneously inhibiting neurotransmission in other areas. Lethal doses produce respiratory and cardiovascular collapse.

11.2 Exposure Situations and Circumstances

The most common source of nicotine is tobacco in forms for smoking, chewing, or use as snuff. Nicotine is also available in an expanding variety of commercial products for nicotine replacement therapy for smoking cessation. These products include transdermal patches, chewing gum, nasal sprays, inhalers, lozenges, and oral dissolvable tablets. Concentrated nicotine solutions in a variety of flavors are sold for use in electronic cigarettes. The extraction of nicotine from tobacco products is commonly discussed in manuals and on Internet sites that target survivalists and militant individuals, and people exploring suicidal methodology. Extraction is also described on Internet sites dealing with natural insecticides for organic gardening.

11.3 Symptoms of Poisoning

Nausea, vomiting, and diarrhea occur within minutes of a nicotine overdose. These symptoms are generally followed by various degrees of agitation, confusion, headache, and perhaps auditory and visual disturbances. Blood pressure usually increases and is associated with an abnormal heart rate. In severe poisoning, symptoms rapidly progress to dyspnea and coma. Death results from paralysis of respiratory muscles or cardiovascular collapse.

11.4 Case Studies

Case: 2014 Trial and Conviction of 1994 Poisoner

In 1994, a 50-year-old woman died unexpectedly in California a few hours after retiring. She had gone to bed around 6 p.m. and was joined by her husband a short time later. Around midnight, the husband noticed that his wife was not breathing and summoned emergency responders who were unable to resuscitate her. An autopsy did not disclose a cause of death, but toxicological testing revealed that she died from nicotine poisoning. There was no explanation for the nicotine exposure and her death was ruled a homicide. From the beginning, the husband was the prime suspect. The couple had met while working together in a Northern California power plant. He worked as an engineer and she was a communication specialist. They had been married for about 2 years when the death occurred. Early in the marriage, the husband had urged his wife to purchase life insurance. Later, the wife began to have episodic bouts of an illness that on at least two occasions required hospitalization. During hospitalization there were indications that the husband may have added substances to the wife's IV fluids. The wife had confided to friends that she was uncomfortable with the insurance issue, and suspected that her husband was poisoning her to collect on the policies. Despite these and other considerations, authorities were unable to obtain direct evidence that linked the husband to the death. Years later, the case was reexamined and more advanced toxicological testing was done on retained autopsy specimens. The results of this testing indicated that the lethal dose of nicotine was administered shortly before death and, since the husband was the only person with the wife for the preceding 6 h prior to death, he was arrested and charged with the murder. In addition, high levels of zolpidem were found in the body and indications of a possible injection site identified. It was surmised that the wife was heavily sedated and subsequently injected with lethal doses of nicotine. The husband was convicted and sentenced in 2014 to life in prison without parole.

Comments

The wife was sedated with zolpidem. This was not a medication she used therapeutically. The nicotine source was not identified but there was reason to suspect that it was obtained by extraction from tobacco.

Case: Nicotine Extracted from Tobacco

In 2008, a 19-year-old male student was found dead in his bedroom by his father. His naked body was lying face down beside the bed. There was considerable vomitus and feces on and near the body. Empty carbonated drink bottles and tobacco packages were found near a saucepan containing a thick brown liquid residue. The cause of death was not apparent, and an autopsy did not provide an explanation. Toxicological tests were negative for all common and illicit drugs except for nicotine, which was detected in lethal levels in tissues and fluids collected at autopsy. The deceased had a history of ethanol and marijuana abuse. Months prior to the death, he had displayed an unusual interest in matters relating to dying. Investigators found information on various methods for committing suicide saved on the deceased's personal computer, which included extracting lethal amounts of nicotine from tobacco. The extraction methodology and use of nicotine were consistent with items collected at the scene. The cause of death was determined to be nicotine toxicity and the manner was suicide.

Comments

Deaths from tobacco extracts are uncommon. The increasing availability of commercial nicotine solutions for e-cigarettes may increase the use of nicotine for intentional poisoning.

Case: Nicotine Patch Suicide

Around 1997, a 31-year-old woman was found dead by her husband. There were signs of vomiting prior to death, but she was found with a plastic bag covering her nose and mouth. There were 18 nicotine patches on her chest and abdomen attached with duct tape and a suicide note near the body. An autopsy was negative relative to an anatomical cause of death. A broad spectrum of toxicological testing identified only nicotine, cotinine, and caffeine. The cause of death was ruled asphyxia and the manner of death was ruled suicide.

Comments

The principal metabolite of nicotine is cotinine. It is commonly identified in testing of samples from smokers. As smoking is common, toxicological testing does not routinely include nicotine and cotinine. In cases where nicotine poisoning is suspected, specific testing should be requested.

Case: Rectal Use of Tobacco Products

Around 2010, a 42-year-old man was taken by relatives to an emergency department of a hospital because of severe nausea, vomiting, and dizziness associated with rectal administration of moist snuff sachets (teabag-like packages of tobacco intended for oral use). The man was a regular user of moist snuff in the typical manner by placing sachets under the upper lip for buccal absorption. He had found that this provided some relief for migraine headaches. On this occasion, he had an unusually severe migraine and decided to use snuff rectally and, because there was little effect, he inserted about 75 sachets within a period of 2 h. He then became alarmed at the increasing toxic symptoms produced and attempted to remove the snuff using a water enema that failed. At this point, he was transported to the hospital. He was nauseated and vomiting, and in an agitated state. The remaining snuff was removed, but the man's condition deteriorated and he became comatose. This necessitated intubation and mechanical ventilation. Plasma and urine levels of cotinine (the metabolite of nicotine) were significantly elevated. He was treated symptomatically over the next 36 h in an intensive care unit. On the second day following admission, his condition had normalized and he was discharged with no further follow-up. It was estimated that more than 150 mg of nicotine had been absorbed from the rectum. Had the man not received medical treatment, this amount of nicotine was life-threatening.

Comments

Nicotine is well-absorbed from oral as well as rectal mucosal surfaces. Perhaps nausea associated with his headache suggested the rectal route of administration. It is not uncommon for medications utilized for alleviating the symptoms of migraine headache to be administered rectally. The massive number of sachets used in this case is remarkable.

Case: Contamination of Hamburger Meat

In 2003, about 100 people became ill after eating ground beef purchased from a supermarket in Michigan. Symptoms included a burning sensation in the mouth, nausea, vomiting, dizziness, and heart rate irregularities. Subsequently the beef was tested for pathogens and potential chemical contaminates. The testing ultimately identified nicotine. Approximately 1700 lbs (pounds) of ground beef sold by the supermarket was recalled and a local and federal investigation was initiated. The investigation led to the indictment of a disgruntled employee who poisoned the beef. On the evening of the poisoning, the employee brought an insecticide containing nicotine to work and added it to a 200-pound batch of ground beef that was later packaged and sold to supermarket customers. His intent was to punish his supervisor. He pleaded guilty to the poisoning and received a 9-year prison sentence and paid $12,000 in restitution.

Comments

Nicotine-containing insecticides are no longer commercially available in the United States. However, products purchased in the past remain in storage areas and will likely continue to surface in forensic circumstances for many years.

Case: Electronic Cigarette Solution Injection

In 2014, a 29-year-old man with a history of depression composed a suicide note and then overdosed by injecting a nicotine solution that he had for refilling his nicotine replacement electronic smoking device. He was not taking any other medications. He was found unconscious by his family who called for emergency medical responders. Resuscitation was initiated and he was transported to a medical facility. Despite aggressive therapy for cardiovascular and pulmonary complications, his condition deteriorated. This was further complicated by persistent seizures that were only moderately controlled. He never regained consciousness and life-support measures were discontinued. Toxicological testing on samples collected when he arrived at the hospital identified only nicotine and cotinine, and the drugs used for his resuscitation efforts. The levels of nicotine and cotinine were consistent with those reported from other nicotine deaths.

Comments

Liquid nicotine products for e-cigarettes pose a hazard for accidental poisonings by children and suicidal poisoning in adults who may ingest or inject the concentrated flavored solutions. The suicide note left by the individual in this case described an intravenous injection; however, the injection site could not be identified.

Case: Electronic Cigarette Solution Ingestion

In 2015, a 24-year-old woman called emergency responders after ingesting a lethal amount of liquid nicotine solution for use in electronic cigarettes. On arrival, responders found the woman unresponsive with no pulse. There were two empty vials (15 ml) of liquid nicotine (100 mg/ml), a partially filled bottle of whiskey, and a suicide note near the woman. There were also prescription containers for trazodone, fluoxetine, and olanzapine but nothing suggested that these medications were involved in the woman's suicidal ingestion. After intensive resuscitation measures, spontaneous circulation returned. Paramedics were unable to obtain intravenous access, so fluids and medications were administered through an intraosseous catheter. After administering succinylcholine and midazolom, she was intubated, ventilated, and transported to a hospital emergency department. On arrival, her pupils were fixed and dilated and she was incontinent of urine and feces, and had whole body myoclonus. The plasma nicotine minutes after her arrival was greater than 1000 ng/ml. Despite aggressive supportive care, she died. MRI imaging showed multiple infarcts consistent with anoxic brain injury.

Comments

Sample dilutions were not performed to determine the specific level above the 1000 ng/ml cutoff level for the standard methodology employed by the analytical laboratory. General toxicological screening in this case did not identify any other potential toxicants deemed relevant to the cause of death.

References and Additional Reading

Appleton S: Frequency and outcomes of accidental ingestion of tobacco products in young children. *Reg Toxicol Pharmacol*, 61: 210–214, 2011.

Bassett RA, Osterhoudt K, Brabazon T: Nicotine poisoning in an infant. *N Engl J Med*, 370: 2249–2250, 2014.

Boulton M, Stanbury M, Wade D, Tilden J, Bryan D, Payne J, Eisenga B: Nicotine poisoning after ingestion of contaminated ground beef—Michigan, 2003. *CDC MMWR*, 52: 413–416, 2003.

Chen BC, Bright SB, Trivedi AR, Valento M: Death following intentional ingestion of e-liquid. *Clin Toxicol*, 53: 914–916, 2015.

Connolly GN, Richter P, Alequas A, Pechacek TF, Stanifill SB, Alpert HR: Unintentional child poisonings through ingestion of conventional and novel tobacco products. *Pediatrics*, 125: 896–899, 2010.

Corkery JM, Button J, Vento AE, Schifano F: Two UK suicides using nicotine extracted from tobacco employing instructions available on the Internet. *Forensic Sci Int*, 199: 9–13, 2010.

Hagiya K, Miztani T, Yasuda S, Kawano S: Nicotine poisoning due to intravenous injection of cigarette soakage. *Hum Exper Toxicol*, 29: 427–429, 2010.

Kemp PM, Sneed GS, George CE: Post-mortem distribution of nicotine and cotinine from a case involving the simultaneous administration of multiple nicotine transdermal systems. *J Anal Toxicol*, 21: 310–313, 1997.

Knudsen K, Strinnholm M: A case of life-threatening rectal administration of moist snuff. *Clin Toxicol*, 48: 572–573, 2010.

Montalto N, Brackett CC, Sobol T: Use of transdermal nicotine systems in a possible suicide attempt. *J Am Board Fam Pract*, 7: 417–420, 1994.

Schneider S, Diederich N, Appenzeller B, Schartz A, Lorang C, Wennig R: Internet suicide guidelines: Report of a life-threatening poisoning using tobacco extract. *J Emerg Med*, 38: 610–613, 2010.

Solarino B, Rosenbaum F, Riebelmann B, Buschmann CT, Toskos M: Death due to ingestion of nicotine containing solution: Case report and review of the literature. *Forensic Sci Int*, 195: 19–22, 2010.

Thornton SL, Oller L, Sawyer T: Fetal intravenous injection of electronic nicotine delivery system refilling solution. *J Med Toxicol*, 10: 202–204, 2014.

Woolf A, Burkhart K, Caraccio T, Litovitz T: Self-poisoning among adults using multiple transdermal nicotine patches. *Clin Toxicol*, 34: 691–698, 1996.

Strychnine 12

12.1 Introduction

Strychnine is derived from the seeds of *Strychnos nux vomica*, which is a small tree native to India. The words *nux* and *vomica* are commonly found on antique apothecary jars and other collectable containers some of which may still contain strychnine. In small doses, strychnine acts as a stimulant and has a long history of use as a performance-enhancing drug, especially in long-distance cycling. It is still listed on the World Anti-Doping Agents Prohibited List. Strychnine was a component of some nonprescription cathartics and tonics until the early 1960s. It is still present in some homeopathic products. Strychnine produces its effects on the body by antagonizing inhibitor neurotransmitters. In toxic doses, this results in generalized seizure-like contractions of skeletal muscles. Death usually results from respiratory failure due to the intense continuing contraction of respiratory muscles.

12.2 Exposure Situations and Circumstances

Strychnine is used as a pesticide primarily in products for the control of rodents and predatory animals in farming and ranching communities. Occasionally, strychnine is encountered as an adulterant in illegal drugs.

12.3 Symptoms of Poisoning

Initial symptoms of strychnine poisoning may include heightened attention and anxiety, and muscle spasms. This may progress to painful generalized convulsions. Typically there is facial grimacing resembling a frozen mask-like grin (*risus sardonicus*) and a rigid arched back (*opisthotonus*) with only the back of the head and heels of feet touching a supporting flat surface. Poisoning victims remain fully conscious while experiencing painful convulsing episodes. Death results from asphyxia due to sustained contracture of respiratory muscles.

12.4 Case Studies

Case: Therapeutic Strychnine

In 2001, a 16-year-old boy was admitted to a hospital in Massachusetts because of mental and emotional disturbances. He was confused, hostile, and increasingly aggressive. A few days preceding his admission, he was feverish and had developed a sore throat with a cough, and began to have diarrhea. He was being treated by his mother with a nonprescription cough and cold product and herbal tea. At the hospital, he received a very comprehensive examination that included an ECG, chest X-ray, a CAT scan of his head, a lumbar puncture, and toxicological screening. The examination did not identify a basis for his illness. He had intermittent muscle fasciculations and twitching in his arms and legs, which progressed to rigidity throughout his body; his jaws were tightly clenched. He remained conscious throughout these episodes. These symptoms were ultimately recognized as being consistent with strychnine poisoning. Specialized toxicology testing was initiated, which identified strychnine in urine samples. The source of the strychnine was the cough and cold product, which was obtained from a relative living in Cambodia. He was discharged after 11 days of hospitalization with a concurrent diagnosis of strychnine poisoning and an unrelated psychiatric disorder.

Comments

In some countries, strychnine is used in traditional health remedies. This is true for Cambodia and occasionally strychnine-containing products are found in Cambodian communities in the United States. These products could be commercially imported but generally are obtained from relatives living in Cambodia. The practice of families obtaining consumer products and medications from relatives and friends living in their country of origin is not uncommon.

Case: Courtroom Suicides

In 2013, a 42-year-old man living in Alabama was found guilty of child sex abuse charges. While in the courtroom, before being taken to jail, he took what he said was his daily medication. When he arrived at the jail, he had a seizure and died within an hour. Autopsy samples revealed that his death was due to strychnine. Oxycodone and amphetamines were also present in his system. The man had been free on bond during the trial and was able to bring the drugs with him when he appeared in court. He was facing a possible prison sentence of up to 20 years. The strychnine was obtained from a family-owned pest control company.

Comments

Other cases of courtroom suicide have been reported that involved cyanide or other toxicants.

Case: Murder or Suicide

In 2009, a 52-year-old woman died in her home near Seattle, Washington. Her death was due to strychnine. Her 63-year-old husband was subsequently arrested and tried for her murder. He and his wife were drinking heavily on the day of her death and they had had a heated argument. He was the only person with her when she died and had waited for a considerable period of time before contacting emergency responders. After 8 days of deliberation following his trial, the jury was unable to reach a unanimous decision. The trial had lasted 7 weeks and was ultimately declared a mistrial after jurors became deadlocked with 9–3 in favor of a guilty verdict. He had given police conflicting and sometimes false information during the death investigations. Investigators did learn that he was pursuing a romantic relationship with his wife's best friend. Moreover, he was the manager of a pest control company that frequently utilized strychnine. Well into the investigation, and after the first trial, a bottle containing strychnine was conveniently found in the wife's collection of decorative bottles. This raised the possibility of suicide. He was later retried and acquitted. After spending more than 2 years in jail since his initial arrest, he was released and rejoined his children and grandchildren. The second trial verdict did not abolish the suspicion harbored by most investigators and many members of the community.

Comments

The strychnine was found among the wife's belongings only after it was apparent that the husband was likely to be convicted of murder. The husband delayed the request for emergency help while the wife suffered an agonizing death. These and other indications of possible intentional poisoning were devalued by the jury in light of the totality of evidence presented during the trial.

Case: Gopher Pellet Suicide

Around 2002, a 52-year-old disabled veteran was found dead on his bed in his home. He had been dead for several days. There was a suicide note, and a drinking glass with residual material. This residue came from commercial strychnine gopher pellets. Additional residue from the same source was found in stomach contents collected at autopsy. The autopsy also identified pulmonary edema and hemorrhaging, and signs of chronic cardiovascular disease. Strychnine was present in all fluids and tissues collected at levels consistent with previous cases of strychnine deaths. No other drugs were detected. Death was due to strychnine poisoning and the manner of death was ruled to be suicide.

Comments

The availability of strychnine and its prominence as a classic poison makes it a likely choice by some individuals for suicide.

Case: Ice Cream Surprise

In 2009, a 34-year-old woman living in Texas was charged with illegal possession and distribution of methamphetamine, and some associated weapon charges. She pleaded guilty to the charges and received a prison sentence of 20 years with 5 years probation. Earlier that same year, her 60-year-old sometimes boyfriend was found unconscious in the yard of his home shortly after she visited. He died before emergency medical responders arrived at the home. His death was ruled to be a homicide and caused by strychnine poisoning. Evidence collected by the investigators indicated that the fatal dose of strychnine was delivered in a bowl of ice cream prepared by the woman, and that the source of the strychnine was a nearby ranch where the woman was staying. She was charged with the murder and, shortly before her trial was to start in 2011, she pleaded guilty and accepted a sentence of 40 years in prison. Her guilty plea was likely influenced by the fact that she was also the only suspect for the 2006 murders of her husband (gunshot) and a former lover (drug overdose).

Comments

Strychnine was identified in blood samples obtained at the time of death, in urine specimens collected at autopsy, and in residue from a chocolate ice cream container recovered from the victim's trash.

Case: Drug Users Beware

In 2014, three teenage boys (ages 16, 16, and 13 years old) living in a small community in California gathered in the backyard of a home and snorted what they believed to be cocaine. Within minutes, they became seriously ill and started to experience severe seizures. An adult living in the home called emergency medical responders who transported the boys to a hospital. One boy died, whereas the others remained hospitalized for more than a week. The survivors are likely to have long-lasting medical and psychological problems. The powder that they had snorted was strychnine. There are many unanswered questions regarding how this tragic event came about. It appears that a younger boy found the powder in the garage at his home and started a rumor that he had cocaine. The parents of the boy who found the powder indicated that they did use strychnine as a rodenticide and stored it in an unmarked container in the garage. The younger boy had himself not utilized any of the powder. This case was closed by local police and was assigned to the juvenile authorities for disposition.

Comments

This case is an illustration of complex issues involving immaturity, experimentation, and risky behavior. Investigative findings relative to the circumstances pertaining to the source of the strychnine were not made public.

References and Additional Reading

Katz J, Prescott K, Wolf AD: Strychnine poisoning from a Cambodian traditional remedy. *Am J Emerg Med*, 14: 475, 1996.

Libenson MH, Yang JM: A 16-year-old boy with an altered mental status and muscle rigidity. *N Engl J Med*, 344: 1232–1239, 2001.

Lindsey T, O'Hara J, Irvine R, Kerrigan S: Strychnine overdose following ingestion of gopher bait. *J Anal Toxicol*, 28: 135–137, 2004.

Parker AJ, Lee JB, Redman J, Jolliffe L: Strychnine poisoning: Gone but not forgotten. *Emerg Med J*, 28: 84, 2011.

Pratt S, Hoizey G, Lefrancq T, Saint-Martin P: An unusual case of strychnine poisoning. *J Forensic Sci*, 60: 816–817, 2015.

Rosano TG, Hubbard JD, Meola JM, Swift TA: Fatal strychnine poisoning: Application of gas chromatography and tandem mass spectrometry. *J Anal Toxicol*, 24: 642–647, 2000.

Sarvesvaran R: Strychnine poisoning: A case report. *Malayian J Pathol*, 14: 35–39, 1992.

Wood DM, Webster E, Martinez D, Dargan PI, Jones AL: Case report: Survival after deliberate strychnine self-poisoning, with toxicokinetic data. *Crit Care*, 6: 456–459, 2002.

Yamarick W, Walson P, DiTragla J: Strychnine poisoning in an adolescent. *Clin Tox*, 30: 141–148, 1992.

Thallium 13

13.1 Introduction

Thallium is an extremely toxic naturally occurring chemical element having a number of specialized industrial uses. It was the dominant ingredient of most commercial rodenticides for more than 45 years until the early 1970s when most countries banned this application because of the human toxicity potential. Thallium is sufficiently uncommon that when forensic investigators encounter it, attention should be directed initially to the possibility of an intentional exposure rather than a natural or an accidental exposure.

Thallium is molecularly similar to potassium and replaces potassium in many vital bodily processes thereby blocking them. In particular, thallium interferes with neurotransmitters and cellular energy production and storage.

13.2 Exposure Situations and Circumstances

Thallium compounds are used in the manufacturing of electronic components and are incorporated into certain types of optical glass. Thallium sulfate was the primary ingredient in the most popular rat poisons and other pesticides throughout the world, but its use continues only in a few countries among which are Russia and China. Products discontinued in other countries will continue to be found in domestic and commercial storage areas. Thallium is also used in some chemical manufacturing processes, and it might be found in industrial or academic chemical research laboratories. The synthesis of some illicit drugs involves thallium compounds, and this sometimes results in drugs being contaminated with thallium. However, there have also been incidents of thallium having been intentionally used to adulterate illicit drug supplies. It is extremely toxic in small doses and is soluble in beverages without noticeably altering the odor or taste. These features enable thallium salts to be easily incorporated into almost any food or beverage. Thallium compounds can be absorbed by inhalation, ingestion, or skin contact. A teaspoonful of thallium sulfate contains sufficient material to kill more than 20 individuals.

A radioisotope of thallium is used for cardiovascular imaging studies. Trace amounts of this radioactive isotope (thallium 201) are used in clinical medicine for the evaluation of coronary artery disease. The amount of the isotope used in imaging studies has insignificant health effects, but the radioactivity can activate security radiation alarms for days or weeks following diagnostic procedures. Individuals who undergo these tests should carry documentation of the testing for presentation to security agents that they might encounter following activation of a radiation detector.

13.3 Symptoms of Poisoning

Thallium poisoning produces nausea, vomiting, and intense abdominal pain. There are often neurologic symptoms such as muscle weakness and pain starting in the lower extremities. Hair loss from the entire body occurs within a few days of toxic exposure. Depending on the amount and frequency of administration, symptoms can occur within hours or after days or weeks. Death may be preceded by delirium, convulsions, muscle weakness, pain, and coma. Death is usually due to respiratory failure or cardiac arrest.

13.4 Case Studies

Case: Agitated Neighbor

In 1988, a 41-year-old waitress living in a small community in Central Florida developed an illness marked by nausea and intense pain in her lower extremities. She was hospitalized and shortly thereafter lapsed into a coma and died 5 months later. She had lived with her husband and their four children and a granddaughter. Two of the children also became ill and were hospitalized, but they recovered. From the symptoms and laboratory testing, it was determined that the family had been poisoned with thallium. Thallium was also identified in blood and urine from the family members who did not develop any toxic symptoms. An investigation into the possible source of the thallium revealed that bottles of a cola beverage that the family consumed during an evening meal had contained toxic levels of thallium, and that the addition of thallium to the cola was a deliberate act. The couple had been married for 6 months and it was common knowledge among their friends that there was significant marital discord. This was the second marriage for each of the parents. The husband appeared to be a viable suspect for the poisoning.

When investigators spoke to others who knew the family, they found that the family had many altercations with their nearest neighbors, a quiet couple without children, over the annoying behavior of the family's children. There were instances involving loud music, all-terrain vehicles riding on their neighbor's property, and dogs threatening the neighbor's cats. The neighbor was an unemployed chemist and computer programmer and his wife was a physician. The neighbor became the focus of an 18-month investigation involving a female undercover police officer who befriended the man. When investigators searched the neighbor's home, they found thallium, bottle-capping equipment, published poison reference materials, and personal journals with notes on thallium poisoning. The neighbor had indications in his background that suggested he was very much interested in poisons and poisoning, and he had also spent time in prison for involvement in illegal drug manufacturing that utilized thallium in the manufacturing process. Ultimately, the neighbor was arrested and tried for murder; he was convicted and sentenced to death.

Comments

Through a series of appeals, this convicted killer has been able to remain on Florida's death row for more than 25 years and continues to profess his innocence. He was convicted of murder and attempted murder as well as product tampering. The thallium compound used was easily added to the cola beverage without altering its taste or appearance. Bottle-capping equipment for home use is easily available commercially for home brewing and canning. The degree of thallium poisoning experienced by each family member was roughly proportional to the amount of cola consumed. The deceased mother drank the largest amount. The husband had only used a small amount of cola in a mixed drink and he had the lowest blood level and no symptoms.

Case: Iced Tea

In 1991, a 32-year-old electrician living in Pennsylvania started to experience aching muscle pain and burning sensations in his hands and feet. He was also having frequent episodes of nausea with vomiting. After he was hospitalized, his condition seemed to stabilize and improve slightly, and he was discharged after 3 days with a tentative diagnosis of food poisoning. Nine days later, he was readmitted. His symptoms had become more severe and now included mental confusion and agitation. Over the next 2 weeks, he gradually improved and then suddenly suffered a cardiac arrest. Resuscitation was unsuccessful and life support was discontinued a few days later. It was determined that his death resulted from thallium poisoning. Prior to his illness, he had been involved in renovating a university chemistry laboratory where thallium was used. His wife and stepdaughter were also tested for thallium and found to have elevated levels. Traces of thallium were also found in a thermos that he used to carry iced tea to his worksite. It was decided to exhume his body in 1994 for a more thorough toxicological analysis. Samples of his hair, toenails, fingernails, and skin were tested for thallium. From a segmental analysis of his hair shafts, a timeline for thallium exposures during the previous year was constructed. This time line demonstrated that the thallium exposure began prior to the husband's work in the university chemistry laboratory. It also indicated that he received a massive amount a few days before he died. The only person who could have carried out this chronic thallium poisoning was his 33-year-old wife. She was arrested and charged with first-degree murder. To avoid a trial and a possible death sentence, she confessed. She received a sentence of 10–20 years in prison. Her motive was a $300,000 life insurance policy. She explained that she had been poisoning her husband for months with a rat poison product that she discovered in their basement. She added small amounts to her husband's work thermos and administered the final lethal dose by adding it to a cola beverage that her husband drank while hospitalized. She did not know it was thallium until she was informed of this by the authorities. She could not explain how both she and her daughter had thallium in their urine samples. It was speculated that either they consumed some of the poisoned iced tea by mistake or that the mother intentionally exposed herself and her child to deflect attention from herself. She completed her 20-year prison sentence in 2016 and was released at the age of 53.

Comments

This case demonstrates the value of a historic record of poison exposures that can be provided with hair analysis. A comparison of exposure times with a victim's activities over the same time period can be very enlightening in terms of poison sources and victim's accessibility for poisoning. This case is also noteworthy in that the poison was chosen simply because it was a poison (rodenticide) rather than a specific toxic substance.

Case: New Jersey Chemist

In 2011, a 39-year-old computer engineer living in New Jersey suddenly became ill and was hospitalized. He died 12 days later. His 44-year-old wife was a chemist and worked for a pharmaceutical company. They had a 4-year-old son. When the husband became ill, the couple was in the process of finalizing a divorce initiated by the husband. A death investigation revealed that the wife had been poisoning the husband for about 2 months with thallium obtained from the laboratory where she worked. Moreover, the poisoning had continued during the husband's hospitalization. Prior to his death, the couple had lived in a spacious home where police had visited more than a dozen times to intervene in domestic disputes. The wife was tried for murder and sentenced to life in prison.

Comments

The chemist had threatened to poison her husband if he ever tried to divorce her. In addition, the husband had checked himself into the hospital and stated that his wife had poisoned him. It seems inevitable that the husband's thallium poisoning death would be swiftly attributed to the actions of the wife. Apparently, stealth and discretion were not components of her plan.

Case: Domestic Suicide with Imported Rodenticide

Around 2007, a 26-year-old man living in California was admitted to a hospital 10 h after he developed nausea, cramping, and bloody diarrhea following the ingestion of a rodenticide. A few hours later he described feelings of pins and needles in his legs, which were followed by pain, burning sensations, and weakness in both his arms and legs. He then became confused, his diarrhea continued, and cardiac abnormalities became apparent with ECG monitoring. It was at this time that the man disclosed that he had ingested rat poison he obtained from Russia. With this information and his clinical condition, a tentative diagnosis of thallium poisoning was made, and specific treatment was initiated. This included hemodialysis and the administration of an antidote. His condition improved over 10 days. Hair loss was first noted around day 10. The man recovered and was discharged from the hospital after about 2 weeks.

Comments

Russia and China are two of the few countries that continue to use thallium commercially as a rat poison. It is unknown whether the thallium was obtained with the intention of using it as a suicidal agent. It seems likely that it was obtained for use as a rodenticide and its availability made it a potential suicide agent.

Case: Toxic Role Model

In 2005, a 16-year-old schoolgirl in Japan was arrested for attempted murder of her mother with thallium. The thallium was administered in food and beverages over a period of months, and continued after the mother was hospitalized. Prior to this poisoning, the teenager was considered a good student with a bright future. The thallium was purchased from a local pharmacy and a chemical supply company under the guise of using it for a school science project. To deflect suspicions, the teenager even ingested thallium herself. Her younger brother was the first to connect her with the poisoning; after he alerted the police, an investigation began. To the surprise of everyone, it was discovered that she carefully documented the toxic features of thallium poisoning that she observed in her mother and posted them on an anonymous blog. The blog also included pictures of her suffering mother and notations about how easy it was to deceive and manipulate her teachers and the individuals who provided the thallium. The features of the case closely mirrored those of infamous Graham Young (1947–1990) who poisoned his stepmother with thallium and meticulously documented his observations. In fact, Graham Young was the teenager's professed role model and she was attempting to emulate his poisoning activities. She had read books about him and watched a movie made about his criminal poisoning life. Interestingly, Graham Young had also studied and idolized infamous poisoners that preceded him. Graham Young poisoned his father, stepmother, sister, and a classmate. For this, he was committed to a mental institution where he spent 9 years. While in the institution, he poisoned other patients and some staff members. Following his release, he continued to poison individuals until he was arrested in 1971. He poisoned more than 50 people and several died. He was tried for murder and sentenced to life imprisonment. He died mysteriously in his cell in 1990. The Japanese teenage girl who poisoned her mother was considered by the court as developmentally disturbed and mandated to be confined to a type of mental facility reform school. The court felt that a structured education would likely be effective in correcting her condition. In 2013, a Japanese movie based on this case was released. It was titled *Poisoning Diary of a Thallium Girl*. This is also strangely similar to the Graham Young case, which resulted in a film in 1995 titled: *The Young Poisoner's Handbook*.

Comments

The teenager in this case was apparently not attempting to kill her mother but using her as an experimental subject to study the effects of thallium.

References and Additional Reading

Al-Hammouri F, Darwazeh G, Said A, Ghosh RA: Acute thallium poisoning: Series of ten cases. *J Med Toxicol*, 7: 306–311, 2011.

Cvjetko P, Cujetko I, Pavlica M: Thallium toxicity in humans. *Arh Hig Rada Toksikol*, 61: 111–119, 2010.

Ghannoum M: Extracorporeal treatment for thallium poisoning: Recommendations from the EXTRIP workgroup. *Clin J Am Soc Nephrol*, 7: 1682–1690, 2012.

Good J, Goreck S: *Poison Mind*. New York: William Morrow, 1995.

Hoffman RS: Thallium toxicity and the role of Prussian blue in therapy. *Toxicol Rev*, 22: 29–40, 2003.

Jha S, Kumar R, Kumar R: Thallium poisoning presenting as paresthesias, paresis, psychosis, and pain in abdomen. *J Assoc Physicians India*, 54: 53–55, 2006.

Li S, Huang W, Duan Y, Xing J, Zhou Y: Human fatality due to thallium poisoning: Autopsy, microscopy, and mass spectrometry assays. *J Forensic Sci*, 60: 247–251, 2015.

Pelclova D, Urban P, Ridzon P, Senholdova Z, Lukas E, Diblik P, Lacina L: Two-year follow-up of two patients after severe thallium intoxication. *Hum Exp Tox*, 28: 263–272, 2009.

Peter ALJ, Viraraghavan T: Thallium: A review of public health and environmental concerns. *Environ Int*, 31: 493–501, 2005.

Rangan C: Thallium poisoning. *California Poison Cont Sys Newslett*, 5: 1–6, 2007.

Rusyniak DE, Furbee RB, Kirk MA: Thallium and arsenic poisoning in a small midwestern town. *Ann Emerg Med*, 39: 307–311, 2002.

Zhao G, Ding M, Zhang B, Lv W, Yin H, Zhang L, Ying Z, Zhang Q: Clinical manifestations and management of acute thallium poisoning. *Eur Neuro*, 60: 292–297, 2008.

Aspirin
14

14.1 Introduction

Aspirin is the common name for acetylsalicylic acid. Derivatives of salicylic acid are collectively referred to as salicylates. Although aspirin is the most familiar salicylate, there are other forms of salicylate utilized in clinical medicine. These include methyl salicylate, which is a component of many analgesic liniment type products used for muscle soreness, and bismuth subsalicylate, which is found in pink colored antidiarrheal products. All salicylates are potentially lethal, and overdoses are considered medical emergencies that require prompt aggressive treatment, often in an intensive care unit of a medical facility.

Salicylates stimulate respiratory centers in the CNS. Increased respiration disrupts the composition of gases carried in blood and alters the acidity of body fluids. Salicylates also block mitochondrial energy storage leading to increased heat production and hyperthermia. These metabolic disturbances result in life-threatening changes in body fluids and electrolytes.

14.2 Exposure Situations and Circumstances

Toxic exposures most often result from either adult suicidal ingestion, excessive utilization of salicylate products in therapeutic situations, or pediatric accidental ingestions. The majority of pediatric aspirin deaths result from administration of excessive amounts by parents or other caregivers for therapeutic reasons. Two main symptoms of aspirin toxicity are hyperthermia and hyperventilation. These symptoms of poisoning are very similar to those of the conditions treated with aspirin. Children with upper respiratory breathing irregularities and fevers associated with childhood colds are sometimes treated with aspirin. As these symptoms increase with excessive aspirin therapy, they can be interpreted as a worsening of the cold and cause even more excessive aspirin administration and a potentially lethal overdose.

14.3 Symptoms of Poisoning

Initial symptoms include tinnitus, nausea, vomiting, diaphoresis, and lethargy. Neurologic and psychiatric symptoms can include: agitation, delirium, hallucinations, slurred speech, and convulsions. Hyperventilation and hyperthermia are hallmarks of salicylate toxicity. Death usually results from pulmonary edema, cerebral edema, and cardiopulmonary arrest.

14.4 Case Studies

Case: Salicylate Liniment

In 2007, a 14-year-old boy was taken to a hospital emergency department because of chest pain, vomiting, and an increased breathing rate. Initial testing revealed elevated blood glucose levels, the presence of glucose in his urine, and other changes that were consistent with diabetes. He was started on insulin and further testing was undertaken. The metabolic changes found during expanded blood testing suggested possible salicylate toxicity. Blood salicylate was then measured and found to be close to 70 ng/ml (therapeutic range is 5–30 ng/ml). The appropriate treatment for salicylate poisoning was successfully employed and the boy was discharged. It was ultimately determined that the toxic levels of salicylate were the result of several days of masturbation using a lubricant that was a topical analgesic liniment containing methyl salicylate.

Comments

The metabolic effects of salicylates are complex and can result in either hypoglycemia or hyperglycemia, which requires evaluation within the context of other observed abnormalities.

Case: Chlorine and Aspirin Suicide

In 2012, a 48-year-old man was found dead in a hotel bed. A plastic bag containing a liquid was found on the floor near the bed. Empty containers of household bleach and toilet bowl cleaner were near the bag, and some empty aspirin packages were found in a trash container. The decedent had discoloration around the mouth indicative of chemical burns, and foam exuding from the mouth indicative of pulmonary edema. An autopsy revealed pulmonary edema and lung congestion, and mucosa ecchymosis throughout the trachea and bronchi. High concentrations of salicylate were detected in samples of blood, urine, brain, lung, liver, and stomach contents. Chloride was present in the contents of the plastic bag.

Standard screening for ethanol and drugs of abuse was negative. Based on the empty packages found at the scene, the estimated dose of aspirin was 30 grams (500 mg × 60). It was assumed that chlorine gas was generated by mixing toilet cleaner (hydrochloric acid) and household bleach (sodium hypochlorite). It was concluded that the cause of death was salicylate poisoning combined with chlorine gas inhalation.

Comments

The rational for using a combination of aspirin and chlorine for suicide by this individual is not known. Perhaps the chlorine exposure was the intended method of causing death while the aspirin was ingested in an attempt to reduce the expected pain associated with the corrosive action of chlorine on the respiratory passages.

Case: Drugged, Confused, Lost

In 2009, a 57-year-old man was found wandering the streets, confused and disoriented. Paramedics transported him to a local hospital for evaluation. Except for the man's obvious confusion, he was in relatively good health and did not have any apparent medical problems. He was breathing faster than normal and had a slight elevation in heart rate. Blood tests indicated elevated white blood cell count as well as elevated blood glucose. A chest X-ray showed some diffuse infiltrates. The initial hospital evaluation suggested pneumonia. He was started on antibiotics and admitted to the hospital for observation and additional testing. At this point, abnormalities in laboratory tests prompted the measurement of a serum salicylate level, which was elevated. He was then successfully treated for salicylate poisoning and discharged the following day. The man had been taking two aspirin tablets 7 or 8 times a day for several weeks due to chronic low back pain.

Comments

Chronic salicylate toxicity generally occurs in older individuals who use excessive doses of aspirin for prolonged periods. This can produce delirium, confusion, slurred speech, tachycardia, and hyperthermia. Since the onset of toxic symptoms can be gradual, the initial medical evaluation of patients can be misleading and suggest other conditions such as congestive heart failure, hyperthyroidism, dementia, and psychosis. Chronic salicylate poisoning is a potentially serious medical emergency that might require intensive therapeutic measures including hemodialysis.

Case: Aspirin Suicide

In 2009, a 28-year-old suicidal man ingested a large number of aspirin tablets. About 4 h later, he was transported to a hospital by emergency medical responders. He was experiencing severe gastric pain, had difficulty breathing, and was somewhat agitated. Except for an elevated heart rate, his examination at the hospital was unremarkable. Laboratory testing for metabolic abnormalities was within normal ranges. Urine toxicology screening did not disclose any common drugs of abuse. Serum salicylate levels confirmed the ingestion of aspirin. Following charcoal administration, IV fluids containing appropriate electrolytes were initiated. About 2 h later, the man became diaphoretic, respiratory rate increased, his agitation worsened, and body temperature continued to increase. Respiratory distress intensified, necessitating intubation and mechanical ventilation. About an hour later, the man had a cardiac arrest, which did not respond to resuscitation attempts.

Comments

This case illustrates the rapid progression of salicylate toxicity following an acute overdose. The complicated hemodynamic, electrolyte, and acid–base disturbances produced by toxic levels of salicylates require immediate intensive medical care that may include hemodialysis.

Case: Delayed Absorption Lethality

In 2009, a 53-year-old man living in Philadelphia went to a hospital emergency department about an hour after ingesting about 200 adult aspirin tablets in a suicide attempt. On arrival, his serum salicylate level was undetectable. Seven hours later, his level was 35 mg/dl. He was monitored for 8 h and then transferred to a psychiatric unit. Seventeen hours after his initial hospital admission, physicians in the emergency department again saw the man when he became diaphoretic, tachypneic, and unable to respond to questioning. At this time, his salicylate level was 128 mg/dl. Intensive treatment was initiated, but the man died 3 h later.

Comments

This case illustrates the unpredictable nature of salicylate absorption and metabolism after oral ingestion of large doses. There are a number of possibilities for explaining delayed absorption following oral ingestion of large quantities of tablets. The tablets may clump together in the stomach, forming a solid concretion that dissolves in an erratic and unpredictable rate.

Aspirin could also cause pylorospasm that would delay transfer from the stomach to the intestine. Characteristics of the particular aspirin formulation such as coatings and tableting materials that might be unimportant in therapeutic dosing can become a critical consideration in poisoning cases in which exposures might involve huge numbers of dosage units.

Case: Dermatological Salicylate Poisoning

In 2007, an 80-year-old bedridden man living in San Francisco received care from a live-in attendant who regularly massaged his legs and feet with oil of wintergreen (35% methyl salicylate). On one occasion, the man mistook a bottle of oil lying on a nightstand for a beverage and drank a mouthful. He immediately vomited, and a short time later had several seizures. Emergency medical responders found him unresponsive. He was not breathing and displayed ECG abnormalities. Resuscitation was initiated while he was transported to a hospital emergency department. The man's medical history included diabetes, renal failure that required regular dialysis and coronary artery disease that required a pacemaker. On arrival at the hospital, he was intubated and gastric lavage was performed and followed by charcoal administration. Clinical and laboratory testing showed marked metabolic and electrolyte abnormalities and complex ECG changes. Appropriate intravenous fluids were administered and hemodialysis was initiated. His serum salicylate level was 74 mg/dl. His condition continued to deteriorate and he expired following a generalized seizure about 9 h after admission. Following an autopsy and toxicology testing, the cause of death was ruled to be salicylate toxicity from oral ingestion and continued dermal absorption from the oil of wintergreen, which was all exacerbated by the patient's chronic renal failure.

Comments

This case illustrates the toxic potential of methyl salicylate by oral and topical administration. Oil of wintergreen contains a high concentration of methyl salicylate and the surface area of the lower extremities presents a large surface area for topical absorption. A major route of elimination of salicylate is through renal excretion. Renal excretion is especially important in overdose situations. The individual's preexisting renal disease contributed to salicylate accumulation that reached lethal levels.

References and Additional Reading

Anderson RJ, Potts DE, Gabow PA, Rumac BH, Schrier RW: Unrecognized adult salicylate intoxication. *Ann Intern Med*, 85: 745–748, 1976.

Carstairs S: Salicylates. *California Poison Cont Syst Newslett*, 7: 1–6, 2009.

Chin RL, Olson KR, Dempsey D: Salicylate toxicity from ingestion and continued dermal absportion. *West J Emerg Med*, 8: 23–25, 2007.

Fertel BS, Nelson LS, Goldfarb DS: The underutilization of hemodialysis in patients with salicylate poisoning. *Kidney Int*, 75: 1349–1353, 2009.

Herres J, Ryan D, Salzman M: Delayed salicylate toxicity with undetectable initial levels after large-dose aspirin ingestion. *Am J Emerg Med*, 27: 1173–1175, 2009.

Lindmark JD, Verive M: Salicylate toxicity in an adolescent presenting as chest pain after chronic topical salicylate use. *Chest*, 132: 720, 2007.

Nishiguchi M, Takahashi M, Nushinda H, Okudaira N, Nishio H: An autopsy case of a nonprescription aspirin overdose and chlorine gas exposure. *J Forensic Res*, 4: 1–4, 2013.

Pearlman BL, Gambhir R: Salicylate intoxication: A clinical review. *Postgrad Med*, 121: 162–168, 2009.

Rivera W, Kleinschmidt KC, Velez LI, Shepard G, Keyes DC: Delayed salicylate toxicity at 35 hours without early manifestations following a single salicylate ingestion. *Ann Pharmacother*, 38: 1186–1188, 2004.

Stinsbury SJ: Fatal salicylate toxicity from bismuth subsalicylate. *West J Med*, 155: 637–639, 1991.

Wong A, Mac K, Aneman A, Wong J, Chan BS: Modern intermittent hemodialysis (IHD) is an effective method of removing salicylate in chronic topical salicylate toxicity. *J Med Toxicol*, 12: 130–133, 2016.

Acetaminophen 15

15.1 Introduction

Acetaminophen is a nonopioid analgesic and antipyretic available in several hundred products with Tylenol being the most well-known. The toxicity of acetaminophen continues to be underestimated by many people despite intense public information campaigns to rectify this impression. It is one of the most common pharmaceutical agents involved in accidental poisonings and suicides. It is the most common cause of fulminant liver failure. Acetaminophen overdose poisoning is a major reason for liver transplants in the United States.

Acetaminophen in therapeutic doses is metabolized to inactive metabolites in the liver. When the metabolizing capacity is exceeded in overdoses, a toxic intermediate metabolite accumulates that destroys liver cells.

15.2 Exposure Situations and Circumstances

The adult therapeutic dose of acetaminophen is one or two adult tablets every 4–6 h with a total daily dose not exceeding 3 g. It has been estimated that the minimum acute adult dose of acetaminophen to cause severe liver damage is in the range of 7–10 g. This equates to 14–20 maximum strength (500 mg) tablets. This is an estimate and can be influenced by many factors such as body weight, health status, fasting state, and concurrent medications. However, it is clear that significant life-threatening toxicity can result from acetaminophen in doses that do not greatly exceed therapeutic doses. Dosing directions on products that contain acetaminophen are product specific: different for adults, children, regular strength, maximum strength, long-acting formulations, drops, solutions, and suppositories. Accidental poisoning can occur when product dosing schedules are not followed, and also when different products containing acetaminophen are used concurrently.

15.3 Symptoms of Poisoning

Initially, individuals who ingest an overdose of acetaminophen do not have alarming symptoms, which tends to delay seeking medical attention. They could experience nausea, vomiting, or fatigue, but physical signs of liver damage usually do not emerge until around 18 h or longer. Characteristically, the impending severe clinical decline in health starts with abdominal pain. Over the next 2 days, liver dysfunction becomes evident by the appearance of jaundice, bleeding problems, lowered blood sugar levels, and mental disturbances. Kidney failure may also occur. Death from multiorgan failure can occur within 4 days from the time of ingestion. N-acetylcysteine is a specific antidote for acetaminophen poisoning, but it needs to be administered within hours of the ingestion. After 24 h, the effectiveness of the antidote significantly decreases. Severe hepatotoxicity is not reversible and survival often necessitates a liver transplantation.

15.4 Case Studies

Case: Delayed Medical Intervention

In 2009, a teenage girl died from acetaminophen-induced liver failure 11 days after she ingested an overdose in an emotional response to an unexpected break up with her boyfriend. The couple had been dating for about a year when the boyfriend decided to end the relationship. They were both students, and the break up happened just before Christmas. After a somewhat emotional last meeting, the girl returned to her home where she lived with her parents and siblings, and ingested approximately 24 or more acetaminophen tablets and 24 ibuprofen tablets. She then sent a string of text messages to her ex-boyfriend indicating what she had done and that without him in her life she wanted to die. In response, the boy called her mother who in turn confronted the girl. She somehow convinced her mother that none of what the boy said was true. Later, she visited a friend near her home and also told her about the overdose. Not long after this conversation, the girl collapsed, emergency responders were called, and she was rushed to a nearby hospital. Despite treatment in an intensive care unit, the girl continued to deteriorate and her name was entered onto an emergency liver transplant list. Her total hospitalization was 10 days, and she was listed for the last 5 days. She died before a transplant could be accomplished. An autopsy confirmed that the death resulted from acetaminophen poisoning.

Comments

This case is representative of an impulsive suicide attempt made using medications that are immediately accessible. The behavior of the deceased and the others who knew about the overdose indicates that they did not appreciate the serious lethal potential of acetaminophen. The delay in recognizing the emergence of toxic symptoms delayed the seeking of medical evaluation. The ibuprofen ingested played no role in this fatal outcome. Deaths from acute ingestions of even massive amounts of ibuprofen are exceedingly rare.

Case: Too Busy to Live

In 2010, a 25-year-old female exercise instructor died from acetaminophen-induced liver failure. Five days before her death, this mother developed a respiratory infection for which she was prescribed antibiotics by her family physician. In addition to the antibiotics, she self-medicated with acetaminophen tablets, a combination cough–cold medication, and cough syrup. As her illness progressed, she became nauseated and vomited often. To compensate for what she perceived as a possible loss of medication through vomiting, she increased her doses of medications. Two days later, she saw another physician complaining of mouth ulcers and difficulty swallowing. This physician prescribed a throat spray and a codeine–acetaminophen combination product for pain. The following day she was found to be confused, had difficulty walking, and was clearly jaundiced. A relative then took her to a hospital, but the wait time was so long that she left. Hours later she returned to the hospital. This time she was seen and tests were ordered, but she again left before they were completed. She returned again in the evening and this time she was admitted. She died later that same night. An autopsy confirmed that she died from acetaminophen poisoning and the death was judged to be accidental.

Comments

This active individual appeared to have a slight, but annoying cold. Approximately 10 days later she died from an acetaminophen overdose. As her condition progressed, she interpreted symptoms of acetaminophen poisoning as increasing severity of the original cold and responded by the increasing doses of her medications. She was taking acetaminophen tablets and other medications that contained acetaminophen. What she was actually experiencing was an increasingly toxic response to her medications. It is troubling to consider that this excessive use of medication would be a rational approach by many people.

Case: Irreversible Liver Damage

In 2010, a 28-year-old woman was brought to an emergency department by her roommate because of lethargy and confusion. Twelve hours earlier she had taken 60 acetaminophen tablets and several methamphetamine tablets along with more than eight bottles of beer. Her overdose was apparently triggered by a recent dissolution of a romantic relationship. She had a history of depression and a seizure disorder, and took medication regularly for both conditions. Weeks prior to the overdose, she was fired from her waitressing job for poor performance. She had many friends. She was a regular drinker and smoked marijuana but did not appear to be dependent on these substances. She also had previous psychiatric hospitalizations and had attempted suicide at least twice, once by wrist slashing and another by barbiturate overdose. On this occasion, her condition was rapidly deteriorating and required intense medical treatment, including intubation and mechanical ventilation. Blood testing indicated severe liver toxicity; toxicology screening for commonly abused drugs was positive for amphetamines, benzodiazepines, and marijuana. Antidotal therapy for acetaminophen toxicity was initiated, but she was not expected to survive without a liver transplant. Due to this patient's history and the limited number of organs available for transplant, considerable discussion and debate among the health care providers preceded a decision to list the patient as a candidate for emergency liver transplantation. Within 36 h of this decision, transplantation took place and she was discharged from the hospital about 3 weeks later. She was compliant with psychiatric and medical treatment conditions imposed by the transplantation providers at the time of this case report was published and physicians were optimistic about her future.

Comments

This case illustrates the potential lethality of acetaminophen in suicidal ingestions, and touches on the complications and ethical consideration in treating individuals having poor prospects for healthy living with organ transplantation when organ donors are limited in number.

Case: Unconscious Man on Public Sidewalk

In 2011, during a community celebration in New England, a 25-year-old man was found unconscious on a sidewalk. There were no signs of trauma or indications of drug use. He was taken by emergency responders to a hospital for evaluation. There were several intoxicated patients in the hospital emergency unit when the man arrived and, after an examination, his altered mental status was attributed to alcohol intoxication and it was decided to observe him until he was sufficiently sober for hospital discharge. When the man's mental status did not improve over several hours, a more intensive evaluation was initiated that included a head CAT scan and laboratory testing. No abnormalities were seen on the scan, but the laboratory tests disclosed toxic levels of acetaminophen. Blood alcohol was undetectable and liver enzymes were elevated. At this point, the intravenous administration of the acetaminophen poisoning antidote (N-acetylcysteine) was initiated. His condition continued to improve over the succeeding days and full hepatic recovery was achieved in about 2 weeks. During recovery, the man reported that in a suicide attempt he had ingested three *bottles* of acetaminophen and one *box* of nonprescription sleep medication.

Comments

This case illustrates how experienced clinicians can misdiagnose ethanol intoxication. The difficulty in identifying and assessing intoxication has been noted in many studies involving evaluations by medical professionals as well as nonmedically trained observers. It is worthwhile to consider what the outcome of this acetaminophen overdose would have been if the individual had collapsed unconscious in an area where he would not have been discovered. The antidote for acetaminophen poisoning becomes much less effective in preventing permanent hepatic damage when administered longer than 8 h following the overdose.

References and Additional Reading

Achaval S, Suarez-Almazor M: Acetaminophen overdose: A little recognized public health threat. *Pharmacoepidemiol Drug Saf*, 20: 827–829, 2011.

Birmingham C, Nelson L: Due diligence in presumed ethanol intoxication. *New York State Poison Center's Toxicol Lett*, 16: 3–4, 2011.

Buck ML: New options for the use of N-acetylcysteine in acetaminophen overdose. *Pediatr Pharmacother*, University of Virginia, 22: 1–4, 2016.

Gyamlani GG, Parikh CR: Acetaminophen toxicity: Suicidal vs. accidental. *Cri Care*, 6: 155–159, 2002.

Heard KJ: Acetylcysteine for acetaminophen poisoning. *N Engl J Med*, 359: 285–292, 2008.

Kavalci C, Kavalci G, Sezenler E: Acetaminophen poisoning: Case report. *Internet J Toxicol*, 6: 1–5, 2008.

Larson AM: Acetaminophen hepatotoxicity. *Clin Liver Dis*, 11: 525–548, 2007.

Lee WM: Acetaminophen toxicity: Changing perceptions on a social-medical issue. *Hepatology*, 46: 966–970, 2007.

Navarro VJ, Senior JR: Drug-related hepatotoxicity. *N Engl J Med*, 354: 731–739, 2006.

Rhodes R, Aggarwal S, Schiano TD: Overdose with suicidal intent: Ethical considerations for liver transplant programs. *Liver Transpl*, 17: 1111–1116, 2011.

Zimmerman HJ, Maddrey WC: Acetaminophen (paracetamol) hepatotoxicity with regular intake of alcohol: Analysis of instances of therapeutic misadventure. *Hepatology*, 22: 767–773, 1995.

Alcohol 16

16.1 Introduction

Alcohol is a general chemical term that is applied to a family of structurally related organic compounds. The most common alcohols involved in toxic exposures are ethanol, methanol, and isopropanol (Table 16.1). However, when the term alcohol is used in medical and forensic situations without further qualification, it refers specifically to ethanol.

The clinical toxicology of isopropanol closely resembles that of ethanol. The toxic potential of methanol far exceeds that of ethanol. Single acute doses of methanol can cause irreversible neurological damage and blindness, and life-threatening metabolic disturbances.

The regular excessive use of ethanol will ultimately lead to decrements in most organ-system function and cause diseases usually related to the gastrointestinal system and the CNS (Table 16.2). Ethanol is also a human carcinogen. The primary focus of this chapter is on acute ethanol intoxication.

16.2 Exposure Situations and Circumstances

16.2.1 Absorption

Some ethanol is absorbed from the stomach but most of the absorption occurs in the upper small intestine. Ethanol is metabolized by the liver but small amounts are excreted unchanged in urine, breath, and perspiration. The levels of ethanol detected in the breath can be correlated with blood levels and can be used to estimate the amount of ethanol consumed. Urine levels of ethanol do not correlate with blood levels and only provide confirmation of ethanol exposure. The rates at which ethanol is absorbed and eliminated from the systemic circulation are variable and are influenced by factors such as the amount consumed, the usage patterns, the concurrent use of drugs, and simultaneous eating or fasting. Many influential factors have been identified and are important considerations in evaluating exposure situations and interpreting testing results.

Table 16.1   Common Alcohols

Chemical Name	Common Name
Ethyl alcohol (ethanol)	Grain alcohol
Methyl alcohol (methanol)	Wood alcohol
Isopropyl alcohol (isopropanol)	Rubbing alcohol

Table 16.2   Some Potential Consequences of Excessive Drinking

Behavioral	Medical
Accidents	Arrhythmias
Anxiety	Cancer
Depression	Cardiomyopathy
Domestic violence	Cirrhosis
Drowning	Hepatitis
Homicide	Hypertension
Risky behavior	Neuropathy
Suicide	Pancreatitis
Sexual assault	Sudden death
Snake bites	Stroke

16.2.2 Exposure

Practices that are structured around consuming large amounts of ethanol products over short periods can have lethal consequences from the toxicity of ethyl alcohol, especially with the lack of realization of the eminent possibility of death by family members, friends, and other bystanders. Consuming large amounts of ethanol during drinking games and contests, forced consumption during hazing, and celebrating events by the rapid consumption of multiple liquor shots can be life-threatening. Similarly, bypassing the usual gastrointestinal disposition pathways of ethanol by using alternate routes of administration such as injections, enemas, and inhalation markedly increases the possibility of lethal overdoses. Acute ethanol poisoning deaths in teenagers and young adults generate considerable public attention because of the age of the decedents and the circumstances of the drinking event. Typically, there is some type of group partying, hazing, or other risky behavior. However, these deaths make up only about 5% of all acute ethanol deaths. The majority of ethanol poisoning deaths in the United States occurs in middle-aged men and generally do not receive much media attention. These acute deaths are usually due to overdoses that occur during binge drinking episodes.

Moonshine is a general term for illegally produced whiskey or liquor. Some commercial products are branded as moonshine and sold in liquor stores, but these products are not actual moonshine as the term is used here.

Thousands of gallons of illegal moonshine are produced each year throughout the United States. These beverages are generally derived from the fermentation of wheat grain. They usually have high ethyl alcohol content (75%). Moonshine can contain toxic impurities or can be adulterated with industrial solvents. The most common impurities are metals that are leached from production equipment. Lead is the most common metal found in moonshine products and is responsible for serious toxic effects. There have been cases in which unscrupulous distillers have added inexpensive methyl alcohol to their products. Methyl alcohol is an extremely toxic substance that is potentially lethal and can also produce permanent blindness. Toxic batches of moonshine are occasionally produced and distributed within the United States and are responsible for poisoning groups of individuals. In many other countries, adulterated illegal moonshine products are much more common and regularly cause poisoning epidemics where thousands of poisoning cases occur with hundreds of deaths.

16.3 Symptoms of Poisoning

Large amounts of ethanol, particularly if consumed rapidly, can produce partial or complete blackouts, which are periods of memory loss for events that transpired while an individual was drinking. Although often confused with passing out or losing consciousness after excessive drinking, blackouts do not involve a loss of consciousness. Indeed, individuals can engage in a wide range of goal-directed activities and complicated behaviors during blackouts, including driving, sexual intercourse, and participating in conversations. Observers are often unaware of the individual's true level of intoxication. Blackouts represent episodes of amnesia. Memories that were formed prior to becoming intoxicated are not affected. People experiencing total blackouts are unable to recall any details whatsoever from events that occurred while they were intoxicated. Among the factors that predispose to blackouts are gulping drinks and drinking on an empty stomach, both of which lead to rapid rises in blood alcohol concentration (BAC). Estimates of BAC levels during blackout periods suggest that they can begin at levels around 0.20% but can also occur at lower blood levels. Blackouts can last from hours to days.

If an individual passes out during heavy drinking, the ethanol consumed will continue to be absorbed during unconsciousness. The individual can become increasingly depressed and blood levels can rise to a lethal range. The first symptom of ethanol poisoning is nausea, followed by vomiting. The signs and symptoms indicative of ethanol poisoning are loss of consciousness, increasing difficulty in awakening unconscious individuals, lack of response to physical stimuli, and slow, shallow breathing.

Table 16.3   Stages of Alcohol Intoxication in Nontolerant Individuals

Blood Alcohol Concentration (g/dL)	Stage of Intoxication
0.01–0.05	Sobriety
0.03–0.12	Euphoria
0.09–0.25	Excitement
0.18–0.30	Confusion
0.25–0.48	Stupor
0.35–0.50	Coma
0.45 and higher	Death

Stages of ethanol intoxication in nontolerant individuals are listed in Table 16.3. With increasing levels of ethanol there is an increased degree of CNS depression that progresses until respiratory centers are completely inactive. The various behavior manifestations of CNS depression reflect its increasing involvement with neuronal pathways within the brain.

Death from ethanol overdose can occur through several physiological mechanisms. When the concentration of ethanol in the brain becomes high enough to depress the brain areas responsible for the control of consciousness and respiration, the drinker lapses into a coma, stops breathing, and dies within minutes. Although tolerance to ethanol can significantly increase the threshold for some toxic effects, the threshold for lethality does not increase in proportion. Vomiting while unconscious can be fatal. While in a deep sleep from the depressant effects of ethanol, an individual may asphyxiate on vomitus. Aspiration of vomited material into the lungs is a serious medical problem, and blocked respiratory passages account for many ethanol overdose deaths.

Lethal ethanol concentrations are generally in the 0.40%–0.50% range. However, there are documented cases of fatal overdoses at lower concentrations. Consuming 10 or more standard drinks in less than an hour may be lethal. Although such high rates of consumption are atypical, participating in drinking games or club initiations often involves this level of consumption. Impaired judgment from intoxication coupled with large amounts of alcohol is a potentially fatal combination.

The concentration of ethanol found in postmortem testing can be the result of ingestion, or the formation of ethanol by fermentation of substances within the body after death. Vitreous humor may be used to differentiate ingested ethanol from postmortem ethanol formation because the processes that produce ethanol after death do not occur appreciably within in the eye.

16.4 Case Studies

Case: Ethanol and Isopropanol

In 2009, a 53-year-old man with alcoholism was found unresponsive outside of a hospital and brought to the emergency department. His vital signs were normal, but he had signs of intoxication including slurred speech, somnolence, confusion, and unsteady gait. He was treated with intravenous fluids, thiamine, folic acid, magnesium, and glucose. A serum alcohol screen revealed isopropanol and its metabolite acetone but was negative for ethanol. A urine drug abuse screen was negative. He was admitted to a general medical unit where his mental status gradually improved. His vital signs and physical examination were unremarkable. The isopropanol intoxication was managed with intravenous fluids and close monitoring. He eventually disclosed that he had consumed a bottle of rubbing alcohol (isopropanol) before admission. During the morning of the second day of hospitalization, he ate breakfast, used the bathroom, and then fell asleep. Approximately 45 min later, a nurse examined him and found that he could not be awakened. The patient's vital signs were normal, but he was unresponsive to painful stimuli. Naloxone and flumazenil were administered intravenously with no effect. The patient was then transferred to an intensive care unit for further treatment. In the intensive care unit, a second serum alcohol screen was performed and revealed a high level of ethanol and a lower level of isopropanol. A urine drug screen was positive for ethanol. The patient was treated conservatively and gradually improved. On the third day of hospitalization, he admitted to ingesting the contents of a pump bottle (500 ml) of ethanol-based sanitizer that was attached to the wall of his hospital room.

Comments

Alcohol-based hand sanitizers containing 60%–95% ethanol are common in healthcare settings and homes. The naxolone and flumazenil are antidotes for overdoses by opioids and benzodiazepines respectively.

Case: Hand Sanitizer and Pediatric Intoxication

In 2011, a 6-year-old girl seemed drowsy to her father when he picked her up after school. The girl continued to become more sedated until she became unresponsive and was taken to a hospital emergency department. Physical and laboratory evaluations did not identify a basis for the child's condition until toxicology testing revealed a serum ethanol level of 205 mg/dL. She was admitted to the hospital for administration of intravenous fluids and observation. She was discharged the following day without any signs of complications. An investigation found that the child had made frequent trips to the restroom during the school day and had ingested small amounts of hand sanitizer in the restroom because she liked the taste.

Comments

Alcohol-based hand sanitizers generally contain ethyl alcohol. Some sanitizers contain isopropyl alcohol but ethyl alcohol is the most common. The products can also be attractively scented, flavored, and packaged. It was estimated that a total of about 2 oz of the sanitizer would have been ingested to provide the ethanol level observed in this case.

Case: Fatal Celebration

In 2007, a female university student was celebrating her 21st birthday with four friends at a popular bar. Her friends and other patrons of the bar bought her exotic alcoholic cocktails and shots during an approximately 2-hour period that she was there. She passed out in the bar and her friends took her to an apartment where she was staying and put her to bed around midnight. She vomited at least twice but otherwise remained unconscious or in deep sleep. The friends ultimately left the apartment and her roommate went to bed. The student was last seen alive about 2:30 a.m. breathing and snoring. She was found dead in her bed the following morning at about 7 a.m. An investigation followed and her death was ultimately ruled as accidental and caused by ethanol poisoning. No criminal charges were filed. The family of the deceased girl filed a wrongful death lawsuit against the owners of the bar for serving the girl who was obviously intoxicated. Prior to trial, a confidential financial settlement was reached between the parents and the bar owners. The bar was permanently closed. The friends who accompanied the girl to the bar were also named in the lawsuit as having contributed to the death by buying drinks and for their negligence in leaving her alone without seeking medical help.

The deceased student had a significant history of alcohol use. Statements provided to police indicated that she was seen drunk at least 100 times in the past year and that she had been put to bed drunk by friends at least 50 times. She also had two convictions for drunken driving. On the evening of the birthday celebration, she was drinking prior to going to the bar. When she passed out at the bar, she was carried out over the shoulder of a male friend who placed her in a car with her friends who also drove to her apartment. He again carried her over his shoulder from the car to the apartment where she died.

Comments

This case raised significant legal questions about the responsibility of drinking companions for providing drinks and contributing to ethanol consumption, and for not seeking aid for a severely intoxicated individual. The individual who died was an experienced heavy drinker who had engaged in drinking episodes similar to the last one many times before. Although the information available cannot point to a specific factor that explains the lethality in this case, it does illustrate that acute alcohol poisoning can occur in chronic heavy drinkers. This case also highlights the apparent lack of appreciation by bystanders of potentially fatal ethanol poisoning. Generally, cases of alcohol fatalities described in media reports tend to imply that these cases mostly involve young, inexperienced individuals. However, the majority of acute alcohol poisoning deaths in the United States occur in middle-aged men who are experienced drinkers.

Case: Night Out on the Town in NYC

In 2006, a 38-year-old mother of three was found unconscious in the entry way of an apartment building in New York City. Emergency medical responders were unable to resuscitate her and she was pronounced dead on arrival at the local hospital. It was later determined that she died from acute cocaine and ethanol intoxication.

The deceased was a well-respected physician who lived with her husband and children on Long Island. She seemingly had a picture-perfect life in terms of family, community activity, and medical practice. On the evening preceding her death, she went to Manhattan for a night on the town with friends. The evening started on a Saturday night around 8 p.m. in a bar on the Lower East Side with drinking and using cocaine. Around 2 a.m., a 51-year-old married TV producer whom she knew well joined her at the bar. She and the man left the bar around 4 a.m. and went to a small walk-up apartment where the man's cocaine dealer lived. At some point, she became incapacitated. Around 8:30 a.m., the men carried her down the stairs to the entrance of the apartment building and called for emergency responders. The men left before police responders arrived. The death was ruled accidental and no criminal charges were filed. Apparently, the deceased did occasionally go out with girlfriends for cocaine-fueled alcoholic binges in New York bars where she was unlikely to be recognized.

Comments

Drug abusers often combine ethanol with cocaine to decrease the feeling of drunkenness and to intensify or modify the cocaine high. Ethanol can also mute some of the unpleasant symptoms experienced with cocaine use. However, ethanol significantly increases the potential lethality of cocaine, and cocaine will enable users to consume lethal amounts of ethanol without feeling the effects.

Case: Wine Enema

In 2014, a 52-year-old man was found dead in his home. He was last seen alone about 2 days prior to the discovery of his body. He was in his bed with a tube in his rectum that was connected to an enema bag containing wine hanging next to the bed. The man was wearing a condom and women's underwear. Empty boxes of white wine and pornographic material were found in the room. Autopsy findings and toxicology testing were consistent with a death from acute ethanol intoxication from the wine enema.

Comments

The rectal absorption of ethanol bypasses the initial metabolism that occurs in the liver following oral administration and can produce higher initial blood levels with increased potential for fatal respiratory depression. The use of the ethanol enema in this case appeared to be more related to erotic fulfillment than to some type of enhanced method of ethanol delivery for intoxication.

Case: Denatured Alcohol

In 2013, a 52-year-old unconscious woman was admitted to a hospital emergency department after ingesting a liter of denatured alcohol with suicidal intent. She was intubated for mechanical ventilation, and intravenous fluids and norepinephrine were administered for cardiovascular stabilization. Blood ethanol on admission was 1.127 mg/dL. She underwent continuous hemodialysis for 21 h. The blood ethanol was 0.044 mg/dL when the dialysis was discontinued. She was discharged from the hospital 8 days later. The time interval between ingestion and treatment initiation, and the previous history regarding ethanol use by the individual was not disclosed.

Comments

Denatured alcohol is ethanol with additives to make it unfit to drink. This is done to make it available for use as paint thinner and other commercial purposes without requiring beverage taxes. There are a number of different additives that can be used to denature ethanol, which are selected to be compatible with the intended use of the denatured product. A common denaturant is methyl alcohol, and these products are sometimes referred to as methylated spirits. The denaturants contained in the product ingested in this case did not include methyl alcohol. This case demonstrates that with early resuscitation and hemodialysis, survival of exceedingly high doses of ethanol is possible.

Case: Methanol in Tempting Containers

In 2012, two men washing delivery trucks at a large beverage company in Canada found a 1.5 L plastic bottle of vodka in the cab of one of the trucks. Both men drank from the bottle, thinking it was some type of flavored vodka. Later, one of these workers took home the remaining vodka and continued drinking it throughout the evening. It was later learned that the blue fluid in the vodka bottle was a commercial windshield wiper fluid containing methanol. The worker who took the vodka bottle home died later from methanol poisoning; his coworker survived following hospitalization and treatment. It had been a common practice of truck drivers working at the company to store wiper fluid in liquor bottles in the truck cabs. The company was fined for negligence in complying with occupational safety regulations related to the handling, storage, use, disposal, and transport of hazardous materials.

Comments

Some flavored commercial vodka products are blue and closely resemble the common blue color of wiper fluids. Methanol has an odor similar to ethanol and can initially produce intoxication that is also similar to the effects of ethanol. However, methanol is extremely toxic and ingestion of small portions can cause permanent blindness, coma, or death. Fatalities similar to the one in this case have occurred after wiper fluids were mistakenly added to punch mixtures or individual cocktails at social events. It is a too common practice to store excess toxic liquids in empty alcoholic beverage containers that are mistakenly consumed later.

Case: Fatal Blood Loss

The police discovered a man dead in his unkempt home after being summoned by concerned neighbors. The man was on his bed with massive amounts of blood in the room and on the body. Blood was tracked from the bedroom to the bathroom, and there were indications of blood splatter near the body. The initial impression was that the man had been the victim of violence and homicide. The cluttered and unkempt home made it difficult to determine the circumstances surrounding the homicide. Forensic investigators at the death scene found no external sign of trauma on the body. It was later determined that the decedent had a long history of excessive alcohol use, and the source of the blood was upper gastrointestinal bleeding. The bleeding had apparently occurred over a sufficient length of time for the man himself to have tracked the blood from the bed to the bathroom. What had appeared to be blood splatter was actually from insects attracted to the decomposing body.

Comments

Suspicious death scene findings can be the result of progressive drug-related diseases caused by chronic abuse.

Chronic alcohol abuse can cause cirrhosis of the liver, which impedes blood flow through the liver. As a result, veins in the esophagus carrying blood to the liver have increased pressure because of the restricted flow. These distended veins (esophageal varices) can burst and lead to critical blood loss.

References and Additional Reading

Caplan YH, Goldberger BA (Eds.): *Garriott's Medicolegal Aspects of Alcohol*, 6th ed. Tucson, AZ: Lawyers & Judges Publishing, 2014.

Darke S, Duflou J, Torok M, Prolov T: Toxicology, circumstances and pathology of deaths from acute alcohol toxicity. *J Forensic Leg Med*, 20: 1122–1125, 2013.

Gilliland MGF, Bost RO: Alcohol in decomposed bodies: Postmortem synthesis and distribution. *J Forensic Sci*, 38: 1266–1274, 1993.

Gossop M, Manning V, Ridge G: Concurrent use of alcohol and cocaine: Differences in patterns of use and problems among users of crack cocaine and cocaine powder. *Alcohol & Alcoholism*, 41: 121–125, 2006.

Hadley JA, Smith GS: Evidence for an early onset of endogenous alcohol production in bodies recovered from the water: Implications for studying alcohol and drowning. *Accid Anal Prev*, 35: 763–769, 2003.

Hunsaker DM, Hunsaker JC: Postmortem alcohol interpretation: Medicalogical considerations affecting living and deceased persons. *Forensic Path Rev*, 1: 307–338, 2004.

Jones AW, Holmgren P: Comparison of blood-ethanol concentrations in deaths attributed to acute alcohol poisoning and chronic alcoholism. *J Forensic Sci*, 48: 874–879, 2003.

Jones AW: Pharmacokinetics of ethanol: Issues of forensic importance. *Forensic Sci Rev*, 2: 91–136, 2011.

Joseph MM, Zeretzke C, Reader S, Sollee DR: Acute ethanol poisoning in a 6-year-old girl following ingestion of alcohol-based hand sanitizer at school. *World J Emerg Med*, 2: 232–233, 2011.

Karch SB (Ed.): *Forensic Issues in Alcohol Testing.* Boca Raton, FL: CRC Press, 2016.

Kugelberg FC, Jones AW: Interpreting results of ethanol analysis in postmortem specimens: A review of the literature. *Forensic Sci Int*, 165: 10–29, 2007.

Li G, Baker SP, Lamb MW, Qiang Y, McCarthy ML: Characteristics of alcohol-related fatal general aviation crashes. *Accid Anal Prev*, 37: 143–148, 2005.

Mahdi AS, McBride AJ: Intravenous injection of alcohol by drug injectors: Report of three cases. *Alcohol Alcoholism*, 34: 918–919, 1999.

Marek E, Kraft WF: Ethanol pharmacokinetics in neonates and infants. *Curr Ther Res Clin Exp*, 76: 90–97, 2014.

McDonough M: Alcohol use disorders: Implications for the clinical toxicologist. *Asia Pac J Med Toxicol*, 4: 13–24, 2015.

Molina DK: A characterization of sources of isopropanol detected on postmortem toxicologic analysis. *J Forensic Sci*, 55: 998–1002, 2010.

Peterson T, Rentmeester L, Judge BS, Cohle SD, Jones JS: Self-administered ethanol enema causing accidental death. *Case Rep Emerg Med*, 2014: 1–3, 2014.

Pressman MR, Caudill DS: Alcohol-induced blackout as a criminal defense or mitigating factor: An evidence-based review and admissibility as scientific evidence. *J Forensic Sci*, 58: 932–940, 2013.

Robinson E, Minera MG: Accidental acute alcohol intoxication in infants: Review and case report. *J Emerg Med*, 47: 524–526, 2014.

Sanap M, Chapman MJ: Severe ethanol poisoning: A case report and brief review. *Crit Care Resusc*, 5: 106–108, 2003.

Shetty BSK, Rastogi P, Kanchan T, Palimar V: Postmortem diagnosis of esophageal variceal bleeding—A case of sudden death. *J Punjab Acad Forensic Med Toxicol*, 9: 96–98, 2009.

Simpson SA, Wilson MP, Nordstrom K: Emergency department management of alcohol withdrawl. *J Emerg Med*, 51: 269–273, 2016.

Slaughter RJ, Mason RW, Beasley DM, Vale JA, Schep LJ: Isopropanol poisoning. *Clin Toxicol*, 52: 470–478, 2014.

Stout RG, Farooque RS: Claims of amnesia for criminal offenses: Psychopathology, substance abuse, and malingering. *J Forensic Sci*, 53: 1218–1222, 2008.

Templeton AH, Carter KLT, Sheron N, Gallagher PJ, Verrill C: Sudden unexpected death in alcohol misuse: An unrecognized public health issue? *Int J Environ Res Public Health*, 6: 3070–3081, 2009.

Thanarajasingam G, Diedrich DA, Mueller PS: Intentional ingestion of ethanol-based hand sanitizer by a hospitalized patient with alcoholism. *Mayo Clin Proc*, 82: 1288–1289, 2007.

Tsokos M, Turk EE: Esophageal variceal hemorrhage presenting as sudden death in outpatients. *Arch Pathol Lab Med*, 126: 1197–1200, 2002.

White AM: What happened? Alcohol, memory, blackouts, and the brain. *Alcohol Res Health*, 27: 186–196, 2003.

Opioids 17

17.1 Introduction

Opioids are indispensable in medical practice because of their ability to relieve pain irrespective of the source. Opioids also produce sedation and euphoria, which can foster misuse and abuse leading to addiction. The most important toxic effect of opioids is their dose-dependent depression of respiration. With repeated use, tolerance can develop and increasing doses becomes necessary for pain relief as well as for the euphoric effects. Tolerance also develops to the respiratory depressant effects, but at a slower rate than for other effects. With escalating doses of opioids, levels are reached which can be dangerously close to doses that produce lethal respiratory failure. Many factors can decrease or eliminate the narrow margin of safety between high opioid doses required for analgesia, euphoria, or suppression of withdrawal symptoms, and doses that produce respiratory failure and death. Some of these factors are reviewed in this chapter and highlighted with case studies.

17.2 Exposure Situations and Circumstances

The abusive use of opioids in variable doses in erratic dosing schedules combined with the concurrent use of other stimulant or sedative drugs can have life-threatening consequences. This is an especially dangerous practice when substances are administered by injection, or produced illegally. Some of the other risk factors for opioid lethality are listed in Table 17.1. A particularly important factor is tolerance, which can wax and wane with usage patterns and predispose users to unexpected toxicity. There is usually cross-tolerance between different opioids but it can be variable and not complete, and therefore cannot be easily applied in a quantitative manner when switching to

Table 17.1   Some Risk Factors for Opioid Lethality

- Use of illicit opioids
- Use of opioids by injection
- Daily morphine-equivalent doses exceeding 100 mg
- Concurrent opioid use with alcohol, cocaine, benzodiazepines, or other sedatives
- Resumption of opioid use at previously tolerated doses following periods of abstinence during incarceration, hospitalization, or participation in detoxification and rehabilitation programs
- Use of opioids in individuals with pulmonary diseases
- Unavailability of emergency treatment resources
- Using long-acting opioids
- Abuse of fentanyl and fentanyl analogs
- Escalating doses because of tolerance

different opioids in clinical situations. Some characteristics of opioids relative to abuse and poisoning patterns are summarized below:

Morphine is the prototype opioid and the standard to which all other opioids are compared in research and therapeutic applications. The most common route of administration of morphine in medical settings is intravenous injection. Oral administration undergoes extensive first-pass metabolism that reduces the effective dose to about 50% of that achieved with parenteral administration.

Heroin is more potent than morphine. The chemical structure of heroin facilitates its entrance into the brain after systemic absorption. After entrance into the CNS, heroin is rapidly converted into morphine. Thus, its increased potency compared to morphine is believed to be due to the increased speed of delivery to the brain. Heroin can be inhaled, snorted, smoked, or injected. Death from a heroin overdose results most often from respiratory depression. Occasionally, immediate deaths occur during heroin injections. Although these deaths can be the result of heroin overdoses, many involve other mechanisms. Factors that have been studied in an effort to understand acute death with heroin injection include the following: (1) fluctuations in tolerance, (2) allergic phenomenon, (3) toxic adulterants in heroin products, (4) drug interactions, and (5) a host of other susceptibility changes at unpredictable intervals. These rapid deaths are not easily explained in many cases and probably often involve fluctuations in use patterns and tolerance, and the concomitant abuse of other substances.

Fentanyl is commercially available in dosage forms for administration by sublingual, buccal, nasal, transdermal, and intravenous routes. On account of widespread therapeutic use, there has been considerable toxicological interest on the transdermal patch. The fentanyl patch is a drug delivery system designed to deliver fentanyl to the systemic circulation at a constant rate for several hours. Fentanyl patches continue to be used for diversion for misuse and abuse. Abusers use patches in a variety of ways, which include intravenous injection of the fentanyl gel extracted from patches, inhalation of fumes from heated patches, ingestion of the gel matrix, application of patches to the oral mucosal surfaces, and drinking liquids in which patches have been steeped, similar to tea bags. The sources of patches used by abusers include theft of new patches, retrieval of used patches discarded carelessly, and theft of patches from the bodies of living or dead patients. The design of patches is based on the diffusion of fentanyl from a reservoir through a membrane in contact with the skin. This diffusion is mass driven and the residual amount of fentanyl in the reservoir even 72 h after the application is significant and can exceed a lethal human dose in a nontolerant individual. Fentanyl and fentanyl analogs are also manufactured illicitly and available throughout the country. The high potency of fentanyl relative to other opioids is a major factor in the increasing number of deaths from opioid abuse. Fentanyl is often substituted for a number of illicit drugs. The substituted products often lead to opioid overdoses.

Fentanyl is about 50 times more potent than heroin. Fentanyl and fentanyl analogs (e.g., acetyl fentanyl, butryryl fentanyl) are produced illegally and often substituted for heroin and other opioids by illegal drug suppliers because it is cheaper and easier to obtain. On account of its high potency, there is an increased incidence of fentanyl-related deaths in experienced users expecting to receive less potent opioids such as heroin.

Methadone is used both for the treatment of pain and for replacement therapy in opioid addiction treatment programs. Dosing issues arise because the pharmacological properties of methadone are complex and significantly different from most other opioids. Methadone's duration of analgesia is generally 4 to 8 h, but its elimination half-life may be anywhere from 8 to 60 h or longer. Methadone's peak respiratory depressant effects typically occur later and persist longer than its peak analgesic effects. Dosing methadone based on subjective effects can lead to an accumulation of drug within the body, which can ultimately raise lethal levels. There are also several clinically relevant drug interactions with methadone.

Oxycodone is used therapeutically most often as oral tablets, which are available in immediate release and long-acting formulations. The immediate release tablets have a faster onset of action and a shorter duration of action than the controlled-release products. This distinction is not appreciated by many individuals who self-medicate with different formulations, each of which are commercially available in a number of strengths. This can lead to overmedication with increasing incidents of toxicity and more rapid development of tolerance and dependence. The euphoric properties of oxycodone have resulted in its becoming one of the most commonly abused prescription drugs in the United States. Diverted oral prescription products are commonly snorted, inhaled, and injected. The brand name for the controlled-release formulation (long lasting) of oxycodone is OxyContin. The controlled-release formulation contains a large amount of oxycodone that is designed to release small amounts over an extended period. Drug abusers, however, chew or crush the tablets to get an immediate release of the total amount of the drug present. Crushed tablets can also be sniffed, smoked, or injected. Newer formulations of oxycodone are designed to reduce this misuse by other routes of oral preparations. However, excessive oral use of oxycodone is not prevented by the newer formulations.

Hydrocodone in combination with acetaminophen has been one of the most prescribed oral medications in the United States for years. This extraordinary therapeutic availability has resulted in widespread misuse and abuse. Recreational use of hydrocodone combination products can result in addiction and overdose lethality comparable to that of morphine. In addition, the excessive use commonly associated with abuse carries a significant risk of acetaminophen toxicity and hepatic failure. Single ingredient hydrocodone products are also commercially available.

Buprenorphine is 25–40 times more potent than morphine. Buprenorphine has a ceiling dose effect for respiratory depression that is lower than maximal analgesic doses. It is used for both treating pain and for replacement therapy in opioid addiction treatment. It is commercially available in a variety of formulations that include oral tablets, transdermal patches, transmucosal tablets and films, injectables, and subdermal implants. Oral formulations of buprenorphine combined with naloxone are commonly used for analgesia and addiction replacement therapy. Naloxone is an opioid antagonist that is not effective when administered orally, but when tablets are crushed then injected or snorted, the naloxone blocks the effects of buprenorphine. Parenteral use of naloxone combination products may also precipitate withdrawal symptoms in opioid-dependent individuals.

Deaths involving buprenorphine are rare. Those that have been reported generally occur after intravenous use with concurrent use of ethanol, benzodiazepines, or psychotherapeutic medications.

Codeine is most often prescribed for pain relief in the form of tablets containing both codeine and acetaminophen. These combination tablets pose a significant danger of hepatic failure from the acetaminophen when consumed in large quantities by individuals who misuse or abuse them. Codeine is a prodrug that is metabolically converted to morphine in the body. The analgesic effects of codeine are therefore due to morphine. The rate of enzymatic conversion can vary with essentially little or no conversion in some individuals to an extremely rapid conversion in others. In the latter case, the unexpected elevated morphine levels can be life-threatening. Concurrent medications can also influence the rate of conversion of codeine to morphine and markedly influence the analgesic effects of codeine as well as its toxicity.

17.3 Symptoms of Poisoning

The three principle symptoms of an opioid overdose are miosis, unconsciousness, and respiratory depression. These and other symptoms are listed in Table 17.2. Clinical poisonous situations can be complicated by the concomitant utilization of other drugs such as ethanol, benzodiazepines, cocaine, muscle relaxants, and other psychotherapeutic or recreational drugs. Mixed intoxication can involve withdrawal symptoms of opioids or of other substances. The most common symptoms of opioid withdrawal are shown in Table 17.3.

Table 17.2   Symptoms of Opioid Overdose

- Depressed mental status
- Depressed respiratory drive
- Decreased gastrointestinal mobility
- Coma
- Bradycardia
- Hypotension
- Hypothermia
- Miosis
- Evidence of injection
- Exceptional snoring

Table 17.3 Symptoms of Opioid Withdrawal

- Piloerection
- Agitation
- Vomiting
- Diarrhea
- Mydriasis
- Diaphoresis
- Hypertension
- Tachycardia
- Tachypnea
- Yawning
- Muscle cramps

17.4 Case Studies

Case: Murder–Suicide with Patches and Strangulation

Around 2012, a 78-year-old woman and her husband were found dead lying side-by-side on their bed. There were 13 fentanyl patches and 40 buprenorphine patches on the woman's body, and ligature marks on her neck. The husband had a noose around his neck that had been fashioned from self-locking plastic cable ties. A suicide note written by the husband indicated that the woman had terminal breast cancer. Toxicological testing of blood and urine from the woman revealed lethal levels of fentanyl and buprenorphine; no other drugs were detected. Her death was ruled to be due to a combination of strangulation and opioid poisoning. Investigators postulated that the husband had applied the patches, and then strangled his comatose wife. He subsequently committed suicide by autostrangulation with plastic cable ties. Autopsy findings were consistent with this explanation.

Comments

The supposed explanation for the homicide was euthanasia and this was followed by suicide possibly because of lost companionship or avoidance of criminal responsibility.

Case: Football Player

In 2011, a 21-year-old talented college football player died while attending an open house party hosted by some casual acquaintances in a Florida beach community. He arrived at the party via cab close to midnight and was last seen alive about 3 h later. His body was discovered early the following morning on an open second-floor balcony of the five-bedroom home where the party was held. His death was ruled to be accidental and caused by multiple drug toxicity. Toxicological testing identified methadone, oxycodone, diazepam, carisoprodol, cannabinoids, and relevant metabolites. The athlete had a history of substance abuse issues beginning in high school and participated in rehabilitation programs. Four adults, in their early 20s, lived in the home where the party occurred. They were arrested because at least 15 of the attendees using drugs and alcohol at the home were underage. It was determined that the athlete had purchased the methadone that he used from the cab driver who transported him to the party. The cab driver, who was a known drug dealer, was arrested and charged with manslaughter and trafficking in controlled substances. He pled guilty and received 2 years in prison, 2 years of house arrest, and 10 years of probation. The source of the other substances that contributed to the death could not be determined.

Comments

This case involves a mature individual who was familiar with drug use and the types of group settings in which multiple individuals utilize a variety of drugs. In this party setting, circumstances were such that he consumed several drugs and likely became lethargic or sedated, went to a quiet area of the home to regain his composure, and then passed out, lapsed into a coma, and subsequently died.

Case: Methadone Snorting

In 2009, a 25-year-old single man living with his mother in Iowa developed cold symptoms that were sufficiently troublesome that he went to his physician for treatment. The physician prescribed an antibiotic. The man spent the remainder of the day at home with his mother. They were together until around 10 p.m. when the mother retired for the night. The next morning the mother left the home before the son awoke. When she returned in the afternoon, she was surprised that the son's bedroom door was still closed and he had not gotten up. She found him in bed, clothed, unresponsive, and cold. Emergency medical responders subsequently arrived and declared the son dead at the scene. Prescription medications on his nightstand included lorazepam, buspirone, and sertraline, plus an empty methadone tablet container that had not been prescribed for him, marijuana with smoking paraphernalia, and a grinding device for shredding marijuana. At autopsy, no needle sites were identified. Microscopic examination of the lungs revealed particles consistent with unevenly ground tablet fragments. Toxicological studies identified and quantitated THC and metabolites, sertraline and metabolites, nicotine and metabolites, and methadone. The levels were such that the cause of death was ruled to be from drug interactions and the manner of death accidental. The decedent had no known history of methadone use or abuse.

Comments

Death from presumed unspecified drug interactions in polysubstance abuses is frequently ruled to be the case when no anatomic cause of death is identified at autopsy. This individual was under a physician's care and being treated for depression and anxiety, as well as other conditions such as the upper respiratory symptomatology that was evaluated the day prior to his death. The totality of the information available from this case suggests that both the methadone and its administration by insufflating were experimentation and escalation of drug abuse behavior. The presence of preexisting respiratory issues that prompted a visit to a physician the day before the death could indicate methadone snorting in increasing amounts starting a few days prior to the terminal event with accumulation and interaction with sertraline.

Case: Long-Acting Opioid Tablets

In 2010, a 26-year-old suicidal man with a history of substance abuse went to a hospital emergency department 1 h after ingesting 10 morphine tablets (100 mg each). He was somewhat depressed but his vital signs were normal. Urine screening was positive for cocaine and opioids. Vital signs remained normal for a 6-hour observation period and then he transferred to an inpatient psychiatric ward. About 6 h later, he became apneic and pulseless. Following attempted resuscitation, he was maintained on life support for 14 days and ultimately died from hypoxic complications. It was unknown at the time of admission that the morphine tablets were a modified release formula that could delay the onset of overdose symptoms.

Comments

Opioids are marketed in many forms and strengths. Long-lasting oral tablets and capsules can pose an increased risk of toxic overdose when used therapeutically without medical follow-up and dosage adjustments.

Case: IV Use of Fentanyl Patches

In 2004, a 41-year-old man was found dead in his home by a friend. A syringe and an empty fentanyl transdermal patch were found near the body. A week later, a 42-year-old man was found dead by friends in the same home. Again, a syringe was found with packaging from a fentanyl transdermal patch. Postmortem toxicology results for the first man revealed fentanyl, morphine, ethanol, amphetamine, and cannabinoids. The cause of death was determined to be a combination of fentanyl, morphine, and ethanol intoxication. Postmortem toxicology results for the second man revealed fentanyl, sertraline, ethanol, and a metabolite of clonazepam. The cause of death was determined to be fentanyl intoxication. Both men were drug addicts and had purchased the patches from an individual whose parents were physicians.

Comments

The fentanyl patches in this case contained 10 mg of gelled fentanyl in a reservoir that can be extracted from the patch with a syringe.

Case: Emerging Recreational Opioid

In 2014, an 18-year-old man with a history of substance abuse was found unresponsive on the bathroom floor of a residence he shared with a roommate who had seen him alive 12 h earlier. He was pronounced dead at the scene. He had a tourniquet on his arm and a syringe was found nearby. Autopsy was consistent with a hypoxic death from respiratory failure with no contributory natural diseases. Postmortem toxicology testing revealed lethal levels of acetyl fentanyl and its metabolites. Samples tested included blood, gastric contents, urine, liver, and vitreous fluid. Acetyl fentanyl was also identified in a syringe. The cause of death was determined to be acetyl fentanyl intoxication, and the manner was ruled accidental.

Comments

Acetyl fentanyl is an illegal fentanyl analog. There have been many deaths in the United States attributed to acetyl fentanyl.

References and Additional Reading

Aromatario M, Flore PA, Cappelleti S, Bottoni E, Ciallella C: Methadone related deaths: Identifying the vulnerable patients. *J Forensic Toxicol Pharmacol*, 2: 1–4, 2013.

Boyer EW: Management of opioid analgesic overdose. *N Engl J Med*, 367: 146–155, 2012.

Chugh SS, Socoteanu C, Reinier K, Waltz J, Jui J, Gunson K: A community-based evaluation of sudden death associated with therapeutic levels of methadone. *Am J Med*, 121: 66–71, 2008.

Collett BJ: Opioid tolerance: The clinical perspective. *Br J Anaesth*, 81: 58–68, 1998.

Cone EJ, Fant RV, Rohay JM, Caplan YH, Ballina M, Reder RF, Haddox JD: Oxycodone involvement in drug abuse deaths. II. Evidence for toxic multiple drug-drug interactions. *J Anal Toxicol*, 28: 616–624, 2004.

Cunningham SM, Haikal NA, Kraner JC: Fatal intoxication with acetyl fentanyl. *J Forensic Sci*, 61: 276–280, 2016.

Dahan A, Aarts L, Smith TW: Incidence, reversal, and prevention of opioid-induced respiratory depression. *Anesthesiology*, 122: 226–238, 2010.

Dahan A, Yassen A, Romberg R, Sarton E, Teppema L, Olofsen E, Danhof M: Buprenorphine induces ceiling in respiratory depression but not in analgesia. *Br J Anaesth*, 96: 627–632, 2006.

Davis GG: Recommendations for the investigation, diagnosis, and certification of deaths related to opioid drugs. *Acad Forensic Pathol*, 3: 62–76, 2013.

DeLuca F, Focardi EB, Defraia B, Vaiano F, Mari F: An unusual homicide involving strangulation after transdermal fentanyl and buprenorphine intoxication. *J Forensic Toxicol Pharmacol*, 2: 1–4, 2013.

Goldberger BA, Maxwell JC, Campbell A, Wilford BB: Uniform standards and case definitions for classifying opioid-related deaths: Recommendations by a SAMHSA consensus panel. *J Addict Dis*, 32: 231–243, 2013.

Kapur BM, Hutson JR, Chibber T, Luk A, Selby P: Methadone: A review of drug-drug and pathophysiological interactions. *Crit Rev Clin Lab Sci*, 48: 171–195, 2011.

Klintz P: Deaths involving buprenorphine: A compendium of French cases. *Forensic Sci Intern*, 121: 65–69, 2001.

Krinsky CS, Lathrop SL, Crossey M, Baker G, Zumwalt R: A toxicology-based review of fentanyl-related deaths in New Mexico (1986–2007). *Am J Forensic Med Pathol*, 32: 347–351, 2011.

Lee D, Chronister CW, Broussard WA, Utley-Bobak SR, Schultz DL, Vega RS, Goldberger BA: Illicit fentanyl-related fatalities in Florida: Toxicological findings. *J Anal Toxicol*, 40: 588–594, 2016.

Lilleng PK, Mehlum LI, Bachs L, Morild I: Deaths after intravenous misuse of transdermal fentanyl. *J Forensic Sci*, 49: 1–3, 2004.

Madden ME, Shapiro SL: The methadone epidemic: Methadone-related deaths on the rise in Vermont. *Am J Forensic Med Pathol*, 32: 131–135, 2011.

Marinetti LJ, Ehlers BJ: A series of forensic toxicology and drug seizure cases involving illicit fentanyl alone and in combination with heroin, cocaine, or heroin and cocaine. *J Anal Toxicol*, 38: 592–598, 2014.

McCance-Katz EF, Sullivan LE, Nallani S: Drug interactions of clinical importance among the opioids, methadone and buprenorphine, and other frequently prescribed medications: A review. *Am J Addict*, 19: 4–16, 2009.

Milone MC: Laboratory testing for prescription opioids. *J Med Toxicol*, 8: 408–416, 2012.

Nelsen JL, Marraffa JM, Jones L, Grant WD: Management considerations following overdoses of modified-release morphine preparations. *World J Emerg Med*, 1: 75–76, 2010.

Nelson L, Schwaner R: Transdermal fentanyl: Pharmacology and toxicology. *J Med Toxicol*, 5: 230–241, 2009.

Palmer RB: Fentanyl in postmortem forensic toxicology. *Clin Toxical*, 48: 771–784, 2010.

Palmiere C, Brunel C, Sporkert F, Augsburger M: An unusual case of accidental poisoning: Fatal methadone inhalation. *J Forensic Sci*, 56: 1072–1075, 2011.

Pelissier-Alicot AL, Sastre C, Baillif-Couniou V, Gaulier JM, Kintz P, Kuhlmann E, Perich P, Bartoli C, Piercecchi-Marti MD, Leonetti G: Buprenorphine-related deaths: Unusual forensic situations. *Int J Legal Med*, 124: 647–651, 2010.

Polkis J, Polkis A, Wolf C, Hathaway C, Arbefeville E, Chrostowski L, Devers K, Hair L, Mainland M, Merves M, Pearson J: Two fatal intoxications involving butyryl fentanyl. *J Anal Toxicol*, 40: 703–708, 2016.

Rastogi R, Swarm RA, Patel TA: Case scenario: Opioid association with serotonin syndrome: Implications to the practitioners. *Anesthesiology*, 115: 1291–1298, 2011.

Sturup J, Caman S: Homicide-suicide offences: Description, classification and short case studies. *J Crim Psychol*, 5: 177–187, 2015.

Traqui A, Kintz P, Ludes B: Buprenorphine-related deaths among drug addicts in France: A report on 20 fatalities. *J Anal Toxicol*, 22: 430–434, 1998.

Wolff K: Characterization of methadone overdose: Clinical considerations and the scientific evidence. *Ther Drug Monit*, 24: 457–470, 2002.

Antidepressants 18

18.1 Introduction

Antidepressants are among the medications most often prescribed in the United States. In addition to depression, these agents are used to treat a broad spectrum of anxiety disorders, menstrual and menopausal symptoms, pain disorders, and nicotine dependence. One should expect to encounter antidepressants often in forensic situations, either incidentally or possibly implicated in some fashion in the events under consideration. Familiarity with these agents and their toxic potential can be an investigative asset. The majority of antidepressants that are most often prescribed can be divided into two main groups: (1) tricyclic antidepressants (TCAs) and (2) selective serotonin reuptake inhibitors (SSRIs). There are, however, a number of antidepressants that fall outside these groups. A list of common antidepressants is provided in Table 18.1. TCAs have chemical structures based on three connected molecular rings; SSRIs share a marked selectivity in their effect on brain serotonin. TCAs are much less selective in their effects on neurotransmitters. This is an important difference relative to potential toxicity. Although both groups have comparable therapeutic efficacy, TCAs are associated with more significant side effects and greater potential for serious toxicity, especially cardiotoxicity. The focus of this chapter is on the use of antidepressants to treat depression because depression is a risk factor for suicide, which frequently involves lethal overdoses.

18.2 Exposure Situations and Circumstances

Depression is a spectrum disorder that can involve treatment with complicated mixtures of antidepressants and other types of medications that increase toxic possibilities. Clinical depression can range from mild to severe forms that may be emotionally paralyzing and might include psychotic features. The severity of depression in an individual often fluctuates with highly variable episodes that have inconsistent responses to treatment. Some individuals appear to be stabilized with an appropriate dose of an antidepressant for long periods, whereas others require frequent dose adjustments and medication changes. All of these complexities in drug treatment can result in

Table 18.1   Antidepressants

Generic Name	Common Brand Name
Selective Serotonin Reuptake Inhibitors	
Citalopram	Celexa
Escitalopram	Lexapro
Fluoxetine	Prozac
Paroxetine	Paxil
Sertraline	Zoloft
Tricyclic Antidepressants	
Amitriptyline	Elavil
Desipramine	Norpramin
Doxepin	Sinequan
Imipramine	Tofranil
Nortriptyline	Pamelor
Other Antidepressants	
Duloxetine	Cymbalta
Venlafaxine	Effexor
Bupropion	Wellbutrin
Mirtazapine	Remeron
Trazodone	Desyrel

patients having a medicine cabinet full of an assortment of various strengths of many different drugs. This medication availability can be a significant risk factor for intentional overdoses.

Antidepressants require many days and often weeks to become fully effective. When suicide is a possibility, this delayed onset of action necessitates close clinical monitoring and interim measures such as hospitalization or other treatment modalities until an effective drug regimen is established. The delay in the onset of action precludes taking these agents on an as-needed basis similar to the way one might take headache medication. Nevertheless, some individuals self-medicate and take antidepressants in this fashion. This is frequently encountered with substance abusers and others who obtain these drugs through sources that do not include medical supervision. In such cases, any therapeutic antidepressant benefit is highly unlikely and exposes individuals to medications with serious toxic potential. The vast majority of patients prescribed antidepressants do not abuse them. When abuse does occur, the most common intent is to achieve psychostimulating effects.

There is a clear relationship between depression and substance abuse disorders. Whether substance abuse leads to depression or the reverse, the risk for intentional or unintentional mixed-drug overdoses is greatly enhanced in individuals who abuse drugs. Immediate and long-term toxicity from combining antidepressants with other drugs or alcohol can create life-threatening situations.

18.3 Symptoms of Poisoning

Tricyclic antidepressants: TCA poisoning is becoming less common as these drugs are replaced with newer antidepressants, particularly the SSRIs. However, TCA poisoning remains an important cause of death in suicides resulting from overdose. Death from TCA overdose usually occurs within a few hours after ingestion and may result from ventricular fibrillation, cardiogenic shock, or status epilepticus with hyperthermia. Sudden death several days after apparent recovery from an overdose has been reported. Poisoning symptoms are shown in Table 18.2.

Selective serotonin reuptake inhibitors: SSRIs are considerably less toxic in overdose than the TCAs. There is no specific treatment for SSRI poisoning. Symptomatic and supportive therapy is usually effective for the successful management of overdose cases that received medical attention. SSRI poisoning symptoms are shown in Table 18.3.

Table 18.2 Symptoms of Poisoning with Tricyclic Antidepressants

Common	Uncommon
Drowsiness	Coma
Mydriasis	Hyperreflexia
Tachycardia	Hypotension
Xerostomia	Hypothermia
	Increased muscle tone
	Respiratory depression
	Rhabdomyolysis
	Seizures
	Urinary retention
	Ventricular fibrillation

Table 18.3 Symptoms of Poisoning with Selective Serotonin Reuptake Inhibitors

Common	Uncommon
Agitation	Arrhythmias
Confusion	Renal failure
Drowsiness	Respiratory failure
Mydriasis	Rhabdomyolysis
Nausea	Seizures
Tachycardia	
Tremor	
Vomiting	

18.4 Case Studies

Case: Suicide Following Discontinuation of Medication

A 53-year-old male with a history of suicidal threats was found unresponsive in his home. Empty containers of prescribed sertraline (SSRI) and alprazolam were found together with a suicide note. He was transported to a medical facility where resuscitation efforts were unsuccessful. During autopsy, no evidence of violence or anatomic cause of death was detected. No tablet fragments were found in the gastric contents. Toxicological screening of postmortem samples was negative for common substances of abuse and medications, except for sertraline and its metabolite, and alprazolam. The levels of alprazolam were consistent with therapeutic use. The sertraline levels were consistent with levels found in previously reported cases of overdose deaths. Based on the toxicological findings, the cause of death was ruled to be due to multiple drug intoxication following an acute sertraline overdose. The mechanism of death could not be determined. The manner of death was suicide.

Comments

The individual in this case ingested an SSRI and a benzodiazepine. An analysis of the relative concentrations of sertraline and its metabolite in various autopsy samples suggested that death occurred shortly after ingestion and that the deceased was not following the daily regimen of sertraline therapy as prescribed by his physician. There is no way to determine with any certainty whether compliance with the antidepressant therapeutic regimen would have prevented the suicide.

Case: Suicide with Second Thoughts

In 2008, a 40-year-old suicidal man living in a town in Kentucky ingested approximately 19 g of venlafaxine (antidepressant) that had been prescribed in the form of extended release tablets for the treatment of his depression. He then went to the emergency department of a nearby hospital. On arrival, about 1 h following the ingestion, he was asymptomatic except for nausea and an elevated heart rate. He was administered charcoal, and whole-bowel irrigation was initiated with polyethylene glycol. He became more nauseous with accompanying vomiting and exhibited a degree of sedation. At 2 h postingestion, he was transported to a nearby medical facility having more advanced care resources. During transport, the man had a major seizure. Nausea and vomiting continued and he experienced another seizure soon after his arrival at the second medical facility. Supportive care continued for approximately 9 h from the time of ingestion until he developed refractory ventricular fibrillation and died. Antemortem and postmortem blood testing confirmed the lethal venlafaxine overdose; no other substances were detected.

Comments

The symptoms of the individual described in this case were consistent with those previously reported in similar cases: seizure, arrhythmias, CNS depression, and hypotension. It was estimated that the individual ingested about 165 tablets of extended release venlafaxine tablets of two different strengths (75 and 150 mg). This large number of tablets, designed to slowly release the drug over a period of hours, prompted the initiation of whole-bowel irrigation in an attempt to flush the tablets through the gastrointestinal tract prior to their disintegration and absorption. Despite this decontamination effort, a lethal amount was absorbed.

Case: Tricyclic Antidepressant Overdose

In 2014, a 43-year-old suicidal man was found in his home unresponsive and without a pulse by emergency medical responders. There were indications that the man had ingested approximately 60 amitriptyline tablets (50 mg $\times$ 60). Resuscitation measures were initiated and he was transported to a hospital where immediate intubation for mechanical ventilation took place. ECG monitoring showed arrhythmias and he exhibited seizure activity. Sodium bicarbonate was administered intravenously. He died soon after arrival at the hospital. Urine toxicology testing was positive for tricyclic antidepressants.

Comments

Life-threatening arrhythmias and death from tricyclic antidepressant overdoses usually occur within 24 h of ingestion. ECG changes can be more predictive than blood levels for toxicity evaluation in overdoses. The cardiotoxicity caused by tricyclic antidepressants in turn leads to a number of major metabolic changes, which further complicates the management of poisoning cases. Sodium bicarbonate is an appropriate initial treatment for arrhythmias and hypotension produced by tricyclic antidepressants.

Case: Mixed-Drug Suicide

In 2011, a 36-year-old suicidal woman who had ingested multiple drugs was taken to a hospital about 5 h after the ingestion. Based on the amounts of medications missing from containers in her home, it was estimated that she ingested about a 10-day supply of fluoxetine (SSRI), moclobemide, propranol, estazolam, bromazepam, aprazolam, lorazepam, and midazolam. On arrival, gastric lavage was performed and followed with the administration of charcoal. She then became comatose, developed generalized muscle twitching, and became hypotensive with bradycardia. These symptoms were appropriately treated and then she was intubated and placed on mechanical ventilation. Body temperature was elevated and marked diaphoresis was noted. ECG tracings disclosed a number of abnormalities. Despite treatment, her condition continued to deteriorate to irreversible hypotension with continuing cardiac arrhythmias, and uncontrollable bleeding abnormalities. Approximately 22 h following the ingestion, she died. Antemortem drug levels confirmed the multiple drug overdoses.

Comments

This case is typical of mixed-drug suicidal overdoses in which individuals ingest large amounts of a variety of medications that are easily accessible to them.

Case: Homicide of Bedridden Wife

In 2003, a 57-year-old man living in a small town in Ohio called emergency responders about 5 a.m. when he found his 58-year-old bedridden wife was not breathing. She was found dead by the responding paramedics. She had been ill for about 5 years with a pulmonary disease and complications of diabetes. During the illness, there were periods of time when the woman was in a nursing home, but at the time of her death she was at home being cared for by her husband and regular home nursing visits. As the woman's health issues were progressively deteriorating, it was assumed the death was due to natural causes. However, the state health care providers requested an investigation due to an accumulated history of questionable and unacceptable behavior of the husband while caring for his wife. There was a clear pattern of abusive practices, as well as considerable heated confrontations with the home care providers. There were formal complaints on file from the nursing staff and other reports from service providers and law enforcement agencies. On three previous occasions the husband had been charged with domestic violence, one of which resulted in an 11-month prison sentence. Based on results from the wife's autopsy, toxicology testing, and interviews with the health care providers, the death was ruled as a homicide due to a toxic combination of sertraline (SSRI) and tramadol. The husband was arrested and charged with aggravated murder, involuntary manslaughter, failing to provide for a functionally impaired person, and domestic violence. Investigators learned that during the woman's protracted illness, all medications prescribed were always secured in a locked storage area and no one other than the husband administered them. Thus, the husband was the only person who could have administered the lethal amounts of medication. The husband was found guilty of all charges and sentenced to life in prison.

Comments

This case is illustrative of abusive behavior toward a helpless individual that is solely dependent on a family member for care. It also illustrates how significant alerting events and behaviors can fail to illicit timely and appropriate corrective action from responsible observers.

Case: Selective Serotonin Reuptake Inhibitor Overdose

In 2015, a 35-year-old woman was questioned by her male partner about a previously full prescription container for citalopram (SSRI) that he found empty. This woman denied taking the medication, but a short time later she began to have seizures, which progressed to being cyanotic with a barely detectable pulse. Emergency medical responders arrived and initiated resuscitation measures that included IV fluids and assisted ventilation. She was then transported to a hospital emergency department where she was intubated and placed on mechanical ventilation. She had a history of depression, which was being treated with citalopram. There was a past history of methamphetamine abuse but she was currently using only the antidepressant, ethanol, and marijuana. She was hypotensive with increased heart rate. ECG tracings were abnormal. Urine toxicology screening was positive for cannabinoids and negative for amphetamines, barbiturates, benzodiazapines, cocaine, and opioids. She was transferred to an intensive care unit where she was treated for her cardiac arrhythmias and midazolam was administered for seizure control. Body temperature continued to increase despite active cooling measures. Cardiac irregularities became more serious and did not respond to corrective measures. After about an hour of continuous CPR, she expired. This was approximately 6 h after her arrival at the hospital. Toxicology testing of samples collected at autopsy was positive for citalopram and THC.

Comments

Citalopram is an SSRI, which has potential cardiac and neurologic toxicities. This case represents a massive overdose with marked hemodynamic instability, hyperthermia, and seizures that could not be controlled with intensive medical treatment. Fatalities following citalopram overdoses without coingestion are rare. It was estimated that the overdose occurred approximately 1 h prior to requesting assistance from emergency responders. It is likely that seizures and her cardiac arrest before resuscitation began resulting in hypoperfusion of her brain and caused irreversible neurologic damage and contributed significantly to her death.

References and Additional Reading

Bosse GM, Spiller HA, Collins AM: A fatal case of venlafaxine overdose. *J Med Toxicol*, 4: 18–20, 2008.

Dams R, Benijts THP, Lambert WE, Van Bocxlaer JF, Van Varenberg D, Van Peteghem C, De Leenheer AP: A fatal case of serotonin syndrome after combined moclobemide-citalopram intoxication. *J Anal Toxicol*, 25: 147–151, 2001.

De Meester A, Carbutti G, Gabriel L, Jacques JM: Fatal overdose with trazodone: Case report and literature review. *Acta Clinica Belgica*, 56: 258–261, 2001.

Evans EA, Sullivan MA: Abuse and misuse of antidepressants. *Subt Abuse Rehabil*, 5: 107–120, 2014.

Goeringer KE, Raymon L, Christian GD, Logan BK: Postmortem forensic toxicology of selective serotonin reuptake inhibitors: A review of pharmacology and report of 168 cases. *J Forensic Sci*, 45: 633–648, 2000.

Hargrove V, Molina DK: A fatality due to cyproheptadine and citalopram. *J Anal Toxicol*, 33: 564–567, 2009.

Kraai EP, Seifert SA: Citalopram overdose: A fatal case. *J Med Toxicol*, 11: 232–236, 2015.

Liebelt EL: An update on antidepressant toxicity: An evolution of unique toxicities to master. *Clin Ped Emerg Med*, 9: 24–34, 2008.

Martinez MA, Ballesteros S, Sanchez de la Torre C, Almarza E: Investigation of a fatality due to trazodone poisoning: Case report and literature review. *J Anal Toxicol*, 29: 267–268, 2005.

Milner DA, Hall M, Davis GG, Brissie RM, Robinson CA: Fatal multiple drug intoxication following acute sertraline use. *J Anal Toxicol*, 22: 545–548, 1998.

Parsons AT, Anthony RM, Meeker JE: Two fatal cases of venlafaxine poisoning. *J Anal Toxicol*, 20: 266–268, 1996.

Pilgrim JL, Gerostamoulos D, Drummer OH: Deaths involving contraindicated and inappropriate combinations of serotonergic drugs. *Int J Legal Med*, 125: 803–815, 2011.

Wu M, Deng J: Fatal serotonin toxicity caused by moclobemide and fluoxetine overdose. *Gung Med J*, 34: 644–649, 2011.

Benzodiazepines 19

19.1 Introduction

Benzodiazepines are among the most widely prescribed medications in the world. They are a chemically related group of compounds, which have rather selective antianxiety properties, and an unusually broad margin of safety. They are used in treating anxiety, panic disorders, phobias, obsessive compulsive disorders, insomnia, and some forms of depression. They can be used to reduce anxiety associated with various diagnostic or medical procedures, and are commonly combined with other agents to facilitate surgical anesthesia. Beyond their antianxiety indications, they can provide significant muscle relaxation and have anticonvulsant properties. Benzodiazepines are the primary medications for controlling seizures in emergency situations regardless of the underlying cause of the seizure. The most common benzodiazepines are listed in Table 19.1.

Individual benzodiazepines can have pharmacological or toxicological features that might be clinically relevant in certain situations but, as a first consideration, the various benzodiazepines can be considered interchangeable except for potency (dose), and onset and duration of action. Perceived differences between benzodiazepines are often based on marketing objectives rather than on pharmacological considerations. After appropriate adjustments for pharmacokinetic factors (dose, onset, and duration), the effects of benzodiazepines administered concurrently can be considered additive. When differences might be an important consideration, this is generally highlighted in common references that provide drug-specific information. Benzodiazepines alone are almost never the cause of an overdose death, but they are very often a contributing factor in multiple drug deaths.

19.2 Exposure Situations and Circumstances

Due to the widespread use and abuse of benzodiazepines, there is a high probability that they will be encountered in forensic investigations. Their presence might be incidental, or an important consideration for the investigation. In addition to the large number of benzodiazepines available commercially

Table 19.1 Benzodiazepines

Generic Name	Popular Brand Name
Alprazolam	Xanax
Clorazepate	Tranxene
Chlordiazepoxide	Librium
Clonazepam	Klonopin
Diazepam	Valium
Flunitrazepam	Rohypnol
Flurazepam	Dalmane
Lorazepam	Ativan
Midazolam	Versed
Nitrazepam	Mogadon
Oxazepam	Serax
Temazepam	Restoril
Triazolam	Halcion

for therapeutic applications, there is a growing source of illegally produced benzodiazepines that include unique designer versions.

Death can result from the ingestion of massive quantities of benzodiazepines but recovery after prolonged coma is the usual outcome. Lethal drug combinations with opioids, ethanol, or other CNS depressants can occur in clinical situations as well as in abuse or misuse situations. Psychological and physical dependence can develop with use over prolonged periods. Withdrawal symptoms include confusion, anxiety, agitation, restlessness, insomnia, and seizures. Due to the long half-lives of some benzodiazepines, withdrawal symptoms may not occur until a number of days after discontinuation. Benzodiazepines with a short elimination half-life induce more abrupt and severe withdrawal reactions.

19.3 Symptoms of Poisoning

The symptoms of benzodiazepine toxicity following an acute overdose begin within a few hours and resemble those seen with alcohol intoxication. Symptoms include impaired balance and motor functions, ataxia, and slurred speech. On occasions, paradoxical symptoms may occur, which include anxiety, delirium, hallucinations, and aggression. Large overdoses may produce coma, respiratory depression, and cardiac arrest. However, life-threatening effects are rare when no other substances are involved.

All benzodiazepines can produce anterograde amnesia in which memory is impaired relative to events that occur after the drug is administered. The dose and route of administration are important factors. The amnesic effect is seldom recognized or of clinical significance in therapeutic situations involving oral administration. High oral doses combined with ethanol or intravenous administration consistently produce varying degrees of amnesia.

19.4 Case Studies

Case: Man in the Bamboo

In 2003, a 57-year-old male was found dead in a bamboo thicket near his home. It was winter and it was estimated that he died 2 or 3 days prior to discovery. Autopsy findings were consistent with asphyxia. Toxicological screening identified triazolam and its metabolite in stomach contents, blood, urine, bile, and organ samples. The history, circumstances of the death, and levels of triazolam and its metabolite in various samples suggested that the victim died soon after ingesting a lethal amount of triazolam. The position of the body indicated that respiration was severely compromised by the obstruction of the nose and mouth of the man when he fell to the ground in his comatose condition. The cause of death was found to be postural asphyxia secondary to triazolam overdose.

Comments

Death from postural or positional asphyxia occurs in circumstances in which a victim's body assumes an abnormal position that causes mechanical obstruction of airways.

Case: Zolpidem Overdose and Diazepam Withdrawal

In 2009, a 43-year-old woman was brought to a hospital emergency department by a family member because of her unusual behavior and apparent hallucinations. She was believed to have taken several zolpidem tablets for insomnia. Her blood pressure was elevated, but other aspects of a physical examination were unremarkable. Laboratory tests were normal except for a urine drug screen, which was positive for benzodiazepines. After admission, blood pressure and pulse continued to increase and her behavior was abnormal. Approximately 12 h after admission, she began to have episodes of shaking. During hospitalization, she received a variety of medications for seizure prevention, blood pressure control, psychosis, and possible systemic infections. These medications had little effect on her condition. Approximately 14 h after admission, she developed acute respiratory failure, which was unresponsive to resuscitative measures. An autopsy did not disclose any evidence of natural disease, trauma, or drug toxicity. Toxicology screening was carried out on antemortem and postmortem blood samples and was essentially negative except for trace amounts of medications used in her treatment. No zolpidem was detected. She was somewhat obese and had mild heart enlargement. From past medical records and conversations with the victim's psychiatrist, it was discovered that up until about 10 days before her death, she had been taking diazepam for several years. The psychiatrist had discontinued the diazepam and prescribed 2 mg alprazolam three times a day in its place. Her concurrent medications included ziprasidone, citalopram, and zolpidem. She had taken 100 alprazolam (2 mg each) tablets over 6 days and then stopped when her prescription supply was exhausted. Four days later, when her insomnia was intolerable, she took 60 mg zolpidem (usual dose is 5–10 mg). A review of her clinical presentation, medical history, and autopsy findings strongly suggested acute withdrawal from benzodiazepines rather than zolpidem overdose as the likely cause of her symptomology. The cause of death was ruled to be a complication of chronic benzodiazepine use. It was speculated that the terminal event was a fatal arrhythmia induced by benzodiazepine withdrawal.

Comments

The acute withdrawal symptoms from benzodiazepine are very similar to those seen with ethanol withdrawal and can be fatal. In this case, the withdrawal was not recognized when she arrived at the hospital. Her immediate history and symptoms strongly suggested to the emergency physician that she was likely suffering from a suicidal overdose of zolpidem.

Case: Alprazolam Suicide

In 1997, a 44-year-old woman was found dead in her bed. She had a history of psychiatric problems and was being treated with alprazolam, lorazepam, fluoxetine, venlafaxine, and phenytoin. No natural cause of death was identified at autopsy. Comprehensive toxicological screens were performed on postmortem samples. Four drugs were identified in urine: (1) alprozalam, (2) chlorpheniramine, (3) dextromethorphan, and (4) doxylamine. Only alprazolam was found in blood samples. High levels of alprazolam were also found in bile, vitreous humor, liver, kidney, and stomach contents. Based on the findings of the death investigation, it was concluded that the death was caused by acute alprazolam intoxication and the manner of death was ruled as suicide.

Comments

The psychotherapeutic agents prescribed for the woman in this case included two antidepressants, an anticonvulsant-mood stabilizer, and two benzodiazepines. Toxicological testing, however, identified only one of these medications. High levels of alprazolam were found in all samples of fluids and tissues tested. Although the actual dose of alprazolam ingested could not be determined, the levels found in the fluid and tissue samples were not consistent with an accidental overdose. Chlorpheniramine, dextromethorphan, and doxylamine are the typical ingredients of popular cough–cold combination products. The medications that were prescribed indicated that the woman was being treated for a major depressive disorder. Her lack of compliance in using medications to alleviate or modulate her depressive symptoms might have contributed to the intentional overdose.

References and Additional Reading

Belviso M, DeDonno A, Vitale L, Introna F: Positional asphyxia: Reflection on 2 cases. *Am J Forensic Med Pathol*, 24: 292–297, 2003.

Charlson F, Degenhardt L, McLaren J, Hall W, Lynskey M: A systemic review of research examining benzodiazepine-related mortality. *Pharmacoepidemol Drug Saf*, 18: 93–103, 2009.

Drummer OH, Ranson DL: Sudden death and benzodiazepines. *Am J Forensic Med Pathol*, 17: 336–342, 1996.

Goulle JP, Anger JP: Drug-facilitated robbery or sexual assault: Problems associated with amnesia. *Ther Drug Monit*, 26: 206–210, 2004.

Jann M, Kennedy WK, Lopez G: Benzodiazepines: A major component of unintentional prescription drug overdoses with opioid analgesics. *J Pharm Prac*, 27: 5–16, 2014.

Jenkins AJ, Levine B, Locke JL, Smialek JE: A fatality due to alprozalam intoxication. *J Anal Toxicol*, 21: 218–220, 1997.

Jones JD, Mogali S, Comer SD: Polydrug abuse: A review of opioid and benzodiazepine combination use. *Drug Alcohol Depend*, 125: 8–18, 2012.

Koski A, Ojanpera I, Vuori E: Alcohol and benzodiazepine in fatal poisoning. *Alcohol Clin Exp Res*, 26: 956–959, 2002.

Lann MA, Molina, DK: A fatal case of benzodiazepine withdrawal. *Am J Forensic Med Pathol*, 30: 177–179, 2009.

Lukasik-Glebocka M, Sommerfield K, Tezyk A, Zielinska-Psuja B, Panienski P, Zaba C: Flubromazolam—A new life-threatening designer benzodiazepine. *Clin Toxicol*, 54: 66–68, 2016.

Mejo SL: Anterograde amnesia linked to benzodiazepines. *Nurse Pract*, 17: 49–50, 1992.

Moosmann B, King LA, Auwarter V: Designer benzodiazepines: A new challenge. *World Psychiatry*, 14: 248–249, 2015.

Muriya F, Hashimoto Y: A case of fatal triazolam overdose. *Leg Med*, 5: 91–95, 2003.

Repplinger D, Nelson LS: Withdrawal: Another danger of diversion. *Emerg Med*, 48: 77–79, 2016.

Stimulants

20

20.1 Introduction

Stimulants increase both energy and alertness and engender a euphoric sense of well-being. Although various stimulants have many common traits, each has its own unique mechanism of action and spectrum of activity. They all influence neurotransmitters in the brain, and generally produce varying degrees of cardiovascular toxicity. Most are addicting, but the time course of the development of dependence as well as the resistance of addiction to treatment is very different for each stimulant. Dosages, routes of administration, and patterns of use are important determinants of toxicity, which can be life-threatening. Some prototypical stimulants are reviewed in the following sections (Table 20.1). New and emerging stimulants are reviewed in Chapter 21.

20.2 Exposure Situations and Circumstances

Stimulants can be ingested, injected, snorted, or smoked. Illegal substances are typically adulterated and misrepresented. The composition, quality, and potency of substances vary not only in different areas of the country but also within the same community. It is convenient to discuss stimulants, as well as other abused substances, as if they were used in isolation. However, multiple drug use is almost always a feature of abuse situations. Substances other than the most obvious can be significantly more responsible for the actions and the events under consideration by forensic investigators. The possibility of multiple substance involvement in toxic situations that include stimulants should be evaluated.

20.3 Symptoms of Poisoning

Symptoms of toxicity from stimulants can wax and wane in intensity, and can be expressed differently among abusers. Characteristic symptoms of stimulant overdose are provided in Table 20.2.

Table 20.1   Stimulants

Amphetamine
Methamphetamine
MDMA
Methylphenidate
Cocaine
Cathinone
Caffeine

Table 20.2   Stimulant Overdose Symptoms

Agitated delirium
Diaphoresis
Hallucinations
Hypertension
Hyperthermina
Mydriasis
Paranoia
Rhabdomyolysis
Seizures
Tachycardia

The term amphetamine is often used in a general sense to describe a group of drugs chemically related to amphetamine that produce pronounced stimulation of the CNS. However, various amphetamines have striking differences in their stimulant properties, toxic potential, and patterns of abuse. The prototype stimulants are reviewed as follows.

Amphetamine and dextroamphetamine can be considered identical in terms of their actions. Dextroamphetamine is an isomer of amphetamine twice as potent as the racemic mixture. Amphetamine is used clinically almost exclusively for treating attention deficit hyperactivity disorders (ADHD). In the past, amphetamine was often used to treat some facets of depression, narcolepsy, and for appetite control, but this is rarely done today. The toxic effects of amphetamines are largely dose-related. Large doses can produce delirium, paranoia, hallucinations, and seizures. Lethal overdoses produce hyperthermia, cardiac arrhythmias, and intracranial hemorrhage. Amphetamine psychosis with paranoia can occur with heavy abuse and sometimes even with long-term therapeutic doses. Symptoms of psychosis are similar to those seen with schizophrenia, but they are reversible with abstinence and psychiatric treatment modalities.

Methamphetamine is a more potent and longer acting stimulant than amphetamine with fewer cardiovascular effects. It is, however, significantly more toxic when used in high doses. It can be smoked, injected, snorted, or ingested. When smoked or injected, methamphetamine produces an immediate pleasurable rush followed by euphoria lasting from 8 to 24 h. Methamphetamine can be used to engage in extended socializing, sexual activity, work productivity, and long-distance driving. Intravenous use is sometimes almost continuous for extended binges lasting for days until drug supplies are exhausted. Continuing heavy use produces major physical and mental deterioration. Methamphetamine intoxication can produce bizarre, paranoid behavior with wild raging actions with hallucinations. Individuals can be highly agitated and present serious risks to themselves and others. In addition to the extreme behavioral changes, methamphetamine can produce life-threatening seizures, hyperthermia, and cardiac arrhythmias. Death usually results from multiple organ failure.

Methylenedioxy-methamphetamine (MDMA) is a popular stimulant because it can impart a general sense of well-being, increase emotional warmth and sensory perception, and enhance empathy toward others. There appears to be a general belief that, compared to other abused drugs, MDMA is a relatively safe drug for occasional use. In reality, MDMA can produce a variety of adverse effects that include hypertension, panic attacks, coma, and seizures. In some circumstances, MDMA can produce life-threatening hyperthermia and kidney failure. Sudden deaths can occur in MDMA users from cardiac arrhythmias. This possibility is greater for individuals with preexisting cardiovascular disorders. Users commonly ascribe toxic effects of MDMA to lack of purity or a bad batch of illegal MDMA, but most of the products distributed as MDMA (Ecstasy, Molly) are knowingly manufactured with substances other than MDMA and generally are significantly more toxic.

Methylphenidate tablets are most often prescribed for the treatment of ADHD. Tablets are commonly diverted from legal distribution channels and crushed for abuse by snorting or injecting. The potential for abuse and attendant toxic effects of methylphenidate is similar to amphetamine. Methylphenidate is often mentioned in popular web discussion groups as a nontoxic cognitive performance-enhancing agent. Snorting methylphenidate markedly increases the possibility of serious adverse effects that include agitation, paranoia, and seizures.

Cocaine can produce euphoria, energy, talkativeness, mental alertness, and a decreased need for food and sleep. These characteristics can overshadow the likelihood of extreme negative cardiovascular and behavioral effects. The intensity and duration of these effects depend on how much cocaine is administered and the route of administration. After smoking, effects may last up to 10 min, and perhaps up to 30 min after snorting. This short duration of action necessitates frequent dosing and often extends into binging. Cocaine can significantly elevate body temperature, heart rate, and blood pressure. These effects become more pronounced with increasing doses that can also trigger irritability, paranoia, violent aggressive behavior, and other manifestations of neurotoxicity. Cardiovascular effects can include arrhythmias and malignant hypertension. Cocaine-related deaths are often the result of cardiac arrest or seizures followed by respiratory arrest. Sudden deaths can occur after the first use of cocaine or unexpectedly at any point during future use.

Cathinone is a stimulant found in an evergreen shrub (*Catha edulis*) that grows in East Africa. The leaves, known as khat, are chewed for its stimulant effect in countries such as Yemen, Somalia, Ethiopia, and where individuals from these countries have relocated. Cathinone is present only in fresh leaves and therefore chewing them for stimulant effects must be done within a few days from harvesting. Despite this limitation, harvested plants are occasionally exported to distant countries including the United States. The effects of cathinone are similar to those seen with amphetamine. Many synthetic derivatives of cathinone have recently been introduced for illegal recreational use. Some examples are mephedrone, methylone, and pyrovalerone. The emerging cathinone-related stimulants are reviewed in Chapter 21.

Caffeine elevates catecholamine neurotransmitters and blocks adenosine receptors, which result in an increased respiratory rate, increased heart rate, and hypotension. It may also cause hyperglycemia and stimulate gastric acid secretion. In overdose situations, cardiac arrhythmias and seizures can be fatal. Oral doses of caffeine in the neighborhood of 5–10 g are considered lethal. Caffeine is a frequent addition or adulterant in illegal drugs. It is also generally the major component of many energy-type dietary supplements and counterfeit stimulant prescription drugs.

Energy Dietary Supplements can contain synthetic psychostimulants chemically related to amphetamine. These stimulant-containing supplements are usually marketed for weight loss, energy, or as sports-enhancing supplements. These stimulants may produce neuropsychiatric problems and contribute to cardiovascular diseases such as hypertension and strokes. Most stimulant components of supplements are banned by agencies that oversee performance-enhancing substances. The most common synthetic stimulants that have been identified in supplements are dimethylamylamine (DMAA), dimethylbutylamine (DMBA), and beta-methylphenethylamine (BMPEA).

20.4 Case Studies

Case: Terminal High

In 1999, a single-engine, two-seat private airplane (Cessna 1404) crashed in an isolated area near the Idaho–Oregon border. The plane was flying in heavy snow and fog with poor visibility. The plane departed from a landing strip on a ranch less than a mile from the crash site. The 44-year-old male pilot was alone. He did not survive the crash impact. His seatbelt and shoulder harness had not been buckled. No evidence of engine malfunction or instrument failures were identified by crash investigators. An autopsy did not reveal any medical issues that might have contributed to the man's death. Toxicological analysis of tissue samples and fluids identified amphetamine and methamphetamine. No other substances were found. The findings were consistent with a recent oral ingestion of methamphetamine. The National Transportation Safety Board ruled the cause of the accident as the result of meteorological conditions obscuring the pilot's visibility and incapacitation due to illegal substances.

Comments

Methamphetamine is metabolized to amphetamine and the finding of both drugs in toxicology testing is indicative of methamphetamine use.

Case: Eight Ball Hyperthermia

In 2000, a 19-year-old man was arrested and jailed following a traffic violation. About 2 h later, he was diaphoretic and shivering. He told his cellmate that he had ingested eight balls of methamphetamine. Emergency medical responders were requested and, following their assessment, he was transported to a hospital emergency department. On arrival, he was diaphoretic; body temperature was 108°F, respiration 45, pulse 180, and blood pressure 186/96. His pupils were dilated; he displayed diffuse rigidity and tremulousness. He did not respond to verbal or painful stimuli. Aggressive symptomatic therapy was initiated that included external cooling with ice packs, intravenous fluids, medications to control tachycardia, and intubation. Decontamination was attempted with gastric lavage and charcoal. Chest radiograph and a CAT scan of the head were normal. Clinical laboratory tests were essentially normal except for indications of metabolic acidosis. Drug screening was negative for ethanol and positive for cannabinoids and amphetamines. His temperature was reduced to 103°F. Over the next 2 days, his condition continued to deteriorate with indications of organ damage, bleeding problems, and acid–base disturbances. On day 4, dialysis was initiated. However, his neurologic status never improved; he had multiple cardiac arrests with a fatal cardiac arrest on hospital day 16.

Comments

It was estimated that the man swallowed approximately 8 g of methamphetamine shortly before his arrest to avoid detection of the drug by police. This was consistent with toxicology testing results. Death from methamphetamine commonly results from intracerebral hemorrhage, cardiac arrhythmias, or hyperthermia. The hyperthermia in this case persisted despite aggressive medical therapy.

Case: Massive Caffeine Overdose

In 2001, a 41-year-old woman arrived at a hospital emergency department 3 h after ingesting 250 caffeine tablets (200 mg each). Her blood pressure and pulse rate were elevated. Soon after arrival, her blood pressure dropped and ECG tracings indicated various cardiac abnormalities. This was closely followed by seizures. Over the next 5 h, cardiopulmonary resuscitation was performed intermittently and several drugs were administered to combat cardiac arrhythmias and maintain blood pressure. Following 5 h of hemodialysis, she was stabilized without drug support. However, she developed pneumonia, rhabdomyolysis, and multisystem organ failure necessitating continued intensive therapy. She did survive and was discharged 24 days after arrival and made a full recovery.

Comments

Intentional caffeine overdoses commonly occur with suicidal intentions. It was not clear whether the caffeine was specifically selected for the suicide or whether its availability was the basis for its use.

Case: Caffeine for Lunch

In 2014, an 18-year-old high school senior living in a small town in Ohio died soon after ingesting one or two teaspoons of caffeine powder. A popular student and a varsity athlete, he died a few days before graduation. He had purchased caffeine powder on the Internet and was using it as a preworkout supplement. The boy had gone home from school for lunch and ingested the caffeine powder. His body was discovered that afternoon by his brother. Death was ruled as an accidental caffeine overdose. It was postulated that the death resulted from cardiac arrhythmias and seizures. Toxicology testing at autopsy was consistent with this finding. No other drugs were detected.

Comments

The powder used by the athlete as a preworkout dietary supplement was essentially pure caffeine. It had been purchased on a website that sold a variety of vitamins and dietary supplements to consumers. For some reason on the fatal day, the boy ingested more than he usually did, or perhaps he used an excessive amount directly rather than his usual practice of mixing it with some type of beverage.

Case: Multiple Drug Suicide

In 2013, a 47-year-old woman was admitted to a hospital 2 h after ingesting several prescription medications in a suicidal effort. The medication included antidepressants, antipsychotics, sedatives, and methylphenidate. The estimated total amounts of the specific medications ingested were methylphenidate (3000 mg), duloxetine (360 mg), chlorprothixene (200 mg), quetiapine (400 mg), zopiclone (15 mg), and mirtazapine (60 mg). The medications were taken with 1 L of an alcoholic beverage (40% alcohol). All the medications had been prescribed for her except the methylphenidate, which had been prescribed for her teenage son. On arrival at the hospital, the patient was comatose and in cardiovascular shock. The treatment and resuscitation measures initiated included gastric lavage, administration of charcoal, intravenous administration of a lipid emulsion, charcoal hemoperfusion, and hemodialysis. Many drugs were administered to facilitate procedures and provide symptomatic treatment for metabolic and cardiovascular disturbances. The woman recovered after hospitalization for approximately 1 month but remained severely depressed with continuing suicidal thoughts. She was discharged for psychiatric follow-up and treatment.

Comments

It would appear that this woman, with courage provided by ethanol, embarked on an impulsive suicide attempt involving the ingestion of all available medications.

Case: Molly at the Electric Zoo

In 2012, a product called Molly was supplied to many attendees of the Electric Zoo Music Festival at Randall's Island in New York City. Many people who used the drug became seriously ill and at least three people died as a direct result of the product. One of the individuals who died was a 23-year-old university graduate. Toward the end of the music concert, he started to feel bad, then collapsed, and had a seizure. Emergency responders transported him to a hospital where he died shortly after arrival. His death was ruled to be due to the combined effects of MDMA, methylone, and hyperthermia. About 130,000 attended the 3-day music festival. After 2 days, the festival was canceled. One of the drug distributors was arrested and charged with drug trafficking and conspiracy.

Comments

During the same week as the Electric Zoo Festival in New York City, other deaths related to Molly occurred in Washington, DC and in Boston. All the seven known deaths involved products containing methylone, which is an illegal designer stimulant.

References and Additional Reading

Banerjee P, Ali Z, Levine B, Fowler DR: Fatal caffeine intoxication: A series of eight cases from 1999 to 2009. *J Forensic Sci*, 59: 865–868, 2014.

Bjarnadottir GD, Haraldsson HM, Rafnar BO, Sigurdsson E, Steingrimsson S, Johannsson M, Bragadottir H, Magnusson A: Prevalent intravenous abuse of methylphenidate among treatment-seeking patients with substance abuse disorders: A descriptive population-based study. *J Addict Med*, 9: 188–194, 2015.

Cantrell FL, Ogera P, Mallett P, McIntyre IM: Fatal oral methylphenidate intoxication with postmortem concentrations. *J Forensic Sci*, 59: 847–849, 2014.

Carvalho M, Carmo H, Costa VM, Capela JP, Pontes H, Remiao F, Carvalho F, Bastos L: Toxicity of amphetamines, an update. *Arch Toxicol*, 86: 1167–1231, 2012.

Chaturvedi AK, Cardona PS, Soper JW, Canfield DV: Distribution and optical purity of methamphetamine found in toxic concentrations in a civil aviation accident pilot fatality. *J Forensic Sci*, 49: 832–836, 2004.

Cohen PA, Zeijon R, Nardin R, Keizers PH, Venhuis B: Hemorrhagic stroke probably caused by exercise combined with a sports supplement containing β-methylphenylethylamine (BMPEA): A case report. *Ann Intern Med*, 162: 879–880, 2015.

Eichner S, Maguire M, Shea LA, Fete MG: Banned and discouraged-use ingredients found in weight loss supplements. *J Am Pharm Assoc*, 56: 538–543, 2016.

Gill JR, Hayes JA, deSouza IS, Marker E, Stajic M: Ecstasy (MDMA) deaths in New York City: A case series and review of the literature. *J Forensic Sci*, 47: 121–126, 2002.

Green SL, Kerr F, Braitberg G: Review article: Amphetamines and related drugs of abuse. *Emerg Med Australas*, 20: 391–402, 2008.

Jabbar SB, Hanly MG: Fatal caffeine overdose: A case report and review of the literature. *Am J Forensic Med Pathol*, 34: 321–324, 2013.

Jansen T, Hoegberg LCG, Gregersen JW, Filipouski I, Johansen SS: Severe methphenidate intoxication: Charcoal hemoperfusion as an aid in treating the patient. *J Clinic Toxicol*, 3: 153–154, 2013.

Kalant H: The pharmacology and toxicology of "ecstasy" (MDMA) and related drugs. *Can Med Assoc J*, 165: 917–928, 2001.

Lang RA, Hillis LD: Cardiovascular complications of cocaine use. *N Engl J Med*, 345: 351–358, 2001.

Logan BK: Amphetamines: An update on forensic issues. *J Anal Toxicol*, 25: 400–404, 2001.

Logan BK: Methamphetamine: Effects on human performance and behavior. *Forensic Sci Rev*, 14: 133–151, 2002.

Lucena J, Blanco M, Jurado C, Rico A, Salguero M, Vazquez R, Thiene G, Basso C: Cocaine-related sudden death: A prospective investigation in south-west Spain. *Eur Heart J*, 31: 318–329, 2010.

O'Connor AD, Padilla-Jones A, Gerkin RD, Levine M: Prevalence of rhabdomyolysis in sympathomimetic toxicity: A comparison of stimulants. *J Med Toxicol*, 11: 195–200, 2015.

Pilgrim JL, Gerostamoulos D, Drummer OH: Involvement of amphetamines in sudden and unexpected death. *J Forensic Sci*, 54: 478–485, 2009.

Quigley K, Shanks K, Behonick G, Terrell A: A guide for the interpretation of post-mortem methamphetamine findings: A series of case reports. *J Forensic Toxicol Pharmacol*, 3: 1–5, 2014.

Schwartz BG, Rezkalla S, Kloner RA: Cardiovascular effects of cocaine. *Circulation*, 122: 2558–2569, 2010.

Stewart MJ, Fulton HG, Barrett SP: Powder and crack cocaine use among opioid users: Is all cocaine the same? *J Addict Med*, 8: 264–270, 2014.

Wallace ME, Squires R: Fatal massive amphetamine ingestion associated with hyperpyrexia. *J Am Board Fam Med*, 13: 13–15, 2000.

Yamamoto T, Yoshizawa K, Kubo S, Emoto Y, Hara K, Waters B, Umehara T, Murase T, Ikematsu K: Autopsy report for a caffeine intoxication case and review of the current literature. *J Toxicol Pathol*, 28: 33–36, 2015.

Emerging Recreational Psychotropics 21

21.1 Introduction

During the past few years, hundreds of new illegal psychoactive chemicals have become available for recreational use. These chemicals can produce profound changes in behavior, mood, and consciousness, and have significant toxic potential. Users can obtain these chemicals in mass-produced packaging, in capsules, or in the plastic bags and small bundles typically utilized by drug dealers. Regardless of their physical appearance, these products are rarely pure and almost never what they are purported to be. Moreover, the composition changes frequently. Even within the same batch of products, purchased at the same time or within short time intervals, there can be significant differences in substances, quantities, and purity.

There is an understandable tendency to group the emerging psychoactive substances by their chemical similarity to other more well-known substances. For example, a substance may be a derivative or an analog of amphetamine. This might imply to users that the new substance is merely a stronger or more potent form of amphetamine. This is not generally the case. Small modifications in the chemical structure of a compound can produce significant changes in the spectrum of effects that the newer compound might produce. The newer compound might be more potent, but it might also have effects that are qualitatively much different from the parent compound. When chemical structures of psychoactive chemicals are presented side-by-side in a pictorial format, some may appear very similar to one another but the similarity usually ends there. Their effects can vary significantly.

Some synthetic psychotropic drugs are commonly combined with mixtures of plant materials and packaged with labeling implying that the material is a form of mild incense or a relatively safe natural herbal tranquilizer. In reality, these products can contain a variety of dangerous chemicals with the potential for causing disturbing and intolerable mental changes and life-threatening alterations in major organs. As these products are widely used by many individuals without any serious consequence, there is a sense among users that, for the most part, they are relatively safe and considerably safer than older substances such as heroin or cocaine. Many users discount repeated deaths with newer substances as due to something other than what they personally use, or believe the more familiar self-directed refrain of *not to worry,*

Table 21.1   Some Features of Emerging Psychotropic Drugs

- Usual effects are minor or moderate, but can be lethal
- Composition and potency of products change frequently
- Unpredictable responses
- Effects can last hours or days
- Not detected on routine drug abuse screens
- Can produce profound mental alterations
- Can cause multisystem organ failure
- Craving can be intense
- Multiple drug exposures are common
- Exposures tend to occur in groups
- Hyperthermia, seizures, serotonin syndrome, and hyponatremia are among the most serious effects

I do this all the time. Deaths resulting from emerging psychotropics often occur in situations that attract considerable media attention and community outrage. Less well known and appreciated are the hundreds of near-death drug cases that crowd hospital emergency departments throughout the country. Some features of emerging psychotropic drugs are listed in Table 21.1.

21.2 Exposure Situations and Circumstances

Emerging recreational drugs in flashy attractive packages were initially sold openly in head shops and convenience stores such as gas stations. With the continuing enactment of federal and local laws to prohibit the sale of these drugs, their availability has been somewhat reduced. Some retail sales outlets continue to discreetly sell banned drugs and newer substances not yet controlled by regulations, but most drug products, which have been formally designated as illegal, are now sold to users clandestinely.

Most emerging psychotropics are available on the Internet. There are numerous websites where drugs can be purchased in amounts that might be required for distributors or in smaller amounts for personal use. Specific drugs can be purchased in bulk powder form, or prepackaged in units for resale. The ease of buying the drugs with a credit card, and the delivery times, are sometimes equal to or better than what might be expected when purchasing clothing or household items from an established online retail store.

Some laboratories that supply illegal drugs are commercial chemical companies that produce bulk chemicals for a variety of industrial uses, whereas others only produce illegal drugs. The location of the production laboratories might be in any country and the distribution of substances can involve many intermediaries before a particular dose reaches the end user.

On account of the increasingly complex distribution paths of substances and products, the composition and potency of substances available to abusers is extremely variable and inconsistent.

Newer synthetic drugs can be cheaper and more easily available than older drugs such as cocaine, MDMA, heroin, and LSD. Newer drugs are commonly substituted for the older, more familiar drugs and sold by dealers as whatever drug is in demand, or may be used to cut more expensive drugs that are supplied.

More than 600 different illegally produced psychoactive drugs have been identified in the past few years. The number of emerging synthetic drugs is challenging the resources of analytical laboratories, regulatory agencies, medical professionals, and law enforcement units. Even the most dedicated individuals involved in dealing with this growing issue struggle with the increasing availability of information on the emerging psychotropic drugs. It is becoming increasingly difficult to discern which information is actually new and not a duplicate review or refinement of the existing knowledge. References to these substances in clinical literature conveniently group them broadly into two classes: (1) cathinones and (2) cannabinoids.

> *Cathinones*: Cathinone is the active stimulant component of the khat plant (*Catha edulis*) and is very similar in activity and potency to amphetamine. Some emerging psychotropic drugs are derivatives of cathinone. These include mephedrone, methylone, α-PVP, and MDPV. These substituted cathinones now represent only a small class of the emerging synthetic psychotropic drugs that produce various degrees of stimulating and hallucinogenic effects. There are currently more than 200 of these drugs grouped into more than 15 chemical classes. A collective slang term for these substances is *bath salts*.
>
> *Cannabinoids*: The psychoactive components of natural marijuana are chemically related and referred to as cannabinoids. Many cannabinoids have been isolated from marijuana, but the one most responsible for the psychoactive effects is tetrahydrocannabinol or THC. Synthetic cannabinoids are derivatives of the naturally occurring compounds but differ significantly in potency, effects, and toxicity. Synthetic cannabinoids are not laboratory copies of natural cannabinoids. They are new compounds that never existed in marijuana plants. More than 200 synthetic cannabinoids have been identified. Synthetic marijuana is produced by adding synthetic cannabinoids to various blends of plant material. The resulting product is then sold as an herbal marijuana substitute to be used in the same manner as marijuana to allegedly achieve similar effects. A collective slang term for these substances is *spice*.

There are also synthetic designer opioids beginning to emerge on the illegal drug market as well as illegally produced prescription opioids such as fentanyl and carfentanil. A more recent emerging drug problem is the appearance of counterfeit versions of well-known prescription drugs such as OxyContin, Xanax, Norco, and Percocet. To date, these counterfeit products have been found most often to contain fentanyl.

21.3 Symptoms of Toxicity

The effects produced by recreational psychoactive chemicals can be extreme, intense, and relatively nonspecific (Table 21.2). Although the circumstances of a situation can point to the possible involvement of a particular substance or a particular class of substances, one does not usually know with reasonable scientific certainty what the causative substance is until an analytical laboratory identifies the substance. Clearly, trends occur in particular regions that can be useful for predicting what agents are most likely involved in any given situation, but chemical analysis of biological samples and, if possible, analysis of physical samples is necessary prior to assigning causation to a specific agent or class.

Table 21.2   Potential Toxic Effects of Emerging Stimulant-Hallucinogenic Drugs and Cannabinoids

Aggression
Agitation
Chest pain
Delusions
Excited delirium
Hallucinations
Hypertension
Hyperthermia
Kidney failure
Liver failure
Myocardial infarction
Panic attacks
Paranoia
Psychosis
Rhabdomyolysis
Seizures
Self-mutilation
Serotonin syndrome
Stroke
Suicidal behavior
Tachycardia
Violent behavior

21.4 Case Studies

Case: Colorado Black Mamba Outbreak

In 2013, patients began showing up at emergency departments in Denver, Colorado with severe symptoms after smoking a synthetic marijuana product. In a period of slightly less than a month, about 200 cases of exposure were identified statewide. The majority of patients were young men with altered mental status, variable abnormal heart rates, and had experienced seizures. Symptoms included disorientation, delirium, confusion, anxiety, lethargy, agitation, paranoia, and hallucinations. Around 10 different branded products (e.g., Black Mamba) were found to be involved, but they all contained a synthetic cannabinoid known technically as AB-PINACA. Most patients were treated symptomatically in emergency departments and discharged within 24 h, but some required admission to intensive care units and there were three deaths.

Comments

AB-PINACA is a potent synthetic cannabinoid that can produce serious behavioral changes and other effects that are potentially life-threatening.

Case: Two Users, One Survivor

In 2009, two men in their early twenties started using multiple drugs one evening and continued well into the night. They lived close to one another and this was something they had done many times before. The following morning, one of the men was found unresponsive. Emergency responders began resuscitation efforts and transported the man to a nearby hospital where resuscitation was unsuccessful. An autopsy was carried out and samples were collected for toxicological testing. Except for multiple needle marks on the body, there were no pathological indications of drug use identified. Syringes and other paraphernalia were collected from the residence where the man was found. The man, who had used the drugs with the deceased in much the same way and in the same amounts, was not seriously affected. He described how they both had used a bath salt-type substance by snorting, injecting, and swallowing. In addition, in the early morning hours they injected heroin. He also provided a urine sample for analysis. Based on the circumstances and the results from autopsy samples and the urine sample from the survivor, the medical examiner concluded that the cause of death was multiple drug toxicity and the manner of death was accidental. The drugs involved were mephedrone and heroin.

Comments

Mephedrone is a synthetic stimulant that is sold illegally in various forms under a variety of names. It can be purchased on the Internet, and has been promoted as a legal high. Its effects are often described as comparable to those produced by cocaine. Its appearance in the United States began sometime in 2009. This case illustrates the complexity of multiple drug use relative to lethality. In this case, two individuals used similar drugs and one died. Why one survived and one died is not known. Moreover, why the outcome did not occur in the reversed order is a mystery.

Case: Smokin Slurry Scrubba

In 2012, 44-year-old Glenn and his long-time girlfriend, Rachael, 44, started using a bath salt-type drug that they purchased in an adult novelty shop in their community. Both had been using stimulant-type substances for a number of years. Glenn was a long-distance truck driver and Rachael generally traveled with him staying in motels or in the sleeping compartment of the truck. On their first visit to the store that sold the drug products, they were shown a bewildering assortment of commercially packaged substances with creative brand names. Ultimately, the salesperson recommended a product, based on his personal experience, and suggested ways that it might be used. The name of the product was Smokin Slurry Scrubba. The couple later injected portions of the product. The effects of the substance were so disturbing that they disposed of the remaining portion of the supply they had purchased. Despite this deeply concerning initial experience, they returned to the store on several occasions and purchased more of the same product. They both experienced hallucinations of menacing individuals and situations, and exhibited bizarre behavior. Their body temperatures rose to levels that were so alarming that, shortly after an injection, they removed all their clothing in hopes of cooling themselves. All of these effects, as well as changes in heart rate, blood pressure, and less perceptible alterations lasted for hours. After their last purchase of Smokin Slurry Scrubba, they drove to a stretch of highway outside the town and injected the newly purchased substance. A short time later, Rachael stumbled out of the truck. She was naked from the waist up. She was screaming and began running in a very erratic fashion. She covered a considerable distance before being discovered by motorists and subsequently taken by ambulance to a nearby hospital. Glenn emerged from the truck completely naked moments after Rachael. He ran in the opposite direction until he encountered an industrial facility. He scaled an 8-foot security fence topped with barbed wire, and then purposely went through the compound until he discovered an administration building where he was breaking through a glass door when a security guard caught up with him. Another employee soon arrived and an intense struggle took place that included falling down a flight of stairs. After the two men succeeded in pinning Glenn to the ground, he began to become considerably less aggressive and by the time police and paramedics arrived, he had stopped breathing. Resuscitation began immediately and was continued while he was transported to a hospital's intensive care unit. He never regained consciousness. Life-support measures were discontinued on his second hospital day and he died.

Comments

This case occurred in Australia; however, similar cases occurred in the United States and elsewhere. The specific ingredient in the bath salt product involved in this case was alpha-PVP. The individuals had what they described as a very bad and disturbing experience and yet continued to purchase and use the same substance. They had other options and could have used more familiar drugs. The unbearable heat that the couple described, which caused them to remove their clothes, is common for this class of drugs. Hyperthermia is real, it is uncomfortable, and it is deadly.

Case: Young Entrepreneur

In 2012, the 20-year-old son of a state legislator was sentenced to 16 years in prison for leading a drug ring that imported methylone from China and sold it throughout the United States, mostly at parties attended by young adults. He and six other members of the group, ranging in age from 18 to 23 years old, pled guilty to charges that included money laundering, possession of a controlled substance, and distribution of illegal drugs. The activities of the group had attracted the attention of the authorities on several occasions, but investigative efforts intensified when one member of the group died as a result of a methylone overdose. The circumstances of the death led authorities to the activities of the drug ring. The day prior to the death, the group had received a shipment of bulk methylone powder and repackaged it in capsules for sale to users. Potential buyers had been invited to a weekend party at the apartment of the deceased. During the party the individual took what others felt was an excessive number of capsules, became visibly ill, and eventually retired to his bedroom where he was found dead the following day.

Comments

The business model illustrated by this case is very common. It is now very easy for an individual or small group of individuals to obtain substances at competitive prices using the Internet and operate small profitable distribution units. The benefit is that they are not associated with organized crime and the harsh practices involved with illegal drug distribution.

Case: Buyer Beware

In 2012, a 24-year-old female ingested two capsules of ecstasy at a concert. A short time later, she lost consciousness and paramedics at the concert transported her to a hospital emergency department. A history evolved that indicated that the woman was otherwise healthy and that she had minimal exposure to marijuana and cocaine in the past; she was not a chronic drug user. On arrival, she was comatose, her body temperature was rising, heart rate and blood pressure were elevated, she had slowed respirations, and there was some jerking of the extremities. Some symptomatic improvement was seen with treatment but this was not sustained, and multisystem organ failure led to her death on the second day of hospitalization. Autopsy revealed evidence of generalized bleeding, liver abnormalities, and brain damage. Toxicology testing was negative for recreational drugs except for methylone and butylone. The remaining capsules from her supply were also analyzed and found to contain a mixture of methylone and butylone in substantial amounts.

Comments

The capsules purchased at the concert by the individual in this case were purported to be ecstasy. In the past, ecstasy was the common street name for MDMA.

Case: Delusional Man Inadequately Dressed

In 2012, police found a 34-year-old man wandering around outside his home in Baltimore. He was delusional, talking to himself, and not dressed adequately for the winter weather. He was taken to a local hospital emergency department for evaluation and treatment. His history included depression, back pain, and chronic drug and alcohol abuse. At the time of this incident, he was using bath salts orally and possibly other substances. Soon after his arrival at the emergency unit, he became agitated and developed troubling cardiovascular problems that necessitated admission to an intensive care unit where he was sedated and intubated.

Despite efforts to normalize his cardiac function and rising body temperature, he died approximately 12 h after arrival at the hospital. An autopsy did not disclose any diagnostic abnormalities. Toxicological screening identified MDPV as the cause of this accidental death.

Comments

The rapid progression of an ambulatory delusional individual to death despite the relatively early and aggressive medical treatment is striking. Death was due to cardiac arrhythmias and elevated body temperature.

Case: Dragonflies and N-Bombs

In 2014, a 24-year-old man attending an arts festival and concert series in New York ingested an illegal drug known as dragonfly and became significantly disoriented and agitated. He was then transported to a nearby hospital emergency department by emergency medical responders. On arrival, he had elevated blood pressure, heart rate, and body temperature. His respiratory rate was high and his agitated behavior was progressing to the point of becoming potentially violent. The emergency medical staff suspected that the substance ingested was a synthetic psychedelic from the substituted phenethylamine chemical class in the NBOMe series. The individual was administered escalating doses of a benzodiazepine until his behavior was somewhat neutralized, then he had a generalized seizure, which was terminated with additional benzodiazepine administration. His body temperature remained elevated despite cooling measures. At this point, the man was intubated, started on an infusion of propofol, and admitted to an intensive care unit where he remained until his temperature was normalized and he could be weaned from a ventilator. Three days after his arrival at the hospital, he was discharged in stable condition.

Comments

This case illustrates the potentially life-threatening consequences that can result from illegal psychotropic drug use. The individual in this case was undoubtedly expecting an enhanced experience at a public art–music festival but instead received an enhanced medical experience that included an induced coma in an intensive care unit. Emergency medical care in situations of this nature requires immediate intervention to support life functions and neutralize or reverse escalating toxic drug effects. The specific drug was not confirmed by laboratory analysis, as is commonly the case in such situations.

Case: Synthetic Cannabinoid and Self-Mutilation

In 2011, a 23-year-old man was found dead in his room by a sibling. His body had indications of blunt force injuries and a number of stab wounds. The room was in uncharacteristic disarray and there was damage to the walls and glass windows. Drugs and paraphernalia in the room included a typical marijuana smoking pipe, a foil package of plant material labeled Mad Hatter Incense, and a commercially made package of scored rectangular tablets labeled ZAN-X Extra Relaxation. An investigation revealed that the decedent had no history of mental illness or seizure disorders, he was not using any therapeutic medications, and his family was unaware of any use of illicit drugs. Several hours prior to the discovery of his body, he had lunch with a family member and did not seem in any way abnormal. However, the individual who discovered the body heard stomping noises coming from the decedent's room lasting for about 30 min. Postmortem evaluation of the body indicated that the injuries resulted from the decedent's punching walls and other objects, or were otherwise self-inflicted. A complex stab wound in the neck was believed to have been the fatal injury. Extensive toxicological testing of postmortem specimens and the drug materials collected at the death site were conducted. High concentrations of a synthetic cannabinoid (AM 2201) were found in the biologic samples and in the smoking material and the drug paraphernalia. The investigative conclusion was that the psychiatric abnormalities induced by the synthetic cannabinoid resulted in the decedent's self-mutilation that included blunt force trauma and sharp object stabbing.

Comments

This case provides an example of an acute psychotic episode produced by a synthetic cannabinoid.

Case: Dilemma—Rohypnol or Something Else?

In 2008, about 40 individuals with similar symptoms were seen over a period of a few months in emergency facilities in Oslo, Norway. Most were confused, agitated, and hallucinating. They had dilated pupils with vital signs generally in normal ranges. However, seven of the individuals were comatose on arrival. They were all regular users of illicit drugs and all had developed their symptoms following the use of illegally purchased Rohypnol (flunitrazepam) tablets. In some cases, other substances had been used concurrently. The individuals were most frequently diagnosed as having unspecified drug-induced psychosis. They were treated symptomatically with a variety of therapeutic agents that included naloxone, flumazenil, haloperidol, and diazepam. Some individuals were admitted

Table 21.3 Anticholinergic Toxidrome (Scopolamine Toxicity)

Delirium

Dry mucous membranes

Flushing

Hallucinations

Hyperthermia

Mydriasis

Picking imaginary objects from the air

Seizures

Tachycardia

Urinary retention

to hospitals, but the majority recovered and were discharged or left the facility against medical advice. Tablets provided by patients and serum samples from some initial patients were sent to an analytical laboratory for testing, but the results were not available until the majority of individuals had been treated and discharged. The tablets, which were physically indistinguishable from commercial Rohypnol tablets, were found to contain scopolamine (0.6 mg/tablet) with no other active ingredients. Scopolamine was also identified in the serum samples tested.

Comments

Scopolamine poisonings are rare, but the anticholinergic toxidrome it produces is well known (Table 21.3). Until the results of the toxicology testing became available, no diagnosis of anticholinergic poisoning was made. Even though the symptoms of most cases were highly suggestive of anticholinergic poisoning, the physicians involved had never seen the syndrome before. As the patients were known substance abusers, it was assumed that the agent involved was a common substance, most likely an amphetamine derivative. Scopolamine has been identified in the past as a contaminant of other illegal drugs, such as heroin. With multiple drug exposures, the clinical diagnosis of possible anticholinergic poisoning can be especially difficult.

References and Additional Reading

Anwar M, Law R, Schier J: Kratom (*Mitragyna speciosa*) exposures reported to poison centers—United States, 2010–2015. *CDC MMWR*, 65: 748–749, 2016.

Baumann MH, Solis E, Witterson LR, Marusich JA, Fantegrossi WE, Wiley JL: Bath salts, spice, and related designer drugs: The science behind the headlines. *J Neurosci*, 34: 15150–15158, 2014.

Boulanger-Gobeil C, St-Onge M, Laliberte M, Auger PL: Seizures and hyponatre-
    mia related to ethcathinone and methylone poisoning. *J Med Toxicol*, 8: 54–61,
    2012.
Brandt SD, King LA, Evans-Brown M: The new drug phenomenon. *Drug Test
    Analysis*, 6: 587–597, 2014.
Bretteville-Jensen AL, Tuv SS, Bilgrei OR, Fjeld B, Bachs L: Synthetic cannabinoids
    and cathinones: Prevalence and markets. *Forensic Sci Rev*, 25: 7–26, 2013.
Castellanos D, Gralink LM: Synthetic cannabinoids 2015: An update for pediatri-
    cians in clinical practice. *World J Clin Pediatr*, 5: 16–24, 2016.
Cohen J, Morrison S, Greenberg J, Saidinejad M: Clinical presentation of intoxica-
    tion due to synthetic cannabinoids. *Pediatrics*, 129: 1064–1067, 2012.
Dargan PI, Wood DM: *Novel Psychoactive Substances: Classification, Pharmacology,
    and Toxicology*. Waltham, MA: Academic Press, 2013.
Dickson AJ, Vorce SP, Levine B, Past MR: Multiple-drug toxicity caused by the
    coadministration of 4-methylmethcathinone (mephedrone) and heroin.
    J Anal Toxicol, 34: 162–168, 2010.
Fratantonio J, Andrade L, Febo M: Designer drugs: A synthetic catastrophe.
    J Reward Defic Syndr, 1: 82–86, 2015.
Gunderson EW, Kirkpatrick MG, Willing LM, Holstege CP: Intranasal substituted
    cathinone "bath salts" psychosis potentially exacerbated by diphenhydramine.
    J Addict Med, 7: 163–168, 2013.
Gurney SMR, Scott KS, Kacinko SL, Presley BC, Logan BK: Pharmacology,
    toxicology, and adverse effects of synthetic cannabinoid drugs. *Forensic Sci
    Rev*, 26: 53–75, 2014.
Harris CR, Brown A: Synthetic cannabinoid intoxicating: A case series and review.
    J Emerg Med, 44: 360–366, 2013.
Hill SL, Thomas SH: Clinical toxicology of newer recreational drugs. *Clin Toxicol*,
    49: 705–719, 2011.
Jerry J, Collins G, Streem D: Synthetic legal intoxicating drugs: The emerging
    "incense" and "bath salt" phenomenon. *Cleveland Clinic J Med*, 79: 258–264,
    2012.
Kasper AM, Ridpath AD, Arnold JK, Chatham-Stephens K, Morrison M, Olaniyi
    O, Parker C, Galli R, Cox R, Preacely N et al.: Severe illness associated with
    reported use of synthetic cannabinoids: Mississippi, April 2015. *CDC MMWR*,
    64: 1121–1122, 2015.
Kesha K, Boggs CL, Ripple MG, Allan CH, Levine B, Jufer-Phipps R, Doyon S, Chi P,
    Fowler DR: Methylenedioxypyrovalerone ("Bath Salts"), related deaths: Case
    report and review of the literature. *J Forensic Sci*, 58: 1654–1659, 2013.
Khey DN, Stogner J, Miller BL: *Emerging Trends in Drug Use and Distribution*. New
    York: Springer, 2014.
Liechti ME: Novel psychoactive substances (designer drugs): Overview and phar-
    macology of medulators of monamine signaling. *Swiss Med Wkly*, 145: w14043,
    2015.
McNeely J, Parikh S, Valentine C, Haddad N, Shidham G, Rovin B, Herbert L,
    Agarwal A: Bath salts: A newly recognized cause of acute kidney injury. *Case
    Rep Nephrol*, 560854:1–5, 2012.
Meijer KA, Russo RR, Adhvaryu DV: Smoking synthetic marijuana leads to self-
    mutilation requiring bilateral amputations. *Orthopedics*, 37: 391–394, 2014.

Meyer MR: New psychoactive substances: An overview on recent publications on their toxicodynamics and toxicokinetics. *Arch Toxicol*, 90: 2421–2444, 2016.

Miotto K, Striebel J, Cho AK, Wang C: Clinical and pharmacological aspects of bath salt use: A review of the literature and case reports. *Drug Alcohol Depend*, 132: 1–12, 2013.

Monte AA, Bronstein AC, Heard KJ, Iwanicki JL: An outbreak of exposure to a novel synthetic cannabinoid. *N Engl J Med*, 370: 389–390, 2014.

Moran J, Seely K: Bath salts: Understanding a pervasive designer drug. *Clin Lab News,* 40:8, 2014.

Murray BL, Murphy CM, Beuhler MC: Death following recreational use of designer drug "bath salts" containing 3,4-methylenedioxypyrovalerone. (MDPV) *J Med Toxicol*, 8:69–75, 2012.

Nelson ME, Bryant SM, Aks SE: Emerging drugs of abuse. *Emerg Med Clin North Am*, 32: 1–28, 2014.

Patton AL, Chimalakonda KC, Moran CL, McCain KR, Radominska-Pandya A, James LP, Kokes C, Moran JH: K2 toxicity: Fatal case of psychiatric complications following AM2201 exposure. *J Forensic Sci*, 58: 1676–1680, 2013.

Penders TM: How to recognize a patient who's high on "bath salts." *J Family Prac*, 61: 210–212, 2012.

Prosser JM, Nelson LS: The toxicology of bath salts: A review of synthetic cathinones. *J Med Toxicol*, 8: 33–42, 2012.

Schneir AB, Baumbacher T: Convulsions associated with the use of synthetic cannabinoid product. *J Med Toxicol*, 8: 62–64, 2012.

Schwartz MD, Trecki J, Edison LA, Steck AR, Arnold JK, Gerona RR: A common source outbreak of severe delirium associated with exposure to the novel synthetic cannabinoid ADB-PINACA. *J Emerg Med*, 48: 573–580, 2015.

Sellors K, Jones A, Chan B: Death due to intravenous use of α-pyrrolidino-pentiophenone. *Med J Aust*, 201: 601–603, 2014.

Spiller HA, Ryan ML, Weston RG, Jansen J: Clinical experience with an analytical confirmation of "bath salts" and "legal highs" (synthetic cathinones) in the United States. *Clin Toxicol*, 49:499–505, 2011.

Tait RJ, Caldicott D, Mountain D, Hill SL, Lenton S: A systematic review of adverse events arising from the use of synthetic cannabinoids and their associated treatment. *Clin Toxicol*, 54: 1–13, 2016.

Vallersnes OM, Lund C, Duns AK, Netland H, Rasmussen I-A: Epidemic of poisoning caused by scopolamine disguised as Rohypnol tablets. *Clin Toxicol*, 47: 889–893, 2009.

Waldrop MR, Nacca NE, Nelson LS: Case studies in toxicology: You can't see dragonfly or hear NBOMe, but they can still hurt you. *Emerg Med*, 47: 13–16, 2015.

Warrick BJ, Wilson J, Hodge M, Freemon S, Leonard K, Aaron C: Lethal serotonin syndrome after methylone and butylone ingestion. *J Med Toxicol*, 8: 65–68, 2012.

Weaver MF, Hopper JA, Gunderson EW: Designer drugs 2015: Assessment and management. *Addict Sci Clin Practice*, 10: 1–8, 2015.

Wilson B, Tavakoli H, DeCecchis D, Mahadev V: Synthetic cannabinoids, synthetic cathinones, and other emerging drugs of abuse. *Psych Ann*, 43: 558–564, 2013.

Food Poisoning

22

22.1 Introduction

Food poisoning is caused by either naturally occurring toxic components of food, chemical contamination, or microbial agents. Most often symptoms are confined to the gastrointestinal tract, but in some cases the initial symptoms may involve other organ systems. When several individuals simultaneously develop an illness, consideration is almost always given to the possibility of a common exposure to a toxicant and, depending on the circumstances, the primary culprit considered will be food. When an isolated individual develops an illness from a foodborne toxicant it presents much more of a diagnostic challenge.

Some common food poisoning exposure situations and causative agents are reviewed in this chapter. The material presented is relevant to contemporary forensic investigations of poisoning cases, but it is only a small sampling of the poisoning possibilities associated with food consumption.

22.2 Exposure Situations and Circumstances

Foods may be accidentally contaminated with toxic substances during any phase of production: growing, harvesting, processing, storing, shipping, and preparation for consumption. In addition, there exists a real possibility that terrorists or others could intentionally contaminate food. Some terrorist organizations are known to be considering contaminating water and food supplies with chemical and biological substances. Both ricin and cyanide are frequently mentioned as possible food contaminators in terrorist documents. The idea of contaminating food is certainly not a new one. For example, in 1984, members of a cult group in Oregon actually contaminated salad bars with *Salmonella*, which sickened hundreds of people.

**Table 22.1   Epidemiological Indicators for Deliberate
Infectious Disease Outbreaks**

- Unusual event with large number of casualties without plausible explanation
- Higher morbidity or mortality than is expected for a particular disease
- Uncommon disease for a particular area
- Point-source outbreak (quick onset—plateau—quick drop in new cases)
- Multiple epidemics at different locations
- Dead animals
- Spread from humans to animals
- Unusual manifestations of a familiar disease
- Cases clustered in a downwind plume pattern
- Cases distributed along travel patterns

Table 22.1 provides a list of epidemiological indicators that could be considered during the investigation of infectious disease outbreaks deliberately caused by biological agents dispersed directly or added to food.

22.3 Symptoms of Poisoning

Bacterial infections resulting from food poisoning can sometimes be mild with relatively little discomfort. Young children, older adults, and people who have impaired immune systems are most likely to have severe infections. The infections can, in some cases, progress to fatal stages. Many serious complications, while not necessarily life-threatening, can also develop and cause permanent organ damage. Table 22.2 summarizes the typical or usual symptoms of some common bacterial food poisonings.

Seafood poisoning is responsible for about 25% of all foodborne diseases in the United States, and most of these diseases are due to raw oysters with deaths due to one bacterium, *Vibrio vulnificus* (Table 22.3).

Allergic reactions to food can occur with very small amounts of the food and develop within minutes. Symptoms can be cutaneous, gastrointestinal, respiratory, circulatory, or neurologic (Table 22.4). Anaphylaxis is a severe multiorgan system allergic reaction that can be fatal; there is rapid progression of symptoms that include airway blockage, shock, respiratory failure, and cardiac arrest. The majority of food-induced anaphylaxis deaths in the United States are caused by peanuts and tree nuts (walnuts, almonds, hazelnuts, cashews, and pecans).

Table 22.2   Food Poisoning from Microbial Contamination

Salmonella
Diarrhea, abdominal cramps, fever, vomiting, headache, body aches
Onset usually 12–72 h
Duration usually 3–7 days

Staphylococcus aureus
Nausea, vomiting, stomach cramps, diarrhea
Onset 30 min to 6 h
Duration usually 1–3 days

Escherichia coli
Abdominal cramps, watery diarrhea
Onset 1–10 days
Duration 5–10 days

Shigella
Diarrhea, fever, stomach cramps, and rectal spasms
Onset usually 1–3 days
Duration usually 5–7 days

Clostridium botulinum
Nausea, vomiting, fatigue, dizziness, double vision, dry mouth, muscle weakness, and paralysis
Onset usually 12–72 h
Duration 1–10 days with treatment. Full recovery often weeks or months. A 35%–65% chance
of death without immediate treatment

Listeria
Fever, diarrhea, systemic disease
Onset 1–3 days
Duration days to weeks

Norovirus
Nausea, vomiting, fatigue, cramping, diarrhea, fever, and headache
Onset 12–48 h
Duration 1–3 days

Table 22.3   Poisoning from Contaminated Seafood

Scombroid Poisoning
Improper refrigeration of certain fish can cause bacterial conversion of some tissue components
to histamine. When these fish are consumed they can produce flushing, dizziness, blurry
vision, and swelling of the tongue and mouth. This is not an allergic reaction; it is a histamine
overdose. Most commonly occurs with tuna, mackerel, and mahi-mahi.

Ciguatera Poisoning
Large predatory tropical reef fish may contain toxins that can produce gastrointestinal
symptoms, muscle weakness, dizziness, unusual sensory perception, and hallucinations.
Symptoms can persist for weeks but ciguatera poisoning is rarely fatal. Most common fish that
might contain the toxins are grouper, sea bass, snapper, and barracuda.

(Continued)

Table 22.3 (*Continued*) Poisoning from Contaminated Seafood

Shellfish Poisoning

Several toxins can be found in certain shellfish (mussels, clams, oysters, lobsters, and others)
  obtained in various locations involving different water depths and temperatures. These toxins
  can produce symptoms that are relatively mild and related to the gastrointestinal tract, or
  more serious life-threatening symptoms such as muscle paralysis and respiratory failure.

Table 22.4 Symptoms of an Allergic Reaction

Organ System	Symptoms
Skin	Pruritus, flushing, urticarial, and angioedema
Gastrointestinal	Oral pruritus, abdominal pain, cramping, vomiting, and diarrhea
Upper respiratory	Sneezing, nasal congestion, coughing, hoarseness, throat tightening, and difficulty swallowing
Lower respiratory	Wheezing, shortness of breath, cyanosis, and respiratory arrest
Cardiovascular	Tachycardia, hypotension, arrhythmia, bradycardia, and cardiac arrest
Neurologic	Anxiety, feeling of doom, dizziness, and loss of consciousness
Other	Metallic taste, uterine cramping, and urinary urgency

22.4 Investigative Considerations

Depending on the number of victims involved, food illness outbreak inves-
tigations can involve several local and state public health agencies, and
could include federal agencies such as the Centers for Disease Control
and Prevention, the Food and Drug Administration, the United States
Department of Agriculture's Food Safety and Inspection Service, and the
Environmental Protection Agency. Investigations may also extend to the
Federal Bureau of Investigation and the Department of Homeland Security.
Forensic investigators in a particular jurisdiction might function initially in
large outbreaks in a role akin to an investigative first responder. Later, this
role would likely switch to one of collecting investigative information from
other agencies and culling out specific aspects that apply to individual cases
requiring disposition at a local level.

22.5 Case Studies

Case: Green Onions and Hepatitis

In November 2003, a large foodborne outbreak of hepatitis A was associated with eating at a restaurant in Pennsylvania. There were about
600 individuals infected over a period of 3 months; 124 were hospitalized and 3 died. When meals consumed by sickened individuals were

compared, five menu items became suspect: (1) mild salsa, (2) bar beverages, (3) grilled chicken fajitas, (4) ground beef burritos, and (5) an enchilada platter. Mild salsa was most often consumed by the infected patrons. Both hot salsa and mild salsa were complimentarily provided to everyone. Both versions of the salsa were prepared with the same ingredients except that only mild salsa contained green onions. The green onions were determined to be the source of the hepatitis virus. These onions were traced to two farms in Northern Mexico where contamination apparently occurred either before or during packing into shipping boxes at the farms. When harvested, each onion's outer layer is stripped off and discarded by workers and then they are hand-bundled with rubber bands and packed on ice in shipping boxes. These boxes were imported into the United States, passed through two distributors without any repacking, and then delivered to the restaurant where the outbreak occurred. The viral contamination may have occurred through contact with infected workers during harvesting and processing or perhaps through contact with contaminated water used for irrigation, rinsing, and icing. The source of the contamination in this particular case was not identified.

Comments

Hepatitis A virus is transmitted by the fecal–oral route and is highly contagious. It causes an inflammatory liver disease with symptoms that include nausea, diarrhea, fever, fatigue, and jaundice, which may last for several weeks. A relatively small microbial exposure can easily spread through large amounts of onions because of the extensive handling and mixing during harvesting, packaging, and preparation for use. In restaurants, onions are mixed during washing, chopping, and bulk storage. Microbial contamination from produce such as onions can also be spread to other food items in kitchen preparation areas. This outbreak occurred in a restaurant that belonged to a restaurant chain that was in financial difficulty due to other factors prior to this incident. Following the substantial legal liability for settlements from this incident, the entire restaurant chain ceased all operations permanently.

Case: Peanut Butter and *Salmonella*

In 2008, *Salmonella* was diagnosed in more than 700 people in 46 states and in Canada. Hundreds were hospitalized, and more than nine died. The outbreak was traced to the contamination of peanut butter produced by a large company located in Georgia. The outbreak included the company's peanut butter and processed foods produced by other manufacturers that contained the company's peanut butter or paste. Food products included cookies, crackers, cereal, candy, ice cream, and pet foods. It was determined that the company shipped peanut butter and paste that it knew was contaminated with *Salmonella*. Investigators found unsanitary conditions in the company's plant, faked laboratory testing results, and records showing that products confirmed to be contaminated with *Salmonella* were shipped to customers. In 2014, the 61-year-old owner of the company, the company's quality control manager, and a food broker were tried and found guilty of several federal felony charges related to the introduction of adulterated food into interstate commerce with the intent to defraud or mislead. The owner was sentenced to 28 years in prison, the food broker 20 years, and the quality control manager 5 years.

Comments

Salmonella is one of the most common intestinal infections in the United States. The infection results from eating food contaminated with fecal material from animals or humans who carry the bacteria. Contaminated foods may include eggs, meat, poultry, fruits, or vegetables.

Case: Black Pepper Cabbage Salad

In 1998, 14 employees became ill shortly after eating homemade food at a company lunch in Louisiana. Their symptoms were mostly gastrointestinal (nausea, diarrhea, and cramps) and neurological (dizziness, muscle fasciculations, and blurred vision). Ten received treatment in a hospital emergency department and two required hospitalization. The meal consisted of pork roast, rice, cabbage salad, biscuits, and soft drinks. The cabbage salad was identified as the most likely cause of the illness. The employee who made the salad used precut packaged cabbage, which was mixed in a bowl with vinegar and ground black pepper. The black pepper had been obtained from one of the employee's relatives. The lunch event was the first time that the pepper had been used. The granular contents of the pepper container were analyzed and found to be a commercial pesticide containing aldicarb. The relative of the employee was a crawfish farmer who, unbeknownst to the employee, had added the aldicarb to an empty pepper container to sprinkle bait for killing wild dogs and raccoons that regularly destroyed fishing nets and other items necessary for crawfish farming. The employee acquired the pepper container and its contents, along with many other items, after the farmer had died.

Comments

Aldicarb is a restricted-use pesticide sometimes used in agriculture for soil treatment. This case is an example of unintentional poisoning resulting from transferring substances from original containers to other containers that might be more convenient or facilitate their use. Putting the granular pesticide product into an empty black pepper sprinkler container for application would probably not seem illogical to the farmer. It would probably not have occurred to him that the pepper could ever find its way to a food kitchen and be used to make cabbage salad for an employee lunch.

Case: Fish Allergy or Fish Poisoning

In 2002, three adults at a restaurant developed generalized urticaria, experienced palpitations, and were feverish shortly after eating tuna. They subsequently went to a hospital emergency department. On arrival, they were tachycardiac, tachypneic, and erythema was noted over their faces and trunk. Due to the simultaneous symptoms in three individuals, a diagnosis of histamine fish poisoning was made, and they were treated with an antihistamine and a nebulized bronchodilator. All symptoms resolved within 2 h.

Comments

As the symptoms of histamine fish poisoning mimic those of an allergic reaction, the poisoning can be misdiagnosed. This poisoning is caused by histamine in the specific fish meal consumed at the time. Poisoned individuals generally have no history of hypersensitivity and are therefore not likely to have a subsequent reaction to the offending type of fish.

References and Additional Reading

Attaran RR, Probst F: Histamine fish poisoning: A common but frequently misdiagnosed condition. *Emerg Med J*, 19: 474–475, 2002.

Balistreri WF: Unsafe at any lunch? *Medscape*, February 8, 2016.

Bock SA, Munoz-Furlong A, Sampson HA: Further fatalities caused by anaphylactic reactions to food, 2001–2006. *J Allergy Clin Immunol*, 119: 1016–1018, 2007.

Dembek ZF, Kortepeter MG, Pavlin JA: Discernment between deliberate and natural infectious disease outbreaks. *Epidemiol Infect*, 135: 353–371, 2007.

Edlow JA: *The Deadly Dinner Party & Other Medical Detective Stories*. New Haven, CT: Yale University Press, 2009.

Farley TA, McFarland L, McClelland J: Aldicarb as a cause of food poisoning: Louisiana, 1998. *CDC MMWR*, 48: 269–271, 1999.

Jantschitsch C, Kinaciyan T, Manafi M, Safer M, Tanew A: Severe scrombroid fish poisoning: An underrecognized dermatologic emergency. *J Am Acad Derm*, 65: 246–247, 2011.

Maki DG: Don't eat the spinach: Controlling foodborne infectious disease. *N Engl J Med*, 355: 1952–1955, 2006.

Oliver JD: *Vibrio vulnificus*: Death in the half shell. A personal journey with the pathogen and its ecology. *Microb Ecol*, 65: 793–799, 2013.

Painter JA, Hoekstri RM, Ayers J, Tauxe RV, Branden CR, Angulo FJ: Attribution of foodborne illness, hospitalization, and death to food commodities: United States 1998–2008. *Emerg Infect Dis*, 19: 407–415, 2013.

Perl TM, Bedard L, Kosatsky T, Hockin JC, Todd EC, Remis RS: An outbreak of toxic encephalopathy caused by eating mussels contaminated with domoic acid. *N Engl J Med*, 322: 1775–1780, 1990.

Scallan E, Hoekstra RM, Angulo FJ, Tauxe RV, Widdowson M-A, Roy SL, Jones JL, Griffin PM: Foodborne illness acquired in the United States: Major pathogens. *Emerg Infect Dis*, 17: 7–15, 2011.

Wheeler C, Vogt TM, Armstrong GL, Vaughn G, Weltman A, Nainan OV, Dato V, Xia G, Waller K, Amon J et al.: An outbreak of hepatitis A associated with green onions. *N Engl J Med*, 353: 890–897, 2005.

Plants and Mushrooms 23

23.1 Introduction

Most plants are relatively safe when ingested in small amounts. Due to their irritating qualities, they can cause gastrointestinal disturbances leading to nausea, vomiting, and diarrhea. In contrast, some plants contain components that are among the most toxic substances known to man. Small quantities of these plants can sometimes produce death in a few hours. Poisonous plants can be found in gardens and in the wild. An insidious feature of some plant toxins is that the onset of toxic symptoms, often nonreversible, can be delayed for hours or days. Possible exposure to toxic plants is more common than most individuals suspect. The natural growth patterns of certain toxic plants can be limited to particular areas, but plants with attractive foliage or desired medicinal qualities are often planted elsewhere in gardens or in containers in homes.

The identification of plants can be daunting and it is often difficult to distinguish between toxic and nontoxic varieties. There are many inconsistencies with plant names in different regions and sometimes even within the same community. Fortunately, many sites on the Internet provide descriptions and pictures of plants that can be consulted for plant identification. The concentration of toxins found in plants can vary in different portions of the plant, as well as in the entire plant when grown in different locations or under different environmental conditions. In general, plant toxicants are not destroyed or inactivated by cooking.

This chapter is a review of some of the more common poisonous plants. Familiarity with these plants and their potential toxicity can be very valuable both personally and professionally. Although not comprehensive, this review provides an idea of the scope of possible toxicities that can be produced by plants. It is designed to assist in judging the potential involvement of plant poisoning in circumstances that might have forensic implications.

23.2 Exposure Situations and Circumstances

Accidental toxic plant exposures most often involve either young children exploring their environment or adults foraging for edible wild plants. Poisoning situations may also arise from contamination or misidentification of plants and herbs collected and used for cooking or for dietary supplements with purported health benefits. Occasionally, toxic plants find their way into home food gardens and are overlooked or mistakenly identified and harvested for use in salads or for seasoning. Serious overdoses of toxic plant materials are a rather common occurrence in individuals who use plants recreationally for their hallucinogenic effects. Poisonous plants are sometimes consumed with suicidal intentions and occasionally employed as homicidal weapons.

23.3 Symptoms of Poisoning

23.3.1 Angel's Trumpet (*Brugmansia suaveolens*)

Angel's trumpet is a large ornamental shrub with trumpet-shaped attractively colored flowers that point downward. All parts of the plant contain toxic tropane alkaloids, but the highest concentrations are in the seeds located within the blooming flowers. Toxic effects include hallucinations, dry mouth, delirium, hypertension, tachycardia, seizures, and mydriasis. This plant is used recreationally, usually smoked or as a tea, for hallucinogenic effects. There is a long history of use as a ritualistic hallucinogen in sorcery and black magic. Hallucinations can be visual and auditory and are usually more terrifying than pleasurable. There is a high risk of toxic overdoses and exposures often requiring hospitalization. Toxic exposures often occur in group settings. It is very common for individuals using Angel's trumpet initially for hallucinogenic purposes to be so disturbed by their initial experience that they never attempt to repeat it again.

23.3.2 Castor Bean Plant (*Ricinus communis*)

Castor plants are substantial agrocrops grown for their oil content, which has industrial applications as a lubricant, and for some chemical processes. Plants also grow wild and are a favorite residential landscaping choice. They grow in full sun with minimal water and present as a large bush with attractive leaves and brightly colored flowers. Seeds are also very attractive and sometimes used for making souvenir necklaces. Castor bean seeds are extremely toxic. When chewed, less than a dozen seeds can be fatal. Ricin is the toxic component of castor bean plants and can be extracted by simple techniques described on several sites that are easily accessed on the Internet. The dose of pure ricin required to kill an individual is roughly equivalent to the size of a single salt crystal. There have been many reports of ricin extraction from castor beans for use in criminal or terrorist activities. The symptoms of ricin poisoning depend on the route of exposure and the dose received. Ricin exposure by respiration or injection is significantly more lethal than oral ingestion. Many organs can be affected and death can occur within 36 to 72 h. The most consistent symptom is gastroenteritis. This is manifested by vomiting and diarrhea, which can produce dehydration, hypotension, and seizures.

23.3.3 Deadly Nightshade (*Atropa belladonna*)

Deadly nightshade is a flowering, branching berry bush that can grow several feet high. It has bell-shaped brown–violet flowers and large pointed green leaves. It has green berries about the size of cherries. It is rarely grown for ornamental reasons and is most often found in shady, moist locations in the wild. The plant contains toxic alkaloids that include atropine, hyoscyamine, and scopolamine. Small amounts of any parts of the plant can contain lethal quantities of these alkaloids. The attractive berries have somewhat of a sweet taste and pose a danger to children; fewer than six berries can be lethal. Nightshade has an extensive history of use in natural medicines, witchcraft, sorcery, religious rituals, and recreational use. Symptoms of nightshade poisoning include the following: dry mouth, slurred speech, light sensitivity, visual disturbances, urinary retention, memory decrements, seizures, confusion, and hallucinations. Death results from cardiopulmonary arrest. Nightshade is most often ingested as a tea, but ingesting seeds or other plant parts and smoking dried leaves is not uncommon. Clusters of poisonings occur regularly among adolescents who have used the plants for their hallucinogenic effects. Typically, hallucinatory trips start well with perceived psychic enlightenment and usually progress to frightening sensations with severe life-threatening toxic effects, which necessitate terminating the trip in a hospital's intensive care unit. Individuals who survive these hallucinatory adventures seldom elect to repeat them.

23.3.4 Glory Lily (*Gloriosa superba*)

Glory Lily is a showy, brightly colored, unique flower that is often grown in and around homes. It also grows in the wild. It has been used in suicides and homicides. All parts of the plant are poisonous, but especially the tuberous rhizome. The most toxic component of the plant is colchicine. The tubers (bulbs) have been mistaken for sweet potatoes and onions. Some bulbs are difficult to distinguish from large onions and have been incorporated into salads and other food items and resulted in deaths. Colchicine interferes with essential biological functions such as cell division, secretions, protein synthesis, and myocardial contraction. Poisoning symptoms can begin with severe gastrointestinal symptoms and progress to multiorgan failure.

23.3.5 Foxglove (*Digitalis purpurea*)

Foxglove is a popular ornamental plant grown around homes and also potted for indoor decor. It has a central stalk with drooping, closely spaced, thimble-shaped flowers that are available in a large variety of appealing colors. Plants contain several cardiotoxic components. The principal one is digitalis. Foxglove is the source of medicinal digitalis, which is used extensively in modern medicine for the treatment of congestive heart failure. The dose of standardized formulations of digitalis used for medical purposes is very precise because the margin between safe therapeutic doses and toxic doses is narrow. When moderate amounts of plant materials are ingested, there is a certainty that the amount of digitalis, as well as other toxic plant components, will induce significant toxicity that is often life-threatening. Following ingestion, individuals experience severe nausea, vomiting, cramping, and diarrhea. Toxic symptoms could also include confusion and colorful visual disturbances. Death is preceded by cardiac arrhythmias that impede the flow of blood to vital organs including the brain and the kidneys. Toxicity can result from teas brewed from plant parts, or ingesting any plant parts for some inappropriate medical goal. Accidental, suicidal, and homicidal poisonings with foxglove plants are not unusual.

23.3.6 Poison Hemlock (*Conium maculatum*)

Poison hemlock is a tall plant with finely divided lacy leaves with clusters of small white flowers. Once one sees the plant or pictures of it, it is easily recognizable in natural settings. It contains coniine, which produces toxicity very similar to that seen with nicotine. Coniine can produce CNS stimulation, seizures, ascending paralysis, coma, and death from respiratory failure. Death results from lack of oxygen due to paralysis of the respiratory muscles.

23.3.7 Water Hemlock (*Cicuta douglasii*)

Water hemlock has small compound leaves, small white or green flowers, and tuberous large hollow roots. It can be confused with wild carrots, parsnips, wild celery, ginseng, and other edible plants. It contains cicutoxin, which can cause nausea, vomiting, abdominal pain, and death from untreatable, continuous severe seizures not responsive to treatment.

23.3.8 Monkshood (*Aconitum napellus*)

Monkshood is an attractive ornamental flowering plant. The flowers are shaped like the hood on a monk's robe, and it is available in a variety of bright colors, typically yellow or blue. The flowers are closely spaced on stout single, unbranched stems. Relative to the flowers, the smooth green leaves generally go unnoticed. Monkshood is one of the most toxic plants known to man. All parts of the plants are extremely toxic. The primary toxic component is aconitine (or aconite), which is both a neurotoxin and a cardiotoxin. Monkshood plants are used extensively in Chinese medicine, and it has been identified as an ingredient of some herbal products available in the United States. The estimated lethal dose in humans is 2 mg of pure aconitine or 1 g of plant material. There is a large body of information dealing with toxicity and fatal poisonings resulting from accidental, suicidal, and homicidal aconitine poisonings. Acute poisoning usually appears rapidly within 2 h of ingestion. Symptoms can include dizziness, intense pain, and generalized muscle weakness that can progress to hypotension and cardiac arrhythmias. Death is caused by respiratory paralysis or cardiovascular collapse.

23.3.9 Oleander (*Nerium oleander*)

Oleander is a tall evergreen shrub with attractive clusters of colored flowers. It is frequently planted along roadways, and it is often used in the landscaping of private homes, parks, and communal areas of businesses and developments of every kind. It is also popular for indoor potting. Oleander contains oleandrin, which is a cardiotoxic compound with actions similar to that of digitalis. Ingesting a few leaves can be lethal. Initially, a poisoned individual will experience gastrointestinal disturbances reflected by nausea, vomiting, and diarrhea. This can progress to drowsiness, unconsciousness, and various types of cardiac arrhythmias. Death is preceded by convulsions and respiratory failure.

23.3.10 Rosary Pea (*Abrus prechtorius*)

Seeds from this plant are bright red with a black spot covering one end. They are very attractive and are often used to make beaded jewelry. The seeds contain abrin, which blocks protein synthesis causing cell death and multiple organ failures. Abrin is one of the most potent toxins known to man. Intact seeds are not poisonous, but if scratched, broken, or chewed, they are extremely toxic. There is more than enough abrin in one seed to kill an adult. Initial symptoms of poisoning can occur within hours or can be delayed for 1 to 3 days. Fever, cough, nausea, and tightness in the chest usually precede pulmonary edema, respiratory failure, and death. The ingestion of whole seeds usually produces mild gastrointestinal symptoms because the seed shell prevents absorption and also because digestive enzymes tend to destroy abrin due to its protein structure. However, grinding the seeds prior to ingestion will most assuredly guarantee a fatal outcome.

23.3.11 Mushrooms

Wild mushrooms grow almost anywhere and can appear overnight in wilderness areas as well as on lawns and in gardens. They can be distinctly colored and shaped in sizes from a button to jumbo. Of the thousands of species of mushrooms, about 250 are known to be poisonous and about a dozen are considered deadly. Accidental mushroom poisoning is usually the result of misidentification or the application of erroneous folklore to select edible species. For example, it is a myth that poisonous mushrooms blacken silver coins; no known mushrooms react with silver. Toxicity can be limited to the gastrointestinal system (nausea, vomiting, diarrhea), which may be severe and require hospitalization, to lethal neurotoxicity, organ failure, liver damage, or kidney failure. The onset of fatal organ damage can be days or weeks after ingestion.

Most mushroom poisoning deaths are due to mushrooms belonging to the *Amanita* species. Typically, gastrointestinal symptoms start several hours after ingestion and subside after several days, and then death from liver failure occurs a few days later. There is a high mortality rate, even with aggressive treatment, and generally requires a liver transplant within days of exposure.

The intentional or accidental consumption of native hallucinogenic mushrooms rarely results in life-threatening symptoms. However, mushrooms sold for their hallucinogenic properties could be fortified with synthetic designer drugs having significant toxic potential.

23.4 Case Studies

Case: Deputy's Wife

In 2008, a 42-year-old woman poisoned her husband with foxglove. They had a troubled marriage and there may have been elements of domestic abuse involved. She claimed her intention was only to create discomfort and illness. They had been married for 14 years and lived in Colorado, where he was a sheriff's deputy, with their 3-year-old daughter. After an evening meal that included a salad made from a variety of different kinds of lettuce, her husband experienced stomach cramps and heart palpitations that lasted throughout the night. Several things about his wife's behavior triggered suspicions that his wife may have poisoned him. He had noticed new potted plants on their deck having leaves similar to those included in the dinner salad. He also found that his wife had used their computer to research the toxicity of foxglove. Subsequently, he reported the suspected poisoning to the authorities and went to a hospital where testing revealed serum levels of digitoxin. Initially, the wife was charged with attempted murder, but after an investigation lasting almost 2 years, she accepted a plea bargain and pleaded guilty to felony assault with a sentence of 5 years in prison.

Comments

Foxglove is a popular ornamental plant found in many flower gardens. There are many varieties that produce a spectrum of colorful attractive flowers. They contain cardiotoxic glycosides. These glycosides act primarily on the heart, but they also produce effects in the neurological and gastrointestinal systems. Digitoxin is one of the cardiotoxic glycosides found in foxglove. Lethal levels of digitoxin produce death by dysrhythmias and refractory hyperkalemia. Deaths from unintentional foxglove plant exposures are rare.

Case: Trail Food

A healthy 75-year-old man took a short hike with friends through a wooded area near the place they were vacationing. The man regularly hiked and camped. On this day, he picked some wildflowers and blackberries for snacking, which he was accustomed to doing. About 2 or 3 h after eating some of the flowers and berries, he became nauseous and experienced abdominal pain. This rapidly progressed to vomiting and then he suddenly collapsed and died. This was about 4 h after eating the plants. At autopsy, all organs were severely congested with pronounced bleeding and edema in the lungs. Toxicological screening was negative for commonly abused drugs. However, samples of the flowers he had ingested were identified as monkshood (*Aconitum napellus*). The principal toxic component of monkshood was found in toxic concentrations in blood and urine samples.

Comments

Aconitine is a rapidly acting poison that typically produces nausea and vomiting, dizziness, and hypotension that progress to paralysis, cardiac arrhythmias, shock, coma, and death. Most poisonings due to aconitine are due to misuse in herbal medications, but there are reports of its use in homicides and suicides. Aconitine poisoning from eating unknown plants in the wild is very unusual.

Case: Unhealthy Choice

In 1992, two adult brothers were foraging for wild ginseng in a wooded area near the coast of Maine. They collected several plants growing in a swampy area and tasted a root from one of the plants. The first brother only bit into a root; the second brother took three bites. Within 30 min, the second brother started vomiting and having convulsions. They were able to contact rescue services who arrived at their location within 15 min. At this point, the second brother was unresponsive and cyanotic, and he was having severe tonic–clonic seizures followed by periods of apnea. They were both transported to a hospital where the second brother ultimately died. His death occurred approximately 3 h after ingesting the plant root. The other brother began having seizures and exhibited delirium while at the hospital, but this was successfully managed medically and he was ultimately discharged without any residual effects. The root ingested by the brothers came from water hemlock.

Comments

Water hemlock is similar in appearance to parsnips, smells like fresh turnips, and tastes sweet. It contains cicutoxin, which is present throughout the plant but mostly concentrated in the root. Water hemlock causes the majority of fatalities attributed to the misidentification of edible plants in the United States.

Case: Lawn Mushrooms

In 2011, a man living in Oregon died after eating mushrooms found growing on his lawn. After cooking, the man ate approximately five; his wife and daughter only tasted small bite-sized portions. Later the family developed nausea and vomiting with bloody diarrhea. The daughter went to a local emergency department where she was treated symptomatically. Later, the mother arrived at the emergency department for treatment. It was at this point that the connection to a potential poisonous mushroom ingestion was made. The father never sought treatment and died at home, while his family was being treated at the hospital. Both the wife and daughter developed significant liver toxicity and coagulopathy, but they recovered after hospital treatment.

Comments

Symptoms of mushroom poisoning range from gastric irritation, drowsiness, and confusion to signs of cardiac, renal, or hepatic damage. The majority of mushroom deaths are due to *Amanitas*, which can easily be mistaken for edible mushrooms. Symptoms may not appear for many hours after ingestion.

Case: Wild Garlic

In 2011, a previously healthy 39-year-old man was seen in a hospital emergency department because of an acute onset of nausea, diarrhea, and abdominal pain. The only atypical food he had eaten was some harvested garlic that he had with breakfast 9 h before. His symptoms were attributed to food poisoning and he was discharged. Four hours later, his symptoms intensified and he returned to the hospital. His vital signs and ECG tracings were normal. Samples were collected for laboratory analysis, antiemetics were administered, and intravenous rehydration was initiated. Laboratory results were within normal ranges except for some changes in hematology tests and elevated levels of liver enzymes. Based on the information available at this time, a diagnosis of infectious gastroenteritis was made and the man was transferred to the infectious disease ward where antibiotics were administered. Symptoms improved over the following 30 h, and then the man suddenly developed severe dyspnea and respiratory distress. Aggressive therapy that included endotracheal intubation was initiated. Cardiopulmonary resuscitation continued for about an hour until the man was declared dead. Autopsy findings included pulmonary edema and congestion, and mild coronary arterial stenosis. There were histopathological abnormalities seen in cardiac and hepatic tissues. Specimens were collected for general toxicological screening that included common drugs of abuse, alcohols, metals, and cyanide. Results were negative for all tested substances. Plants from which the wild garlic was obtained were collected and identified as *Colchicum persicum*, and an analysis of an extract from the plant confirmed the presence of colchicine. The death was ruled accidental.

Comments

There are several kinds of wild garlic that are harvested for personal consumption. These plants can easily be mistaken for other poisonous plants as was illustrated in this case. The man had mistaken meadow saffron plants (lily of the valley) for wild bear's garlic. The saffron plant contains colchicine, which is extremely toxic and acts by blocking cellular division in all tissues. Colchicine is used clinically for the treatment of gout. It also has uses in agriculture and in molecular biology research. Thus, colchicine availability is not limited to the plant world, and the purified form found in other settings can be encountered in accidental or intentional lethal exposures with forensic implications.

Case: Vegans Lacking Survival Skills

In 2004, the bodies of a male and a female, approximately 30 years old, were found near a forester's cabin in a wooded area near Pisa, Italy. It was winter and the couple was shabbily dressed and showed signs of severe malnutrition; there were no documents, money, or food found with the bodies. There were no signs of trauma and nothing to suggest that anyone else had been with the couple. It was estimated that death might have occurred 2–3 days prior to the discovery. An autopsy did not reveal an anatomic cause of death. Partially digested plant material was found in the gastric contents. There were gastric lesions, pancreatitis, histological alterations of myocardial and hepatic cells, and hemorrhagic lesions in some other organs. Some of these findings were believed to be due to chronic hypothermia. Toxicological screening was negative except for the presence of oleandrin, which was inferred from positive radioimmunoassay tests for digitoxin. Oleandrin is the major toxic component of oleander (*Nerium oleander*), which grew in abundance in the area where the bodies were found. The identity of the couple remained unknown for 4 years until the female was recognized by her parents from a photograph shown on a television show dedicated to missing persons. Their daughter had gone off with a friend who belonged to an extreme vegetarians group dedicated to not eating or using any products derived from animals. They chose to live only on natural products that they could find in the wild. It was postulated that the oleander was consumed inadvertently because of a desperate attempt to locate edible plant materials.

Comments

Since the individuals described in this case were dedicated to those living on natural vegetation, it is difficult to understand how they could be unaware of the serious potential toxicity of the oleander plants common in this area.

Case: Castor Bean Extract Injection

In 2009, a 49-year-old man arrived at a Belgium hospital emergency department approximately 24 h after injecting himself intravenously and subcutaneously with an extract of castor beans with suicidal intent. He had nausea, vomiting, diarrhea, and labored breathing. He was dehydrated due to fluid loss and in hypovolemic shock. Liver enzymes were elevated. His condition continued to deteriorate with indication of liver failure, renal failure, and hematological dysfunction. Despite efforts to stabilize and reverse his deteriorating condition, he died from multiple organ system failures 9 h after admission. An autopsy was not done. Toxicological analysis identified ricinine in postmortem samples of blood, urine, and vitreous humor, and in the castor bean extract.

Comments

Ricinine is a component of castor beans that can be used as a biomarker to assess exposure to castor beans or unpurified ricin.

Case: Botanical Garden

In 2016, a 22-year-old woman collapsed shortly after visiting a botanical garden in California. She appeared to have had a generalized seizure and was pulseless and apneic. Bystanders initiated cardiopulmonary resuscitation until emergency medical responders arrived and shifted her to a hospital emergency department. On arrival, she was unresponsive and apneic with a very weak pulse. There were remnants of green plant material in her mouth. The woman had significant cardiac arrhythmias with persistent cardiovascular deterioration despite aggressive medical treatment and supportive measures. She expired approximately 1.5 h after arrival at the hospital. A small amount of plant material was found in the woman's purse. It was identified as the common yew evergreen plant (*Taxus baccata*). Cardiotoxic alkaloids from the yew were identified and quantitated in perimortem samples of serum and gastric contents.

Comments

The ingestion of small quantities of the common yew evergreen shrub can cause severe toxicity marked by seizures, cardiac arrhythmias, and refractory cardiac collapse. In this case, the yew ingestion was intentional and the plant was presumably obtained from an exhibit in a public botanical garden in a large city in Southern California. However, this plant is common and easily available throughout the United States.

References and Additional Reading

Amrollahi-Sharifabadi M, Seghatoleslami A, Amrollahi-Sharifabadi M, Bayani F, Mirjalili M: Fatal colchicine poisoning by accidental ingestion of *Colchicum persicum*: A Case report. *Am J Forensic Med Pathol*, 34: 295–298, 2013.

Arens AM, Anaebere TC, Horng H, Olson K: Fatal *Taxus baccata* ingestion with perimortem serum taxine B quantification. *Clin Toxicol*, 54: 878–880, 2016.

Audi J, Belson M, Patel M, Shier J, Osterloh J: Ricin poisoning: A comprehensive review. *JAMA*, 294: 2342–2351, 2005.

Beuhler MC, Sasser HC, Watson WA: The outcome of North American pediatric unintentional mushroom ingestions with various decontamination treatments: An analysis of 14 years of TESS data. *Toxicon*, 53: 437–443, 2009.

Chan TY: Aconite poisoning. *Clin Toxicol*, 47: 279–285, 2009.

Coopman V, DeLeeuw M, Cordonnier J, Jacobs W: Suicidal death after injection of a castor bean extract (*Ricinus communis*). *Forensic Sci Int*, 189: 13–20, 2009.

Cunningham N: Hallucinogenic plants of abuse. *Emerg Med Aust*, 20: 167–174, 2008.

Finkelstein Y, Aks SE, Hutson JR, Juurlink DN, Nguyem P, Dubnov-Raz G, Pollak U, Koren G, Bentur Y: Colchicine poisoning: The dark side of an ancient drug. *Clin Toxicol*, 48: 407–414, 2010.

French LK, Hendrickson RG, Horowitz BZ: *Amanita phalloides* poisoning. *Clin Toxicol*, 49: 128–129, 2011.

Glatstein MM, Alabdulrazzaq F, Garcia-Bournissen F, Scolnik D: Use of physostigmine for hallucinogenic plant poisoning in a teenager: Case report and review of the literature. *Am J Therapeut*, 19: 384–388, 2012.

Hamelin EL, Johnson JC, Osterloh JD, Thomas JD: Evaluation of ricinine, a ricin biomarker, from a non-lethal castor bean ingestion. *J Anal Toxicol*, 36: 660–662, 2012.

Lim CS, Chhabra N, Leikin S, Fischbein C, Mueller GM, Nelson ME: Atlas of select poisonous plants and mushrooms. *Disease-a-Month*, 62: 42–67, 2016.

McClain JL, Hause DW, Clark MA: *Amanita phalloides* mushroom poisoning: A cluster of four fatalities. *J Forensic Sci*, 34: 83–87, 1989.

Nelson LS, Shih RD, Balick MJ: *Handbook of Poisonous and Injurious Plants*, 2nd ed. New York: Springer, 2007.

Papi L, Luciani AB, Forni D, Giusiani M: Unexpected double lethal oleander poisoning. *Am J Forensic Med Pathol*, 33: 93–97, 2012.

Perju-Dumbrava D, Morar S, Chiroban O, Lechintan E, Cioca A: Suicidal poisoning by ingestion of *Taxus baccata* leaves: Case report and literature review. *Rom J Leg Med*, 21: 115–118, 2013.

Schep LJ, Temple WA, Butt GA, Beasley MD: Ricin as a weapon of mass terror: Separating fact from fiction. *Environ Int*, 35: 1267–1271, 2009.

Sweeney K, Gensheimer KF, Knowlton-Field J, Smith RA: Water hemlock poisoning—Maine, 1992. *CDC MMWR*, 43: 229–231, 1994.

Weakley-Jones B, Gerber JE, Biggs G: Colchicine poisoning: Case report of two homicides. *Am J Forensic Med Pathol*, 22: 203–206, 2001.

Pesticides 24

24.1 Introduction

Pesticides are chemicals used to kill, control, or repel pests. Target pests can include insects, worms, weeds, mollusks, birds, mammals, fish, and plant pathogens. There are many types of pesticides with diverse chemical structures that are formulated into many different products with human toxicity. The inert constituents and solvents in pesticide products can also be toxic, sometimes more toxic than the pesticide. In the United States, there are more than 1000 individual pesticides marketed in approximately 20,000 products. The complexity and diversity of pesticide products necessitate that they be specifically identified in exposure situations. This can be difficult because pesticides are often transferred from their original packaging to other containers that are smaller and more convenient to use. Pesticide products are heavily regulated by federal and local laws that specify how they can be marketed, who can purchase them, and how they must be used. Some examples of common pesticides are provided in Table 24.1.

24.2 Exposure Situations and Circumstances

Individuals involved in the manufacturing, transportation, or application of pesticides are the most susceptible to accidental exposure, and they can expose family members through contaminated clothing. Emergency workers such as firefighters and paramedics can also be exposed to pesticides from accidents and from burning storage structures. The effects of exposure can be delayed and not immediately associated with exposure incidents.

Agricultural pesticides are used in approximately one-third of all suicides worldwide. Many cases of suicide appear to be impulsive acts undertaken during stressful events and therefore pesticide availability strongly influences their use for suicide.

Homicides using pesticides most often occur in developing countries where they are frequently the only toxic substance available. Pesticides are generally potent, fast-acting poisons, but they are often formulated into pellets, sprays, and other forms that can be difficult to disguise for administration in food and beverages. In addition, most pesticides have a very

Table 24.1   Pesticide Categorization

Category	Example
Algicides	Polyquate
Fungicides	Chlorothalonil
Herbicide	Diquat, 2, 4-D, atrazine
Insecticides	Malathion, permethrin
Miticides	Aldicarb
Molluscicides	Metaldehyde
Nematicides	Diamidafos
Rodenticides	Brodifacoum

unpleasant taste and a sharp, pungent odor that make them very difficult to administer surreptitiously. Victims are often children or an individual with some degree of cognitive dysfunction associated with decreased taste and smell that permits them to ingest repulsive pesticide products.

Pesticide products are generally prominently labeled as poisons, and individuals seeking a poison for use in some criminal activity can be led to these products. A perpetrator might choose a rat poison without any knowledge of what the product ingredients are or the type of toxicity it might produce. Adults have been known to do this, but it might be expected more often with younger perpetrators who attempt to poison a family member or teacher using an easily accessible rodenticide product.

24.3 Symptoms of Poisoning

The spectrum of poisoning symptoms that might be produced by pesticides includes most symptoms produced by common medical conditions and requires evaluation based on detailed medical and occupational histories. The most frequently encountered pesticide poisonings involve insecticides, rodenticides, and herbicides.

In terms of toxicity, the most important insecticides are organophosphates and carbamates. These agents act by blocking the action of the enzyme that regulates the amount of acetylcholine available for neurotransmission. Since neurons that utilize acetylcholine as a neurotransmitter are located throughout the body, the effects of these insecticides are widespread. Principal symptoms of toxicity include abnormal muscle contractions, behavioral disturbances, increased pulmonary secretions, and respiratory depression. A listing of possible symptoms for organophosphate poisoning is provided in Table 24.2.

Many different types of poisons have been used to control rodents such as rats, mice, gophers, and moles. Older rodenticides contained arsenic, thallium, or strychnine. These are still used in some countries. In the United States,

Table 24.2 Symptoms of Organophosphate Poisoning

Anxiety and confusion
Diaphoresis
Difficulty breathing and pulmonary congestion
Hypertension or hypotension
Miosis
Muscle weakness, fasciculations, and paralysis
Nausea, vomiting, and diarrhea
Tachycardia and other arrhythmias
Tremors and convulsions

only strychnine is still used in restricted situations. Most rodenticides used today are warfarin-type anticoagulants, which result in the death of rodents from uncontrolled internal bleeding.

Metal phosphide compounds are commonly used by licensed exterminators. These compounds react with moisture and produce phosphine gas, which is extremely toxic. Phosphine blocks many cellular processes and causes multisystem organ failure leading to death. Other commercially available rodenticides act as either neurotoxins, cardiotoxins, or disrupt critical metabolic processes. Rodenticides are rather nonspecific and can poison birds and other wildlife, pets, and humans. Older rodenticides containing discontinued and unlicensed substances can still be found in barns, attics, and other neglected storage areas. Unapproved pesticide products can also be imported illegally by individuals who obtain them from friends or relatives living outside the United States.

Many herbicides used throughout the world are derivatives of dinitrophenol. Some of these compounds were studied in 1930s for use as potential weight-loss products but were quickly abandoned because of severe toxic effects. These agents do, however, remain available through the Internet. They are illegally promoted for weight loss and included in some bodybuilding products. There have been a number of deaths associated with these products. Prominent symptoms of toxicity include hyperthermia and increased respiration and heart rate.

24.4 Case Studies

Case: Hazardous Wine

In 1999, two middle-aged men were clearing out the storage area in the semifinished basement of a home in New Jersey in preparation for listing the house for sale. One man had inherited the house from his father.

The other was a coworker who had a pick-up truck to haul away discarded items. They were both married with families and had worked together in the same large company for several years. Among the stored items were 6 gallon-bottles of red wine from a well-known California winery. Four gallons were still sealed in the original cardboard shipping container. One of the other two bottles had been opened, but was nearly full. The wine was obviously old and the men were concerned about it still being palatable. To pursue this, the truck owner tasted a small amount. It was extremely bad and he spit out most of it. They continued working for a short time, and then the man with the truck drove home—about 30 min away. By the time he arrived, he was seriously ill and paramedics were called to transport him to a nearby hospital. Soon after arrival at the hospital, the man died. From the description of events that occurred prior to arriving at the hospital, the medical personnel suspected some type of pesticide poisoning. The death was reported to police and triggered an immediate response from local health authorities and HAZMAT specialists. The police investigation was initially focused on the possibility of homicide. Toxicology testing of autopsy samples revealed only dinoseb, a toxic herbicide. The physical findings of the autopsy were consistent with dinoseb poisoning. The police investigation was prolonged because of inconsistent descriptions of the events that occurred on the evening of the poisoning. The homeowner and his family members were concerned about possible liability for the death. The family of the deceased was suspicious of the homeowner's involvement and pursued legal action for wrongful death. This became further complicated by the possible involvement of an exterminating company who had recently treated the property. Ultimately, a wrongful death suit was brought by the family of the deceased individual and was settled through coverage by the homeowner's insurance. From the investigation of the circumstances surrounding the death, it was concluded that the cause was poisoning and the manner of death was accidental.

Comments

Dinoseb is an extremely toxic herbicide that has been banned from use in the United States since 1986. This case occurred 13 years after dinoseb products ceased being marketed. From the investigation it was clear that the dinoseb had been transferred to the wine bottle years before, but the circumstances were not discovered. This case illustrates how old products that have not been commercially available for long periods can still surface in forensic investigations. It also produces an example of the possible consequences of storing substances in containers other than the original ones.

Case: Rebecca and Rachel

In 2010, a family living in a town in Utah contacted a pest control company to eradicate an infestation of field mice that were damaging their lawn and shrubbery. Around 8 a.m. on a Friday, a technician from the exterminating company arrived at the home and applied Fumitoxin pellets to several mouse burrowing holes. The parents and their four children were away from the home most of the day. When they returned, they noticed a strong odor and attempted to contact the exterminator but were unsuccessful. They then contacted the fire department who came and checked for any possible carbon monoxide. They ruled out carbon monoxide exposure and subsequently left the home. On Saturday, the family developed nausea and vomiting and other flu-like symptoms and was hospitalized. They were discharged on Sunday. At this point, it was speculated that the family had food poisoning. That Sunday evening, 4-year-old Rebecca was taken to a hospital where she suffered a cardiopulmonary arrest, which was not responsive to resuscitation efforts. Later, 15-month-old Rachel was hospitalized in critical condition. She died on Tuesday. Emergency responders quickly expanded to include police, firefighter, HAZMAT teams, local and federal regulatory agencies, and National Guard hazardous material specialists. Ultimately, it was determined that the deaths resulted from phosphine gas liberated from aluminum phosphide contained in the Fumitoxin that had migrated into the home from areas of application near the house. The amount of Fumitoxin used, as well as the proximity of use near the home, was in clear violation of federal pesticide regulations. Several other aspects of the misuse of the rodenticide were also identified. The technician that applied the pesticide was formally charged with violations of federal regulations. He pleaded guilty to the charges and was sentenced to 3 years probation and 100 h of community service. The exterminating company was fined $3000 and barred from doing business for 3 years. A wrongful death suit against the technician and the exterminating company was settled for an undisclosed amount.

Comments

The Utah deaths were not the first children to die from phosphine gas poisoning under these circumstances. This has occurred in other states and in other countries. As a direct result of this case, regulations were strengthened and Fumitoxin use is no longer permitted in residential areas. Treated areas must now be marked with conspicuous signs warning of the danger, and reentry into a treated area is not permitted for 48 h.

Case: Herbicide Suicide

In 2011, a 29-year-old man was admitted to a hospital after he had intentionally ingested about 300 ml (10 oz) of an herbicide product containing glyphosate. He was agitated and had compromised respiration that required immediate intubation and mechanical ventilation. He had significant hypotension that was resistant to treatment and persistent cardiac arrhythmias. He was started on hemofiltration in an attempt to remove the glyphosate from his circulation. Laboratory testing indicated a variety of metabolic imbalances. Following resuscitation from a cardiac arrest, he was placed on life support. He continued to show signs of multiple organ failure and after 2 days life support was discontinued.

Comments

Glyphosate-containing herbicides are probably the most widely used herbicide products in the world. General-purpose herbicide products used in both household and commercial environments contain glyphosate. It acts by blocking key steps in cellular metabolic activity. This results in cellular damage to vital organs, which are expressed most prominently in the cardiovascular and respiratory systems.

Case: Strawberry Smoothie

In 2014, a 32-year-old woman living in a small town near Aspen, Colorado, intentionally poisoned herself and her two daughters aged 8 and 11 years. The poison was a rodenticide product containing brodifacoum purchased from a local hardware store. She blended the product into strawberry smoothies, which she gave to her unsuspecting children and then consumed herself. She was deeply disturbed over the possibility that her estranged husband might move out of the country with the children and somehow reasoned that killing the children and herself was a solution to the dilemma. Her expectation was that the deaths would occur quickly after ingestion of the rodenticide. When this did not happen, she mentioned what she had done during a visit to her health care provider the following day. This resulted in her and the children being taken to a local hospital for treatment. They all recovered without any lasting effects. The mother was arrested and charged with two counts of attempted first-degree murder and child abuse. Each attempted murder count has a potential sentence of 16 to 48 years in prison.

Comments

Brodifacoum is a long-acting anticoagulant, sometimes referred to as a superwarfarin, which blocks the coagulation process and causes death in rodents from internal bleeding. Death usually occurs after several days of continued feeding on pellets or grain containing the anticoagulant. Although the same effect can occur in humans, the delay in effect provides a margin of safety for accidental poisoning from single exposure. The use of a rat poison product for suicide or homicide often occurs without consideration or knowledge of the ingredients contained in the products. Their selection in many cases is based on the fact that they are poisons as prominently stated on the product labeling. Young children and teenagers who poison family members, teachers, or rivals might use a product simply because it is labeled as a poison and easily available. Likewise, individuals with limited education, language issues, or marginal intelligence tend to employ rat poison for intentional poisoning. Generally, the expectation of these individuals is that the poison will cause death and that it will occur quickly.

References and Additional Reading

Beswick E, Millo J: Fatal poisoning with glyphosate-surfactant herbicide. *J Intensive Care Soc*, 12: 37–39, 2011.

Bradberry SM, Proudfoot AT, Vale JA: Glyphosate poisoning. *Toxicol Rev*, 23: 159–167, 2004.

Bumbrah GS, Krishan K, Kanchan T, Shama M, Sodhi GS: Phosphide poisoning: A review of literature. *Forensic Sci Int*, 10: 1–6, 2012.

Grundlingh J, Dargan PI, El-Zanfaly M, Wood DM: 2, 4-Dinitrophenol (DNP): A weight loss agent with significant acute toxicity and risk of death. *J Med Toxicol*, 7: 205–212, 2011.

Kumar L, Agarwal SS, Chavali KH, Mestri SC: Homicide by organophosphorus compound poisoning: A case report. *Med Sci Law*, 49: 136–138, 2009.

Langley RL, Mort SA: Human exposures to pesticides in the United States. *J Agromedicine*, 17: 300–315, 2012.

Lemoine TJ, Schoolman K, Jackman G, Vernon DD: Unintentional fatal phosphine gas poisoning of a family. *Pediatr Emerg Care*, 27: 868–871, 2011.

Miranda EJ, McIntyre IM, Parker DR, Gary RD, Logan BK: Two deaths attributed to the use of 2, 4-dinitrophenol. *J Anal Toxicol*, 30: 219–222, 2006.

Palmer RB, Alakija P, de Baca JE, Nolte KB: Fatal brodifacoum rodenticide poisoning: Autopsy and toxicological findings. *J Forensic Sci*, 44: 851–855, 1999.

Rancic D, Dordevic D, Marinkovic N, Brajkovic G: Fatal dinoseb intoxication: Case report. *MD Medical Data*, 6: 99–103, 2014.

Roberts JR, Reigart JR: *Recognition and Management of Pesticide Poisoning*, 6th ed. Washington, DC: Office of Pesticide Programs, United States Environmental Protection Agency, 2013.

Simpson WM Jr., Schuman SH: Recognition and management of acute pesticide poisoning. *Am Fam Physician*, 65: 1599–1604, 2002.

Poisoning

This section focuses on circumstances, whether accidental, homicidal, or suicidal, in which poisoning might occur. It also highlights the diversities and capabilities of poisoners. These poisoning situations can be viewed as models and can be used initially to form a framework for investigations.

As in previous chapters, accompanying cases were selected to emphasize the circumstances to help investigators distinguish accidental, homicidal, and suicidal situations that they might not otherwise have considered as involving poisons.

III

Poisoning

Accidental Poisoning 25

25.1 Introduction

Most accidental poisonings occur in children. Although the majority of pediatric exposures do not have serious or fatal consequences, some involve life-threatening exposures and require medical evaluation. Accidental poisoning in adults, especially in the elderly, tends to be more serious. Adult exposures usually involve medications, substances in the workplace, and products utilized in crafts, hobbies, and gardening. A particularly serious common toxic exposure for all age groups is carbon monoxide from a variety of sources. The leading cause of all accidental poisoning deaths is opioid overdoses. Other important toxicants involved in accidental deaths are listed in Table 25.1.

Accidental poisonings are discussed throughout this book in chapters that focus on specific poisons or typical poisoning circumstances. A general familiarity with common accidental poisonings can significantly facilitate progress in investigations in which the distinction between accidental and suicidal or homicidal poisoning is not obvious. Important risk factors for accidental poisonings are listed in Table 25.2. Some accidental poisoning case studies that may be of particular interest to forensic investigators are presented in Section 25.3 of this chapter.

25.2 Exposure Situations and Circumstances

25.2.1 Pediatric Poisoning

There are several classes of adult medications that can be lethal to toddlers who ingest even one or a few standard pills or teaspoonfuls. The exposure circumstances might involve toddlers encountering unattended medication containers in the home or perhaps discovering a pill that was previously lost by a parent or grandparent. Medications in purses, travel containers, or on nightstands are common targets for toddler exploration. Examples of the pharmacological classes of drugs that have single dose lethality potential in toddlers are listed in Table 25.3. This topic is raised here to emphasize that small doses, sometimes a single pill, of a large number of adult medications can kill a young child. Some medications are available in a wide range of

Table 25.1 Common Toxicants Involved in Accidental Poisoning Deaths

- Analgesics
- Psychiatric medications
- Street drugs
- Cardiac medications
- Alcohols
- Industrial chemicals
- Gases and fumes
- Cleaners
- Automotive products
- Pesticides

Table 25.2 High Risk Factors for Accidental Poisoning

- Look-alike product confusion
- Lack of attention or supervision of children
- Product removed from original containers and stored in the empty container from a different product
- Ingesting products without reading the labels
- Children visiting grandparents or vice versa
- Children medicated with adult medication
- Taking medication in the dark
- Parents sedating children with ethanol or other depressants
- Ingesting wild plants or mushrooms without assured identification

Table 25.3 Medications That Can Kill a Toddler with One or a Few Doses

Tricyclic antidepressants
Antipsychotics
Antimalarials
Anti-arrhythmics
Calcium channel blockers
Opioids
Oral hypoglycemics

dosages that could differ in strength as much as tenfold from the lowest to the highest dose per tablet. Ingesting a few tablets of a lower strength could be fatal, and this possibility is amplified with increased tablet strength. Other medications that are especially toxic to young children include topical analgesic ointments and liniments containing salicylates, iron supplements, nicotine replacement products, eye drops, illegal drugs, and ethanol.

Table 25.4 Household Items Generally Regarded as Nontoxic

Personal Use Items	Medications
Bath oil	Antacids
Bubble bath	Antibiotics (with some exceptions)
Cosmetics	Calamine lotion
Deodorants	Oral contraceptives (without iron)
Eye make-up	Corticosteroids
Hairspray	Hydrogen peroxide 3%
Hand lotion	Homeopathic medications
Lipstick	Mineral oil
Moisturizers	Zinc oxide
Petroleum jelly	Zirconium oxide
Shampoo	A&D ointment
Shaving cream	Cold pack
Suntan lotion	Glycerin
Toothpaste	Lanolin
	Lip balm
	Vitamins without iron

Art Supplies and Toys	Miscellaneous
Ballpoint pen ink	Ashes
Chalk	Dehumidifying packets
Clay	Candles without insect repellants
Crayons (marked A.P. or C.P)	Latex paint
Magic markers	Newspaper
Paste and white glue	Potting soil (unfertilized)
Pencil lead	Styrofoam
Plaster of Paris	Sweetening agents
Play-Doh	Incense
Silly Putty	Thermometers (caution with broken glass)
Teething rings	Book matches (less than 1/2 book)
Watercolors	Lubricating oil
	Fabric softener sheets
	Household bleach (2%–5%)

25.2.2 Therapeutic Misadventures

A therapeutic misadventure refers to a toxic outcome from a well-intended but inappropriate therapeutic measure. In other words, an individual does something that he or she may feel is entirely appropriate but in actuality is dangerous and has toxic consequences. Examples might include administering adult medications to children or treating a child with some type of alternative therapy supplement that has inherent toxicity or might aggravate the condition for which it is being used.

25.2.3 Drug Combinations

The toxic side effects of a single drug may be tolerable or even unnoticeable when used alone, but when combined with other drugs that produce similar adverse effects, the effects can be additive and result in a potentially lethal combination. Combinations of psychotropic drugs with opioids are of particular concern. The combined toxic effects of these drugs on respiration and cardiac function can be life-threatening. When drugs are added to a treatment regimen at different times, or when different physicians in different medical specialties prescribe drugs without overall monitoring responsibilities assumed by any one prescriber, the possibility of potentially lethal combinations is increased.

25.2.4 Nontoxic Ingestions

Table 25.4 lists some substances that are generally considered nontoxic when accidentally ingested in small amounts by otherwise healthy children. There could be toxic exceptions and circumstances, which require consideration, but familiarity with the items listed might be useful in initial evaluations. The primary concern with many of the products listed is possible obstruction of respiratory passages.

25.2.5 Children Living with Substance Abusers

Children living with their parents or other adults with substance abuse disorders are at a heightened risk for accidental poisoning because of the availability of toxic substances as well as the often irresponsible and risky behaviors of their caregivers. The toxicants in the child's surroundings can include the chemicals used for producing illegal drugs. This can involve rather small-scale drug manufacturing processes for substances used by an individual or larger chemical operations for amounts intended for distribution. Toxic agents include precursor chemicals and reagents, and the chemical fertilizers and growing materials for plant cultivation.

25.3 Case Studies

Case: Healthy Choice

In 2003, a 58-year-old man living in Florida arrived home from work earlier than usual and decided to have a snack before dinner. He made a salad with lettuce, tomatoes, cucumbers, onion, and carrots. This he tossed with oil and vinegar and seasoned with salt and pepper and then topped with a handful of croutons. Later he ate a dinner of fried grouper, a blend of vegetables, and red wine. About 2 h after the dinner, he started having burning pains in his stomach. This was followed by severe vomiting and bouts of blood-tinged diarrhea. He was taken to a hospital emergency department. On arrival he was unconscious and in hypovolemic shock. He had severe petechial hemorrhages over his chest and abdomen, and oliguria. Symptomatic and supportive treatment was provided, but he developed multiple complications and died on the second day of hospitalization. Autopsy findings included inflammation of the stomach wall, numerous hemorrhagic points throughout his intestines, and petechial hemorrhages over the surface of his heart, lungs, and cerebral hemispheres. The stomach contents and blood and tissue samples did not reveal any common poisons. An investigation ultimately determined that the man's wife had purchased several Glory lily bulbs (*Gloriosa superba*) earlier in the day of the incident and had placed them on a windowsill in the kitchen where she customarily placed fruits and vegetables for ripening. The man had apparently mistaken them for onions and incorporated a bulb into his salad.

Comments

All parts of the Glory lily are extremely poisonous, especially the tubers which are bulb-like roots. The principle toxic component is colchicine, which blocks cellular division in all tissues. Death from hemorrhagic complications and multiorgan failure can occur within 24 h of ingestion.

Case: IV Use of Oral Methadone

Around 2004, a 43-year-old male IV drug abuser was admitted to a university medical center hospital for evaluation of a seizure disorder of recent onset, and a number of other neurological problems that included ataxia, progressive cognition decline, and a significant impairment of his ability to write and speak. His drug history included cocaine, heroin, methadone, and lorazepam. He was treated initially with anticonvulsants. Extensive neurological evaluation and laboratory testing revealed a number of abnormalities. The most striking blood abnormality was a high level of aluminum. Aluminum toxicity was undoubtedly responsible for the majority of the neurological deficits. He was subsequently treated with appropriate chelating agents to reduce the body load of aluminum. He improved over the next several months, but not all the neurological symptoms were eliminated. For about 4 years, prior to his hospital admission, the man had been regularly injecting a concentrated form of oral methadone. An oral formulation of methadone dispensed by a treatment program was heated in an aluminum pot to reduce the volume for intravenous injection. The acidic methadone formulation and lengthy heating times facilitated the leaching of aluminum from the cooking pot. This would not have presented a problem if the contents of the pot were ingested rather than injected. In healthy individuals, absorption of aluminum after oral ingestion is minimal (less than 0.1%). However, intravenously administered aluminum is totally bioavailable and can produce toxic neurologic effects.

Comments

This case provides an example of how the route of administration can influence the toxicity of a substance. When administered orally, aluminum is essentially not absorbed. Intravenous drug use exposes abusers to a host of health problems that extend beyond those inherent in the particular drugs used.

Case: Therapeutic Misadventure—Alcoholism

In 2013, a 34-year-old man was admitted to a medical center hospital in Boston because of a sudden onset of nausea, vomiting, and diarrhea accompanied by severe abdominal pain. He spent the previous night drinking with friends at a neighborhood bar and became ill shortly after returning to his home where he lived with his wife and children. He was intoxicated when he got home and went to bed after drinking some lemonade. His symptoms started soon after, persisted for several hours without abatement, and ultimately led him to seek medical help at an emergency department of a hospital. His condition continued to deteriorate in the hospital. Within 3 days of admission, the man had advancing signs of liver failure, kidney failure, and cardiotoxicity. When confronted with the likely possibility that the man would not survive unless the cause of his condition was identified and treated specifically, the man's wife revealed that she had mixed a packet of powder into the lemonade, which was purported to contain a substance that would induce vomiting and somehow stop her husband's future drinking. She obtained the substance from friends in a country in Central America. The substance was antimony potassium tartrate. Antimony is a poisonous chemical element with toxic properties similar to those of arsenic. It was determined that the man had ingested a potentially lethal dose of antimony in the lemonade. He survived after aggressive treatment over the following 11 days and was able to resume working a few days after hospital discharge.

Comments

The antimony compound ingested by this individual is sold in some countries for use as a form of aversion therapy for substance abuse. Other cases have been reported with similar products from other countries. The victim in this case had ingested a lethal amount of antimony that required aggressive medical treatment, which itself carries risks. Had the poison not been identified early in the course of treatment, or if the treatment was delayed, the individual would not have survived. It might be of interest to speculate on the outcome of a death investigation that might have been initiated if the man had died at home.

Case: Therapeutic Misadventure—Suspected Drug Abuse

A previously healthy 14-year-old boy returned home from a party and stated that he may have ingested a pill, but he was unsure what pill he may have taken. There had also been alcohol at the party. His parents tried to induce vomiting with saltwater (5 tablespoonfuls of table salt in a glass of water). They boy collapsed approximately 30 min after drinking the saltwater and emergency medical responders were called. En route to a hospital, the patient had two seizures. When he arrived at the hospital he was comatose, hypertensive, hyperthermic, tachycardic, and tachypenic. He was given thiamine, naloxone, diazepam, ceftriaxone, and intravenous fluids. Gastric lavage was performed. A screen for typically abused drugs was negative. Prior to transportation by a helicopter to a second hospital having more advanced care resources, the boy was endotracheally intubated. Another seizure occurred en route. He arrived at a tertiary care hospital 3.5 h after his initial presentation to the first hospital. His pupils were equal and reactive, and he was tachycardic and hypertensive. Comprehensive toxicology testing of blood and urine detected only agents used for his treatment. His temperature rose and he had another seizure. He was treated with lorazepam, phenobarbital, sodium bicarbonate, charcoal, and acetaminophen. The patient suddenly developed profound hypotension, which was unresponsive to therapy. Over the next 24 h, he had fluctuating blood pressure but no further seizures and no further signs of neurological activity. A neurological examination was consistent with brain death and life support was ultimately discontinued. The death was due to hypernatremia.

Comments

Hypernatremia is an elevated sodium level in the blood. In this case, the elevated sodium was due to salt poisoning. Table salt is sodium chloride. The initial treatment in this case was symptomatic, focused on seizure control, cardiovascular stabilization, and antidotal therapy for likely drug toxicity because of the history provided by the parents. It was only later that the saltwater ingestion was identified as the causative agent. Toxicity testing for possible drug use was negative. The medical deterioration of the boy was consistent with hypernatremia due to salt poisoning.

Case: Therapeutic Misadventure—Cancer Prevention

In 1998, a 41-year-old woman chewed and swallowed about 30 apricot pits from a bag she had purchased at a health food store. Within 20 min, she became weak and had difficulty breathing and swallowing. Emergency medical responders found her moaning and unresponsive to painful stimuli. She was hypotensive, tachycardiac, dyspenic, diaphoretic, and had pale skin. It was presumed that she was having an anaphylactic reaction and she was treated with oxygen, epinephrine, fluids, corticosteroids, and diphenhydramine. However, her condition remained unchanged while she was transported to a hospital emergency department where an examination revealed that she was likely experiencing cyanide intoxication. This was later confirmed by laboratory testing. Antidotal therapy was initiated and there were immediate signs of improvement. The woman made a complete recovery and was discharged on the third hospital day.

Comments

Apricot pits contain amygdalin, which is a cyanogenic glycoside that releases cyanide when chewed. Products containing amygdalin have been sold under the name Laetrile and promoted as being effective for cancer treatment. The ineffectiveness of Laetrile for cancer therapy has been known for many years. Nevertheless, it continues to be sold in some countries and is available on the Internet. Individuals continue to purchase Laetrile as well as natural sources such as apricot pits, and sporadic cases of cyanide poisoning and death continue to occur.

Case: Button Batteries

In 2009, a 2-year-old bled to death 3 weeks after a button battery lodged in her esophagus. The battery came from a hand-held electronic game. When the girl swallowed the battery, she developed chest pain and was taken to a hospital for X-ray and removal of the battery. She was discharged after 4 days. Fourteen days later she was found on her bathroom floor coughing up blood. She was again rushed to a hospital where, despite aggressive treatment, she bled to death from erosion of her esophagus. The initial corrosive action of the battery had so damaged the esophagus that it ultimately perforated.

Comments

As many as 10% of children who swallow button batteries die. About 3000 people of all ages swallow button batteries each year in the United States. They can be found in many devices that include hearing aids, key fobs, watches, calculators, remote control units, and in musical greeting cards. Batteries lodged in the esophagus can cause severe burns in just 2 h. Within 6 h, the battery can erode through the esophagus or any other organ they are lodged against, and within 8–10 h, they can cause fatal injury.

Case: Poison Lurking in Gardens

In 2004, a 53-year-old woman went to an urgent care clinic because of persistent nausea and vomiting over the preceding day. Her examination revealed that, in addition to her gastrointestinal symptoms she was hypotensive and had a marked decrease in heart rate. From the urgent care facility, she was transferred to a hospital emergency department for an in-depth evaluation. Abnormalities were noted on ECG tracings and laboratory testing disclosed electrolyte imbalances. Her previous medical history and current use of medications did not suggest any explanation for her current condition. Initial concern was for the possibility that she had an acute cardiac infarction, but this concern shifted to a possible exposure to a cardiotoxic drug. There were no apparent issues suggesting recreational drug use or abuse. Initial toxicological screening of serum and urine was negative. Her heart rate remained low, ECG abnormalities were nonspecific, and nausea and vomiting continued. During continued probing of her previous history, it was reported that she had eaten freshly prepared dandelion salad on two occasions prior to the onset of her symptoms. Dandelion leaves in salads are generally considered relatively safe and even an extreme ingestion would not produce cardiotoxicity. Her condition did not improve with symptomatic treatment and about a day after admission, she had a syncopal episode. Diagnostic laboratory and clinical testing were not informative. On the third day of hospitalization, the presence of digoxin in samples of her serum was noted. There was no explanation for this finding and repeated testing confirmed that the finding was not due to laboratory error. Attention was then directed to the possibility of herbal medications that could have been ingested. Eventually, the source of the digoxin was traced to foxglove growing in the woman's garden that she had incorporated into the salad. The lady's symptoms gradually improved and she was discharged on the 9th hospital day.

Comments

The serum immunoassay for digoxin in this case reacted with digitoxin, which is the principal toxic cardiac glycoside in foxglove plants. The clinical symptoms of poisoning with cardiac glycosides from plants can be diverse and misleading and, as in this case, delay diagnosis and treatment.

References and Additional Reading

Bar-Oz B, Levichek Z, Koren G: Medications that can be fatal for a toddler with one tablet or teaspoonful. *Pediatr Drugs*, 6: 123–126, 2004.

Casavant MJ, Fitch JA: Fatal hypernatremia from saltwater used as an emetic. *Clin Toxicol*, 41: 861–863, 2003.

Finkelstein Y, Aks SE, Hutson JR, Juurlink DN, Nguyen P, Dubnov-Raz G, Pollak U, Koren G, Bentur Y: Colchicine poisoning: The dark side of an ancient drug. *Clin Toxicol*, 48: 407–414, 2010.

Friesen MS, Purssell RA, Gair RD: Aluminum toxicity following IV use of oral methadone solution. *Clin Toxicol*, 44: 307–314, 2006.

Greene SL, Dargan PI, Jones AL: Acute poisoning: Understanding 90% of cases in a nutshell. *Postgrad Med*, 81: 204–216, 2005.

Konstantopoulos WM, Ewald MB, Pratt DS: Case 22-2012: A 34-year-old man with intractable vomiting after ingestion of an unknown substance. *N Engl J Med*, 367: 259–268, 2012.

Martin TC, Racque MA: Accidental and non-accidental ingestion of methadone and buprenorphine in childhood: A single center experience, 1999–2009. *Curr Drug Saf*, 6: 12–16, 2011.

Maxwell MJ, Muthu P, Pritty PE: Accidental colchicine overdose. A case report and literature review. *Emerg Med J*, 19:265–267, 2002.

Michael JB, Sztajnkrycer MD: Deadly pediatric poisons: Nine common agents that kill at low doses. *Emerg Med Clin N Am*, 22: 1019–1050, 2004.

Mowry JB, Spyker DA, Brooks DE, Zimmerman A, Schauben JL: 2015 Annual report of the American Association of Poison Control Centers' National Poison Data System (NPDS): 33rd annual report. *Clin Toxicol*, 54: 924–1109, 2016.

Newman LS, Feinberg MW, LeWine HE: A bitter tale. *N Engl J Med*, 351: 594–599, 2004.

Suchard JR, Wallace KL, Gerkin RD: Acute cyanide toxicity caused by apricot kernel ingestion. *Ann Emerg Med*, 32: 742–744, 1998.

Suicidal Poisoning 26

26.1 Introduction

Suicide is a leading cause of death in the United States, and most result from gunshot, hanging, or poisoning. Suicides constitute a significant portion of the cases encountered by forensic investigators and pathologists.

The focus of investigations is to collect sufficient information to allow a distinction between suicides and other manners of death. In many cases, the circumstances are such that the sole basis for differentiating accidental from suicidal deaths is the intent of the deceased. Homicide investigations are often complicated by the misinformation provided by perpetrators. This chapter reviews some features of suicidal poisoning that might facilitate recognition and suggests investigative approaches that could aid in gathering various types of relevant information.

26.2 Exposure Situations and Circumstances

26.2.1 Impulsivity

Suicide may be preceded by deliberation and planning over a period of time, or be more impulsive with only minutes or hours of contemplation. When collecting evidence to construct a possible suicide scenario, one should not be limited by a perceived likelihood that an individual would be unlikely to intentionally self-administer a particular substance with suicidal intent. In suicides having a strong impulsive component, the choice of a toxic substance may be more of an indication of availability rather than cognitive reflection on the toxic features of the substance.

26.2.2 Internet

There are many discussion groups, newsgroups, and suicide methodology sites on the Internet that are directed to individuals contemplating suicide. Some of these provide step-by-step suicide guides as well as emotional support and validation for suicide. Information is available on how to obtain and use toxic substances in a format that allows one to compare the features of different toxicants to one another, and also to rate the efficacy of toxicants and other methods of suicide. These sites are continuously expanding their scope of information and types of assistance provided. Some sites even include editorial help with suicide notes and suggestions for funeral planning.

26.2.3 Poisons

Suicidal poisoning may involve virtually any chemical substance attainable by an individual. This might include medications, household or industrial products, recreational drugs, pesticides, and well-known poisons such as cyanide or arsenic. Usually, these agents are ingested but other routes of administration may be utilized. The range of possible toxic substances employed by individuals with suicidal intent is exhaustive. Illustrative of the heterogeneous scope of substances that might be involved in suicidal deaths is a listing of some of the nonmedication substances that have been self-injected by suicidal individuals (Table 26.1).

For many years, carbon monoxide from various sources was the most commonly employed gas used as a suicidal agent. Other gases are now being encountered in suicidal investigations. These include inert gases, which act by blocking access to oxygen, and reactive gases that prevent utilization of inspired oxygen. Some of the more common gases that have been utilized for suicide are listed in Table 26.2. In the past few years, there has been an

Table 26.1 Substances That Have Been Self-Injected Intravenously with Suicidal Intent

Arsenic
Castor bean extract
Copper sulfate
Charcoal lighter fluid
Fresh flower preservative
Gasoline
Household bleach
Hydrochloric acid
India ink
Insecticides
Insulin
Kerosene
Lamp oil
Lighter fluid
Metallic mercury
Nicotine
Potassium chloride
Snake venom
Sodium cyanide
Toluene

Table 26.2   Suicide Gases

Carbon dioxide
Carbon monoxide
Helium
Hydrogen sulfide
Nitrogen

Table 26.3   Examples of Acidic Products and Sulfur-Containing Products That Produce Hydrogen Sulfide When Combined

Products Containing Acid	Sulfur-Containing Products
Disinfectants	Artist oil paint
Muriatic acid	Bath salts
Stone cleaners	Garden fungicides
Toilet bowl cleaners	Selenium shampoo
Tub and tile cleaners	Some latex paints
	Some pesticides
	Spackling pastes

increase in suicides using hydrogen sulfide generated from combinations of common household products. By combining acidic products with sulfur-containing products in confined spaces, lethal levels of hydrogen sulfide can be produced quickly (Table 26.3). Death from hydrogen sulfide can occur after only a few breaths.

26.3 Investigative Considerations

Many factors are known to influence suicidal thinking and suicidal acts. Influential factors can impact an individual differently at various times in their lives, and at times multiple factors can converge to precipitate suicidal actions. Some potential suicidal precipitation factors are listed in Table 26.4. With the understanding that suicide is complex and that most people confronted by the factors listed do not commit suicide, familiarization with these and other aspects of stressful situations and circumstances can guide investigations and enhance opportunities for acquiring additional relevant information.

Table 26.4   Possible Suicide Precipitating Factors

Alcoholism and substance abuse
Chronic health problems
Chronic pain
Debilitating or terminal illness
Depression and other mental disorders
Discrimination
Dishonor
Experience of violence
Financial issues
Grief
Homelessness
Intimate partner problems
Legal difficulties
Military service issues
Postpartum depression
Recent or pending crisis
Relationship issues
Sexual abuse
Social isolation
Unemployment

26.3.1 Psychotherapeutic Medication

Mental health problems can be a risk factor for suicide, but most individuals with mental health problems do not engage in suicidal behavior or die by suicide. When medications are involved in suicidal investigations, either as a possible cause of overdose death or as a possible precipitating factor due to noncompliance with therapeutic regimens, the role of the medication in the death is not easily addressed. Postmortem toxicology testing results in concert with the autopsy findings, medical and psychological history, and circumstances of the death can lead to an informed opinion regarding the cause of death. However, opinions regarding the state of mind of the deceased based on whether or not prescribed medication was being used are more difficult to address. For example, frequently, individuals who commit suicide have discontinued their medications sometime prior for various reasons. It is possible that had they been appropriately medicated, the suicide would not have occurred. Suicides do occur in individuals receiving appropriate medication, though, and the discontinuation of medication may or may not be a significant factor in determining the manner of death.

26.3.2 Psychological Autopsy

A psychological autopsy is an examination of all available information about a deceased individual to determine the likelihood of suicidal intent. Information is gathered through structured interviews of family members, relatives, friends, and health care professionals, and reviewing records from medical and psychiatric facilities. This information is integrated with the results of the forensic investigation and is evaluated by trained professionals to arrive at a probability for suicidal intention by a deceased individual.

26.3.3 Staging Death Scene

Alteration of death scenes to mislead investigators can be undertaken by perpetrators or others for various reasons. A scene may be staged to make a homicide appear to be an accident or a suicide. In addition, because of the stigma often associated with suicide and the financial implications regarding insurance, suicide scenes may be disguised as accidental or natural deaths. This might be done by the victim or by a well-meaning family member who removes a medication container from the scene. More elaborately, conceived plans involving the deceased individual and friends who witnessed or participated in an end-of-life assisted suicide are also possible.

26.4 Case Studies

Case: Suicidal Alcoholic

In 2002, a 21-year-old male alcoholic living with his parents became progressively more depressed and he spent most of his days sleeping and then staying awake at night. He had been treated with an antidepressant for several months but discontinued taking it because he felt that it was not improving his depression since he had made a suicide attempt while taking the drug. The man's mother regularly checked on him during the night and usually found him awake and acting somewhat appropriately. On the morning of the day he was admitted to the hospital, she noticed that he was slurring his speech and acting strangely. A short time later, he lost consciousness. An empty gin bottle and an empty bottle of nonprescription sleeping tablets (diphenhydramine) were found in his room. Emergency medical responders were called and he was transported to a hospital emergency department. Laboratory tests were initiated that included urine drug screening and plasma ethanol levels. His diagnosis was intentional ethanol intake and diphenhydramine overdose. Several hours after admission, he became extremely agitated and required restraint. The man's condition continued to deteriorate with significant abnormalities in fluid and electrolyte levels as well as cardiovascular instability requiring his transfer to the hospital's intensive care unit for monitoring and aggressive treatment. On hospital day 3, he developed acute renal failure, which necessitated hemodialysis. Laboratory tests indicated that the renal failure resulted from rhabdomyolysis. With continuing dialysis and fluid management, his renal function returned and his overall condition eventually normalized. On hospital day 16, he was transferred to a psychiatric unit for further evaluation and therapy.

Comments

Rhabdomyolysis is a type of muscle tissue breakdown. The components from the injured muscle cells travel through the blood to the kidneys where they lead to kidney failure that can be life-threatening. Many things can produce rhabdomyolysis, including a very large number of drugs. Diphenhydramine is one of these drugs.

Case: Dangerous Working Environment

In 1997, a 45-year-old male employee of a fruit and vegetable packing company was found dead on the floor of a confined room in his workplace. The atmosphere of the room was modified to increase the shelf life of apples. The ambient air contained carbon dioxide (600 ppm) and 3% oxygen. He had no history of psychiatric or medical disorders. Subsequently, a suicide note was discovered in his home that indicated significant marital discord. His autopsy did not reveal injuries or lesions that might explain the death. Toxicology testing revealed an arterial carbon dioxide level of 204 mmHg (normal 40–60) and an oxygen level of 38.6 mmHg (normal 60–95). Death was attributed to asphyxiation caused by carbon dioxide intoxication and oxygen depletion.

Comments

Carbon dioxide deaths usually occur in work-related industrial accidents that take place in the ship holds, large brewing vats, silos, tunnels, and sewer shafts where small amounts of carbon dioxide can be produced and accumulate over a period of time.

Case: Carefully Planned Suicide

In 2003, a 19-year-old woman was found dead in the back seat of her car lying on her back with a helium tank on the floor. A tube connected the tank's valve to a commercial air filter mask coated with a substance to make it impermeable. The mask was sealed over her face with duct tape. There was a warning sign posted on a car window that advised first responders of the presence of a toxic gas within the car. A suicide note and directions for constructing the helium-suicide system were found in the car. An autopsy did not reveal any cause of death other than asphyxiation. Routine toxicology tests were negative.

Comments

Suicide by asphyxiation using helium is a widely promoted method of ending one's life by right-to-die advocates. Helium is available in many party stores where it is sold for use in inflating balloons used in celebrations.

Case: Misguided Solution for Personal Crisis

In 2008, a 50-year-old divorced man living alone in a trailer park was found dead by police who were responding to a suicide threat. The victim was clothed, lying on his bed, with his head in a breathing tent constructed from a plastic milk crate, a shower curtain, and duct tape. A tube from the tent was connected to an industrial cylinder of nitrogen gas. Nearby were suicide notes, a loaded handgun, and instructions for constructing the suicide system. He had been despondent over his divorce, was struggling with sexual identity issues, and was facing charges of child molestation. His autopsy and toxicology testing revealed nothing that would indicate death from anything but nitrogen-induced asphyxia.

Comments

In some locations, efforts have been made to reduce the availability of helium or modify its composition to deter its use for suicide. This has led to recommendations by right-to-die advocates for the use of nitrogen as an alternate inert gas for suicide.

Case: Loss of Refrigeration

In 2004, a 34-year-old man purchased a 100-pound block of dry ice from a local ice house. The dry ice was split into four parts and each piece was packaged in a brown paper bag. The bags were placed in the front seat of the man's pick-up truck. Windows were closed and the air-conditioner system was set to recirculation. After driving approximately one-fourth of a mile, the man had shortness of breath, and breathing difficulty increased as he drove about another mile. He called his wife (who in turn called 911) and pulled off the road and stopped. His wife and emergency responders located the truck and found the man unconscious. As soon as the truck door was opened, the man began to awaken. He ultimately recovered completely. This was an accidental exposure, but it could have had more severe consequences.

Comments

This case illustrates how asphyxia from carbon dioxide released from dry ice can occur in confined spaces. It is interesting to speculate how inexperienced responders might evaluate the situation if the individual was discovered dead in his truck with nothing but a few empty brown paper bags.

Case: Suicide, Homicide, or Product Tampering

In 1989, a high school student grabbed a yogurt from the refrigerator in his New Jersey home and rushed out the door to join his friends who were picking him up for a ride to school. As they drove, the student ate about half of the flavored yogurt before he began convulsing and then sank into a coma from which he never recovered. He died several weeks later after life support was discontinued. After a lengthy investigation, his death was ruled to be a suicide caused by cyanide poisoning. Initially, investigators assumed that the death was the result of random product tampering. Later it was determined that the cyanide was added to the yogurt after it was opened shortly before it was consumed by the teenager. In addition, an empty vial that had contained the cyanide was discovered in household trash outside the house. The chemical form of the cyanide used was accessible to the student in a chemical laboratory where one of his parents worked.

Comments

The investigation of this case involved local authorities as well as the Federal Bureau of Investigation, and findings were evaluated by both the county and state medical examiners as well as by a grand jury. There was no question as to the cause of death being cyanide poisoning but the manner of death being suicide was vigorously contested by the parents of the teenager. They rejected the possibility that the boy's intention was to end his life.

When the possibility of product tampering was initially considered, the manufacturer of the yogurt product involved had the yogurt removed from all retail store shelves in five states. Although this is the usual practice in tampering situations of this nature, it was a significant undertaking in terms of human and monetary resources.

Case: Snake Venom Injection

In 2006, a 14-year-old boy was transported to a hospital emergency department in Texas after he had injected himself with rattlesnake venom. On arrival, he was confused and agitated. His lips and tongue were swollen. His pulse was barely detectable and his blood pressure was too low to be measured. He was immediately intubated and started on IV fluids and medication to raise his blood pressure. He had major hematological abnormalities and was bleeding internally at many sites. Clotting factors and antivenom were administered in an attempt to stem the bleeding and neutralize the snake venom. During this period, he was sedated with lorazepam and morphine and paralyzed with vecuronium. Over about 3 days, his abnormalities approached normal ranges and sedation was slowly reduced and he was extubated. On day 5, he was considered mentally stabilized and transferred to a psychiatric facility. The boy had a history of psychiatric disorders, substance abuse, and two previous suicide attempts with a benzodiazepine overdose and with laceration of his wrist. In this instance, he killed a rattlesnake from a relative's collection, milked venom from the severed head, and injected it into a vein in his arm.

Comments

The symptoms of rattlesnake venom poisoning observed in this case were similar to those described in reports of rattlesnake envenomation into a vein. Envenomations in which fangs directly penetrate veins are exceedingly rare.

Case: Turkey Baster

In 2005, a 48-year-old man was found dead by police in a locked bedroom of a home near Syracuse, New York that he shared with his 39-year-old wife and two daughters. His body was lying on the bed with containers of cranberry juice, brandy, and antifreeze on the nightstand next to the bed. His death was ruled to be suicide from self-administered antifreeze. He was buried next to his wife's previous husband who had died 5 years earlier of an apparent heart attack. The death investigation was continuing after the burial because of evolving evidence that implicated the wife. Her fingerprints were found on the nightstand containers and, surprisingly on a new turkey baster found in the kitchen trash can that contained the husband's DNA on the tip and traces of antifreeze within the baster. She was placed under surveillance and her phone calls were monitored. Subsequently, the body of her first husband was exhumed and it was discovered that he had also died from antifreeze poisoning. At this point, the wife attempted to poison her 20-year-old daughter with drinks containing zolpidem, methylphenidate, and opioids. The daughter was found comatose with a suicide note beside her. The note contained a confession of her killing her father and stepfather. The daughter survived. There was an abundance of evidence that the mother poisoned her daughter and forged the suicide note. The motive for the murders was insurance and other assets. The wife was tried and convicted of murder, attempted murder, and forging her husband's will. She received a sentence of 51 years in prison.

Comments

This case illustrates how easily misinformation provided by the perpetrator can impact the initiation and progress of investigations of apparent suicides. The wife died in prison and continued to maintain her innocence until her death.

Case: Internet-Assisted Suicide

In 2003, a 19-year-old female college student in Florida ingested a lethal amount of cyanide and died alone in a motel room near her school. Prior to her death, she had arranged for delayed e-mail messages to go to her parents and friends. She also had messages to go to the police that described what she had done and where her body was. Unbeknownst to people around her, she had been suicidal for years and was being treated with antidepressant medication. It was determined that she had communicated with members of an online group she had been involved with for a month. This Internet discussion group promoted suicide as a healthy lifestyle choice. The group had provided her with technical information on obtaining cyanide and using it, suggestions for and even the editing and critiquing of the messages sent after her death. She was a very good student and attending an out-of-state university on a full scholarship. She had a boyfriend. Her suicide e-mails to family and friends were lengthy and upbeat and even provided her wishes for music at any memorial services. Her suicide was a complete shock to those who knew her.

Comments

There are many suicide sites on the Internet that provide detailed instructions on methods of suicide. The particular site involved in this case has been accessible for more than 10 years.

Case: Body in Car Trunk

In 2010, an attractive 38-year-old female social worker in San Diego was found dead in the trunk of her locked car. The car was parked on the street of a residential neighborhood several blocks away from the home she shared with her fiancé. Following an investigation, the medical examiner ruled her death as a suicide caused by diphenhydramine and ethanol intoxication. The woman had recently lost her job and was contemplating legal action against her former employer for wrongful termination. The evening before her death, she had a heated argument with her fiancé, which escalated to her being locked out of their home. She left in her car and during the next hour purchased a supply of over-the-counter sleeping pills in two separate transactions. Over the next 3 h, she exchanged text messages with her fiancé and posted a message to her family. The content of the messages pointed to the finality of her life. During this time, she ingested the sleeping pills with four small bottles of wine. Ultimately, she folded down the backseat of her locked car and curled up in the trunk where she was found dead. Items found in the car included empty wine bottles, prescription medications that included an antidepressant, empty sleeping pill containers with dated receipts for their purchases, a dead cellular phone, and a laptop computer.

Comments

The individual involved in this case was a college graduate who worked with abused children and victims of domestic violence. She did volunteer work and had caring friends. She is said to have liked cooking and music. She had attended a party with colleagues 2 days before her death and was remembered as upbeat and excited about her upcoming wedding.

Case: Flower Power Gone Bad

In 2007, a 28-year-old woman was admitted to a Northern Florida hospital's emergency department after she was found unconscious in her home. She was awake and oriented on arrival at the hospital and informed the hospital staff that she had dissolved a fresh-flower preservative packet in water and injected it intravenously. The specific commercial preservative packet was not identified but most of these types of products contain citric acid and a few other ingredients. She had a history of fabricating ailments, had a bipolar disorder, and had been seen in the hospital about 2 weeks earlier with complaints of abdominal pain. Initially, she had mild alterations in vital signs and a few laboratory-testing abnormalities. However, her condition rapidly deteriorated and she became obtunded with hypertension, elevated heart rate, and labored breathing.

Emergency department staff initiated supportive treatment, and the patient was intubated and mechanically ventilated. Her condition continued to decline and she had a cardiac arrest, which was unresponsive to resuscitation attempts. She expired approximately 11 h after injection of the flower preservative. There was some question as to the motive for the self-administration of the flower preservative, and her appreciation of the potential for a lethal outcome. The cause of death was ruled to be due to lactic acid acidosis and diffuse intravascular coagulopathy, and the manner of death was ruled as suicide.

Comments

Floral preservatives usually consist of various mixtures of carbohydrates, acidifying agents, and compounds to reduce bacterial growth. The focus of this case is not on the toxicology and potential lethality of those types of products, but on the use of available products of any nature to self-administrate for various effects. This individual had a history of fabricating medical conditions for medical attention. This injection may have been a misguided attempt to garner attention.

References and Additional Reading

Adcock JM, Chancellor AS: *Death Investigations*. Burlington, MA: Jones & Bartlett, 2013.

Anderson AR: Characterization of chemical suicides in the United States and its adverse impact on responders and bystanders. *West J Emerg Med*, 17: 680–683, 2016.

Arun M, Palimar V, Kumar GNP, Menezes RG: Unusual methods of suicide: Complexities in investigation. *Med Sci Law*, 50: 149–153, 2010.

Botello T, Noguchi T, Sathyavagiswaran L, Weinberger LE, Gross BH: Evolution of the psychological autopsy: Fifty years of experience at the Los Angeles County Chief Medical Examiner-Coroner's Office. *J Forensic Sci*, 58: 924–926, 2013.

Daine K, Hawton K, Singaravelu V, Stewart A, Simkin S, Montgomery P: The power of the web: A systematic review of studies of the influence of the internet on self-harm and suicide in young people. *PLOS One*, 8: 1–8, 2013.

Dedouit F, Tournel G, Robert AB, Dutrieux P, Hedouin V, Gosset D: An apple a day does not always keep the doctor away. *J Forensic Sci*, 53: 1434–1436, 2008.

Demirci S, Dogan KH, Erkol Z, Deniz I: A series of complex suicides. *Am J Forensic Med Pathol*, 30: 152–154, 2009.

Docker C: *Five Last Acts—The Exit Path. The Arts and Science of Rational Suicide in the Face of Unbearable, Unrelievable Suffering*, 2nd ed. Charleston, SC: CreateSpace Independent Publishing, 2010.

Gallagher, KE, Smith DM, Mellen PF: Suicidal asphyxiation by using pure helium gas. Case report, review, and discussion of the influence of the internet. *Am J Forensic Med Pathol*, 24: 361–363, 2003.

Gilson, T, Parks BO, Porterfield CM: Suicide with inert gases. Addendum to Final Exit. *Am J Forensic Med Pathol*, 24: 306–308, 2003.

Gupta A, Pasquale-Styles MA, Helper BR, Isenschmid DS, Schmidt CJ: Apparent suicidal carbon monoxide poisoning with concomitant prescription drug overdoses. *J Anal Toxicol*, 29: 744–749, 2005.

Haas, CE, Magram Y, Mishra A: Rhabdomyolysis and acute renal failure following an ethanol and diphenhydramine overdose. *Ann Pharmacother*, 37: 538–542, 2003.

Harding BE, Wolf BC: Case report of suicide by inhalation of nitrogen gas. *Am J Forensic Med Pathol*, 29: 235–237, 2008.

Howard MO, Hall MT, Edwards JD, Vaughn MG, Perron BE, Winecker RE: Suicide by asphyxiation due to helium inhalation. *Am J Forensic Med Pathol*, 32: 61–70, 2011.

Humphry D: *Final Exit: The Practicalities of Self-Deliverance and Assisted Suicide for the Dying*, 3rd ed. Junction City, OR: Norrise Lane Press, 2002.

Jacobs D, Klein-Benheim M: The psychological autopsy: A useful tool for determining proximate causation in suicide cases. *Bull Am Acad Psychiatry Law*, 23: 165–182, 1995.

Kimball T, Eubank P, Lewis-Yonger C: Flower power gone bad. *Clin Toxicol*, 46: 606–607, 2008.

Klonsky ED, Qui T, Saffer BY: Recent advances in differentiating suicide attempters from suicide ideators. *Curr Opin Psychiatry*, 30: 15–20, 2017.

Loggers ET, Starks H, Shannon-Dudley M, Back AL, Appelbaum FR, Stewart FM: Implementing a death with dignity program at a comprehensive cancer center. *N Engl J Med*, 368: 1417–1424, 2013.

Morgan DL, Blair HW, Ramsey RP: Suicide attempt by the intravenous injection of rattlesnake venom, *South Med J*, 99: 282–284, 2006.

Musshoff F, Hagemeier L, Kirchbaum K, Madea B: Two cases of suicide by asphyxiation due to helium and argon. *Forensic Sci Int*, 223: e27–e30, 2012.

Nine JS, Rund CR: Fatality from diphenhydramine monointoxication: A case report and review of the infant, pediatric, and adult literature. *Am J Forensic Med Pathol*, 27: 36–41, 2006.

Reedy SJ, Schwartz MD, Morgan BW: Suicide fads: Frequency and characteristics of hydrogen sulfide suicides in the United States. *West J Emerg Med*, 12: 300–304, 2011.

Rockett IRH, Smith GS, Caine ED, Kapusta ND, Hanzlick RL, Larkin GL, Naylor CPE, Nolte KB, Miller TR, Putnam SL et al.: Confronting death from drug self-intoxication (DDSI): Prevention through a better definition. *Am J Public Health*, 104: 49–55, 2014.

Sastre C, Baillif-Couniou V, Kintz P, Cirimele V, Bartoli C, Christia-Lotter MA, Piercecchi-Marti MD, Leonetti G, Pelissier-Alicot AL: Fatal accidental hydrogen sulfide poisoning: A domestic case. *J Forensic Sci*, 58: S280–S284, 2013.

Scott CL, Swartz E, Warburton K: The psychological autopsy: Solving the mysteries of death. *Psychiatr Clin N Am*, 29: 805–822, 2006.

Stone G: *Suicide and Attempted Suicide*. Boston, MA: Da Capo Press, 2001.

Timmermans S: Suicide determination and the professional authority of medical examiners. *Am Soc Rev*, 70: 311–333, 2005.

Tucker M, Eichold B, Micher K, Schier J, Belson M, Patel M, Rubin C: Brief report: Acute illness from dry ice exposure during Hurricane Ivan—Alabama. *CDC MMWR*, 53: 1182–1183, 2004.

Wong PW-C, Fu K-W, Yau RS-P, Ma HH-M, Law Y-W, Chang S-S, Yip PS-F: Accessing suicide-related information on the internet: A retrospective observational study of search behavior. *J Med Internet Res*, 15: 1–19, 2013.

Homicidal Poisoning

27

27.1 Introduction

Criminal homicidal poisoning is a murder in which poison is the murder weapon. Poisoning homicides are rare and in some cases likely go undetected. There are a total of about 16,000 homicide deaths reported per year in the United States, and less than 1% of these are the result of intentional poisoning. As the symptoms of poisoning are often difficult to distinguish from those of natural diseases, intentional poisoning deaths can be easily misdiagnosed or attributed to an acute illness. Homicide poisoning deaths can also appear to be accidental or due to suicidal behavior. Beyond the difficulty in diagnosing poisoning deaths, the circumstances surrounding the death may include false information provided by the perpetrator of the crime.

Homicidal poisoning is difficult to investigate and often requires advanced technology and skills, and a significant commitment of investigative resources. This chapter is an overview of some of the main considerations in homicidal death investigations involving poisoning.

27.2 Exposure Situations and Circumstances

Poisons are neither difficult to obtain nor difficult to administer. Novels and television shows often present plausible poisoning scenarios with sufficient detail for individuals to adapt to real-life situations. Fictional poisoning cases generally identify flaws in the murder plan that ultimately leads to the identification and prosecution of the murderer. Some individuals could understandably reason that they could successfully implement the plan if they avoided those flaws.

27.2.1 Poisons

Individual substances used for poisoning homicides have distinguishing properties such as how quickly they act, the symptoms they produce prior to death, and their analytical detectability. These characteristics can provide useful information for investigative purposes. However, sometimes poisons are selected without any consideration of their toxicological features. A rodenticide, for example, might be used to poison someone because it was, in fact, identified on the label as a poison. A particular poison might also be chosen because it happened to be easily accessible. For example, poisoning with therapeutic medications might be selected with little regard for specific mechanisms.

27.2.2 Poisoners

Poisoners are frequently characterized as individuals who are cunning, sneaky, and creative, have superior intelligence, and are likely to be females. These descriptors may very well fit some poisoners, but many poisoners tend to be individuals with ordinary skills and average intelligence. They do not seem to preferentially select exotic or rare substances for poisoning. They usually poison individuals they know or with whom they are in some way connected. Probably the most generalizable feature of poisoners is the desire to eliminate someone for an identifiable reason without being caught. It is especially important to apprehend the individual responsible because of the real possibility that, because a poisoning murder goes undetected, the poisoner gains confidence from the success and later poisons another person.

27.2.3 Poisoning

The circumstances surrounding an individual's death are important determinants in establishing the cause and manner of suspected poisoning deaths. In some cases, a retrospective examination of a decedent's medical history can be enlightening. Some poisoners are known to have experimented with various doses as well as with individual poisons prior to an exposure with a fatal outcome. There could be a history of illness occurring at irregular intervals that reflect this. The illness might have been unexplained or diagnosed as a disease.

Poisonings most frequently involve premeditation and a degree of planning. However, there are cases in which planning might occur rather quickly and the poisoning is somewhat impulsive. For example, someone might simply decide to kill someone and use a convenient poison, such as a rodenticide, as he or she is preparing a meal. Also, individuals may have considered how they might poison someone as a random thought while they were watching television or reading a novel and then, perhaps years later, they encountered some situation or opportunity and acted on that thought.

27.3 Investigative Considerations

27.3.1 Death Investigation

Each jurisdiction has specific requirements regarding the type of death that requires reporting to a medical examiner or a coroner. These would include the following: unexplained or suspicious deaths; accidental, suicidal, and

Table 27.1   Types of Deaths Reported to Medical Examiners

- Sudden, unexplained deaths
- Deaths in individuals not under the care of physicians
- Deaths of individuals who are incarcerated or in police custody
- Deaths due to suicide, homicide, trauma, disaster, or violence
- Deaths due to drowning, suffocation, burns, electrocution, lightning, radiation, chemical exposure, starvation, environmental exposure, or neglect
- Substance abuse fatalities
- Poisoning deaths
- Deaths occurring in institutions that do not have medical personnel
- Deaths of mothers or neonates in known or suspected abortion cases
- Deaths in individuals that occur during the course of a criminal act

Table 27.2   Possible Indicators of Homicidal Poisoning

- Interference with victim's access to medical evaluation or treatment
- Disposal of decedent's food, beverages, or medicines
- Interference with visitations by friends or relatives
- Insistence on no autopsy
- Insistence on rapid cremation
- Inappropriate grieving behavior
- Delayed request for emergency responders or other medical attention
- Attempts to misdirect or obstruct investigation
- Obvious financial incentives
- Conflict within romantic or business relationships
- Evidence of information research on poisons and poisoning

homicidal deaths; and deaths with public health implications. Deaths that are generally reported are listed in Table 27.1. Possible indicators of homicidal poisoning are provided in Table 27.2.

All information associated with the death should be collected. This might include information obtained at the location where the death occurred, records from law enforcement personnel, emergency services responders, medical records from health care facilities and physicians, eyewitness accounts, and interviews with friends, relatives, or others with information relevant to the investigation.

An autopsy of the deceased is carried out to discover any pathological evidence or physical anomalies that might explain why the death occurred. In the case of poisoning, there can be unique pathological findings that are indicative of either a particular toxic substance or more general toxic effects that might be caused by various toxic exposures. There can also be situations in which poison deaths result from functional disturbances that are not evident from anatomical examinations. Findings are evaluated to ascertain whether death was solely the result of poisoning or possibly due to a combination of toxicity and natural disease processes.

The scope of the toxicological testing carried out during death investigations is governed by information regarding the death and autopsy findings. The testing can be somewhat of a standardized screening that is ordinarily done in suspicious deaths, or can be more extensive and targeted if there is something that suggests a particular poison or class of substances. In some death investigations, depending on a variety of factors, there may be no toxicological testing undertaken.

Toxicology testing of tissue samples and fluids collected at the autopsy can specifically identify and quantitate the amounts of substances and, by comparing the findings from samples from various organs and fluids, information may be obtained that suggests the amount of substance involved in the exposure, the time it was absorbed into the circulations, and the likely route by which the substance was administered.

The determination that a death resulted from poisoning is based on a consideration of the circumstances surrounding the death, autopsy findings, and toxicological testing. Other possible causes of the death should be examined and ruled out. The specific poison must be identified and the lethal amount present should be determined. The history of the decedent, the circumstances of the death, and the signs and symptoms that preceded the death should be consistent with death due to the poison. The evidence usually required to support poisoning as the cause of death is summarized in Table 27.3.

A murder investigation should start as soon as the first law enforcement officer becomes aware of a death that is clearly a murder or suspected to be a murder. The investigation then typically expands to include crime scene investigators, a medical examiner, and homicide detectives. It continues until sufficient evidence is collected to support the arrest and prosecution of the individual responsible. When the murder weapon is a poison, there could be a significant time delay before initiating an investigation because a poison

---

Table 27.3   Evidence of Death by Poisoning

- Evidence of toxic exposure and absorption of a specific substance. This generally consists of analytical testing results that identify the toxicant in postmortem blood and tissue samples.
- The degree of exposure was sufficient to cause death.
- The symptoms that preceded death are consistent with those known to be caused by the punitive toxicants.
- Autopsy findings are consistent with death caused by the punitive toxic substance.
- Other possible causes of death are excluded.

---

death may not be immediately recognized or raise suspicions. The involvement of a poison may first be identified through a medical examiner's death investigation and testing.

27.4 Case Studies

Case: Toxic Swine Flu

In 2010, a 2-year-old child from a small town in New York near the Pennsylvania state line was found dead in his crib by his father. Initially, the death was thought to be due to swine flu because of several cases reported in the area weeks prior to the death. No anatomical cause of death was found at autopsy, and both viral and bacterial testing were negative. Toxicological testing of blood, vitreous humor, urine, liver, bile, and gastric contents were negative except for the presence of methanol in all tissues and fluids. This finding initiated an investigation to determine the source and circumstances of exposure to methanol.

In the days preceding the death, the child had been in three homes under the care of eight different adults. Three days before, the child was with his mother in the morning in her home with two other adults, and then he spent the afternoons with his grandparents in their home. Nothing unusual about the child's behavior was noted throughout this day. In the evening of the following day, the child was picked up by his father and stepmother for a scheduled visitation. The child slept during the drive to his father's house and was put to bed on arrival. The next day the child was noticeably lethargic, often stumbling and falling, and he ate little. There were three adults staying in his father's home. By early evening, the child was having difficulty staying awake and was put to bed around 7 p.m. His crib was in a room where the 6-month-old child of the father and stepmother also slept. The following morning around 7 a.m., the child was found dead in his crib.

This history and apparent lack of accessibility to any methanol products at any of the locations where the child spent the preceding days suggested that the child had been intentionally poisoned. The postmortem toxicology findings and an analysis of residual fluid in the child's drinking cup were consistent with a timeline that indicated that the poisoning occurred in the father's home. Computer searches and discussions with friends prior to the death pointed to the stepmother as the likely poisoner. Ultimately, the stepmother admitted to giving the child a beverage containing automobile windshield wiper fluid on the first evening of his visitation to the father's home. She was convicted of first-degree manslaughter and received a 20-year prison sentence plus 5 years probation.

Comments

The toxicity of methanol is due to its metabolites and therefore death can be delayed while metabolism is occurring and the metabolites accumulate. The initial symptoms of poisoning are nonspecific and could include CNS depression, weakness, nausea, and other abnormalities that are commonly produced by many childhood diseases. The complicated history of the days preceding death presented a formidable investigative challenge for unraveling the likely time and place of toxic exposure. The analytical testing process carried out to locate and identify trace amounts of methanol in this case was extraordinary.

Case: Chemistry Lesson

In 1993, a 38-year-old postman living with his daughter in Texas unexpectedly died from what was later ruled to be a heart attack. He had been married to his high school sweetheart, but they had divorced. The divorce seemed to be precipitated by the husband's change in behavior over the years. He had bouts of depression, which made it difficult for him to hold jobs and he started to become jealous of his wife and on occasions became angry for no apparent reason. Their only child lived with the mother following the divorce. Subsequently, the mother married a man who was also divorced and had children of his own who came with him to the new family. Issues developed within this family that resulted in the daughter moving to live with the father. At the time of the father's death, the daughter was a popular teenager finishing high school and about to go to college. On the day of his death, the father picked up some Mexican food on his way home from work for dinner, which he ate with his daughter. After dinner, he went to an evening service at his church. When he returned, he had stomach pains and began to vomit. He became sufficiently ill that his daughter went to a neighbor for help. The neighbor found the father in a very weak condition and having difficulty in breathing because of increasing secretions blocking his airways. The neighbor immediately called for emergency responders who transported him to a hospital near their home. He died shortly after arrival at the hospital.

Following her father's death, the daughter went to live with her grandparents, who lived near her father's home, so she could continue in the same high school. The daughter had a very close relationship with another girl in her class who shared many of her interests and had a similar divorced family situation. One evening toward the end of the school year, the daughter confided to her friend that she had killed her father. Her girlfriend was shocked and related the revelation to her mother who more or less dismissed it and felt that her daughter's friend made the whole thing up for some reason. The girlfriend also discussed what she had been told with a few of her friends who also reacted with disbelief. Eventually she went to a high school counselor and asked that the police be contacted. The police also felt that the story was not believable, but relayed the story to the medical examiner who agreed to have some samples retained from the autopsy undergo more extensive toxicological analysis. For many reasons, this process took months and by the time the results became available the daughter was attending college. The test had shown that the father had died from poisoning by barium. The daughter had taken barium acetate from her high school chemistry laboratory and added it to the refried beans included with the Mexican meal that the father bought for their last evening meal.

Comments

Barium is a highly toxic chemical element. It is used in a number of industrial processes, and it is commonly found in chemical research laboratories in schools and industrial settings. Barium deaths are due to cardiac arrhythmias and respiratory failure caused by respiratory muscle paralysis.

Barium is available in several salt forms that differ significantly in their solubility. Toxicity is almost always associated with the soluble forms. The barium acetate used in this case is a soluble salt. In contrast to the soluble forms, barium sulfate is an insoluble salt and is used in clinical suspensions administered orally as a contrast agent for gastrointestinal diagnostic procedures.

Case: Likely Murder and Obvious Suspect

In 2009, a 47-year-old man living in Christchurch, New Zealand was found dead in his bed. He was discovered by his 50-year-old wife. He had apparently taken his life by ingesting a large amount of medication. In preparation for his suicide, he wrote a note for his wife, and had also texted a message to her indicating that he was having difficulty coping with life. The husband had a history of depression, and some friends and coworkers had noticed that he had recently not been functioning with his usual enthusiastic approach to things. The couple had been married for about 4 years. Both had children from their past relationships. He worked as a driver for a local delivery company. There was a police investigation and an autopsy was performed. The general view from the beginning was that the death was a suicide. However, when all the information regarding the death was reviewed at a coroner's inquest, the conclusion was reached that the evidence was not sufficient to support a finding of suicide. At this point, the police reopened the case as a possible homicide.

Family members, including the wife's parents, had advised the police that they felt very strongly that the wife had killed her husband, but this was apparently ignored by the initial investigation. It was widely known that the wife had on a number of occasions discussed killing her husband. She had discussed drugging him with the idea that he might have a fatal accident while driving, or the possibility of employing another person to kill her husband, the efficiency of suffocating him while he slept, and other ways to rid herself of her husband. These discussions were so open and bizarre that her friends referred to her as the Black Widow. Evidence was subsequently obtained that showed that she had purchased the medication that was used in her husband's overdose.

The wife's criminal history included convictions for theft, false allegations of attempted murder by her son, and attempted murder of her previous partner. The case that was presented at the trial following her arrest was that she had added the contents of many Phenergan capsules to her husband's evening meal. Later when he was sufficiently sedated, she suffocated him with a pillow. She staged the death scene, sent herself the text message, and wrote the suicide note. She was found guilty of murder and sentenced to life imprisonment. The police offered to compensate the family for their investigative negligence. The offer was rejected. The family intends to seek damage for the inept police work through civil lawsuits.

Comments

Apparently inexperienced investigators conducted the initial investigation and formed a theory for the circumstances of the death prematurely; they then proceeded as if there were no other possibilities.

Case: Airman and Veterinarian

In 2005, a 26-year-old unmarried mother of a 2-year-old met a 24-year-old man in a bar in a small town in Texas. They spent the night together; she subsequently became pregnant following that single encounter. This was the third known pregnancy for the woman. She was a veterinarian who had a private clinic in the town, and he was a U.S. Air Force staff sergeant stationed at a nearby base. The couple somewhat reluctantly married, to the surprise and dismay of their families. They had been married for about 4 months when the wife reported him missing to the police and military authorities. She said that he may have deserted because of an upcoming scheduled deployment of his unit to Afghanistan, and that he had likely headed for Canada. The day after she reported him missing, she filed for divorce. The police and the Air Force launched a parallel investigation that initially focused on areas near the veterinary clinic where the man might be hiding. About 2 months later, his body was found submerged in a pond on a ranch in the area where the wife kept horses. The body was weighted with cinder blocks, a boat anchor, and various automobile parts that were all firmly attached with fishing line, wire, rope, and plastic ties. The cause of death was determined to be an overdose of pentobarbital. The body had numerous cuts that were made after the death to allow gases from decomposition to escape, so that the body would not surface. Investigators amassed a considerable amount of evidence implicating the wife as the perpetrator of the homicide. She was arrested and charged with murder and tampering with evidence. She denied any involvement in the killing, and claimed that she had discovered her husband's body and assumed one of her family members had killed him and she hid the body to protect the family member. The wife's mother made no secret of her dislike for her son-in-law and even told police that she hated him. A few days before the wife's trial was to begin she consented to a no-contest plea agreement that stipulated a 25-year prison sentence for the murder charge and two 10-year sentences for evidence-tampering charges, with all the sentences being served concurrently.

Comments

There is very limited availability of pentobarbital for use in clinical medicine. However, injectable formulations of pentobarbital for veterinary use are readily available and widely used.

Case: Fatal Attraction

In 2005, a 24-year-old university student was found dead in her off campus residence in Florida. She was discovered by the police after failing to contact her fiancé who lived in her hometown. Except for an injection site on her arm, the body had no external signs of trauma or other indications suggestive of a cause of death. A grocery store bag containing a syringe and two empty propofol vials was found discarded near garbage cans outside the residence. No abnormalities were found at autopsy. Toxicological testing identified propofol present in blood samples at levels consistent with those expected in fatalities. Due to the distance between the discarded propofol vials and the body, it was not possible for the victim to have self-injected the fast-acting propofol and have discarded the vials. The death was ruled a homicide.

From the lot numbers on the vials found at the death scene, the propofol was traced to a 29-year-old male nurse who worked at a surgical intensive care unit at a nearby medical center. Subsequently, DNA from the male nurse was found on the discarded syringes, which also had traces of the victim's blood.

One day after the body was discovered, the nurse resigned from his position and left the country. An arrest warrant for murder was issued and the nurse was apprehended and extradited to the United States to stand trial for first-degree murder. He was found guilty and sentenced to life in prison without the possibility of parole.

Investigators determined that the nurse had met the victim through a mutual friend a few months prior to the death. Unbeknownst to the victim, the nurse was obsessed with the woman and when he discovered that she got engaged to her long-term boyfriend, he became enraged and planned her death. The woman had chronic migraine headaches and apparently trusted the nurse to relieve her symptoms with propofol.

Comments

It is surprising that this trained medical professional carried out a premeditated murder of this nature and provided such an obvious and incriminating trail of evidence leading directly to himself.

Case: Stepdaughter

In 2008, a 65-year-old man living in a small community in Alabama died in his home of what appeared to be a heart attack. His body had been discovered by his 32-year-old stepdaughter who lived close by with her husband and their two children. Months after the man's burial, investigators obtained toxicology testing results from blood samples collected at the time of the death that indicated the death was likely due to propofol. At this point, a homicide investigation began, which included exhumation, autopsy, and additional toxicology testing. Investigators soon learned that the stepdaughter had been taking money from the decedent's bank accounts and had also been using his wife's identity for credit purchases. Moreover, she was a nurse and worked at an outpatient surgery unit with access to propofol and other drugs. She was arrested and charged with first-degree murder. On the day that her trial began, she pleaded guilty to a lesser charge and was sentenced to 20 years in prison.

Comments

The case that was to be presented at her trial, based on the evidence and expert testimony, was that the deceased received vecuronium and succinylcholine orally and then received a lethal injection of propofol. It is extremely unlikely that these agents would be available to and administered by someone without medical training.

Case: Insulin Homicide

In 2002, the body of an 8-year-old boy was found by a jogger and her dog in a field near the boy's home in a town in Washington State near the Canadian border. The young boy had been missing since the previous evening. He was naked and his hands and feet were bound with duct tape, his mouth was taped, and there were many deep razor blade gashes on his body. He had been beaten and choked. A syringe and an empty insulin vial were found near the body. The death was ruled to be due to acute insulin poisoning. The boy was not a diabetic.

The individual believed to be the last person to have seen the missing boy was a teenage neighbor. When police questioned him, he remembered seeing the missing boy but did not know where he might have gone. After the boy was discovered, police again questioned the teenager who ultimately confessed to the murder and described in detail what he had done. His explanation for the killing was essentially that he considered the boy a pest and a nuisance who had constantly annoyed him.

The teenager had psychiatric problems and had a history of arson, burglary, and theft. At the time of the murder, he was supposedly on court-ordered home confinement and was only permitted to leave to attend school. He was charged with kidnapping and murder. Following conviction of these charges, he was sentenced to life in prison without the possibility of parole.

Comments

Death from an insulin overdose does not occur rapidly. It could take hours before the victim expires. There was an indication on the body of choking and strangulation, and of cutting—all within a rather short period of time. A possible explanation is that the intention was to poison the boy with insulin, but the teenager became impatient with the time it was taking and strangled the child.

Case: Failed Suicide after Pediatric Homicides

In 2000, a 28-year-old licensed practical nurse in Arkansas received the death penalty for the murder of her children, aged 2 and 5 years old. The children were first sedated with amitriptyline (antidepressant) to facilitate intravenous injections of a potassium chloride solution. However, the injections proved to be exceedingly painful to the children and difficult to administer, so she decided to instead smother the children with a pillow. She then ingested a large amount of amitryptyline and injected herself with potassium chloride. Her suicidal overdose was unsuccessful and she was discovered unconscious by a relative about 20 h later. Also discovered was a suicide note.

She had been suffering from severe depression and decided to end her life but was concerned about the fate of her children after she died. In particular, she feared that the children would be separated and raised independently as they had different fathers. She apparently decided that the death of the children provided a better alternative.

Comments

A lethal intravenous dose of potassium chloride produces death by cardiac arrest. Even though the woman was a caregiver in a medical facility, she had limited knowledge about the medications she utilized. She selected the drugs mainly because they were easily available on the last day she worked at the medical facility. Her plan was to sedate the children and then provide a quick, painless death with the potassium; however, she had neither the knowledge nor the skill to carry out the plan.

References and Additional Reading

Adcock JA, Chancellor AS: *Death Investigations*. Burlington, MA: Jones & Bartlett, Learning, 2013.

Ananda S, Shaohua Z, Liang L: Fatal barium chloride poisoning: Four case reports and literature review. *Am J Forensic Med Pathol*, 34: 115–118, 2013.

Battefort F, Dehours E, Vallé B, Hamdaoui A, Bounes V, Ducassé J-L: Suicide attempt by intravenous potassium self-poisoning: A case report. *Case Rep Emerg Med*, #323818, 2012.

Beno JM, Hartman R, Wallace C, Nemeth D, LaPoint S: Homicidal methanol poisoning in a child. *J Anal Tox*, 35: 524–528, 2011.

Bhoelan BS, Stevering CH, Van Der Boog ATJ, Van Der Heyden MAG: Barium toxicity and the role of the potassium inward rectifier current. *Clin Toxicol*, 52: 584–593, 2014.

Cordless C: Criminal poisoning and the psychopathology of the poisoner. *J Forensic Psych*, 1: 213–226, 2008.

Crellin SJ, Katz KD: Pentobarbital toxicity after self-administration of Euthasol veterinary euthanasia. *Case Rep Emerg Med*, : #6270491, 2016.

Fenning D: *A Poisoned Passion*. New York: St. Martin's Press, 2009.

Finnberg A, Junuzovic M, Dragovic L, Ortiz-Reyes R, Hamel M, Davis J, Erickson A: Homicide by poisoning. *Am J Forensic Med Pathol*, 34: 38–42, 2013.

Holstege CP, Neer TM, Saathoff GB, Furbee RB: *Criminal Poisoning: Clinical and Forensic Perspectives*. Sudbury, MA: Jones & Barlett, 2011.

Johnstone RE, Katz RL, Stanley TH: Homicides using muscle relaxants, opioids, and anesthetic drugs: Anesthesiologist assistance in their investigation and prosecution. *Anesthesiology*, 114: 713–716, 2011.

Kirby RR, Colaw JM, Douglas MM: Death from propofol: Accident, suicide, or murder? *Anesth Analg*, 108: 1182–1184, 2009.

Krusz JC, Scott V, Belanger J: Intravenous propofol: Unique effectiveness in treating intractable migraine. *Headache*, 40: 224–230, 2000.

Marks V: Murder by insulin: Suspected, purported and proven—A review. *Drug Test Analysis*, 1: 162–176, 2009.

Pettler LG: *Crime Scene Staging Dynamics in Homicide Cases.* Boca Raton, FL: CRC Press, 2016.

Shepherd G, Ferslew BC: Homicidal poisoning deaths in the United States 1999–2005. *Clin Toxicol*, 47: 342–347, 2009.

Sibbald KN, Holstege CP, Furbee B, Neer T, Saathoff GB: Homicidal poisoning in the United States: An analysis of the Federal Bureau of Investigation Uniform Crime Reports from 2000–2009. *Clin Toxicol*, 49: 568–569, 2011.

Steck-Flynn K: Just a pinch of cyanide: The basics of homicidal poisoning investigations. *Law Enforcement Technol*, 34: 118–126, 2007.

Trestrail JH: *Criminal Poisoning: Investigational Guide for Law Enforcement, Toxicologists, Forensic Scientists, and Attorneys,* 2nd ed. Totowa, NJ: Humana Press, 2007.

U.S. Department of Justice, Office of Justice Programs, National Institute of Justice: *Death Investigation: A Guide for the Scene Investigator.* Washington, DC: Technical Update, June 2011.

Westveer AE, Jarvis JP, Jensen CJ: Homicidal poisoning: The silent offence. *FBI Law Inforcement Bull*, 73: 1–3, 2004.

Poisonous Women

28

28.1 Introduction

Poisoning is often portrayed as the work of evil, cunning, secretive, and physically weak women. The evil, cunning, secretive, and physically weak men are generally assigned more violent tools for killing, such as guns, knives, or strangulation. In fact, poisoning is not a gender-specific murder weapon. Individuals who choose poisons to kill are most often interested primarily in eliminating someone from their lives without getting caught. This appears to be the defining characteristic attracting both men and women to employ poison as a murder weapon. Poisons provide the possibility of a murder being undetected with the death mistakenly attributed to natural causes. The similarities between men and women who kill their victims with poison are greater than their differences. There are likely major differences in the psychological characteristics and motives that bring men and women to the point of taking the life of another individual, but the methodology employed to accomplish this appears to be a pragmatic consideration based on their individual perception of factors that maximize the chances of eluding authorities.

The focus of this chapter is on women poisoners. It seems that even though women are portrayed as the most likely to poison and should be prime suspects, they are able to commit remarkable murders, sometimes involving several victims, and escape detection for long periods. The reason they are able to avoid apprehension probably lies not in failure to consider women as suspects but in failure to consider the deaths as possible homicides. The case studies presented were chosen to represent a spectrum of women poisoners with various levels of intelligence and education, and provide examples of poisoning in a variety of social situations. Emphasis is placed on the particular toxicant each of these women used to kill their victims and, where possible, how it was selected and acquired.

28.2 Exposure Situations and Circumstances

In their traditional roles as caregivers and food providers in family settings, women occupy an advantageous position in terms of criminal poisoning. This can provide access to individuals and facilitate chronic poisoning and experimentation with various substances. Poisons may be included in food or beverages at varying intervals and in varying amounts. Chronic poisoning may be intentional to create the appearance of a lingering illness rather than an unexpected sudden death. Food items can also be used for poisoning victims outside the home through common practices such as taking food to institutionalized individuals, or gifting specialty food items.

28.3 Case Studies

Case: Blanche

In 1965, 18-year-old Blanche married James to escape the abuse of her alcoholic father. They had two children. During the marriage, Blanche worked in a supermarket where she had a series of affairs with coworkers and supervisors. In 1966, Blanche attempted to reconcile her differences with her father and visited him when he became ill with a lingering cardiovascular disorder. She nursed and comforted him until he died of a heart attack fostered by chronic emphysema. Blanche was very active in her church and also devoted much of her time to caring for her bedridden mother-in-law. Her mother-in-law eventually died and, not long after that death, Blanche's husband died while hospitalized for treatment of a rare neurological disease known as Guillain–Barré syndrome. His health had fluctuated for about 3 months until he died from renal and respiratory failure. Throughout her husband's long illness, Blanche maintained a long-time affair with a coworker who had left his wife and children to be with Blanche. He moved into a small apartment and Blanche visited him every morning to prepare his breakfast.

In 1989, Blanche married the pastor of her church. While returning from their honeymoon, the pastor became ill and was hospitalized for what doctors believed to be a viral infection. His condition improved and he was discharged. A few days later, his symptoms returned and were more intense. He was again hospitalized and underwent a battery of tests including toxicology screening. Testing revealed that he had received a large dose of arsenic. This resulted in a police investigation. The pastor survived but sustained permanent neurological damage. The investigation progressed to a point where the bodies of Blanche's husband, her lover, her father, and her mother-in-law were exhumed; all were found to contain large amounts of arsenic. Blanche was arrested, tried, and convicted of murder and sentenced to death by lethal injection. It was shown that Blanche had poisoned her victims with arsenic from a rat poison product that she added to their food. The food included milkshakes that she took to hospitals when she visited.

Comments

Arsenic is tasteless and odorless, and it is deadly in small doses. Depending on the doses and frequency of administration, the symptoms of arsenic poisoning are quite diverse and can result from dysfunction of many organ systems. This broad spectrum of symptoms can easily be attributed to a variety of natural illnesses. The difficulty in distinguishing arsenic poisoning from a host of medical disorders is illustrated in this case.

Case: Cruel and Callous Wife

Angelina met her fourth husband, Frank, in Montebello, California in February 2000. They married in April. He was 41 and she was 32. In July, she urged Frank to purchase a $250,000 life insurance policy with her as the sole beneficiary. In August, she started an affair with an old friend. In September, Frank became ill and was taken to a local emergency room for treatment. Two days later, Frank died from ethylene glycol poisoning. Angelina was arrested, tried, and convicted of murder, and sentenced to death. She had initially tried to kill her husband with oleander plants, but when that failed, she used antifreeze (ethylene glycol). Her motive was life insurance. Records indicate that at around 10 a.m. on the morning of her husband's death she contacted her insurance company to inquire about getting the settlement for her husband's death. During the investigation of her husband's murder, it was determined that she had killed her 13-month-old baby years earlier by choking it with a pacifier. She subsequently brought a suit against the manufacturer of the pacifier and received a $710,000 settlement. As she did in the case of her husband, she had purchased life insurance for the child months before the death.

Comments

Angelina was an angry, hostile woman throughout her trial and challenged the judge at times. She continues to deny her guilt even though legal authorities consider that it was proven with absolute certainty.

Case: Disturbed and Distressed Wife

With her fourth marriage in crisis, 61-year-old Australian Annemarie was a woman on the verge of a nervous breakdown. Not knowing whom to turn to, she approached a clairvoyant for advice. Included in the reading she received were some suggestions that her husband would not enjoy a long life. In her unstable state, Annemarie took this as an instruction to kill him. She decided to poison him with oleander. After purchasing several plants from the local garden store, she boiled the roots and leaves and added the resulting extract to her husband's coffee and orange juice on several occasions. The poison produced severe toxicity but, torn between a cold-hearted killer and a dutiful wife, she nursed her husband back to health after each dose. Severely troubled by her dilemma, she turned to a neighbor for comfort. The neighbor alerted police, and she was arrested and charged with attempted homicide. At trial, the judge acknowledged her deteriorated mental state and borderline personality disorder and treated her crime leniently. She was sentenced to 4 years in jail for administering an injurious substance likely to endanger life.

Comments

Oleander is an attractive ornamental plant and a deadly poison. The plant contains cardiac glycosides, which produce toxic changes in the gastrointestinal system and life-threatening cardiac arrhythmias.

Case: Romantic Toxicologist

Kristin was an attractive blonde with a promising future who worked as a toxicologist in the laboratories of the medical examiner in a major city in California. She had graduated with honors from a state university with a degree in chemistry. Her husband was a researcher in a local university laboratory. In 2000, Kristin called 911 to report that her husband was unconscious and she was unable to rouse him. When police and medical emergency responders arrived, they found her husband dead and covered with rose petals. A wedding picture was close by. Kristin told authorities that she had recently informed her husband that she wanted a divorce and believed that, in response to this news, he committed suicide. The forensic death investigation revealed that her husband died from an overdose of fentanyl. Subsequent investigation revealed that Kristin was an active methamphetamine addict, was having an affair with her married boss who was an expert on fentanyl, and that both methamphetamine and fentanyl were missing from the laboratory where she worked. Kristin was charged with first-degree murder, tried, and subsequently sentenced to life in prison without parole. It was speculated that Kristin had likely sedated her husband with clonazepam and oxycodone and then injected him with fentanyl. She knew that fentanyl was not a drug typically included in toxicology testing. The rose petals found on the body were likely related to scenes from her favorite movie: *American Beauty*. Although she indicated that the rose petals were likely a romantic gesture conceived by her husband to demonstrate his dying love for her, evidence was obtained that indicated she had purchased a red rose from a local supermarket on the day of the death. After losing his job at the medical examiner's office, her lover left the United States. He has repeatedly denied any involvement in the murder. The investigation into his involvement remains open and there is an arrest warrant filed against him for conspiracy to commit an act injurious to the public. Presumably, if he returns to the United States, he would be arrested and face this charge, which carries a possible prison sentence of 3 years.

Comments

Kristin was aware that toxicology testing likely to be carried out by the medical examiner's laboratory where she worked would not include tests for fentanyl. However, because of her relationship with the deceased, the medical examiner felt that testing should be carried out by an independent laboratory. The scope of testing by the selected laboratory included fentanyl and these findings initiated the homicide investigation.

Case: Spousal Terrorism

Carol was a microbiologist who worked in a research laboratory. She became enraged when she learned that her husband was the father of her best friend's baby. She expressed her rage by applying caustic chemicals to surfaces such as door handles and mailboxes that her husband's mistress would likely touch. No serious injuries resulted from the chemicals and authorities initially reacted by treating the incidents as forms of aggravated domestic problems. Eventually, several law enforcement agencies became involved and the incidents seemed to escalate in importance. After authorities videotaped her applying chemicals to mailboxes on numerous occasions, she was indicted by a Federal Grand Jury for using a chemical weapon in violation of a federal anti-terrorism law. She pleaded guilty to the charges and was sentenced to 6 years in prison. The wisdom of dealing with this crime by applying federal chemical weapons terrorism laws generated considerable criticism from lawyers and a number of government agencies. Through appeals, this case rose to the level of the United States Supreme Court, which issued a unanimous ruling in 2014 that the chemical weapons charge did not apply to Carol's poisoning of a woman who slept with her husband.

Comments

Infidelity, anger, revenge, and poisoning are not trivial matters, but they are also not terrorism.

Case: Poisoned Kiss

Xia and Mao were long-term lovers in the central province of Henan in China and had entered into a pact that stipulated that if either one of them cheated on the other, the unfaithful individual would have to die. When Xia found that Mao had been unfaithful, she decided to poison him. She filled a small capsule with an extremely toxic rat poison and, immediately before they had their next meeting, hid the capsule in her mouth. When they kissed, she maneuvered the capsule into his mouth. He swallowed the capsule and died a short time later. Xia was tried for murder in 2007 and sentenced to death.

Comments

Rodenticides are common substances employed for murder and suicide in China. The specific poison in this case was tetramine. It is considerably more toxic to humans than cyanide. The human lethal dose is less than 10 mg. On account of its extreme toxicity, tetramine has been banned worldwide. Despite the ban, sporadic cases continue to be reported in China and other countries including the United States. The potential for tetramine to be used as a chemical weapon has not gone unnoticed by terrorists or security professionals. This substance is tasteless, odorless, soluble in liquids, and is extremely lethal in small amounts.

Case: The Curry Killer

In 2009, a 45-year-old woman living in London with her husband and three children poisoned her young lover after he ended their 16-year extramarital affair to marry a younger woman. She went to her former lover's home while he was away and added aconite (seeds of the monkshood plant) to a curry stew that he and his fiancée were planning to have for dinner that evening. Following their meal, the couple became violently ill and they were rushed to a hospital. He died shortly after arrival; his fiancée survived. The police investigation of the poisonings uncovered the couple's long affair, which had included two abortions during their years together. Ultimately, the woman was arrested and tried for murder and grievous bodily harm. She was convicted and sentenced to life in prison.

Comments

Aconite is a constituent of a flowering plant commonly known as monkshood (*Aconitum napellus*). All parts of the plant are extremely poisonous. Symptoms of poisoning usually appear within 2 h and include numbness in the mouth, dizziness, intense pain, and generalized muscle weakness.

There is also vomiting, nausea, and diarrhea. Death is caused by respiratory failure or cardiovascular collapse.

Case: Toxic Medical Love Triangle

In 2014, a 43-year-old female physician was found guilty of poisoning her 50-year-old physician lover. Both were oncologists working in a world-class cancer treatment center in Texas. Their affair began in 2011 and continued while the male physician maintained a long-term relationship with another woman. Subsequently, he attempted to terminate the newer relationship when his partner became pregnant. During this period, the newer interest invited him to her home for a special coffee blend that she wanted him to taste. He drank two cups of coffee despite its unusually sweet flavor, which he disliked. A short time later, he became disoriented and started to have difficulty in walking and talking. This progressed quickly and resulted in his admission to the hospital emergency department where he was treated for renal failure with cardiopulmonary complications. This was diagnosed quickly as ethylene glycol poisoning. He recovered after appropriate treatment that included hemodialysis, but he sustained permanent kidney damage. An investigation resulted in an arrest of the physician with charges of aggravated assault. A significant amount of damaging evidence was obtained from over 5 h of recorded phone messages between the physician and the victim following the poisoning. Her conviction led to the permanent loss of her license to practice medicine and a prison sentence of 10 years.

Comments

Ethylene glycol is a sweet-tasting liquid solvent that is commonly used in hospital laboratories. It is also the primary ingredient in most automotive antifreeze products. Following the ingestion of the coffee containing ethylene glycol, the physician experienced increasingly more severe symptoms throughout the day. He first experienced slurred speech, poor balance, and loss of fine motor skills. When he was admitted to the hospital, he was diagnosed with central nervous system depression, cardiopulmonary complications, and renal failure.

Case: Mother and Daughter Poisoners

In 2012, Diane was 50 years old and her husband was 61 years old. They lived in a small town in Missouri with their four children. Diane was a nurse and worked as a clinical supervisor for a medical insurance company and her husband performed in a local band. Following a short illness, her husband died. His death was ruled to be due to natural causes and no autopsy was performed. A few months after the death, the family moved to another section of the town. It was here, 5 months after the father's death that her 26-year-old son died after a short illness. Nothing seemed suspicious and the death was also ruled to be due to natural causes and no autopsy was performed. Two months later, her 23-year-old daughter suddenly became ill and was hospitalized. About this time, authorities received an anonymous tip that questioned the two deaths and the daughter's illness, all of whom were previously in good health. The physicians treating the daughter were also suspicious and suspected poisoning. Authorities then questioned Diane about these issues and this led to her confession. She admitted that she had added antifreeze to Gatorade and cola drinks that she gave to her husband and children. Diane stated that she killed her husband because *she hated him* and her son because he was *worse than a pest* and she wanted to kill her daughter because she *would not get a job*. The poisoned daughter survived but had permanent neurological damage. The remaining daughters, 20 and 9 years old, had not been poisoned; however, when the 20-year-old daughter was confronted with the evidence of her mother's guilt, she admitted to participating. Diane and this daughter had planned, researched, and committed the crimes together. Both were charged with first-degree murder and assault. The daughter pleaded guilty to two counts of second-degree murder and assault charges and received two concurrent 30-year sentences followed by two concurrent 20-year sentences. The sentences were contingent on the daughter testifying at her mother's trial. Diane pleaded guilty to first-degree murder and assault charges and was sentenced to life in prison without parole.

Comments

The mother and daughter planned the murders for at least a year prior to the husband's death. The plan included killing the father and three children. Antifreeze was chosen because of its sweet taste, which facilitated mixing with beverages.

Case: Audrey

Audrey was born in 1933 in a small town in Alabama. At 12, she was elected the prettiest girl in her junior high school class. At 17, she married Frank. At 19, her son Michael was born, and at 26 her daughter Carol was born.

When Audrey was 41, Frank developed what appeared to be a viral gastroenteritis. Audrey treated Frank with injections of medications that she allegedly obtained from a friend who was a nurse. Frank's symptoms intensified and he was hospitalized. He died 2 days later. Based on his symptoms prior to death and the results of an autopsy, the cause of death was listed as infectious hepatitis. No postmortem toxicology testing was done. Audrey used most of Frank's life insurance to buy a car, a motorcycle, and new furniture for the entire house.

At 43, Audrey's home, which was insured, was destroyed by fire. At about the same time, her mother died from cancer. Until her mother's death, Audrey had been nursing her mother with injections of analgesics. Audrey was the beneficiary of her mother's insurance. Three years after Frank's death, Audrey obtained life insurance for her daughter, Carol. A few months later, Carol began having violent bouts of nausea and was eventually hospitalized when symptoms progressed to include numbness of her extremities. Audrey treated her daughter with injections of anti-nausea mediation prior to hospitalization and while hospitalized. During the last of several hospitalizations, toxicology testing revealed that Carol's symptoms were due to chronic arsenic poisoning. This initiated a forensic investigation that included the exhumation of Frank's body and the discovery that his death was due to chronic arsenic poisoning. Subsequently, Audrey was indicted for the murder of her husband and the attempted murder of her daughter. While free on bail and awaiting trial, Audrey disappeared. She eluded authorities for about 3 years by changing her identity, moving to different states, and marrying a man she met in a bar during her travels. When she staged the death of one of her assumed identities, the information provided for a newspaper obituary was questioned and aroused the suspicion of the authorities. She was questioned and ultimately confessed to being the missing fugitive. Audrey was tried, convicted, and sentenced to life in prison. After 4 years as a model prisoner, Audrey was able to escape. She was found 4 days later in a wooded area suffering from exposure to freezing rain; she died in a hospital that same day from a cardiac arrest. She was 53.

Comments

Testing of hair and toenail samples indicated that both the husband and daughter had been poisoned with increasing doses of arsenic for months. It was not clear where the syringes used for the injections originated, but the arsenic was believed to have come from an arsenic-containing rodenticide that was found in the woman's home.

References and Additional Reading

Anthes E: Lady killers. *The New Yorker,* May 9, 2015.

Ginsburg P: *Poisoned Blood.* New York: Charles Scribner's Sons, 1988.

Keefe PR: Did a murderer in waiting go undetected because she was a woman? *The New Yorker,* February 14, 2013.

Mann CR: *When Women Kill.* Albany, NY: SUNY Press, 1996.

Rother, C: *Poisoned Love.* New York: Pinnacle, 2005.

Schurman-Kauflin, D: *The New Predator: Women Who Kill.* New York: Algora Publishing, 2000.

Schutz, J: *Preacher's Girl: The Life and Crimes of Blanche Taylor Moore.* New York: William Morrow, 1993.

Scrine C: "More deadly than the male": The sexual politics of female poisoning: Trials of the thallium women. *LIMINA,* 8: 127–143, 2002.

Swatt ML, He NP: Exploring the differences between male and female intimate partner homicides: Revisiting the concept of situated transactions. *Homicide Stud,* 10: 279–292, 2006.

Zhang Y, Su M, Tian DP: Tetramine poisoning: A case report and review of the literature. *Forensic Sci Int,* 204: 24–27, 2011.

Health Care Serial Poisoners

29

29.1 Introduction

There are case studies of poisoning murders provided in other chapters of this book that involve health care professionals as perpetrators and as victims. They involved murders committed outside of a health care setting, and the individuals were not in a caregiver–patient relationship. The focus of this chapter is on health care providers who poison multiple patients in the course of their regular professional practice, most often in treatment facilities. The poisoners in the majority of the reported cases are nurses, but they include physicians, specialized treatment technicians, orderlies, and other individuals who have regular access to patients and can administer poisons while performing their normal care-giving duties.

29.2 Exposure Situations and Circumstances

Sudden unexpected deaths are always of concern to health care supervisors and administrators. When they occur, the possibility of intentional homicide is not usually among the potential explanations that might be pursued. Generally, disease processes follow a predictable clinical course that is familiar to the health care providers in dealing with patients under their care who die. When deviations from the expected course occur, it should signal concern and a search for an explanation. However, sometimes, in the complicated and demanding delivery of health care to patients with serious conditions requiring hospitalization, the time and resources available to routinely explore in-depth the occasional patient anomaly may not be available.

Intentional hospital homicides perpetuated by health care providers are exceedingly difficult to detect. Unless there is some very unusual basis for considering otherwise, an unexpected death is likely to be attributed to a medical aberration or some unrecognized underlying medical condition. When deaths occur regularly or in clusters, suspicions leading to a more formal examination of the circumstances are likely to be initiated. Even when

Table 29.1 Examples of Medications Utilized by Serial Healthcare Poisoners

Medication	Lethal Effect
Digoxin	Cardiac arrhythmia
Epinephrine	Cardiac arrest
Insulin	Diabetic coma
Lidocaine	Seizure/respiratory arrest
Opioids	Respiratory failure
Pancuronium	Muscle paralysis and respiratory failure
Potassium chloride	Cardiac arrest
Rocuronium	Muscle paralysis and respiratory failure
Succinylcholine	Muscle paralysis and respiratory failure

the real possibility of a serial health care murderer is addressed, it is very difficult to pinpoint a likely suspect.

Deaths in hospitals are expected to occur in some patients with life-threatening disorders who are unresponsive to therapeutic intervention. Hospital deaths also occur due to medical errors. Some of these deaths may come to the attention of forensic investigators. The number of intentional homicidal deaths from serial health care poisoners is small compared to the backdrop of deaths that occur for other reasons. The point here is to emphasize the difficulty in identifying and investigating these deaths.

Some of the medications that have been utilized by health care serial poisoners are shown in Table 29.1. The agents are generally administered by injection through existing patient IV lines. Although the medications are often selected because of their assured lethality in a relatively short period of time, there are cases in which medications already being administered to the patient as part of their medical treatment program were administered in larger toxic doses, or doses of several drugs comprising the patient's therapeutic medications were individually increased such that the mixture became lethal.

The motives of health care poisoners are complex and often remain mysterious. In most cases, there can be clear indicators of unusual behavior reflecting deep-seated mental disorders, as well as cases of psychopathic individuals who perform and behave in ways that do not suggest anything unusual, and can even be admired by coworkers. Some possible motivations that have been postulated to explain some cases of medical homicide are listed in Table 29.2.

Table 29.2 Possible Motives of Health Care Serial Killers

- Attention seeking
- Elimination of demanding or annoying patients
- Elimination of perceived inferiors
- Experimentation
- Financial or material gain
- Manifestation of mental disorder
- Pleasure, excitement, or thrill
- Power and control
- Relieve suffering

29.3 Investigative Considerations

The investigation of health care serial poisoning is usually a multidisciplinary effort that is resource intensive. Volumes of medical records from many patients will need to be reviewed by individuals having both the medical expertise and the investigative training. They need to be able to identify information that might be relevant for a developing picture of the actions of a serial killer who dispatched an unknown number of victims, over an unknown period of time, in possibly several institutions that could be in different jurisdictions. Investigations are almost always initiated long after the deaths have occurred and the victims have been buried or cremated.

Since the murders and related crimes in serial health care poisoning cases generally occur in an institutional setting, there is usually significant criminal and civil liability associated with the parent organization and the management of the institution. This can further complicate an investigation.

29.4 Case Studies

Case: Charles—Nurse Terminated Rather than Investigated

In 2003, Charles confessed to killing more than 40 patients in different hospitals where he worked as a nurse. The hospitals were located in Pennsylvania and New Jersey, and the killings were carried out over a period of about 16 years. Charles dropped out of high school and enlisted in the United States Navy where he served aboard a submarine and a supply ship for about 6 years until his discharge in 1984. He then attended nursing school. In 1987, he started his first hospital job in New Jersey. He married that same year and ultimately fathered two children. He started poisoning patients in 1988. Around this time he began changing jobs frequently because of conflicts with employers due to suspicious behaviors and questionable nursing practices. He had a troubled marriage and his wife ultimately filed domestic violence complaints against him and they were divorced in 1993. Charles had a long history of depression, suicidal behaviors, alcoholism, treatment in psychiatric facilities, bizarre antisocial behavior, and was generally considered as an individual with serious mental disturbances. Despite this, he was able to keep his nursing license and obtain nursing jobs at hospitals where he poisoned dozens of patients.

In 2003, pharmacy personnel in the hospital where Charles worked consulted the regional poison center about the possibility of herbal tea products containing cardiac glycosides in amounts that could be fatal when consumed in excessive amounts. The hospital pharmacist was attempting to explain a nearly fatal digoxin overdose in a patient who was not receiving digoxin as part of her therapy in the hospital. The herbal tea was ruled out as a possibility, but the inquiry tied in with another similar consultation a short time later, which also pertained to an unexplained digoxin overdose. On further discussion between the hospital pharmacist and poison center staff, it became known that two other unexplained incidents involving overdoses had also occurred, and all the patients involved were being treated in the same intensive care unit. The medical director of the poison center contacted senior hospital officials and discussed the implications of the poisonings and the necessity of an investigation that included law enforcement inquiries. Months passed and several more suspicious deaths occurred before hospital administrators contacted police who initiated a criminal homicide investigation.

Comments

The perpetrator in this case had demonstrated many observable features of mental instability and worked in positions involving critical medical care where he was associated with unexpected fatalities. There were hospitals that suspected that the nurse was harming or killing patients but failed to take appropriate action.

Case: Kristen—Nurse Enjoyed Excitement of Poisoning

In 2001, a former nurse of a Veterans Affairs Hospital in Massachusetts was convicted of four murders and two attempted murders of patients under her care at the hospital. She was suspected of killing many more patients. She was sentenced to 4 consecutive life terms without the possibility of parole plus 20 years.

This nurse was married and had two children. She was admired by many friends and coworkers and was highly skilled in nursing. Her superiors gave her high ratings and noted that she performed especially well in medical emergency situations. She often organized social functions for birthdays and other holidays and seemed to be generally interested in group activities. Something changed after a few years of marriage and Kristen eventually left her husband and children and became seriously involved with another man who worked at the hospital. Coworkers also began to take notice of the increasing number of patients who died whenever she was working. She was associated with most of the emergency codes that occurred and more than half of all the hospital deaths occurred on her ward. It also came to light that stocks of epinephrine ampoules continued to be depleted and replaced even though there was no documented use of these ampoules for patients. These ampoules contained unit doses of epinephrine that were used for filling syringes for administration to patients. Epinephrine was used in emergency situations in the hospital, but it was always from commercially prefilled syringes.

Comments

Epinephrine is used primarily for the treatment of allergic reactions and for cardiac resuscitation. In this case, epinephrine was used to create a severe cardiovascular emergency situation, which resulted in emergency resuscitation efforts that would include the administration of more epinephrine, resulting in a fatal overdose.

Case: Kimberly—Nurse Poisons Annoying Patients

In 2008, an official of an emergency services department of a town in Texas near Houston wrote to the State Health Department about a dialysis clinic that was requesting emergency services at an alarming frequency. In the preceding month, paramedics had been called about 30 times and had transported 16 patients with cardiac issues to hospitals; 4 of the patients had died. In the previous year, there were only two calls from the dialysis center. An investigation was initiated almost immediately by health authorities and the dialysis clinic administrators. However, even before investigators had time to gather much information, two patients at the dialysis clinic observed 34-year-old Kimberly filling syringes with common cleaning bleach (sodium hypochlorite) and injecting the bleach into the dialysis lines of two patients. She was quickly fired and arrested, then charged with murder. In 2012, she was found guilty of the murders of five dialysis patients and injuring five others. She was sentenced to life imprisonment for the murders and

60 years for aggravated assault. It is believed that she injured or killed more patients than those named in her indictment.

Kimberly was a licensed practical nurse and had been working at the clinic for 8 months. She was married and had two children. She was a drug abuser and had been fired at least four times from previous jobs in health care facilities. Her history included public intoxication and various forms of domestic disturbances.

Comments

Since dialysis treatment involves direct contact of blood from patients with the dialysis filtrating system, it is extremely important that the dialysis machines and the associated tubing connections be clean and sterile. Accordingly, between uses by different patients, the equipment is thoroughly cleaned and disinfected and then tested to insure that the cleaning process was effective and no residual cleaning materials are present prior to use. Regular household bleach (3%–8% sodium hypochlorite) is very safe and effective for this task when used appropriately. In an emergency, household bleach can even be used to purify drinking water (usually about 1/2 teaspoonful per 5 gallons of water). Children swallowing a mouthful of bleach is a common occurrence reported to poison control centers, but it is very rare for someone to swallow enough to require medical treatment. The injection of bleach directly into the circulatory system is quite another matter. There have been other incidents of bleach poisoning in dialysis patients that has resulted from accidental as well as deliberate contamination. In almost all cases, testing safeguards have prevented patient exposure to bleach.

Case: Efren—Respiratory Therapist Killed Patients

In 2002, a 32-year-old respiratory therapist, who had been working in a large hospital in a Los Angeles suburb, pleaded guilty to murdering six elderly patients. He was sentenced to seven consecutive life sentences. He had previously confessed to killing more than 40 patients over an 8-year period. He killed most often by restricting the oxygen supply to ventilators or injecting muscle paralyzing agents (succinylcholine, pancuronium), which would prevent breathing. Almost 200 of the deaths that occurred while the therapist was working were reviewed by investigators, but only 20 bodies were exhumed for toxicological testing. Of these, evidence of poisoning was found in the remains of six patients. His victims were almost always elderly and usually seriously ill. There had been rumors within the hospital for some time about the therapist engaging in mercy killing or hastening death in patients likely to die soon of natural causes.

Comments

Efren killed patients at three different hospitals. At the hospital where he worked prior to his arrest 1050 patients died. All deaths were attributed to natural causes. In his last 2 years there, 171 patients died and of those 54 had been cremated. From the buried patients, 20 were selected for exhumation and toxicological analysis. Unexplained traces of Pavulon (pancuronium bromide) were found in six patients who had died while Efren was working. This evidence was the basis of the murder charges to which he pleaded guilty.

Case: Donald—Nurse's Aide Poisoned Patients, Friends, and Co-workers

Donald was arrested in Kentucky in 1987 and charged with multiple murders. He was 35 years old and had killed more than 50 people since his first victim in 1970 when he was 18. He is currently serving multiple life sentences in an Ohio prison.

Donald dropped out of high school and was enlisted in the United States Air Force; he was discharged after 11 months for nondisclosed issues. He then began working in hospitals as a nurse's aide or in junior technician positions. He fathered at least two children with different women and had a number of long-term relationships with men. His past includes a number of encounters with law enforcement prior to his murder charges. These included arson, burglary, and other crimes that are indicative of his disturbed mental state. Most of his victims were patients in hospitals, but he also killed friends and lovers outside of the medical setting. He killed with drug overdoses, poison administration, or mechanical methods such as tampering with life-support machines. He also administered infectious microorganisms, and inflicted traumatic damage to the internal organs of some patients that resulted in bleeding or other lesions that led to death.

Comments

Donald was suspected of killing people in the early stages of his serial killings, but his coworkers and hospital administrators were apparently unable to accept the real possibility that this charming, helpful person could be a killer.

Case: Michael—Physician Fascinated by Poisons

Michael was born in Washington in 1954, graduated from medical school in Illinois, and was sentenced to life in prison in 2000 for four murders. He is believed to have fatally poisoned more than 50 patients and colleagues.

Michael graduated from high school and college with honors and was among the top candidates for acceptance into a prestigious medical school. He did fairly well on class work without much effort but performed poorly in clinical training assignments. His overall poor performance and actual cheating and falsification of clinical records raised serious concerns by the faculty; nevertheless, he was allowed to graduate after repeating some assignments and clinical rotations. Even with his poor performance in medical school, he was accepted into a surgical internship of a Big-10 university medical program, which was to be followed by a residency in neurosurgery. During his internship, nurses started to notice that apparently healthy patients began dying with alarming frequency wherever Michael was working. This was reported, but he was cleared of any wrongdoing by a rather cursory investigation. However, he was not accepted as a resident physician when his internship ended. From this internship Michael went to work as an emergency medical technician for an Illinois county ambulance service. One year later, he was convicted of exaggerated battery for poisoning coworkers with arsenic and received a 5-year prison sentence. After prison, Michael worked at several nonmedical jobs while forging documents that would allow him to continue practicing medicine. He was successful and worked at medical hospitals in three states. More patients died, the FBI became involved, and Michael fled the country. He began working in a hospital in Zimbabwe and again patients began dying unexpectedly. These deaths led to charges and an arrest in Zimbabwe. While awaiting trial, Michael left the country and was on his way to Saudi Arabia when he was arrested during a layover of his flight in Chicago. Michael was charged with murder, assault, mail and wire fraud, and numerous other crimes in the United States, and five poisoning deaths in Zimbabwe. He pled guilty to murder to avoid the possibility of a death penalty and extradition for trial in Zimbabwe.

Comments

It is very troubling that this individual was able to practice medicine and kill patients in prestigious medical centers.

Case: Harold—Made House Calls and Poisoned Patients

Harold was a general practitioner in a small town in England. He practiced for almost 30 years and was respected by both patients and colleagues. He is known to have killed at least 200 of his patients and suspected of killing many more. Most deaths were caused by lethal doses of heroin (a legally prescribed drug in England). Most victims were elderly women who had no life-threatening conditions and their deaths were unexpected. He administered the heroin injections during home visits, which were a very popular feature of his practice. Suspicions were only aroused when an 81-year-old patient, who was a prominent individual in the community, was found dead, unexpectedly, a few hours after a home visit by the doctor. The patient's will had been recently redrafted to leave all of her assets to the doctor. Subsequently, it was determined that the death was due to a heroin overdose and the will was a forgery. This death triggered a massive investigation of deaths that had occurred over a period of approximately 23 years. After a 4-month trial in 2000, he was convicted of 15 counts of murder and sentenced to 15 life sentences to run concurrently. He never admitted guilt nor explained his thinking. In 2004, Harold committed suicide by hanging himself in his prison cell using bed sheets.

Comments

This physician consistently denied his guilt and never made statements about his motives. It was only after his conviction that his wife began to suspect his guilt.

References and Additional Reading

Barros AJS, Rosa RG, de Borba Telles LE, Taborda JGV: Attempted serial neonaticides: Case report and a brief review of the literature. *J Forensic Sci*, 61: 280–283, 2016.

Clarkson W: *The Good Doctor*. New York: St. Martin's Press, 2002.

Esmail A: Physician as serial killer—The Shipman case. *N Engl J Med*, 352: 1843–1844, 2005.

Field J, Pearson A: Caring to death: The murder of patients by nurses. *Int J Nurs Pract*, 16: 301–309, 2010.

Foxjohn J: *Killer Nurse*. New York: Berkley Books, 2013.

Furbee RB: Criminal poisoning: Medical murderers. *Clin Lab Med*, 26: 255–273, 2006.

Graeber C: *The Good Nurse: A True Story of Medicine, Madness, and Murder*. New York: Twelve, 2013.

Kalin JR, Brissie RM: A case of homicide by lethal injection with lidocaine. *J Forensic Sci*, 47: 1135–1138, 2002.

Kaplan RM: *Medical Murder: Disturbing Cases of Doctors Who Kill.* Crows Nest NSW, Australia: Allen & Unwin, 2009.

Lubaszka CK, Shon PC, Hinch R: Healthcare serial killers as confidence men. *J Investig Psych Offender Profil*, 11: 1–28, 2014.

Perper JA, Cina SJ: *When Doctors Kill: Who, Why, and How.* New York: Copernicus Books, 2010.

Pyrek KM: *Healthcare Crime: Investigating Abuse, Fraud, and Homicide by Caregivers.* Boca Raton, FL: CRC Press, 2011.

Ramsland, K: *Inside the Minds of Healthcare Serial Killers: Why They Kill.* Westport, CT: Praeger, 2007.

Soothill K, Wilson D: Theorizing the puzzle that is Harold Shipman. *J Forensic Psychiatry Psychol*, 16: 685–698, 2005.

Stewart JB: *Blind Eye: The Terrifying Story of a Doctor Who Got Away with Murder.* New York: Touchstone, 1999.

Yorker, BC, Kizer KW, Lampe P, Forrest ARW, Lannan JM, Russell DA: Serial murder by healthcare professionals. *J Forensic Sci*, 51: 1362–1371, 2006.

Hospitalized Patients Poisoned by Visitors 30

30.1 Introduction

Homicidal poisonings can occur almost anywhere. Hospitals are an important example of the seemingly unlikely places where one might encounter intentional poisoning. This chapter draws attention to the possibility of criminal poisoning of hospital patients by visitors. Hospital staff may sometimes perceive visitors as being eccentric, weird, overbearing, or unusual in some way, but it is unlikely that they would be viewed as potential murderers. Although extremely rare, poisoning by visitors does occur. This chapter provides examples of cases involving poisoning in hospitals that were perpetrated by individuals not affiliated with the hospital. The variety of circumstances and toxicants that might be encountered in hospital visitor poisoning cases is illustrated by the examples provided in Table 30.1. Some of these examples are expanded with more details through case studies in Section 30.4.

30.2 Exposure Situations and Circumstances

It is common for friends and family to bring food or candy to hospitalized patients. Sometimes people bring things for patients even when strictly prohibited by hospital policy or forbidden because of the specific medical condition of the patient. Visitors may be genuinely unaware of any restrictions in this area, and most probably feel that bringing some favorite food item to a friend would be a rather trivial infraction of hospital policy. This practice and lack of close policing of food items brought to patients can make it easy for individuals to bring poisoned items to patients. Generally individuals who bring things to patients are viewed as caring and attentive. Seldom, if ever, would the possibility of homicidal intentions on the part of the visitor be suspected. When hospitalized patients manifest increasing degrees of illness, this is almost always attributed to the illness that resulted in their hospitalization.

Many of the reported cases of patients having been intentionally poisoned while hospitalized involve spouses, and the poisoning was a repeat or continuation of poison administration prior to hospitalization. As hospitalization often occurs unexpectedly, and the conditions within the hospital cannot usually be

Table 30.1 Examples of Hospitalized Patients Poisoned by Visitors

Poisoner (age)	Poisoned (age)	Presumptive Motive	Poison	Method	Outcome (year)
Wife (66)	Husband (60)	Unhappy marriage	Fecal bacteria	IV Line	Survived (2014)
Mother (19)	Son (infant)	Unwilling to care for disabled child	Ethanol	Feeding tube	Death (2012)
Female (young adult)	Friend's children	Psychiatric disorder	Medications	Food	Survived (2010–2013)
Wife (44)	Husband (39)	Unhappy marriage	Thallium	IV Line	Death (2011)
Mother (38)	Children (4 & 6)	Insurance	Clonidine	IV Line Feeding tube Food Beverages	One death One survival (2006)
Wife (31)	Husband (37)	Financial issues	Ethylene glycol	Beverages	Survived (2005)
Husband (38)	Wife (41)	Anger	Cyanide	Feeding tube	Death (1998)
Wife (33)	Husband (32)	Insurance	Thallium	Iced Tea	Death (1991)
Husband (47)	Wife (52)	Dissolution of marriage	Environmental bacteria	IV Line	Death (1997)
Wife (57)	Husband (57)	Dissolution of marriage	Strychnine	Food	Survived (1993)
Wife (57)	Husband (50)	Insurance	Arsenic	Milkshakes	Death (1989)
Drug Dealer (33)	Drug abuser (Adult)	Drug sale	Fentanyl	IV Line	Survived (2015)
Male (Adult)	Male (41)	Insurance fraud	Propofol Midazolam Vecuronium	IV Line	Death (2015)
Mother (30)	Daughter (infant)	Therapeutic misadventure	Methadone	Food	Death (2010)
Mother (21)	Son (infant)	Mental disorder	Table salt	Nasogastric tube	Survived (2010)

predicted, continued poisoning within the hospital is usually not well planned or executed. Anybody could conceivably poison someone in a hospital using a variety of substances administered in a variety of ways. Patients are often administered intravenous fluids continuously, and they sometimes also have indwelling feeding tubes or other portals convenient for administering poisons.

When individuals are hospitalized in specialized facilities for treatment of substance abuse disorders, a great deal of effort is expended on preventing drugs from being brought in by visitors, but these efforts are not always successful. In situations where addicted individuals are hospitalized for medical conditions unrelated to abuse and do not disclose their drug use, monitoring is minimal. These hospitalized addicts frequently attempt to maintain their drug use through substances supplied by visitors. Illegal drugs can be used that have variable compositions and potency, and their use within the hospital may occur at erratic intervals when opportunities happen to occur. Hospital deaths have resulted from patients utilizing opioids and other substances supplied by visitors. This can be especially hazardous when illegal drug use is superimposed on therapeutic medications administered in the hospital. Serious medical complications due to the combinations can result. Many substance abusers can appear to others as otherwise ordinary people. Their drug habits are frequently not disclosed, nor are they suspected while hospitalized. It is unrealistic to assume that medical personnel will determine, or always suspect, illegal drug use by patients. Although substance abuse could have a bearing on the reason for hospitalization, it could also be independent from the many diseases or conditions that result in hospitalization.

30.3 Investigative Considerations

When poisoning is initiated within a hospital, it may suggest that the hospitalized patient presented an unexpected opportunity for poisoning. This might also be evident from the particular toxicant used and the administration methodology employed. When poisoning was initiated prior to hospitalization by adding poison to food or beverages, perhaps the same food or beverages will be brought to the patient while in the hospital.

Consideration of previous hospitalizations in evaluating possibilities during poisoning death investigations might also be enlightening. In some chronic poisoning cases, there can be a poison-induced illness that requires hospitalization, which, because the poisoning was interrupted, results in recovery. Subsequently, when the victim is discharged, poisoning resumes and illness returns. This type of cycling is difficult to recognize and is generally discovered only when many other factors lead in this direction. When this occurs, it may suggest some kind of trial and error behavior by the poisoner relative to amounts or substances utilized for poisoning.

30.4 Case Studies

Case: Beating and Poisoning

In 1998, a 41-year-old woman in Syracuse was divorcing her 38-year-old husband. They had two children, ages 9 and 10, and had serious financial problems. They were legally separated but living in the same house until the wife could afford to move. One evening, the husband started an argument, which escalated into a brutal beating with an aluminum baseball bat while their young children watched. The woman was hospitalized with a protective order barring the husband from the hospital. Her injuries were life-threatening, requiring extensive surgery and intensive medical care. The husband was charged with assault, but posted bail and was free awaiting trial. He devised a plan to kill his wife before she recovered sufficiently to enable her to testify against him. He created a fake letterhead for a local company that used cyanide in its manufacturing processes and used it to order cyanide from a chemical supply company. In the order, he specified express delivery, which he could track. This made it possible for him to follow the delivery truck on its rounds until he was able to intercept it and, posing as an employee of the ordering company, convince the driver to give him the package, which was supposedly urgently needed. Having the cyanide, he dressed himself as a maintenance worker and used a fake hospital ID to gain access to his wife's hospital room where he administered potassium cyanide into her feeding tube. She lost consciousness within minutes and died shortly after. At the time of the murder, his wife was in a coma and had been hospitalized for approximately 6 months. He was later arrested and charged with murder with the prosecutor requesting the death penalty. After hearing an overwhelming amount of evidence, he was found guilty of murder and sentenced to 37.5 years to life in prison. The wife's family filed wrongful-death lawsuits against the husband and the hospital security company.

Comments

The poisoner was arrested on the day following the poisoning. Although the victim was discovered gasping for breath soon after the poisoning, attempts at resuscitation were unsuccessful. There was conspicuous white cyanide powder on the victim's face and chest. The poisoner's disguise as one of the janitorial staff was especially poor. Members of the staff remembered the oddly dressed man in glasses who was obviously wearing a wig and had what appeared to be a handmade ID badge. Investigators were able to recover the wig and the remaining cyanide in the poisoner's home, as well as evidence on his personal computer of Internet searches for information on cyanide and how to obtain it.

Case: Developmentally Disabled Baby

In 2012, a 19-year-old woman living in a suburb of New Orleans was eagerly awaiting the birth of her son. She regularly posted pictures and comments on social media that indicated her devotion to the expectant child and her commitment to ensuring that the new child would have a happy, loving life. When her son was born with Down syndrome and serious cardiac defects, things changed. Two months after his birth, the son was hospitalized to undergo a planned surgery to correct heart defects. During this hospitalization, the baby began having seizures, which were soon traced to high levels of blood ethanol. This was reported to authorities who questioned the parents. The baby's 22-year-old father subsequently confessed to adding rum to the baby's feeding tube while in the hospital. He was arrested. About 2 months later, emergency medical responders were summoned to the child's home when he stopped breathing. The baby was rushed to a hospital where he was declared dead on arrival. Samples collected at autopsy revealed high levels of blood ethanol. On questioning, the mother confessed to killing her child by adding an alcoholic hand sanitizer to his feeding tube. She indicated that her goal was to end the child's suffering. She also confessed that the earlier poisoning was done by her and not by her husband. She said that it was not rum as the father indicated, but perfume that she added to the baby's feeding tube over a course of several days. The mother was indicted for first-degree murder. Prior to trial, she pleaded guilty to manslaughter and was sentenced to 40 years in prison without the possibility of parole. Charges against the father were reduced to a misdemeanor for giving a false report to authorities and he was released after spending a year in jail and ordered to pay $850 in fines.

Comments

Young children are particularly susceptible to ethyl alcohol poisoning. In addition to possible lethal depression of respiration, infants and young children are prone to profound hypoglycemia that results in coma and seizures.

Case: Intravenous Fecal Matter

In 2014, a 55-year-old former nurse in Arizona injected fluid contaminated with fecal material into her 66-year-old husband's IV line while he was hospitalized and recovering from heart surgery. She was observed doing this and was detained by the hospital security staff. Later, several contaminated syringes were discovered in her purse. The husband recovered. The wife was charged with attempted first-degree murder.

The husband was a retired police officer and the couple had been married for 30 years. Friends and neighbors were completely surprised with news of the incident and were unable to rationalize the wife's behavior in view of what appeared to all as a sustained loving relationship.

Comments

The poisoner in this case was a former nurse and had previously worked in the hospital where the poisoning occurred. She was familiar with the care and procedures that her husband was experiencing while hospitalized. She was also likely familiar with the risks of infections that might occur in procedures such as her husband's cardiac shunt placement. Infections are very rare with the shunt procedure, but when they occur the outcome can be life-threatening. The circumstances of this case suggest that the woman was well aware of these matters and that the contamination of the IV fluids with bacteria from fecal material was carefully considered and probably based on sound reasoning.

Case: Episodic Pain and Seizures

In 1993, a 57-year-old farmer living in Ireland with his wife and two children consulted a hospital physician about a troubling colicky abdominal pain. He had a history of ulcers and was regularly taking an antacid plus medication to inhibit gastric acid secretion. Nothing was discovered by the physician during his evaluation to explain the abdominal pain, which eventually stopped. Two months later, he developed general muscle weakness and pain accompanied by nausea, vomiting, and dizziness, and he was admitted to a hospital. About 2 weeks after admission, he experienced muscle cramping and became cyanotic for a few hours. He remained hospitalized for 3 months and underwent an extensive evaluation by several medical specialists, but again, no explanation for his symptoms was uncovered and he was discharged. Six days later, his symptoms returned and he had a seizure. He was again hospitalized and again numerous diagnostic tests and radiological examinations revealed no explanation. His symptoms reoccurred intermittently while he was in the hospital. In view of the extensive physical examinations without uncovering an explanation for the man's symptoms, attention turned to a possible psychological basis for his problems. He was anxious and intensely concerned about his extended hospitalization without improvement, but no psychopathology emerged that might account for his physical distress. As a trial, he was started on an antidepressant and a benzodiazepine. There was some improvement after a week and he was discharged. Four days later, he was readmitted after developing profuse diarrhea and recurrent seizures. Both husband and wife were struggling to cope with his continuing serious medical condition. In the hospital, he was treated for the seizures and underwent a thorough neurological evaluation. On this last admission, his evaluations included toxicological screening, and strychnine was identified in urine specimens. The man was informed that a poisonous substance was found in his urine. He denied any intentional poisoning behavior and indicated that no poisonous substances were kept on his farm. Law enforcement authorities were notified, and he was advised not to eat or drink anything not prepared by the hospital until an investigation was concluded. The investigation disclosed that the man's wife was having an affair and that she and her lover had purchased the strychnine used in the poisoning. They admitted to the poisoning, and both received prison sentences. The wife had been adding strychnine to her husband's yogurt in the hospital and to his liquid antacid in their home.

Comments

Possible poisoning should be included in the differential diagnoses of unusual illnesses that wax and wane in intensity and do not respond to conventional therapy for a presumptive illness. This possibility is not necessarily indicative of suicidal or homicidal behavior. Toxic exposures can occur in a variety of ways and investigations into the manner of exposure proceed from the determination that a toxic exposure occurred.

Case: Unexpected Potency

In 2015, a couple in their mid-30s visited a friend who was a patient in a medical center teaching hospital in Northern Michigan. Shortly after the couple left their friend's hospital room, hospital staff found the patient unresponsive and not breathing. Emergency resuscitation was initiated and during this process the patient's respiration was reestablished using naloxone. Naloxone is a specific antagonist of respiratory depression induced by opioids and the patient was not receiving any opioids as part of the treatment of the medical condition for which she was hospitalized. Law enforcement officials were notified of the overdose, and the hospital visitors were arrested the following day. Hospital surveillance cameras had identified the couple's car and this led to their identification. They were drug dealers who had recently been released after serving time for drug possession and delivery charges. It was subsequently determined that the patient was an addict who had likely requested that the dealers bring heroin to the hospital. The drug that the patient received through a hospital intravenous line was fentanyl. Apparently both the patient and the dealers mistakenly believed that the fentanyl was heroin. The circumstances of the case were such that there was a question as to whether the

overdose was accidental or an intended homicide. The couple was initially charged with attempted murder, but they accepted a plea bargain,
and pled guilty to drug possession and dealing, and they received sentences of 4 to 40 years in prison.

Comments

It is not uncommon for hospitalized substance abusers to receive drugs
from friends or dealers who visit them. This is closely monitored in
medical facilities specializing in abuse treatment and, in general, when
patients are known to have drug dependence issues. Patients with hidden
addictions who are hospitalized for medical problems unrelated to drug
use can present problems such as the overdose in this case, or complicate therapeutic and diagnostic measures focused on their treatment. The
heightened possibility of lethal overdose with heroin adulterated with
fentanyl is also illustrated in this case. Had the individual receiving the
fentanyl not been hospitalized at the time, it is likely that it would have
resulted in a fatality.

Case: Episodic Hypernatremia

In 2010, a 21-year-old mother took her 4-month-old infant son to a small
regional medical center in rural Tennessee after about a week of vomiting and diarrhea. The child was severely dehydrated and had been having
seizures. Due to the severity of the child's condition and his failure to
respond to appropriate fluid and electrolyte replacement therapy, he was
transferred to a university medical center in Tennessee for evaluation.
The infant was intubated and maintained on mechanical ventilation. An
MRI of the brain disclosed significant thrombotic injury. Treatment was
initiated with an antithrombotic, anticonvulsants, and antibiotics appropriate for pathogens isolated from stool cultures. The tentative diagnosis was meningitis and sepsis. Antibiotics were continued for 6 weeks.
Pronounced episodic bouts of diarrhea and diuresis continued with
resulting fluctuations in serum sodium. Endoscopic examination of the
child's gastrointestinal tract did not provide insight into the cause of the
diarrhea. The infant was then transferred to another university hospital in Pennsylvania with specialized expertise in treating children with
complex problems similar to those encountered in this case. On arrival
at this medical facility, the serum electrolytes were within the physiological range. Fluid and electrolyte losses were carefully monitored and
replaced. Anticonvulsant medication was continued. The significant central neuronal damage was confirmed with additional imaging studies of
the brain. The infant's father traveled with him to the new hospital; the
mother arrived on day 4. During the first 4 days in the hospital, the child

had improved significantly and was stabilized. Within 24 hours of the mother's arrival, the child developed profuse diarrhea and hypernatremia. Despite elimination of sodium from all replacement fluids and medications, the serum sodium continued to rise. A gastric aspirate obtained from a nasogastric tube contained a significant amount of sodium indicative of oral administration. During intensified visual monitoring, the mother was discovered attempting to administer a concentrated salt solution using a syringe connected to the nasogastric tube. She was arrested by authorities and charged with attempted homicide, aggravated assault, and child endangerment. The mother's backpack contained a syringe, a large commercial container of table salt, and two bottles of concentrated salt solution. She admitted to administering at least five full syringes of salt solution at the first medical center in Tennessee and one or more at the Pennsylvania medical center. It is not clear whether the initial illness was due to poisoning.

The mother had significant preexisting and current psychological disorders and was found to be unfit to stand trial. She had been previously hospitalized for psychiatric problems and was prescribed psychotherapeutic medications, which she had discontinued using. Her charges were reduced from attempted homicide to aggravated assault and endangerment. She pleaded guilty and was sentenced to 5 to 15 years in a psychiatric treatment facility. The child survived, but sustained severe permanent brain damage that included partial blindness.

Comments

Hypernatremic dehydration is common in children who lose fluids from prolonged vomiting and diarrhea. This is generally managed by replacing the lost fluids and, if necessary, treating the condition causing the symptoms. In this case, the child did not respond to conventional medical care, the symptoms occurred episodically, and there was a correlation between the onset and the intensity of symptoms and the presence of the child's mother.

References and Additional Reading

Alt BL, Wells SK: *When Caregivers Kill: Understanding Child Murder by Parents and Other Guardians.* Lanham, MD: Rowman & Littefield, 2010.

Collins M: *While She Slept: A Husband, a Wife, a Brutal Murder.* New York: St. Martins Press, 2005.

Goel N, Munshi LB, Thyagarajan B: Intravenous drug abuse by patients inside the hospital: A cause for sustained bacteremia. *Case Reports Infec Dis,* #1738742, 2016.

Grissinger M: Patients taking their own medications while in the hospital. *PA Patient Saf Advis,* 9: 50–57, 2012.

Katz G, Durst R, Shufman E, Bar-Hamburger R, Grunhaus L: Substance abuse in hospitalized psychiatric patients. *Isr Med Assoc J*, 10: 672–675, 2008.

Moore PW, Palmer RB, Donovan JW: Fatal fentanyl patch misuse in a hospitalized patient with a postmortem increase in fentanyl blood concentration. *J Forensic Sci*, 60: 243–246, 2015.

Nichols L, Chew B: Causes of sudden unexpected death of adult hospital patients. *J Hosp Med*, 7: 706–708, 2012.

Norstrom PE, Brown CM: Use of patients' own medications in small hospitals. *Am J Health Syst Pharm*, 59: 349–354, 2002.

Reardon M, Duane A, Cotter P: Attempted homicide in hospital. *Ir J Med Sci*, 162: 315–317, 1993.

Su E, Shoykhet M, Bell MJ: Severe hypernatremia in a hospitalized child: Munchausen by proxy. *Pediatr Neurol*, 43: 270–273, 2010.

Yu Y, Gong D, Cao Y, Lu M, Huang F, Deng Z: A murder diagnosed as a medical accident: A case report of homicidal poisoning with three anesthetics. *Rom J Leg Med*, 23: 45–48, 2015.

Medical Child Abuse and Homicide 31

31.1 Introduction

Medical child abuse (MCA) is a rare form of child abuse in which caregivers fabricate or induce symptoms of an illness in a child to receive attention. This type of abuse is more commonly referred to as Munchausen syndrome by proxy. The overwhelming majority of MCA cases involve mothers and their children. The motive is not financial or other material gain, or an act of retaliation or punishment. The abuse is an attention-seeking activity to receive some form of emotional gratification.

Increasing awareness of this disorder among health care workers, law enforcement personnel, social workers, and others has increased the possibilities of early detection and remedial action. Unfortunately, this heightened awareness has also increased the possibility of false allegations leading to misdiagnosis. For example, it is becoming rather common for accusations related to MCA to surface in heated divorce and child custody battles.

Victims can have an array of ailments in different organ systems with complex mixtures of seemingly unrelated symptoms. The most common symptoms include abdominal pain, vomiting, diarrhea, weight loss, seizures, apnea, infections, fever, bleeding, and lethargy.

31.2 Exposure Situations and Circumstances

A diagnosis that is vulnerable to manipulation by a parent is especially susceptible to issues regarding MCA. These might include relatively newly recognized disorders, those that are complex and poorly understood, and those that are controversial within the medical community. It is not uncommon with these types of illnesses for there to be conflicts between caring parents and physicians regarding treatment. However, on occasions, elements of MCA can be the basis of the illness.

Misdiagnosis of MCA could happen in circumstances in which there is a legitimate basis for considering this possibility. Errors can be made in good faith and concern for a child's welfare stemming from limited information, incomplete investigation, unrecognized illness, or misunderstandings about caretaker motivation. Guidelines for minimizing the risk of misdiagnoses of MCA can be found in a number of authoritative medical reviews of factitious disorders. An often cited case of misdiagnosis of MCA involved the death of a child suffering from an unrecognized rare medical condition. A mother was accused of killing her child by poisoning with ethylene glycol. This mother was convicted and sent to prison. It was shown later that the child had died because of a rare genetic disorder known as methylmalonic acidemia. This condition produces symptoms similar to those seen with ethylene glycol poisoning.

31.3 Investigative Considerations

Examples of some methods and behaviors that have been employed to induce medical conditions in children in MCA cases are provided in Tables 31.1 and 31.2. Some clinical situations that might heighten suspicion of the possibility of MCA are listed in Table 31.3.

Table 31.1 Examples of Methods Employed in Medical Child Abuse to Induce Illness

Clinical Presentation	Agents and Techniques
Fluid and electrolyte imbalances	Salt
	Diuretics
Internal or external bleeding issues	Anticoagulants
Sudden infant death	Suffocation
	CNS depressants
Lung diseases	Forced aspiration
Neurological signs and symptoms	Phenothiazines
	Antidepressants
	Antipsychotics
Developmental disability	Food restriction
	Suffocation
Manifestations of CNS depression	Barbiturates
	Benzodiazepines
	Chloral hydrate
	Antihistamines
Fever	Contamination of medications with fecal material or other substances
Apnea	Suffocation
Hypoglycemia	Oral hypoglycemics
	Insulin
Gastrointestinal disorders	Ipecac
	Laxatives
	Salt
Hyperthyroidism	Thyroid hormones

Table 31.2   Examples of Behaviors Employed in Medical Child Abuse to Fabricate Illness

- Falsifying medical records or legal documents
- Exaggeration of existing medical problems
- Withholding prescribed medications
- Contamination or substitution of urine or blood samples
- Interference with oxygen or drug administration
- Removal of nutrient solutions from administration devices

Table 31.3   Situations Which May Trigger Suspicion of Medical Child Abuse

- Infant deaths under questionable circumstances
- Illness that involves multiple organ systems, is prolonged, or rare
- Illness that is inconsistent with laboratory testing results
- Extraordinary or unexplained symptoms
- Unexplained recurrence of illness
- Consistently ineffective treatments
- Features of illness absent when mother or other caregiver is absent
- Unrealistic simultaneous multiple allergies

31.4 Case Studies

Case: Abuse or Greed

Judy was a 38-year-old daycare teacher and mother in her second marriage. She had a son (3 years) and a daughter (5 years). The children attended different preschools, neither of which was where the mother worked. On a day in 2005, both children developed stomach flu and were sent home from school. After a few days at home with their mother with no improvement in their incessant vomiting and diarrhea, the children were taken to their pediatrician who then had the children hospitalized for fluid replacement and evaluation. While hospitalized, the condition of the children fluctuated in unexplainable ways that appeared to be unrelated to various treatment modalities. The mother was especially attentive to the children and remained at their bedside throughout hospitalization. After several days in the hospital, the son died, whereas the daughter's condition continued to deteriorate. A few days after the son's death, the hospital was notified that a wrongful death suit was being brought by the family against the hospital. An investigation ensued, which culminated in the arrest of the mother in 2006. She was charged with six felonies that included child abuse and murder. At trial, an overwhelming amount of evidence demonstrated that she poisoned the children. She was found guilty and sentenced to two consecutive life terms in prison.

From an abundance of evidence collected during the investigation, a disturbing story was constructed. The mother had poisoned the children with clonidine. It was one of several prescription medications that she took regularly for therapeutic purposes. Poisonings had begun long before the incident that required the children's hospitalization.

In addition to the clonidine toxicity, an autopsy revealed that a significant factor in the son's death was the pulmonary complications that resulted from the intravenous administration of ground tableting materials. The mother had administered the ground clonidine tablets to the children by multiple routes. This included the children's intravenous lines and nasogastric tubes as well as in their food and beverages. The poisoning was erratic because the opportunities varied due to changes in hospital personnel and scheduling. At trial, the prosecution sought to enter testimony from a psychologist that indicated the mother met the criteria for a diagnosis of MCA. The mother had denied all allegations and indicated that she had no motive to harm her children. The prosecution's intention was to frame the motive as a mental disorder. It was a circuitous form of reasoning. The mental disorder was the reason she committed the crime and the evidence for her mental disorder was the crime. It should be noted that while MCA is a recognized mental disorder and it can be a possible explanation for her actions, MCA is not a mitigating factor of her actions. MCA is a pattern of child abuse, but it does not hinder an individual's ability to distinguish right from wrong behavior.

Comments

The mother's motives were not clear. She started poisoning the children before the hospital incident. It is unlikely that she could have foreseen the opportunity for the wrongful death legal action against the hospital. It appears that she started the poisoning for some purpose and then adjusted her plans continuously as circumstances changed. Once the poisoning was discovered, it was not difficult to review the mother's history and determine that she was not the mother she appeared to be. The investigation uncovered many examples of lying and deceit.

Case: Abuse or Pharmacy Error

After receiving scheduled immunizations from a pediatrician, an otherwise healthy infant had a slight fever, which was treated with acetaminophen. The infant seemed healthy for the next few days, then the fever returned and the infant appeared sufficiently ill for the mother to return to the pediatrician's office. The infant was subsequently admitted to a hospital for testing and observation with a diagnosis of fever of unknown origin. The infant's pediatrician requested that fluid replacement and appropriate antibiotic therapy be provided, and that testing be undertaken for the identification of the microbial basis for the illness. Acetaminophen was continued. Except for a brief time to return home for clothes and toiletries, the mother cared for the infant while in the hospital, changing diapers, giving bottle feedings, and generally assisting hospital staff whenever she could.

Several hours after admission, an intravenous antibiotic solution was piggybacked onto an existing IV fluid line. Minutes after the antibiotic infusion was started, the infant began jerking and screaming, and respiration stopped. Despite intensive resuscitation efforts, the infant could not be stabilized and sustained severe anoxic damage. Life support was ultimately discontinued and the infant expired.

The child's pediatrician and the hospital physicians felt that the death was due to hyperkalemia believed to result from an incorrect level of potassium in the IV fluids. An autopsy was inconclusive regarding the cause of death, but the pathologist supported the view that the death likely resulted from hyperkalemia possibly due to a compounding or dispensing error involving the intravenous fluids administered to the child. The intravenous fluid bag used during the child's stay at the hospital was analyzed and found not to have an elevated concentration of potassium. Records indicated that the child's potassium level was elevated at the time of the cardiopulmonary arrest. No evidence was obtained that indicated or suggested intentional poisoning or accidental medication errors. The elevated potassium was most likely the result of death rather than the cause.

Comments

The level of potassium in plasma is critical for neurotransmission and cardiac function. There is a potassium concentration gradient between the intracellular and extracellular potassium with most of the total potassium being intracellular. The concentration gradient is maintained by an active enzymatic pumping process. A sudden increase in the plasma potassium concentration can produce cardiac arrhythmia and cardiac arrest. After any death, potassium leaks out of cells into plasma and can markedly elevate plasma levels and obscure any elevations that might have occurred before death. These factors severely limit the value of postmortem potassium measurement in discerning the cause and manner of death.

There are drugs, which can alter plasma levels of potassium by various mechanisms and produce cardiotoxicity. The administration of excessive amounts of potassium can also produce fatal cardiotoxicity. High levels of potassium are sometimes administered accidentally because of confusion, misinformation, or formulation errors. Intentional administration of potassium in suicidal and homicidal poisoning has been reported.

References and Additional Reading

Artingstall K: *Munchausen by Proxy and Other Factitious Abuse: Practical and Forensic Investigative Techniques.* Boca Raton, FL: CRC Press, 2017.

Bourget D, Grace J, Whitehurst L: A review of maternal and paternal filicide. *J Am Acad Psychiatry Law*, 35: 74–82, 2007.

Brink FW, Thackeray JD: Factitious illness: Red flags for the pediatric emergency medicine physician. *Clin Pediatr Emerg Med*, 13: 213–220, 2102.

Criddle L: Monsters in the closet—Munchausen Syndrome by Proxy. *Cri Care Nur*, 30: 46–55, 2010.

Eminson M, Postlethwaite RJ Eds.: *Munchausen Syndrome by Proxy Abuse: A Practical Approach.* Oxford: Butterworth-Heinemann, 2000.

Feldman MD: *Playing Sick? Untangling the Web of Munchausen Syndrome, Munchausen by Proxy, Malingering & Factitious Disorders.* New York: Brunner-Routledge, 2004.

Friedman SH, Friedman JB: Parents who kill their children. *Pediatr Rev*, 31: 10–16, 2010.

Friedman SH, Resnick PJ: Child murder by mothers: Patterns and prevention. *World Psychiatry*, 6: 137–141, 2007.

Griest K: *Pediatric Homicide: Medical Investigation.* Boca Raton, FL: CRC Press, 2009.

Isbister GK, Heppell SP, Page CB, Ryan NM: Adult clonidine overdose: Prolonged bradycardia and central nervous system depression but not severe toxicity. *J Clin Toxicol*, 55: 187–192, 2017.

Marshall D: *Effective Investigation of Child Homicide and Suspicious Deaths.* New York: Oxford University Press: 2012.

Roseler TA, Jenny C: *Medical Child Abuse: Beyond Munchausen Syndrome by Proxy.* Elk Grove Village, IL: American Academy of Pediatrics, 2009.

Shoemaker JD, Lynch RE, Hoffmann JW, Sly WS: Misidentification of propionic acid as ethylene glycol in a patient with methlymalonic acidemia. *J Pediatr*, 120: 417–421, 1992.

Stirling J: Beyond Munchausen Syndrome by Proxy: Identification and treatment of child abuse in a medical setting. *Pediatrics*, 119: 1026–1030, 2007.

Talbot M: The bad mother. *The New Yorker*, August 9: 62–75, 2004.

Weintraub P: Munchausen: Unusual suspects. *Psychol Today*, Sept 1: 81–88, 2007.

Welti CV, Davis JH: Fatal hyperkalemia from accidental overdose of potassium chloride. *JAMA*, 240: 1339, 1978.

Drug Abuse Fatalities 32

32.1 Introduction

Deaths from substance abuse usually result from cardiotoxicity, respiratory failure, or both. As with all substances that induce unconsciousness and coma, aspiration of gastric contents can frequently be a major determinant of death. This chapter summarizes the lethal effects of some toxicants that have been reviewed individually in previous chapters along with some other commonly abused substances not specifically addressed elsewhere in this book. These additional toxicants include hallucinogens, inhalants, and non-benzodiazepine sedative-hypnotics. In many abuse fatalities, the causative agent is not immediately obvious, and this succinct overview of possibilities may be useful during preliminary investigation stages.

32.2 Exposure Situations and Circumstances

The descriptive terminology used in substance abuse fatalities can sometimes be misleading. The legality of substances abused can be distinctively different from the legality of the use. Drugs manufactured by legitimate pharmaceutical companies are legal drugs. When these drugs are illegally diverted or abused by individuals, the drug substance remains a legal substance but the misuse becomes illegal. Substances produced and distributed for misuse are always illegal substances. The public is particularly confused by this issue when deaths are reported not to involve illegal substances; the assumption can be that the drugs were prescription drugs and that they were obtained from a physician.

The combined effects of individual drugs used simultaneously can result in a greatly enhanced lethal potential that exceeds what might be intuitively expected. This might result from additive effects of similar drugs or the combined effects of drugs from different classes acting through different toxicological mechanisms. This latter situation would be exemplified by the lethal respiratory depression produced by various combinations of opioids, ethanol, benzodiazepines, muscle relaxants, and other substances with potential for CNS depression. Lethal mixtures can also occur when individual drugs with toxicities related to different organ systems are combined. For example, combining agents having toxic effects primarily on the cardiovascular system with agents having prominent toxic effects on respiration.

Unintended deaths from prescription opioids usually involve the concomitant use of other prescription medications such as benzodiazepines, antidepressants, and antipsychotics. Typically, the antidepressants and antipsychotics are used in a relatively consistent manner with fluctuating dosing patterns of opioids and benzodiazepines. The toxic effect of these drugs can be augmented further by ethanol, which is often consumed in multiple drinking episodes. Ethanol and opioids decrease respiration by different mechanisms and their combined use, in amounts that are not lethal when used individually, can completely stop the breathing of the user. Many substances have sedative effects which, when combined, are at least additive and usually synergistic. Additional factors that can contribute to multiple drug overdose deaths include the use of more than one agent in a pharmacological class simultaneously (e.g., several benzodiazapines, several opioids) and self-administration of the medications in unintended ways while drug impaired.

The dosing intervals of therapeutic drugs are based largely on the known rate of elimination of the drug from the body. Drugs eliminated faster are taken more often than drugs with a slower elimination rate. When drugs are taken more often than dictated by the elimination rate, they tend to accumulate and elevate blood levels, which can reach toxic levels. An important example of this is methadone, which has a relatively long elimination half-life and remains in the body long after its analgesic effects wear off. This can lead to frequently redosing in shortening time intervals resulting in drug accumulation to lethal levels.

Tolerance to the potentially lethal effects of many psychotropic drugs can develop with continued regular use. Tolerant individuals are able to use doses of substances that would be fatal in nontolerant individuals. Tolerance is related to each particular class of drugs and may not quantitatively relate to all drugs within that class. Tolerance can also fluctuate and may be influenced by many environmental and physiological factors.

32.3 Symptoms

The toxic symptoms that precede substance abuse deaths are characteristic of the particular substances involved. These generally are manifestations of extreme depression or excitation of the central nervous system, cardiac

Table 32.1   Substance Abuse Fatalities

Substances	Potentially Lethal Effects
Opioids	• Respiratory depression • Hypotension • Cardiac arrhythmias
Ethanol	• Respiratory depression • Aspiration of gastric contents
Cocaine	• Cardiac arrhythmias • Myocardial infarction • Excited delirium • Hyperthermia
Barbiturates	• Respiratory depression • Cardiovascular collapse
Benzodiazepines	• Respiratory depression
Amphetamines	• Cardiac arrhythmias • Myocardial infarction • Cerebral hemorrhage • Hyperthermia
Hallucinogens	• Agent-dependent mechanism • Fatal behaviors
Inhalants	• Cardiac arrhythmias • Respiratory depression • Aspiration of gastric contents • Suffocation
Emerging psychotropics	• Respiratory depression • Myocardial infarction • Agitated delirium • Hyperthermia • Renal failure

arrhythmias, and cardiovascular collapse. The symptoms have a recent onset and are unexplainable by possible concurrent trauma or natural illness. A summary of many of the most common lethal effects of substances are provided in Table 32.1. Common life-threatening toxic effects associated with substance abuse are described in Table 32.2.

Table 32.2   Examples of Serious Toxic Effects Frequently Encountered in Acute Substance Abuse Fatalities

Life-Threatening Toxic Effects	
Hyperthermia	Significant elevation in body temperature due to hypermetabolic states and failed thermoregulation. This can involve many toxicants acting through a variety of mechanisms. Hyperthermia can lead to multiple organ failure and coagulopathy.
Rhabdomyolysis	Skeletal muscle disintegration with the release of cellular components into plasma, which may lead to acute renal failure.
Agitated delirium	Psychomotor agitation with violent behavior, often with hyperthermia associated with high risk of sudden death.
Serotonin syndrome	Increased serotonergic activity that produces widespread alterations in many organ systems manifested as changes in mental status, cardiovascular function, and neurological control mechanisms. Symptoms can include hallucinations, coma, shock, seizure activity, and hyperthermia.
Cardiac arrhythmias	Irregularities in cardiac function due to abnormal neuroconduction and changes in myocardial contractility that affect heart rate and the synchronized contractions of heart muscles.
Shock	Circulatory failure that results in inadequate oxygen delivery to vital organs. Caused by decreased circulating blood volume and failure of the heart to pump effectively.
CNS depression	Reduced brain function. Depressed neuronal control centers for many vital functions such as respiration and heart rate.
Generalized seizures	Prolonged seizures or continuing seizures in rapid succession preventing respiration.
Withdrawal	Withdrawal from ethanol or sedative hypnotic agents can involve simultaneous hypertensive crises, cardiotoxicity, seizure, and other serious conditions that can be fatal.

32.4 Investigative Considerations

The investigation of drug abuse fatalities requires the integration of information derived from the site where the death occurred, the circumstances under which the death occurred, the medical and social history of the deceased, autopsy findings, and toxicological testing. This information typically includes observations and other relevant information obtained from witnesses or others connected in some way to the fatality.

Although there is almost always some early indication that a death is likely due to abuse or some type of toxic exposure, this is sometimes not evident until toxicology testing results become available. The immediate goal of death investigators is to obtain sufficient information and supporting evidence to determine the cause and manner of death and evaluate the forensic implications. In substance abuse issues, the specifics of the substance involved such as its identity, source, and so on are likely to have implications beyond the death investigation and impact aspects of possible concurrent investigation focused on broader issues such as drug manufacturing, distribution, and organized crime.

32.5 Substances

Most drug abuse fatalities involve opioids, ethanol, cocaine, and benzodiazepines. Deaths also occur with amphetamines, hallucinogens, and newly emerging psychotropic agents. However, class-designating terms like stimulants, depressants, amphetamines, and hallucinogens have become less descriptive as many substances have prominent features that overlap many classes.

To provide a frame of reference for the number and types of substances that might be expected to be identified in all types of law enforcement cases, a listing of the drugs most frequently identified is provided in Table 32.3.

Table 32.3   Drugs Most Frequently Identified by State and Local Forensic Laboratories in the United States in 2015[a]

Cannabis/THC
Methamphetamine
Cocaine
Heroin
Alprazolam
Oxycodone
Hydrocodone
Buprenorphine
Fentanyl
Clonazepam
Amphetamine
Ethylone
Alpha-PVP
AB-CHMINACA
Morphine
XLR11
Tramadol
Diazepam
MDMA
Methadone
Phencyclidine (PCP)
Psilocin/psilocibin
Hydromorphone
Codeine

[a] United States Drug Enforcement Administration, Office of Diversion Control, National Forensic Laboratory Information System, Annual Report, 2016.

The substances are listed in a descending order with respect to the number of cases in which the specific substance was identified. The drugs listed account for about 85% of the almost 1.5 million cases investigated by the laboratories. The top four substances on the list (cannabis/THC, methamphetamine, cocaine, and heroin) were identified in about 70% of the total number of cases. Although the number of emergency psychotropic substances on the list is small, the incidence of particular agents changes often, with different agents appearing and replacing others in the annual compilation. Perhaps this list and similar datasets will be helpful in prioritizing self-education efforts undertaken by investigators.

32.5.1 Opioids

Opioids are involved in the majority of unintentional drug deaths in the United States. These deaths most often occur when opioids are combined with other drugs that include benzodiazepines, alcohol, cocaine, amphetamines, antidepressants, and antipsychotics. Tolerance to respiratory depression develops at a much slower rate than tolerance to analgesics or euphoric effects. For any given drug in a given set of circumstances, there exists a range of doses that are not fatal. By definition, a dose greater than the top nonfatal dose in this range is a lethal dose. In substance abuse situations in which excessive doses of opioids are used, the margin between a nonfatal and a lethal dose can be very small and can be reduced by many changing factors such as tolerance, concurrent drug use, and the type and quality of opioid used.

In about 50% of the deaths due to heroin, pulmonary edema associated with foaming in the mouth and nostrils is observed. This finding is, however, not specific for heroin deaths. Sudden, unexpected deaths in experienced heroin users are not accounted for by overdose in most cases. The mechanisms are not well understood despite ongoing research in this area. Possible explanations for these sudden deaths include toxic contaminants in the heroin, additive effects of drugs used simultaneously, anaphylactic reactions, and enhanced predisposition for cardiac arrhythmias.

Methadone has a long and highly variable elimination half-life compared to other opioids. It remains in the body long after its analgesic or euphoric effects have dissipated. This can lead to individuals increasing the dose or dose frequency such that levels accumulate to lethal levels in a relatively short period of time. Deaths occurring in methadone maintenance programs generally occur during the initiation phase of treatment. These can result from inappropriate dosage selection or from continuing drug use by patients. Typically, the history in this situation indicates that the individual started methadone within a week before death, was asleep and snoring loudly, and then was discovered dead. Methadone also prolongs the QT interval, and has serotonergic effects that increase the possibility of enhanced toxicity when coadministered with other drugs.

Fentanyl is commercially available in a variety of dosage forms which include: injectables, transdermal patches, lozenges, lollipops, buccal films, nasal sprays, and anesthetic gases. It is also produced illegally in clandestine laboratories. There is also a growing number of illicitly produced fentanyl analogs. Both fentanyl and its analogs are being substituted and sold by dealers as heroin and other substances. Fentanyl is significantly more potent than heroin and other opioids and neither the dealers nor the users, in many cases, seem to appreciate the implications of using drugs with lethal potential in very small doses.

32.5.2 Ethanol

Chronic ethanol use can lead to many fatal diseases involving the cardiovascular and gastrointestinal systems. Although ethanol is a carcinogen, the most common terminal event of chronic abuse is liver failure. Acute ethanol overdose deaths are due to respiratory failure, which is often complicated by aspiration of stomach contents. The potential lethality of ethanol is significantly increased with concomitant use of substances that have depressant effects on the central nervous system.

32.5.3 Cocaine

After methadone, cocaine is the second most frequently found substance in drug-related deaths. Deaths from cocaine can be caused by stroke or cardiac arrhythmias and are more frequent in chronic drug abusers. Death can occur within minutes. Ethanol is the most common substance used concurrently by individuals who die from cocaine use.

The use of intravenous cocaine in combination with heroin, termed power balling, is a particularly deadly combination and deaths from this combination result from cardiac arrest.

32.5.4 Benzodiazepines

Very few deaths have occurred in individuals who have only utilized a benzodiazepine. However, combining benzodiazepine with ethanol, opioids, or tricyclic antidepressants markedly increases the possibility of fatal overdose. Symptoms of overdose include hypotension, ataxia, coma, and respiratory depression. Apnea and death are most likely to occur after intravenous administration.

32.5.5 Barbiturates

Toxic doses of barbiturates depress respiration centers and vasomotor centers in the brain, which can progress to death from respiratory failure and cardio-vascular collapse. Barbiturates have limited clinical use and their availability for recreational use is limited. Barbiturates continue to be used medically for treating some types of migraine headaches and certain seizure disorders. Barbiturates have applications in veterinary medicine and are sometimes diverted from animal use to human recreational or suicidal use.

32.5.6 Amphetamines

Deaths from amphetamines can relate to hypertensive cerebrovascular hemorrhage, cardiovascular collapse secondary to ventricular fibrillation, and hyperthermia. Deaths are often preceded by seizures. Fatal reactions to amphetamines are more common in occasional users than in tolerant, chronic, and high-dose abusers.

32.5.7 Hallucinogens

Death from older hallucinogens such as LSD, PCP, and psilocybin almost never occurs. Since users tend to underestimate the lethal potential of GHB, deaths sometimes occur while individuals are presumably sleeping off an intoxication. The behavioral alterations experienced by users do increase their risks for death from accidents, violence, and suicide. However, the number and types of hallucinogenic substances available in the recent years continue to increase, and many of these newer agents have toxic qualities that can be lethal. Signs of serious toxicity include hyperthermia, rhabdo-myolysis, seizures, and cardiovascular instability. Hallucinogenic substances are not easily classifiable because of overlapping chemical structures and effects, and the toxic spectrum of many substances includes hallucinations, but other toxic effects generally overshadow these effects.

32.5.8 Inhalants

Inhalants are volatile organic chemicals or gases that are inhaled to induce psychoactive effects ranging from intoxication similar to that produced by ethanol, to striking hallucinations. Inhalants include individual substances such as butane or propane but most commonly are components of widely used familiar commercial products. (Table 32.4) They are inhaled directly from containers or from some type of vapor chamber such as a plastic bag containing a cloth soaked in a volatile chemical. The various inhalants are remarkably similar with respect to their immediate effects, but with chronic

Table 32.4   Examples of Products Utilized for Inhalant Abuse

- Aerosol cosmetic products
- Air fresheners
- Butane lighters
- Cooking sprays
- Correction fluids
- Degreasers
- Dry cleaning products
- Felt-tip markers
- Gasoline
- Glues and adhesives
- Hairsprays
- Lighter fluid
- Nail polish and removers
- Paints, varnishes, stains, lacquers, thinners, and strippers
- PVC glue
- Refrigerants
- Solvents
- Spray deodorants
- Spray lubricants
- Spray paints
- Whipping cream canisters

use, the inhalants can cause significant permanent damage to organ systems throughout the body. Sudden death can occur with the initial exposure or at any time during the course of inhalant abuse. Immediate death can result from cardiac arrest or from suffocation due to loss of consciousness while inhaling from a bag covering the head. There is also high incidence of aspiration in fatal inhalant abuse cases.

There is a perception that inhalant abuse is a teenage drug problem and most commonly occurs as a phase of experimentation with substance abuse. However, long-term inhalant abuse does occur and can continue into adulthood.

32.5.9 Emerging Synthetic Psychotropic Substances

The growing number of illegal synthetic drugs represents a diverse group of chemicals that can be encountered unexpectedly by both abusers and investigators. They are often misrepresented as more well-known and familiar substances, and are sometimes the active component of counterfeited drugs having the appearance of commercial prescription products such as OxyContin and Xanax. Some of these substances can produce violent self-destructive behaviors. The most recent additions to the growing number of available designer drugs have included opioid derivatives that can produce respiratory arrest with unusually small doses. These emerging drugs are reviewed in Chapter 21.

32.6 Case Studies

Case: Deadly Arrest

Around 2003, a 33-year-old man attending an outdoor music concert started displaying bizarre behavior that included striking other attendees. After a struggle, security guards removed him in handcuffs from the concert grounds and held him until he calmed down sufficiently to allow transportation to a police facility. While being transported, his irrational behavior escalated and he kicked out a window of the police car. He was then removed from the car and placed on the ground in a prone position with his hands still handcuffed behind his back. At this time, his movements began to decrease in intensity until he became motionless and unresponsive. Resuscitation efforts were not successful. The man had no significant medical or psychiatric history, and an autopsy did not uncover a preexisting pathological basis for his death. Toxicological analysis of autopsy specimens identified phencyclidine, ethanol, and diphenhydramine. The cause of death was ruled as asphyxiation associated with phencyclidine intoxication and the manner of death as homicide.

Comments

The sudden and unexpected death of individuals during physical restraint and arrest results from multiple factors. The relative importance of the various factors remains to be elucidated. Deaths of this nature typically involve cocaine. It is uncommon for phencyclidine to be implicated in police-restraint death cases.

Case: 65-Year-Old Huffer

In 2015, a 65-year-old man died in his Florida home while inhaling a volatile solvent for recreational purposes. The deceased was a prominent political activist at both the state and the national level. He had a long-term marriage with children and grandchildren, and he was viewed by many as a mentor and role model. He had a history of solvent abuse and several aerosol solvent containers were recovered at the scene. Autopsy findings and postmortem toxicology testing results were consistent with a ruling of accidental death caused by ethyl chloride intoxication.

Comments

Commercial products containing ethyl chloride are popular for inhalation abuse. There are ethyl chloride products sold that are targeted to abusers. Chronic use can produce significant neurotoxicity. Acute fatalities result from cardiac arrhythmias believed to result from an increased myocardial sensitivity to endogenous catecholamines.

Case: Crazy Monkey

In 2014, a 22-year-old man in Southern California took his dog to a veterinary clinic after it became hyperactive and had a seizure. While at the clinic, the man became ill and then had a generalized seizure. Emergency medical responders found the man awake but his heart rate, blood pressure, respiratory rate, and blood glucose were all elevated. While being examined, the man had another seizure that was treated with midazolam. On arrival at a hospital emergency department, he was unresponsive. Minutes later, he became severely agitated and required restraint by multiple individuals. He was again administered midazolam, intubated, and started on a propofol infusion to maintain sedation. He was transferred to an intensive care unit for monitoring and diagnostic evaluation that included metabolic tests, ECG, head CT scan, and urine toxicology screening. The screen was positive for benzodiazepines and negative for amphetamines, cocaine, THC, barbiturates, methadone, and other opioids. The following morning he was extubated. He remained confused throughout the day and only remembered taking his dog to the clinic because it appeared ill and was not eating. He provided no information on the possible drug exposure for the dog, but he admitted to smoking up to three pots of Crazy Monkey per day. Both the man and the dog recovered after 2 days and were discharged. The Crazy Monkey product was analyzed, and samples of serum and urine were screened for seizure-inducing drugs, common drugs of abuse, synthetic cannabinoids, synthetic cathinones, and other designer drugs. The screening covered more than 700 compounds. Only PB-22 (QUPIC) and trace amounts of UR-144, were detected. These are both synthetic cannabinoids. Three months after this incident, the man was again admitted to a hospital due to smoking Crazy Monkey. His symptoms and the course of hospital evaluation and treatment were almost identical to his first hospital admission, and he again recovered on the second day and left the hospital against medical advice. There were no samples available from the second admission for testing.

Comments

PB-22 (QUPIC) is a synthetic cannabinoid. The individual in this case regularly smoked a plant material product (Crazy Monkey) containing PB-22. He and his dog suffered convulsive episodes from PB-22. The details of the dog's exposure could not be determined. Whether the dog was administered the drug, accidently consumed it, or developed toxicity from inhaling environmental smoke is not known.

Case: Dextromethorphan

Around 2012, four unrelated young adults were living together in an apartment in Washington State where they shared a devotion to a drug culture centered on heavy use of dextromethorphan. For more than a year, they regularly ingested dextromethorphan in pure form obtained from Internet sources, and also medicinal products containing dextromethorphan. Individual doses usually exceeded 500 mg. Their drug-induced behaviors were unpredictable and became so alarming to at least one member of the group that this individual moved out.

One evening the remaining three individuals ingested their usual excessive amount of dextromethorphan and watched a futuristic video that featured individuals with super-human powers and abilities. One of the men present became markedly agitated and began hallucinating. He attempted to emulate the actions of the characters in the video, such as passing through walls and levitating. This bizarre behavior progressed until he started cutting his arms and chest with a kitchen knife. The one woman in the group hugged the man in an effort to calm him. He then stabbed her and himself. Police and emergency medical responders, summoned by the other male in the group, found the hallucinating man dead and the woman seriously wounded. The postmortem blood concentration of dextromethorphan was almost 5000 µg/L. There were deep penetrating stab wounds as well as many, many superficial knife wounds across the chest. The cause of death was ruled as multiple stab wounds in the chest and acute dextromethorphan intoxication. The manner of death was suicide. The individual who summoned emergency responders had a dextromethorphan blood level of 300 µg/L. No criminal charges were filed in this case.

Comments

Dextromethorphan is an antitussive found in many nonprescription cough products and is also used clinically for some types of neurological disorders and occasionally as an adjunct to some analgesic medication regimens. For many years dextromethorphan abuse involved excessive use of commercial cough products, which usually contain 15 mg per dose. Clusters of abusive situations recurred periodically as these medications continued to be rediscovered by experimenting adolescents. There were serious consequences in some cases, and sometimes abuse continued far into adulthood, but this was rare. However, when pure dextromethorphan became easily available from Internet sources, the abusive use of exceeding high doses in continuing patterns markedly elevated the consequences of abuse. Increasingly, abusers are encountered with extreme agitation, psychotic and violent behavior. Abusers often feel invincible and frequently engage in violent and self-destructive behaviors.

Case: Television Viewer

Around 2016, a 45-year-old woman was last seen watching evening television shows. The following day, she was found in her bed unresponsive and not breathing. Emergency medical responders found her dead on arrival. She had a history of anxiety and depression disorders, and previous suicide attempts. She had also been known to have abused oxycodone and ethanol but it was believed she had discontinued using either of them for several months preceding her death. There were indications at the scene of possible inhalant abuse, but this use was not confirmed. Prescribed medications found at the scene included alprazolam, diazepam, promethazine, zonisamide, trazodone, and topiramate. The quantities suggested that they were used as prescribed. There were no indications of any illicit drug use. Autopsy findings included a somewhat enlarged heart, mild nephrosclerosis, edematous lungs containing frothy liquid, and bluish liquid stomach contents. Postmortem toxicological testing of samples of blood, vitreous humor, brain, liver, bile, urine, and gastric contents were identified and quantitated for the levels of butyryl fentanyl, acetyl fentanyl, acetyl norfentanyl (metabolite), alprazolam, and ethanol. Based on the history, autopsy findings, and the toxicology testing results, the cause of death was determined to be intoxication by the combined effects of the substances mentioned earlier, and the manner of death was ruled as accidental. There were no indications of intravenous drug use, which suggested that the exposure route was nasal, oral, or sublingual.

Comments

Acetyl fentanyl and butyryl fentanyl are illicit analogs of fentanyl. Prior to postmortem toxicological testing, there were no indications from the case history or scene investigation that the fentanyl analogs would be detected.

Case: Synthetic Cannabinoid Abuse Death

In 2013, a 27-year-old man in poor health was taken to a hospital emergency department by his girlfriend. After evaluation, he was diagnosed as having acute liver and kidney failure. The man indicated that he had no alcohol abuse problems but smoked marijuana several times per week. He was transferred to an intensive care unit where his symptoms included severe coagulopathy, respiratory failure, and marked metabolic disturbances in addition to the previously noted liver and kidney disorders. His condition continued to deteriorate over the following 12 h, and he expired from cardiopulmonary failure that was unresponsive to resuscitation. Analysis of antemortem serum samples revealed the presence of THC and 5F-PB-22. Based on autopsy findings and the toxicological testing results, the cause of death was determined to be liver failure in a setting of marijuana and 5F-PB-22 exposure. The manner of death was classified as undetermined.

Comments

5F-PB-22 is an illegal synthetic cannabinoid. At the time this case occurred, 5F-PB-22 was being identified only as an additive to plant material sold for smoking. The etiology of the decedent's rapid multiple organ failures could have been the result of exposure to this synthetic cannabinoid, but lack of credible information on the individual's medical history and possible previous exposures to other potential toxicants makes such a determination impossible. The apparently recent onset of the man's failing health and the absence of other substances in serum samples suggests a causal or contributory role of the synthetic cannabinoid or its metabolites. Other cases of unexpected sudden deaths following 5F-PB-22 exposure have been reported. However, in forensic matters, every specific case is unique with respect to cause-and-effect analysis. Perhaps, in this case, the death may not have been as unexpected as it appeared to be.

References and Additional Reading

Behonick G, Shanks KG, Firchau DJ, Mathur G, Lynch CF, Nashelsky M, Jaskierny DJ, Meroueh C: Four postmortem case reports with quantitative detection of the synthetic cannabinoid, 5F-PB-22. *J Anal Toxicol*, 38: 559–562, 2014.

Boyer EW: Management of opioid analgesic overdose. *N Engl J Med*, 367: 146–155, 2012.

Broussard LA, Broussard AK, Pittman TS, Lirette DK: Death due to inhalation of ethyl chloride. *J Forensic Soc*, 45: 223–225, 2000.

Coco TJ, Klasner AE: Drug-induced rhabdomyolysis. *Curr Opin Pediatr*, 16: 206–210, 2004.

Darke S, Deady M, Duflou J: Toxicology and characteristics of deaths involving zolpidem in New South Wales, Australia 2001–2010. *J Forensic Sci*, 57: 1259–1262, 2012.

Djurendic-Brenesel M, Stojiljkovic G, Pilija V: Fatal intoxication with toluene due to inhalation of glue. *J Forensic Sci*, 61: 875–878, 2016.

Glover S, Girion L: Dying for relief: A Times investigation (four-part series on the epidemic of prescription drug deaths). *Los Angeles Times*, November–December, 2012.

Gugelmann H, Gerona R, Li C, Tsutaoka B, Olson KR, Ling D: "Crazy Monkey" poisons man and dog: Human and canine seizures due to PB-22, a novel synthetic cannabinoid. *Clin Toxicol*, 52: 635-638, 2014.

Gunja N: The clinical and forensic toxicology of Z-drugs. *J Med Toxicol*, 9: 155–162, 2013.

Henry JA: Metabolic consequences of drug misuse. *Br J Anaesth*, 85: 136–142, 2000.

Jones JD, Mogali S, Comer SD: Polydrug abuse: A review of opioid and benzodiazepine combination use. *Drug Alcohol Depend*, 125: 8–18, 2012.

Jonsson AK, Soderberg C, Espnes KA, Ahlner J, Eriksson A, Reis M, Druid H: Sedative and hypnotic drugs: Fatal and non-fatal reference blood concentrations. *Forensic Sci Int*, 236: 138–145, 2014.

Katz KD, Leonetti AL, Bailey BC, Surmaitis RM, Eustice ER, Kacinko S, Wheatley SM. Case series of synthetic cannabinoid intoxication from one toxicology center. *West J Emerg Med*, 17: 290–294, 2016.

Krinsky CS, Lathrop SL, Crossey M, Baker G, Zumwalt R: A toxicology-based review of fentanyl-related deaths in New Mexico (1986–2007). *Am J Forensic Med Pathol*, 32: 347–351, 2011.

Lee D, Chronister CW, Broussard WA, Utley-Bobak SR, Schultz DL, Vega RS, Goldberger BA: Illicit fentanyl-related fatalities in Florida: Toxicological findings. *J Anal Toxicol*, 40: 588–594, 2016.

Lee D, Delcher C, Maldonado-Molina MM, Thogmartin JR, Goldberger BA: Manners of death in drug-related fatalities. *J Forensic Sci*, 61: 735–742, 2016.

Logan BK, Yeakel JK, Goldfogel G, Frost MP, Sandstrom G, Wickham DJ: Dextromethorphan abuse leading to assault, suicide, or homicide. *J Forensic Sci*, 57: 1388–1394, 2012.

Martins SS, Sampson L, Cerda M, Galea S: Worldwide prevalence and trends in unintentional drug overdose: A systematic review of the literature. *Am J Public Health*, 105: 29–49, 2015.

Palmer RB: Fentanyl in postmortem forensic toxicology. *Clin Toxicol*, 48: 771–784, 2010.

Pestaner JP, Southall PE: Sudden death during arrest and phencyclidine intoxication. *Am J Forensic Med Pathol*, 24: 119–122, 2003.

Pilgrim JL, Gerostamoulos D, Drummer OH: Deaths involving contraindicated and inappropriate combinations of serotonergic drugs. *Int J Legal Med*, 125: 803–815, 2011.

Schep LJ, Knudsen K, Slaughter RJ, Vale JA, Megarbane B: The clinical toxicology of gamma-hydroxybutyrate, gamma-butyrolactone, and 1, 4-butanediol. *Clin Toxicol*, 50: 458–470, 2012.

Schwartz BG, Rezkalla S, Kloner RA: Cardiovascular effects of cocaine. *Circulation*, 122: 2258–2569, 2010.

Sellors K, Jones A, Chan B: Death due to intravenous use of α-pyrrolidinopentiophenone. *Med J Aust*, 201: 601–603, 2014.

Tamsen F, Thiblin I: Deaths during apprehensions of agitated persons. A review of proposed pathophysiological theories. *Scand J Forensic Sci*, 19: 91–110, 2013.

Templeton AH, Carter KLT, Sheron N, Gallagher PJ, Verrill C: Sudden unexpected death in alcohol misuse: An unrecognized public health issue?. *Int J Environ Res Public Health*, 6: 3070–3081, 2009.

Trecki J, Gerona RR, Schwarz MD: Synthetic cannabinoid-related illnesses and deaths. *N Engl J Med*, 373: 103–107, 2015.

Wilson KC, Saukkonen JJ: Acute respiratory failure from abused substances. *J Intensive Care Med*, 19: 183–193, 2004.

Yacoub I, Robinson CA, Simmons GT, Hall M: Death attributed to ethyl chloride. *J Anal Toxicol*, 17: 384–385, 1993.

Zvosec DL, Smith SW, Porrata T, Strobl AQ, Dyer JE: Case series of 226 gamma-hydroxbutyrae-associated deaths: Lethal toxicity and trauma. *Am J Emerg Med*, 29: 319–332, 2011.

Celebrity Drug Deaths 33

33.1 Introduction

There are many pathways to chronic drug abuse and many individualized patterns of abuse, but the potential lethal consequences of excessive abuse are the same regardless of one's status in life. Wealth and celebrity status can facilitate access to drugs in an environment that conceals and sometimes supports abuse.

The intense attention devoted to celebrity deaths generates a comprehensive body of information on all aspects of celebrities' lives and their deaths, which include expert analysis and commentary. After due consideration for sensationalized and fictional elements, this information provides a rich source of material for investigative considerations that are applicable to death investigations in other circumstances. The case studies provided in Section 33.4 were selected to highlight generalizable aspects of drug abuse deaths.

33.2 Exposure Situations and Circumstances

Many factors have been identified that affect the likelihood of drug abuse, but no single factor or set of factors can adequately explain the abuse by a specific individual. Factors responsible for initiating drug use are not necessarily the same as those that lead to continuing or escalating use. In terms of performance, drugs tend to be used to sleep, to wake up, to mask anxiety, and to provide energy and stamina. The primary focus for investigations is not on how the celebrities come to be abusers, or why they continued, but on the use and circumstances that are relevant to determining what role, if any, the substances played in their death and whether the death was accidental, suicidal, or homicidal.

Recreational drug use can provide users with an artificial state of confidence and well-being. To accomplish this effect, the simultaneous use of several different drugs is often necessary. This leads to physiological and physical dependence, which requires continued use to suppress or prevent withdrawal. Superimposed on this drug use, individuals have unrelated medical issues that may require medication. It would be a significant challenge for trained medical professionals to accomplish this with correct doses and dosing schedules to match changing circumstances.

33.3 Investigative Considerations

The nature of many celebrity lifestyles can facilitate access to virtually any legal or illegal drug, and their friends, support staff, and physicians can include drug abuse enablers and facilitators. An obstacle that can be encountered in celebrity death investigations is the active effort of individuals connected either professionally or socially with the celebrity to minimize or limit the spread of an investigation to other individuals or organizations. This effort is probably more related to damage control than to the concealment of criminal activity. The medical and drug history of celebrities tends to include many physicians and medical facilities, and likely includes incidents of overdose treatment and abuse management. Often the distinction between acute medical treatment of overdoses, medical detoxification, and rehabilitation efforts is not clear in the records. Superimposed on this issue is the popular, more generically applied use of the term detoxification to indicate some type of metabolic cleansing or alternative medicine.

33.4 Case Studies

Case: Philip Seymour Hoffman (1967–2014)

Philip Seymour Hoffman was an Academy Award best actor and director in both films and theater. He appeared in more than 50 movies. He was deeply involved in the activities of his young children who attended public schools. He often spoke publicly about addiction struggles early in his life and career. He had problems with alcohol and drug addiction, but had many drug-free years. Later he began abusing prescription opioids, which escalated to heroin use. His drug use had progressed to the point that it was responsible for his separation from his partner and children and he lived in a nearby apartment. He underwent detoxification for opioids several months before he died but continued to drink and eventually resumed using drugs. After he missed an appointment to pick up his children, friends investigated and found him dead in the bathroom of his Manhattan apartment. He was wearing boxer shorts and a tee shirt. His eyeglasses were still in place and a hypodermic needle was still in his arm. Syringes, heroin packets, and cocaine were found in his apartment along with prescription medications that included clonidine, buprenorphine, hydroxyzine, methocarbamol, and an amphetamine. His death was a result of a lethal mixture of drugs. The actual names and quantities of drugs found in autopsy samples were not made public, but they were reported to have included heroin, cocaine, benzodiazepines, and amphetamines.

Comments

The prescription drugs in his apartment suggest that he was under a physician's care and that he was being treated for his opioid addiction. The combination of cocaine and heroin is common for experienced users and is selected for the combined effects produced. The significance of the syringe in his arm after death is likely the result of losing consciousness before he removed it rather than indicative of an instant death.

Case: Whitney Houston (1963–2012)

Whitney Houston was born in Newark, New Jersey and died in Beverly Hills, California at the age of 49. She was a singer, actress, producer, and model. Whitney had a long history of drug abuse and admissions to rehabilitation facilities. Her drug use ultimately derailed her career and significantly damaged her voice. Whitney was found dead submerged in the bathtub of her hotel suite. She was preparing to attend a Grammy Awards Ceremony later that day. A large number of prescribed medications were found in her hotel suite. Also found were cocaine, nonprescription medications, and a variety of alcoholic beverages. The medical examiner ruled her death as an accident due to drowning secondary to the effects of atherosclerotic heart disease and cocaine use. The drugs identified in the biological samples taken at autopsy included alprazolam, cocaine, marijuana, cyclobenzaprine, and diphenhydramine.

Comments

Chronic cocaine use can cause a buildup of plaque in coronary arteries, disrupt cardiac function, and compromise oxygen utilization by the heart. These effects likely contributed to a major heart attack leading to her drowning. She had a preference for smoking marijuana mixed with cocaine. Cyclobenzaprine is a muscle relaxant with abuse potential.

Case: Amy Winehouse (1983–2011)

Amy Winehouse was a Grammy Award-winning British pop singer–songwriter known for an eclectic mix of musical genres. She had a long public history of heavy drug and alcohol abuse. Drugs included heroin, ecstasy, cocaine, and ketamine. She spent short periods in drug rehabilitation centers and was hospitalized on several occasions for medical conditions related to drug use and abuse. She often performed intoxicated and had tours canceled because of this. She was noted to be a violent person when intoxicated and occasionally slapped or punched her fans. In addition to substance abuse disorders, she was known to have manic depression and an eating disorder. Her heavy tobacco smoking and crack cocaine use led to emphysema. She died from accidental ethanol poisoning. No other drugs were implicated. She apparently resumed drinking after about a month of abstinence. Vodka bottles were found with the body and her postmortem blood alcohol level was well into the lethal range for nontolerant individuals.

Comments

Early speculation following her death was that she died from alcohol withdrawal because she was believed to have been free from drug and alcohol use for several days preceding death. This speculation was clearly incorrect. Her tolerance for alcohol was reduced by the period of abstinence; when she resumed drinking at the amounts she was accustomed to drinking before her period of abstinence, the amount was lethal.

Case: Michael Jackson (1958–2009)

Michael Jackson was the most successful entertainer in history. He sang, he danced, he wrote hit songs, and he orchestrated fantastic performances. He was a global superstar. Michael was intelligent, talented, and unusually creative. He was also immature, troubled, and excessively weird. His one-of-a-kind performances as well as his bizarre behavior and disastrous modification of his facial features captured the attention of the world. After arriving home from a late-night rehearsal, Michael took a shower and went to bed. He died in his bed in the Los Angeles mansion where he lived with his children. The death was ruled a homicide caused by propofol. The propofol was administered by Michael's personal physician, who generally spent the nights with Michael to administer drugs. On Michael's last night, the physician administered doses of diazepam, lorazepam, midazolam, and a slow intravenous infusion of propofol. This resulted in respiratory failure and death. The physician was unquestionably responsible for the death; he lacked both the knowledge and skills required to utilize the medications he was administering, and he practiced medicine recklessly. He was convicted of involuntary manslaughter and went to prison.

Comments

Michael had a long history of substance abuse that included opioids, stimulants, alcohol, and sedative-hypnotics. His use of propofol started around 1997. The propofol was typically administered in hotel rooms and various other nonmedical settings. He had received propofol nightly in his home for at least 2 months prior to his death. It was postulated that on the fatal day he was administered the drugs without close monitoring and his respirations progressively decreased until they stopped; a short time later he had a cardiac arrest. When his physician ultimately discovered Michael not breathing, he lacked both the skill and equipment to resuscitate him.

Case: Heath Ledger (1979–2008)

Heath Ledger was an Australian actor and director. He appeared in 19 films and received numerous national and international acting awards. Heath was found dead in his Manhattan apartment. His accidental death resulted from a lethal mixture of oxycodone, hydrocodone, diazepam, temazepam, alprazolam, and doxylamine. In addition to the drugs found at autopsy, his history of drug use included cocaine, ecstasy, and marijuana.

Comments

The combined respiratory depressant effects of two opioids, three benzodiazepines, and an antihistamine resulted in death. The combined effects of these drugs that might have been used in therapeutic doses are at least additive. The additive effects of drugs are well-known to substance abusers and the possible synergistic effect is one of the reasons for multiple drug use. However, the cumulative toxicity of drug mixtures is underappreciated and usually ignored.

Case: Anna Nicole Smith (1967–2007)

Anna Nicole Smith was a model and television personality probably best known for her flaky sex-goddess appearances and her tabloid lifestyle. Shortly after failing her freshman year in a Houston, Texas high school, she quit school and married a coworker in a local fast-food restaurant. They separated shortly after her son was born. She then moved with her son to Houston where she worked as a topless dancer and eventually became Playmate of the Year in 1993. When she was 26, she married an 89-year-old billionaire who died about a year later (1995). Litigation over Anna's share of her husband's estate was lengthy and intense, and included matters that rose to the level of the United States Supreme Court. In 2006, she gave birth to a girl in a hospital in the Bahamas. While still in the hospital, her son traveled from California to the Bahamas to visit his mother. He died in her hospital room from a drug overdose. About 6 months later, Anna died in a hotel room in Florida from a drug overdose. Her death was ruled to be accidental and due to the combined toxicity of multiple prescription medications. The drugs (or metabolites) identified in postmortem testing included chloral hydrate, clonazepam, diazepam, lorazepam, carisoprodol, diphenhydramine, topiramate, and methadone.

Comments

For medical–legal purposes, the identification and quantification of the specific drugs present in Anna's postmortem tissue samples were extremely important. However, the drugs found represent only a sampling of the possibilities that might have been found in a death investigation carried out at another time. She had access to huge amounts of prescription drugs, which she used excessively for years. They included a number of opioids, benzodiazepines, and sedative-hypnotics, muscle relaxants, and other psychotropic agents. Similarly, she received various other therapeutic agents such as diuretics, antibiotics, antiemetics, and antispasmotics with marginal medical oversight. Her excessive drug use and abuse also included regular uncontrolled injections of vitamins, human growth hormone, and immunoglobulin.

Case: Elvis Presley (1935–1977)

Elvis Presley was a singer, musician, and actor; he was one of the most significant cultural icons of the twentieth century. His performances were electrifying. His energized interpretations of songs made him enormously popular. He was the best-selling solo artist in the history of recorded music. Elvis was introduced to amphetamines in 1959 while serving in the United States Army. His drug use escalated from that point to his eventual fatal overdose. Elvis rarely drank and severely criticized individuals who used illegal recreational drugs. He felt that obtaining prescription drugs from a physician was not drug abuse. He overdosed on barbiturates several times and was hospitalized at least once for meperidine addiction. He continued to perform to sellout crowds even though he was embarrassingly drugged during his performances. He was discovered dead on the bathroom floor of his Graceland mansion in Memphis, Tennessee. He was scheduled to leave that evening to begin a tour. The day before he died, he visited his dentist, played racquetball, and entertained his friends with singing and piano playing. His death was officially attributed to a cardiac arrhythmia, but most experts feel that this was an attempt to cover up an overdose of multiple drugs, which he had used constantly and excessively for years. He was overweight and had an enlarged heart. More than a dozen drugs were identified in blood samples obtained during autopsy.

Comments

Drugs and their metabolites identified during postmortem toxicology testing included the following: codeine, methaqualone, diazepam, ethinamate, ethchlorvynol, amobarbital, pentobarbital, meperidine, phenyltoloxamine, and carbromal. The simultaneous use of these drugs by Elvis was not uncommon in the preceding years of his life. The additive toxicity of multiple drugs was either ignored or not appreciated by the individuals supplying drugs to Elvis. It was well known that Elvis obtained excessive amounts of prescription drugs from his personal physician, and he also obtained additional quantities from other sources. The notion that smaller quantities of several drugs is less lethal than an equivalent amount of a single drug persists today among many drug abusers, and even among many medical professionals who continue to prescribe multiple drugs that are potentially lethal when used simultaneously.

Case: Marilyn Monroe (1926–1962)

Marilyn Monroe was a major screen star and sex idol. She remains one of the most iconic figures in the world. She was married to a United States Merchant Marine sailor, a baseball legend, a literary genius, and had affairs with many of the rich and famous, including a United States President. Marilyn had serious long-term (years) substance abuse problems that involved alcohol, amphetamines, tranquilizers, and several barbiturates and other types of sedative-hypnotic agents. Substances were taken orally as well as by injection. Marilyn was found dead in her bedroom in Los Angeles. She was 36 years old. Her death was ruled to have resulted from acute barbiturate poisoning and was listed as a probable suicide. The principal drugs implicated were Nembutal (a barbiturate) and chloral hydrate. Both drugs were widely prescribed at the time for sleep. In the 50 years since her death, there has been much speculation and controversy regarding the circumstances of her death. There have been numerous books and publications devoted to the analysis of her death. Arguments have been presented to support the manner of her death as being homicide, suicide, or accidental. The most likely explanation for Marilyn's death is that she accidentally overdosed on prescription medications. It is likely that following her usual pattern of heavy drug use during the day, she self-administered an excessive amount of drugs at bedtime.

Comments

In general, the number of tablets or capsules taken and the time of ingestion cannot be determined by postmortem blood levels of drugs. The analytical results suggest that an excessive amount of pentobarbital and chloral hydrate were ingested over a period of hours preceding Marilyn's death. The possibility that other drugs might have been involved was not included in the scope of the testing carried out.

References and Additional Reading

Jones AW, Holmgren P: Comparison of blood-ethanol concentration in deaths attributed to acute alcohol poisoning and chronic alcoholism. *J Forensic Sci*, 48:874–879, 2003.

Lathan SR: Celebrities and substance abuse. *Proc Baylor Univ Med Cent*, 22: 339–341, 2009.

Levy RJ: Clinical effects and lethal and forensic aspects of propofol. *J Forensic Sci*, 57: 142–147, 2011.

Na E, Lee KS, Kim E, Jeon HJ, Yang Y, Roh S: Deaths of celebrities and substance use: A qualitative investigation. *J Add Preven*, 3: 1–6, 2015.

Perper JA, Juste GM, Schueler HE, Motte RW, Cina SJ: Suggested guidelines for the management of high-profile fatality cases. *Arch Pathol Lab Med*, 132: 1630–1634, 2008.

Thompson CC, Cole JP: *The Death of Elvis: What Really Happened*. New York: Delacort Press, 1991.

Viani K: *The Big Book of Celebrity Autopsies*. New York: Skyhorse, 2013.

Wecht CH, Kaufman D: *A Question of Murder*. Amherst, NY: Prometheus Books, 2008.

Drug-Facilitated Crimes 34

34.1 Introduction

Drugs can be used as tools for criminal activity such as sexual assault and robbery. In these crimes, victims are sedated or otherwise affected in ways that render them submissive or compliant with the actions of the perpetrators. The surreptitious administration of sublethal amounts of drugs as a form of punishment and the administration of abortifacients to expectant mothers without their knowledge or consent are also drug-facilitated crimes. Other examples are listed in Table 34.1. Most of the drug-facilitated crimes listed are reviewed in the following sections. Drug-facilitated sexual assault is reviewed separately in the following chapter.

34.2 Exposure Situations and Circumstances

34.2.1 Robbery

Numerous variations of robberies occur that are orchestrated around a victim's expectation of sexual pleasures. This expectation places individuals in situations in which they can be drugged and robbed. Victims may be targets of opportunity or carefully selected based on research and surveillance. Perpetrators may act alone or function as part of a team composed of criminals with special skills applicable to different aspects of the robbery. The increased vulnerability of travelers due to their unfamiliar surroundings is an important risk factor for drug-facilitated robberies.

34.2.2 Sublethal Poisoning

Intentional poisoning for reasons other than homicide could include revenge, punishment, or pranks intended to embarrass or otherwise compromise victims. The objective might be to induce discomfort or illness. An example would be the surreptitious addition of a laxative to an individual's food. Disciplining or punishing children by forcing them to ingest copious amounts of liquids or noxious substances such as spices or hot sauce is another example of sublethal poisoning.

Table 34.1   Drug-Facilitated Crimes

Covert abortion
Drug-facilitated behavioral control
Drug-facilitated interrogation
Drug-facilitated robbery
Drug-facilitated sexual assault
Drug-facilitated sporting advantage
Poisoning for commercial advantage
Sedation of children or elderly by caregivers
Sublethal poisoning for punishment, prank, or attention

34.2.3 Termination of Pregnancy

There are medically approved abortifacient drugs available for use in defined circumstances using a specified dosing schedule. The most common drug used for medical abortion is misoprostol, which is a prostaglandin that induces uterine contractions. Prostaglandins are normal constituents of the body and are involved in a wide variety of functions in different organ systems. For example, in addition to their involvement in uterine contractions, prostaglandins regulate gastric acid secretion and misoprostol is sometimes used therapeutically in nonpregnant individuals for the prevention of gastric ulcers. This use can provide a pretense for obtaining the drug without revealing the actual intended use for covert administration to induce an abortion.

34.2.4 Sedation by Caregivers

The practice of sedating individuals for convenience is viewed by authorities, and society in general, in various ways depending on what the sedating agent is, who administers it, what the objective is, and the consequences. When this occurs in nursing homes, daycare centers, and similar service settings, it is clearly a serious legal and health issue. Less clear-cut, from a medical and legal perspective, are situations involving parents administering sedatives to children in conjunction with activities such as long road trips or airline flights.

34.2.5 Sporting Advantage

Compared to the use of performance-enhancing drugs, drugging sporting opponents is exceedingly rare. Sedating substances, most often benzodiazepines, have been administered surreptitiously to individual opponents and opposing competitive teams in attempts to achieve a competitive advantage.

Inducing a meaningful performance decrement without visible signs of impairment requires precise dosing that would be difficult to accomplish in most competitive sporting environments.

34.2.6 Commercial Advantage

The opportunity for utilizing poisoning for commercial advantage would seem most obviously to involve food in some fashion. However, on a retail level, this almost never occurs. Most localized cases of poisoned or tainted food or beverage products involve a disgruntled employee seeking revenge on his or her employer rather than an act to dissuade patrons from using the outlet and becoming customers of a similar competitive business instead.

34.2.7 Interrogation

Using drugs to extract information from an individual is a common topic in the current climate of homeland security and terrorism. The drugs mentioned most often are thiopental, amobarbital, scopolamine, and ethanol. The efficacy of drug-facilitated interrogation is questionable at best; however, the practice of facilitating conversations with drugs and ethanol is rather common. It is well known that intoxicated individuals often reveal information that they might otherwise not reveal. This observation is likely exploited in some cases for criminal gains.

34.3 Investigative Considerations

Drug-facilitated crimes include many situations where victims are unaware of their exposure to drugs and, due to the amnesic properties of the drugs typically used for these crimes, are unable to recount their experiences. These factors generally delay the initiation of an investigation and also decrease the possibility of identifying the offending drugs in biological samples using conventional analytical methodology.

34.4 Case Studies

Case: Expensive Entertainment

In 2014, five adults in New York City were arrested and charged with grand larceny, conspiracy, assault, forgery, and tampering with evidence relating to their organized scheme for using the credit cards of wealthy male victims to obtain large amounts of money. The conspiracy charged in this indictment involved the theft of approximately $200,000 from four victims over a 3-month period. However, this activity was believed to have been occurring with other victims for quite some time. Wealthy males living in New York were targets that were identified in upscale bars and restaurants and befriended by attractive women who drugged them. They were then taken to a gentlemen's club where they were entertained in a private room while their credit cards were utilized by an experienced team to generate cash. One victim had lost more than $100,000 from charges made on four different occasions. Victims often had no memory of the experience, and those who complained were sent threatening messages that included incriminating photos. The group was headed by a 40-year-old female who employed three younger entertainers and a club manager. The drugs utilized included ketamine, methylone, and cocaine.

Comments

The victims in this case included a hedge fund manager, a banker, a real estate lawyer, and a cardiologist. They learned of the extent of their credit card charges either by checking their monthly statements or by being contacted by their credit card companies.

Case: Nuts on the Bus

In 2001, an adult found unconscious on a public transportation bus was admitted to a hospital in a small town in the Aegean Region of Turkey. The town attracted tourists to view historic sites that were well-connected by railways and motorways. It was quickly determined that the hospitalized patient had been drugged and robbed. Three months later, a second patient was admitted who had similarly been drugged and robbed while traveling using the same public transportation system. Information obtained from these individuals enabled officials to monitor the area of the robberies and ultimately apprehend the perpetrator while in the act of robbing another individual. The thief was a 50-year-old male with a criminal history that included prison time. Each of the victims had sat next to the perpetrator during a trip and had accepted some of the trail mix he offered them from a snack that he was apparently eating. Shortly thereafter, the victims lost consciousness, their valuables were taken, and the perpetrator left the bus unnoticed at the next convenient stop. The mixture consisted of hazelnuts and dried raisins. The hazelnuts had been cut in half, a cavity made to hold clonazepam and the halves were glued back together. When consumed, the taste of the drug in the hazelnuts was masked by the dried raisins.

Comments

This case is a striking example of the ingenuity of criminals. Clonazepam is a long-acting benzodiazepine best known by its brand name Klonopin. It is used in clinical medicine to treat various types of anxiety and seizure disorders, and as an adjunctive medication for other psychiatric conditions. Daily therapeutic doses are generally less than 10 mg. The approximate amount of clonazepam found in each hazelnut in this case was 150 mg.

Case: Visine in Water Bottles

In 2012, a 33-year-old single mother living in Pennsylvania was arrested for poisoning her 45-year-old boyfriend with Visine eye drops over a period of 3 years. Periodically, she added the eye drops to bottled water he drank. Her goal was to gain more attention from her boyfriend. It is not clear how this was intended to work. The poisoning was discovered when suspicions were raised by the man's physician who treated him over the years for unexplained episodic illnesses that included nausea, vomiting, blood pressure fluctuations, and breathing difficulties. The physician had the man's blood tested in a clinical laboratory that identified the poison. Later this was confirmed by authorities with toxicological testing in a forensic laboratory. The woman was charged with assault and reckless endangerment but she pleaded guilty to reduced charges of aggravated assault and was sentenced to 2 to 4 years in prison.

Comments

Many nonprescription eye drop and nasal spray products contain tetrahydrozoline or a closely related ingredient. These agents decrease congestion and reduce eye redness by constricting blood vessels in the areas where they are applied. When these topical products are ingested, they can have serious effects within the cardiovascular system, make breathing difficult, and produce nausea and vomiting. Large doses can induce seizures. There have been a number of unintentional as well as intentional poisonings reported that involve the ingestion of these topical eye and nasal products.

Case: Nanny Poisons Asparagus Soup

In 2010, a 32-year-old nanny was arrested for poisoning her employer's food with automotive windshield washer fluid. The nanny pleaded guilty and received a 1-year prison sentence. The motive was to make the food less palatable and discredit the individual who prepared the food. Initially, she added excess salt to the food, then excess sugar, and finally added a container capful quantity of windshield washer fluid. The salty and sweet meals did generate a great deal of criticism regarding their preparation. The windshield washer-tainted food caused alarm because it was a clearly visible indication that something toxic was added. The tainted food, in this case asparagus soup, was brought to the attention of authorities and subsequently led to the arrest of the nanny.

Comments

Windshield washer fluids can contain methyl alcohol, which is potentially very toxic. It seems likely that the perpetrator in this case happened upon an opportunity in which she was delivering the food and used what was available in her vehicle rather than selectively deciding on the substance to use.

Case: Enthusiastic Tennis Father

Starting in 2000, a 46-year-old retired military pilot drugged a number of his child's tennis rivals and was convicted of manslaughter after one of the players died in a car accident after being drugged. He doped the water bottles of at least 27 players during matches against his son over a period of 3 years. He had apparently become obsessed with this son's tennis career. He had put several benzodiazepine tablets in the deceased player's drink, making him so sedated that he crashed his vehicle when he tried to drive home. On previous occasions, opponents collapsed or felt ill during matches against his son but the connection between the cases was not made. There had been some suspicious behavior by the father, but no one seriously entertained the notion that he might be drugging the athletes. Routine toxicological testing during the car crash death investigation identified lorazepam in the decedent's blood. The son was unaware of his father's actions. He discontinued his participation in tennis competition after the actions of his father came to light. The father confessed to the charges and was sentenced to 8 years in prison.

Comments

It was believed that the father in this case had drugged sporting opponents more than 20 times. He was apparently living vicariously through the accomplishments of his son. There were no financial incentives for his actions.

Case: Physician's Pregnant Mistress

In 2001, a married 35-year-old physician in Ohio was having an affair while he was trying to reunite with his estranged wife. His mistress became pregnant and refused the doctor's requests for her to have a medical abortion. He then decided to abort the child himself, and perhaps rid himself of the mistress by poisoning her. He added anti-ulcer medication (misoprostol marketed as Cytotec) to her drinks. After a couple of weeks, the medication caused a miscarriage of her child. Suspicious that the physician was putting something into her drinks, the mistress contacted the police. Investigators set up a video camera and caught him tampering with her drinks and he was arrested, charged, and convicted for contamination of a substance for human consumption and attempted felonious assault. He was sentenced to 5 years in prison.

Comments

In the United States, the Food and Drug Administration has approved the use of mifepristone and misoprostol in combination for abortion. Either drug is effective alone but their mechanisms differ and complement one another when used together. Misoprostol is also approved for prevention and treating of gastric ulcers. This use is limited to males and women who are not pregnant or likely to become pregnant.

Case: Inconvenient Pregnancy on Active Duty

In 2009, an airman stationed at an Air Force Base in Alaska was tried for the murder of his unborn child after he poisoned his wife, causing her to have a miscarriage. The airman did a computer search for *at-home abortion methods* and found the drug misoprostol. He ordered the misoprostol from sources he found on the Internet and mixed it with his wife's food. One week later, his wife miscarried, thinking it was from natural causes. His wife later determined what her husband had done and reported him to military investigators. He was found guilty of attempting to kill an unborn child and sentenced to 9.5 years in prison.

Comments

Abortions induced by misoprostol are similar to those of spontaneous abortion (miscarriage). In both instances, there can be complications that require medical treatment. Generally, drug-induced abortions cannot be distinguished from miscarriages.

References and Additional Reading

Boussairi A, Dupeyron JP, Hernandez B, Delaitre D, Beugnet L, Espinoza P, Diamant-Berger O: Urine benzodiazepines screening of involuntarily drugged and robbed or raped patients. *Clin Toxicol*, 34: 721–724, 1996.

Cittadini F, Loyola G, Caradonna L, Minelli N, Rossi R: A case of toxic shock due to clandestine abortion by misoprostol self-administration. *J Forensic Sci*, 59: 1662–1664, 2014.

Grimes DA, Benson J, Sing S, Romero M, Ganatra B, Okonofua FE, Shah IH: Unsafe abortion: The preventable pandemic. *Lancet*, 368: 1908–1919, 2006.

Haw C, Stubbs J: Covert administration of medication to older adults: A review of the literature and published studies. *J Psychia Mental Health Nur*, 17: 761–768, 2010.

Khan TM, Mehr MT, Ullah H, Abrar A: Drug-facilitated street and travel related crimes: A new public health issue. *Gomal J Med Sci*, 12: 205–209, 2014.

Kintz P (Ed.): *Toxicological Aspects of Drug-Facilitated Crimes*. Waltman, MA: Academic Press, 2014.

Kintz P, Villian M, Cirimele V: Chemical abuse in the elderly: Evidence from hair analysis. *Ther Drug Monit*, 30: 207–211, 2008.

Latha KS: The noncompliant patient in psychiatry: The case for and against covert/ surreptitious medication. *Mens Sana Monogr*, 8: 96–121, 2010.

Majumder MMA, Basher A, Faiz MA, Kuch U, Pogoda W, Kauert GF, Toennes SW: Criminal poisoning of commuters in Bangladesh: Prospective and retrospective study. *Forensic Sci Int*, 180: 10–16, 2008.

Ramadan ASE, Wenanu O, Cock ADE, Maes V, Lheureux P, Mols P: Chemical submission to commit robbery: A series of involuntary intoxications with flunitrazepam in Asian travelers in Brussels. *J Forensic Leg Med*, 20: 918–921, 2013.

Rocca FD, Pignatiello F, Casacanditella G, Tucci M, Favretto D: Drug-facilitated crime: A diagnosis to remember in the emergency department. *J Toxicol Risk Assess*, 2: 2–3, 2016.

Senol E, Kaya A, Kocak A, Aktas EO, Erbas K, Islam M: Watch out for nuts in your travels: An unusual case of drug-facilitated robbery. *J Travel Med*, 16: 431–432, 2009.

Shbair MKS, Eljabour S, Lhermitte M: Drugs involved in drug-facilitated crimes Part I: Alcohol, sedative-hypnotic drugs, gamma-hydroxybutyrate and ketamine. A review. *Ann Pharm Fran*, 68: 275–285, 2010.

Villian M, Cheze M, Dumestre V, Ludes B, Kintz P: Hair to document drug-facilitated crimes: Four cases involving bromazepam. *J Anal Toxicol*, 28: 516–519, 2004.

Yin S: Malicious use of pharmaceuticals in children. *J Pediatr*, 157: 832–836, 2010.

Drug-Facilitated Sexual Assault

35

35.1 Introduction

Sexual assault encompasses any type of sexual activity with another person without that person's consent. It can include inappropriate touching, intercourse, or attempted intercourse. Various drugs can be employed to render victims physically helpless and unable to refuse sex. Sometimes they are unable to remember the assault. Although drugs may be covertly administered in food or drinks, it is also common for sexual assault to occur after the voluntary consumption of recreational drugs or alcohol. When drugs result in nonconsensual sexual contact, it is legally irrelevant whether the exposure was voluntary or involuntary. The drugs most often associated with drug-facilitated sexual assault (DFSA) are ethanol, GHB, ketamine, and benzodiazepines. Some of the many other drugs that have been used or could be used for DFSA are listed in Table 35.1. The number of drugs actually used in such cases, coupled with the number of drugs, which could be used is large, the toxic qualities of the drugs as a group are generally encompassed by the effects listed in Table 35.2.

35.2 Exposure Situations and Circumstances

The stereotypical DFSA case involves a female drinking alcoholic beverages in a social situation who is surreptitiously drugged by a male and finds herself several hours later in a different location with no memory of events that may have occurred during the missing interval of time. She is then confronted with feelings and physical symptoms that are unexplained and suggestive of sexual behavior (Table 35.3). DFSA cases are often far more diverse and can involve female perpetrators, same sex assaults, and various offenses such as child molestation. The individuals could be related and even be otherwise romantically involved with one another. Sexual assault might happen in almost any setting such as when engaging in risky behaviors such as hitchhiking or when interacting with trusted health care providers.

Table 35.1   Some Drugs That Could Be Used for DFSA

Antihistamines
Barbiturates
Benzodiazepines
Chloral hydrate
Ethanol
GHB
Ketamine
Marijuana
MDMA
Muscle relaxants
Narcotics
Opioids
Phenocyclidine (PCP)
Scopolamine
Zolpiden

Table 35.2   Potential Toxic Effects of Common DFSA Drugs

Less Serious	
Relaxation	Dream-like state
Drowsiness	Movement disturbances
Dizziness	Confusion
Unconsciousness	Memory fragmentation and amnesia
Disinhibition	Inability to resist

More Serious	
Nausea and vomiting	Respiratory distress
Vision disturbances	Tremors
Seizures	Hypotension
Coma	Death

Table 35.3   Observations That Could Be Suggestive of Drug-Facilitated Sexual Assault

- Fragmented memory with portions having sexual overtones
- Missing or disturbed clothing
- Unexplained bleeding, bruising, or soreness
- Awaken in unfamiliar location with intimate partner
- Exaggerated response to familiar beverages including alcohol

Alcohol is the most widely used drug for facilitated sexual assault. It alters judgment regarding risky behavior and decreases one's ability to resist sexual or physical advances. Alcoholic blackouts can occur. It can significantly alter one's ability to remember abusive incidents. It can be used alone or in combination with other drugs.

GHB is used in medicine to treat narcolepsy. It is sometimes used illegally by bodybuilders to stimulate muscle growth. GHB can rapidly immobilize assault victims. There can be sudden loss of muscular control and a victim would essentially drop to the floor, conscious but unable to resist an attacker.

Benzodiazepines are used in medicine for anxiety, sleep, seizure control, and other medical and psychiatric problems. Any of the more than 20 marketed benzodiazepines could be used for DFSA.

Ketamine is used in medicine as an anesthetic for humans and animals. It can produce disturbing dissociative reactions that include hallucinations, lost sense of time and identity, distorted sensory perception, and frightening out of body experiences. It is chemically related to PCP.

35.2.1 Purported Aphrodisiacs

Although there are many drugs such as ethanol and marijuana that can lower an individual's inhibitions and influence receptivity to sexual advances, there are few that specifically arouse or increase sexual desire. Stimulants can provide confidence, focus, and especially endurance. Some products sold with purported aphrodisiac properties, contain ingredients that can cause serious toxicity or even death. Two particularly toxic components of some illegally marketed aphrodisiac products are cantharides and toad venom. Cantharides (Spanish fly) is a corrosive poison that burns the mouth and throat and can cause genitourinary infections, scarring of the urethra, and even death. It has historically been touted as an aphrodisiac. It is actually a very toxic chemical that has produced a number of deaths in individuals to whom it was administered for its alleged aphrodisiac properties. Toad venom has been included in some topical herbal aphrodisiac products sold illegally. It can contain cardiotoxic components capable of causing fatal arrhythmias. Some herbal dietary supplements promoted as sexual enhancers have been found to be adulterated with sildenafil or illegal analogs.

35.3 Investigative Considerations

Blood and urine are the usual specimens obtained following DFSA incidents. The window of detection for drugs in these specimens is narrow, and there is typically some delay in reporting incidents following exposure. In selected cases, segmental hair analysis may be an appropriate method for documenting exposure. Hair analysis can provide information on single or multiple drug exposures and details on the time frame of exposures as they relate to an alleged DFSA incident.

Detection of drugs in DFSA cases is resource intensive and requires sensitive analytical methodology utilized by experienced analysts. The scope of screening must be broad with sufficient sensitivity to detect low levels of substances in samples collected days after exposure.

It is important that sexual assault victims provide an accurate and complete history of their personal drug history. Substances identified by analytical testing, which reflect undisclosed personal drug use can seriously compromise an investigation and possibly negate a victim's accusations and formal testimony.

35.4 Case Studies

Case: Videotapes

In 2003, a 39-year-old attractive man living in a beachfront home near Santa Barbara, California was convicted of 86 felony counts of drug facilitated rape. He was sentenced to 124 years in prison. The man supported himself with an income from a trust fund, and he spent most of his time surfing and fishing. Over a period of several years he had seduced many females using GHB, and he recorded his seductions with a personal video camera. The tapes were recovered by the authorities and substantiated charges brought by his victims. Although under house arrest during his trial, he fled to Mexico; however, the trial preceded and he was found guilty and ultimately sentenced to 50 years in prison. He was later captured and returned to the United States to serve his sentence.

Comments

Most of the victims had no recollection of the incidents and only discovered the seductions by viewing the video tapes. One of the victims, whom he had met in a bar, moved in with him and had a relationship lasting about 4 months. Only after seeing the videotapes years later did she realize that she had been assaulted on their first night together. Many of the women first met the man in bars and willingly went to his home and drank and used drugs but never consented to the video recordings of the sexual assaults.

Case: Foreign Relations

A 24-year-old woman spent about a year in another country living in a college facility for foreign students. During this period, she occasionally woke up on some mornings having headaches, nausea, and noticeable abrasions on her arm. She attributed these things to heavy drinking the previous night. After returning to her native country, she received video clips taken with a cell phone by a friend that showed her having sex with a boy she had met while studying abroad. However, she could not recall the events and noticed that her behavior and state of mind seemed strange. She was convinced that she must have been raped and decided to have toxicological testing done on her hair. This analysis indicated that she had been exposed to GHB and morphine during the period of time she was living in the college facility abroad.

Comments

This case illustrates the amnestic effects of GHB, and it also shows how hair analysis can provide a historic record of drug exposure long after substances are no longer able to be detected in biological fluids.

Case: Vodka Eye Drops

A 19-year-old female was invited by an older male to watch a movie in his home. About 30 min after she had finished a vodka and fruit juice drink, she was provided with a second drink that she only partially drank because it had an unpleasant taste. About 20 min later, she felt light-headed, groggy, and passed out. She woke briefly several times to discover that she was being sexually assaulted. Hours later she woke completely naked in the male's bed; she quickly dressed and left the man's house. She remained nauseous and sedated for several hours until a friend took her to a hospital for treatment and to report the assault. Toxicological screening of urine samples was negative for all drugs except for ethanol and tetrahydrozoline.

Comments

Tetrahydrozoline is a topical vasoconstrictor used in eye drops to constrict dilated blood vessels. When ingested, tetrahydrozoline is a potent depressant with a rapid onset of action. The degree of depression would be expected to be potentiated by ethanol. Effects could include drowsiness, coma, and respiratory depression.

Case: Abuse Allegations Ignored

In 2012, a 46-year-old Oregon physician pleaded guilty to charges of sexual abuse and rape and was sentenced to 23 years in prison. The physician was an anesthesiologist in a large hospital where he practiced for 5 years prior to the criminal charges. He lived in a rural community near the hospital with his wife and two children. The assaults involved anesthetized patients and coworkers. Twelve victims came forward with charges but it is likely that there were others, including some who remained unaware that they had been assaulted. Evidence included descriptions by victims, semen from assault locations, and recorded phone conversations of the physician's admission of guilt. Multiple lawsuits against the hospital have been brought by victims who allege that after learning of the sexual misconduct allegations, senior administrators failed to notify authorities or initiate an internal investigation. Some suits have gone to trial, whereas others were settled for undisclosed financial payments. More than $2 million in compensatory damages have been awarded to the victims.

Comments

This case is an example of sexual abuse perpetrated by a health care professional while practicing medicine and an irresponsible medical institution that failed to take appropriate action after learning about significant professional misconduct and criminal activity.

Case: Drink after Work

In 2009, a 22-year-old single mother was reported missing by her babysitter when she did not come home after finishing her night shift as a manager of a convenience store in a small town in Alabama. She had closed the store shortly after 10 p.m. and was seen leaving alone in her car. In the afternoon of the following day, police located her car in the parking lot of a small business a few miles from her home. Her body was in the backseat wrapped in a blanket. An investigation quickly focused on a 37-year-old man who was a regular customer where she worked and was the last individual in the store the night the woman disappeared. When confronted, the man admitted to drugging the woman without her knowledge. That evening he had invited the woman to drop by after work for a drink at a party at his home. At the party, he gave her beverages containing GHB and a benzodiazepine and had sex with her. A few hours later she died of an apparent overdose. Later, with the help of another male who lived at the house, he wrapped the body in a blanket and drove the woman's car containing the body to the location where it was discovered by police about 5 h later. The man was arrested and charged with drug possession, rape, and murder. His male roommate who helped with the body was charged with obstructing justice.

Comments

This is a case of drug-facilitated assault that was acknowledged by the perpetrator's confession. The potential lethality of the multiple drug ingestions was likely unappreciated. Consuming ethanol, GHB, and benzodiazepines together in varying amounts can produce significant life-threatening respiratory depression.

References and Additional Reading

Anderson C, Anderson D, Harre N, Wade N: Case study: Two fatal case reports of acute yohimbine intoxication. *J Anal Toxicol*, 37: 611–614, 2013.

Bechtel LK, Holstege CP: Criminal poisoning: Drug-facilitated sexual assault. *Emerg Med Clin N Am*, 25: 499–525, 2007.

Beynon CM, McVeigh C, McVeigh J, Leavey C, Bellis MA: The involvement of drugs and alcohol in drug-facilitated sexual assault. A systemic review of the evidence. *Trauma Violence Abuse*, 9: 178–188, 2008.

Brubacher J, Hoffman RS, Bonia T, Ravikumar P, Heller M, Reimer S, Smiddy M, Mojica B: Deaths associated with a purported aphrodisiac—New York City, February 1993-May 1995. *CDC MMWR*, 44: 853–855, 1995.

Dinis-Oliveria RJ, Magalhaes T: Forensic toxicology of drug-facilitated sexual assault. *Tox Mech Meth*, 23: 471–478, 2013.

DuMont J, MacDonald S, Rotbard N, Asllani E, Bainbridge D, Cohen MM: Factors associated with suspected drug-facilitated sexual assault. *Canad Med Assoc J*, 180: 513–519, 2009.

Hall, JA, Moore CBT: Drug-facilitated sexual assault: A review. *J Forensic Leg Med*, 15: 291–297, 2008.

Jones AW, Kugelberg FC, Holmgren A, Ahlner J: Occurance of ethanol and other drugs in blood and urine specimens from female victims of alleged sexual assault. *Forensic Sci Intl*, 181: 40–46, 2008.

Kintz P (Ed.): *Toxicological Aspects of Drug-Facilitated Crimes*. London: Academic Press, 2014.

Lauerma H: Somnophilia and sexual abuse using vaginal administration of triazolam. *J Forensic Sci*, 61: 862–863, 2016.

LeBeau MA, Mozayani A (Eds.): *Drug-Facilitated Sexual Assault: A Forensic Handbook*. London: Academic Press, 2001.

LeBeau MA: Guidance for improved detection of drugs used to facilitate crimes. *Ther Drug Monit*, 30: 229–233, 2008.

Linden JA: Care of the adult patient after sexual assault, *N Engl J Med*, 365: 834–841, 2011.

Montgomery M: Toxicology Evidence. *FBI Law Enfor Bull*, Oct. 2014.

Oiestad EL, Karinen R, Christophersen AS, Vigdis V, Bachs L: Analyses of beverage remains in drug rape cases revealing drug residues: The possibility of contamination from drug concentrated oral fluid or oral cavity contained tablets. *J Forensic Sci*, 59: 208–210, 2014.

Pittel SM, Spina L: Investigating drug-facilitated sexual assault. In Savino J, Turvey B (Eds.): *Rape Investigation Handbook*. London: Elsevier, 2004.

Rossi R, Luncia M, Gambelunghe C, Olivia A, Fucci N: Identification of GHB and morphine in hair in a case of drug-facilitated sexual assault. *Forensic Sci Intl*, 186:9-11, 2009.

Scalzo TP: *Prosecuting Alcohol-Facilitated Sexual Assault*. Special topic series, Alexandria, VA: American Prosecutors Research Institute, National District Attorneys Association, 2007.

Schwartz RH, Miteer R, LeBeau MA: Drug-facilitated sexual assault ("date rape"). *South Med J*, 93: 558–561, 2000.

Spiller HA, Siewert DJ: Drug-facilitated sexual assault using tetrohydrozoline. *J Forensic Sci*, 57: 835–838, 2012.

Xiang P, Shen M, Drummer OH: Review: Drug concentrations in hair and their relevance in drug facilitated crimes. *J Forensic Leg Med*, 36: 126–135, 2015.

Xiang P, Sun Q, Shen B, Chen P, Liu W, Shen M: Segmental hair analysis using liquid chromatography-tandem mass spectrometry after a single dose of benzodiazepines. *Forensic Sci In*, 204: 19–26, 2011.

Drug Product Tampering

36

36.1 Introduction

Drug product tampering is the deliberate alteration of products after they have been produced or manufactured. This applies to the product itself as well as the containers or labeling. Products are typically removed from a point of purchase, taken to another location, carefully opened and contaminated or otherwise adulterated, and then resealed and returned to the display shelf of a sales outlet. Tampering is usually done to alarm consumers or blackmail a company. Both tampering itself and threatening to tamper are criminal offenses, as is claiming tampering has occurred when it has not.

Tampering has a great potential for spreading fear and hysteria, and for doing actual physical harm to large numbers of people. Product tampering reports in the media often inspire copycat cases or threats of tampering. The rate of occurrence of both real and alleged tampering incidents has been linked to the extent of publicity of specific cases. Fictionalized incidents in movies and novels also can trigger tampering. Revenge and mercenary manuals often provide instructions for tampering.

36.2 Exposure Situations and Circumstances

The majority of over-the-counter drugs are required to have at least one indicator or barrier to entry that is capable of providing visible evidence of tampering. Examples of packaging technologies capable of meeting tamper-resistant packaging requirements are listed in Table 36.1. Unfortunately, many consumers do not inspect the packaging or medications prior to using them. Several tampering incidents that have occurred involved products that were visibly altered in ways that were strikingly obvious. For example, in a case involving the addition of cyanide to a long-acting pseudoephedrine capsule product, the colored pellets in the capsules had been replaced with off-white powder, the band seal on the capsules was missing, the blister pack had been slit open, and the lot numbers on the blister pack and box did not match. In spite of these many grossly visible indications of tampering, three people ingested the capsules, and two died.

Table 36.1   Examples of Tamper-Evident Packaging

Film wrappers	Transparent film wrapped around the entire product container
Blister packaging	Each tablet individually sealed in compartments that must be punched open for each dose
Bubble packs	Entire product sealed in a plastic bubble and mounted on a display card
Shrink sealed	Band covering juncture of cap and container
Pouches	Product enclosed in a foil, paper, or plastic pouch that must be torn to obtain the product
Inner seal	Seal over container opening
Breakable caps	Portion of cap must be broken to open the container
Banded capsules	Two-piece capsules sealed with visible gelatin band
Caplets	Solid tablets shaped and colored, so as to appear to be capsules

36.3 Investigative Considerations

Tampering is distinct from other illegal practices involving commercial products such as counterfeiting, violation of manufacturing standards, and diversion of products from intended markets. Tampering and threats of tampering of drug products are federal crimes, and the Federal Bureau of Investigation and the Food and Drug Administration should be consulted when product tampering is encountered or suspected. Both of these agencies have specialized resources dedicated to tampering investigation. Occasionally, products can have manufacturing defects, which attract attention and alarm consumers. Product manufacturers are usually in the best position to distinguish between product defects and intentional tampering. Most major manufacturers have dedicated laboratory resources for investigating and resolving issues related to product abnormalities. Examples of products that have been involved in tampering incidents are listed in Table 36.2.

Table 36.2   Examples of Products That Have Been Adulterated with Poison or Foreign Objects

Product	Poison
Tylenol capsules	Cyanide, strychnine
Visine	Hydrochloric acid
Girl Scout cookies	Pins and needles
Fruit juice	Weed killer
Contact cold medicine	Strychnine
Anacin-3	Cyanide
Extra strength Excedrin	Cyanide
Kool Aid	Cyanide
Sudafed capsules	Cyanide
Baby food	Alleged ground glass

Table 36.3   Motives for Tampering

- Competitive advantage
- Damage company's reputation
- Disguise homicide
- Disguise suicide
- Extortion
- Financial gain
- Hoaxes
- Influence stock market
- Insurance fraud
- Malicious mischief
- Munchausen syndrome
- Psychopathic behavior
- Publicity
- Revenge
- Sabotage
- Terrorism

Offenders have placed tampered products on retail shelves for purchase by random consumers to divert attention from an intentional homicide carried out with a poisoned product. In addition, suicidal individuals have been reported to stage their death to appear to be a tampering incident to disguise the true manner of death, or increase insurance benefits because of an accidental death. Tampering can be used to exert monetary gains for damages, or simply be hoaxes for attention and entertainment. These and other potential motives for tampering are presented in Table 36.3.

36.4 Case Studies

Case: Tylenol Capsules

In 1982, seven people in the Chicago area died suddenly after taking Tylenol capsules that had been laced with potassium cyanide. The poisoned capsules had been added to bottles of Tylenol and placed on the retail shelves of six different stores. Each tainted Tylenol bottle contained 5–10 poisoned capsules. More than 30 million bottles of Tylenol were recalled by the manufacturer at a cost of more than $100 million. The motivation for this crime has never been determined. In 1983, a 29-year-old man was sentenced to 20 years in prison for extortion attempts related to the Tylenol poisoning. He tried to extort $1 million from the drug company to make the killings stop. He was not believed to be responsible for the actual tampering. When the deaths were publicized, he purported that he was the tamperer and would stop if his ransom demands were met.

Comments

Prior to this case, lethal tampering was essentially unheard of. Since this case, there have been many serious tampering cases, and the magnitude of the response to this case became of considerable interest to terrorists.

Case: Pseudoephedrine Decongestant Capsules

In 1991, a 28-year-old woman collapsed in her home minutes after taking an over-the-counter long-acting pseudoephedrine decongestant capsule. She was rushed to a hospital where she was treated for cyanide poisoning. Her condition was critical, but she survived. Within a few days two other people living in the same community also collapsed shortly after taking the same product. Both died from cyanide poisoning. After an 18-month investigation, the surviving woman's husband was charged with product tampering, perjury, and fraud. He had attempted to kill her to collect $700,000 in life insurance. To divert suspicion from himself, he put cyanide in several products and placed them in stores in the area. An additional package of the decongestant containing cyanide was found in the store and another was returned by a purchaser. The husband was convicted and sentenced to two concurrent life terms plus 75 years in prison. He was also ordered to pay $3.5 million restitution to the manufacturer of the product and to pay for his wife's medical bills. The investigation disclosed that the husband was an insurance salesman who had difficulty holding jobs and frequently quarreled with his wife over money. He had expensive hobbies and a history of infidelity. There were occasions of abusive behavior requiring police intervention. Only 10 days before his wife's poisoning, he had increased her insurance policy from $106,000 to $700,000 for accidental death. Using an assumed name and other fake information, he had purchased cyanide from a chemical distributor.

Comments

The tampering of the decongestant product was quite obvious, but the capsules were ingested despite the unusual appearance. The capsules were unsealed and discolored, and the package had signs of having been previously opened. Due to this incident and previous capsule tampering cases, over-the-counter drugs are no longer marketed in capsules. What now appear to consumers to be capsules are actually solid dosage forms made to look similar to capsules. Distinct from over-the-counter drugs, dietary supplements and prescription drugs continue to be available in capsule form.

Case: Calcium Supplement

In 2005, a 36-year-old woman was driving to the movies when she passed out and had a minor accident with another vehicle. Immediately prior to leaving home for the drive, she had taken a calcium capsule that her husband had insisted she take. From the accident scene, she was transported to a hospital where she died within a half hour of arrival. An autopsy revealed her death was due to cyanide; the cyanide was traced to the calcium supplement capsules provided by her husband who was a 41-year-old emergency room physician. At the time of the poisoning, the husband was an alcoholic and had a long and public history of infidelity. He was also facing fraud charges for the activities of a nonmedical communication company he co-owned. His medical license had been previously suspended for substance abuse issues and he was practicing on a probationary basis that included mandatory drug testing. During the investigation of his wife's death he fled the country and was later arrested in Cyprus and extradited to the United States for trial in 2009. He was ultimately convicted of aggravated murder for poisoning his wife and sentenced to life in prison.

Comments

On the day of her death, for some unknown reason, the doctor's wife deviated from her usual route to the movies and took a slower, longer way and likely avoided a high-speed crash that might have resulted in her death and concealed the poisoning. Moreover, shortly before crashing, she had called a friend from her car and told her that she was feeling strange and was wondering if it might be the calcium supplement her husband had insisted that she take. During the trial, there was an attempt by the defense attorney to raise the possibility of the cyanide in the calcium supplement being an act of random tampering.

Case: Excedrin Capsules

Tampering can be staged to appear as if an intentional poisoning was the result of product tampering. An example of staged tampering occurred in Seattle, Washington area in 1986. A 52-year-old man suddenly collapsed after taking two Excedrin capsules. He died that same day in the hospital. After the completion of an autopsy, his death was ruled to be the result of emphysema. Six days after this death, a 40-year-old woman unrelated to the man also collapsed after taking Excedrin. She died later in the same hospital. However, her autopsy revealed that she died from cyanide poisoning. The Excedrin capsules she had taken were found to contain cyanide. When the lot number found on the woman's bottle of Excedrin capsules was publicized, the widow of the deceased man called the police to report that she had a bottle of Excedrin capsules with the same lot number. This led to additional testing of a blood sample from the man and the determination that his cause of death was not emphysema but cyanide poisoning. When the shelves of outlets in the local area were checked, two additional cyanide-laced analgesic products were found. One was Excedrin capsules and the other was an Anacin-3 capsule product.

The investigation of these deaths uncovered a remarkable amount of evidence that led to the federal indictment of the man's widow for product tampering. She was found guilty and sentenced to 90 years in prison. Some of the evidence that was presented at her trial is briefly summarized below:

- The revised cause of death for the deceased man from emphysema to a cyanide death from tampering changed the death from due to natural causes to an accidental death, which added an additional $100,000 to his life insurance benefit.
- In all the tainted capsules collected, the cyanide was found to contain small green crystals. These crystals were determined to be an algicide product that the widow used regularly in her tropical fish tanks.
- Two insurance policies were discovered with forged signatures of the husband.
- Witnesses testified at the trial about conversations they had had with the widow regarding killing her husband.
- The widow's fingerprints were identified on pages in several books at the local library that had specific information on cyanide poisoning.

Comments

The woman in this case considered a number of methods for eliminating her husband. These included using poisonous plants and even the possibility of hiring a professional killer. Possibly, she tried other poisons without success but it is clear that her consideration of the capsule-cyanide method was inspired by the widely publicized Tylenol tampering tragedy.

Case: Diet Cola

In 1991, the FDA was notified of a consumer complaint involving a dead rodent in a 12-fluid oz aluminum can of cola. A female attorney in Somers, New York was reported to have purchased the soft drink and consumed about one half the liquid contents while driving in her car. Sometime later, she discovered that the can contained a mouse. She became nauseated and developed protracted vomiting that lasted several days. She contacted officials at the company that produced the cola and they obtained the can with the contents and initiated an investigation. Company officials sent the frozen can containing the mouse to a private animal hospital where the mouse was removed from the can and shipped to a veterinary pathology laboratory for necropsy and pathological evaluation. Following requests for financial compensation from the woman, the FDA's Office of Criminal Investigations was contacted and subsequently took custody of the can. The consumer related her story and signed an affidavit after she was informed of the Federal Anti-Tampering Act statutes for false reports of a tampering. Overwhelming physical and chemical evidence demonstrated that the mouse had gnawed on the lift tab and around the rim of the mouth opening of the can after the can was opened. The consumer in this case was charged with falsely reporting a product tampering, found guilty, and sentenced to 41 months in federal prison.

Comments

The events preceding this tampering report are not clear, but it was evident that the mouse entered the can after it was opened and that the individual was aware of this when she proceeded to pursue financial compensation from the manufacturer.

Case: Prescription Drug Tampering

In 2012, a 28-year-old male business manager and part-time university student living in Florida was told by his 27-year-old girlfriend that she was pregnant. He urged her to have an abortion but she wanted to have the child. Although expressing support for her decision, he forged a prescription for misoprostol (an abortifacient). After having the prescription filled, he changed the label on the prescription container to indicate that it was a common antibiotic (amoxicillin). He then convinced the girlfriend that she had a minor infection and gave her the mislabeled prescription to treat the alleged infection. After taking a few tablets, the girl became extremely ill with significant cramping, bleeding, and abdominal pain. Concerned, the girlfriend went to a hospital emergency room for treatment. It was there that the contents of the alleged antibiotic prescription tablets were identified. She subsequently had a miscarriage. The man was charged with product tampering and conspiracy to commit mail fraud. He pleaded guilty and was sentenced to 13 years and 8 months in prison. He was initially charged with first-degree murder but reached a plea agreement for the lesser charges.

Comments

This case illustrates how tampering might apply to prescription products. Although the contents of the container were not altered, the label was changed. More often in cases of prescription product tampering, controlled drugs are removed from containers and are replaced with other substances.

References and Additional Reading

Dietz PE: Dangerous information: Product tampering and poisoning advice in revenge and murder manuals. *J Forensic Sci*, 33: 1206–1217, 1988.

Logan B: Product tampering crime: A review. *J Forensic Sci*, 38: 918–927, 1993.

Logan B, Howard J, Kiesel EL: Poisonings associated with cyanide in over the counter cold medication in Washington state, 1991. *J Forensic Sci*, 38: 472–476, 1993.

Olsen G: *Bitter Almonds: The True Story of Mothers, Daughters, and the Seattle Cyanide Murders.* New York: Warner Books, 1993.

Platek F, Ranieri N, Wolnik KA: A false report of product tampering involving a rodent and soft drink can: Light microscopy, image analysis and scanning electron microscopy/energy dispersive x-ray analysis. *J Forensic Sci*, 42: 1172–1175, 1997.

Assassination

37

37.1 Introduction

Covert assassinations usually involve poisons and sophisticated delivery systems to produce deaths that have a high probability of being mistakenly attributed to natural or accidental causes. Assassinations and contract killing of any kind require a forensic investigation to collect evidence and identify perpetrators. However, these homicides are not routinely encountered in any particular jurisdiction, and are extremely unlikely to occur in any investigator's professional career. It is more likely that publicized actual assassinations and fictional assassination will be imitated by individuals and employed in more personalized homicides. In addition, familiarity with actual and fictional killing can be of value to law enforcement officials tasked with the security and protection of high-profile individuals. The case studies presented in this chapter were selected to provide some insight into the complexity of covert assassinations and the technical resources that these poisonings typically require.

37.2 Exposure Situations and Circumstances

The distinction between an assassin and a hit man is made most often on the basis of either the victim's importance or the motive of the killer. An assassin might act on some real or imagined ideological or political motive of a group or be acting alone. A hit man is an individual who kills for money provided by a person or group who may be unable to carry out the killing or attempting to conceal their involvement in the killing.

Targets of assassinations can be political leaders, public commentators, business executives, celebrity entertainers, or other public figures. Unexpected deaths of people of this stature are usually considered suspicious and trigger investigations, which may uncover homicide. The deaths of individuals with less prominence are less likely to arouse suspicions and investigation. This latter group might include teachers, abortion clinic staff, and others whose deaths do not attract extensive public attention. Covert poisoning carried out by individuals unrelated to victims requires planning

Table 37.1 Poisons Implicated in Assassinations

Cyanide
Fentanyl
Gelsemium
Polonium-210
Ricin
Sarin
Succinylcholine
Thallium

that includes identifying possible methods and opportunities for delivering a poison. The particular poison and the method of delivery utilized to avoid detection are factors that, when uncovered, facilitate the identification of perpetrators having the capability for carrying out the poisoning. Some poisons that have been implicated in assassinations are listed in Table 37.1.

37.3 Case Studies

Case: Ricin

In 1978, a Bulgarian novelist and playwright working for the BBC World Services was murdered in London. While in the West, he was extremely critical of the Bulgarian Communist government and its leadership. His harsh criticisms were broadcast weekly on Radio Free Europe and were seen as an inspiration to the dissident movement in Bulgaria. His assassination is believed to have been carried out by agents of the Bulgarian and Russian secret police. While awaiting a bus in London, he was injected with a poison pellet fired from a device disguised as an umbrella carried by a passing pedestrian. He became ill a few hours after the incident and died days later. At autopsy, a small pellet was discovered imbedded in his thigh. The pellet, which was smaller than a pinhead, had contained a lethal dose of ricin. The pellet had two holes forming an X-shaped cavity that held the ricin. The pellet was made of an alloy of platinum and iridium, and the holes could only have been made using sophisticated laser technology.

Comments

There are probably fewer than five realistic possibilities for potent poisons that could have been utilized in this way. Had the pellet not been discovered in this case, the death would likely have been attributed to a viral or bacterial infection.

Case: Castor Beans

In 2014, a 31-year-old man living in Oklahoma plotted the murder of his girlfriend soon after he learned of her untimely pregnancy. The man utilized information obtained from the Internet to extract ricin from castor beans. There is an abundance of information available on ricin, which highlight its use and potential use for murder and terrorism. He then attempted to hire a friend to pose as a pizza delivery driver and provide pizza and soda laced with ricin to his pregnant girlfriend. His friend informed the police and provided them with the ricin. This triggered a huge response from local and national authorities because ricin is considered a biological weapon. The man was arrested and his home was decontaminated by HAZMAT crews. He was charged with two counts of attempted murder and two counts of solicitation to commit murder. He pleaded guilty to the charges and was sentenced to 20 years in prison and fined $10,000.

Comments

The inspiration for the use of ricin in this specific case was the popular TV show: *Breaking Bad.* Castor bean plants and castor beans are legally sold in the United States, but isolated ricin is considered both a biological and chemical weapon and its possession is restricted. The irony of this situation was that the man learned through court testimony that he was not the father of the expectant child.

Case: Dioxin

In 2004, the presidential elections in the Ukraine were especially bitter and violent. Early in the presidential campaign, one of the popular candidates was diagnosed with acute pancreatitis likely caused by a serious viral infection. However, the candidate claimed that he had been poisoned and that the current government was responsible. His face became heavily disfigured; he was also grossly jaundiced. It was later concluded that the changes in the candidate's face were due to dioxin poisoning. Testing revealed that the levels of dioxin in the candidate's blood were 50,000 times above normal. The poisoning was linked to a dinner with a group of senior government officials. This was the first known case of a single high dose of dioxin poisoning. With intense medical treatment, the candidate survived this poisoning and was ultimately elected the president.

Comments

Dioxin is a generic term for a mixture of chemicals that are dioxins. Dioxins are chemical contaminants formed during waste incineration, forest fires, paper pulp bleaching, and herbicide manufacturing. They are not produced intentionally by chemical companies and have no commercial uses. The source of dioxin used for this poisoning has never been identified.

Case: Polonium 210

In 2006, a 44-year-old male Russian dissident met two male friends for drinks in a London hotel bar. Later that evening he had dinner at his home with his wife and, after watching the evening news, went to bed. A few hours later, he began vomiting and had severe abdominal cramps. His condition continued to deteriorate and he went to a hospital for an evaluation. The hospital physicians diagnosed his condition as some type of bacterial gastroenteritis. He was treated symptomatically and sent home. His condition did not improve and 2 days later he went to a second hospital. At this point, it was believed that he had some type of food poisoning, which was likely caused by the sushi he had eaten a few days earlier. He was admitted for treatment and further evaluation. His condition did not improve. Eventually, it was determined that he had been poisoned with radioactive polonium-210. He died 3 weeks after the onset of his gastrointestinal symptoms. It was determined that the radioactive element had been ingested in tea that he drank while meeting with his friends in the London hotel bar. Police had found traces of it in three locations: (1) a sushi bar where he had eaten lunch, (2) a hotel he had visited on the same day, and (3) his home. Polonium-210 is so rare and volatile that the assassin would have needed access to a high-security nuclear laboratory to obtain it. Investigators quickly discovered that the deceased was a former senior officer in the Russian security service. Since leaving Russia he had written and spoken publicly about a number of alleged covert activities carried out by the Russian government.

Comments

Ingesting just 1 μg (one-millionth of a gram) of polonium-210 is lethal. This amount would barely be visible to the naked eye. Once inside the body, polonium's radiation disrupts the DNA in cells, destroying the cells or transforming them into various forms of cancer. Polonium moves through the digestive and circulatory systems spreading the radiation. Death occurs within days. (Polonium is not to be confused with plutonium.)

Case: Succinylcholine

In 2010, a foreign visitor to Dubai was found dead in his 5-star hotel room by a maid. The room was locked from inside, and there was no obvious reason to suspect anything other than that he had died from natural causes, most likely a massive heart attack. The death occurred on the day of his arrival at the hotel. An investigation into the death was initiated only after the identity of the guest was determined. He was a high-ranking Hamas military commander. The key to unraveling the case was the availability of hundreds of hours of surveillance video from cameras located in the hotel and many public areas throughout the city. These video recordings showed that within 4 h following the assassination, the 26 individuals associated with the murder had departed from Dubai. In addition, from hotel security tapes, it was determined that two men actually carried out the assassination and it was accomplished during a 20-min time span. An investigative police report indicates that the victim was first injected with succinylcholine to cause total muscular paralysis and then was smothered with a pillow. His body was discovered 17 h later. The initial autopsy prior to the discovery of his true identity was inconclusive, and it was believed at the time that he died of natural causes.

Comments

Succinylcholine paralyzes all skeletal muscles. When the muscles controlling the rib cage and diaphragm cannot function, breathing ceases. This can occur within a minute after receiving an injection. Consciousness is lost after 3–4 min, and this is followed by cardiac arrest due to anoxia. Deaths from succinylcholine poisoning will appear to have resulted from an unexplained heart attack.

Case: Fentanyl

In 1997, a 41-year-old Hamas Operative in Jordan was exposed to a fentanyl derivative in an assassination attempt. The fentanyl was introduced into his ear with a small specially designed aerosol spray during an orchestrated distraction on a walkway near his office. The intended effect was that he would gradually become tired during the day and ultimately go to sleep and never awaken. The high potency of the drug would leave little trace for detection. The poison was successfully administered, but the attack was observed by bodyguards who subsequently captured the assassins. The incident was immediately elevated to an international crisis that was resolved only after Israeli authorities supplied an antidote for the poison and released several Palestinian prisoners.

Comments

The aerosolized fentanyl was absorbed from the ear canal and the victim developed a respiratory depression that necessitated intubation and ventilation. Emergency physicians surmised that the poison was an opioid and began treatment with naloxone. The political leverage engendered by the possible international repercussions of the incident persuaded the sponsors to reveal the composition of the poison and the antidote to Jordanian physicians.

References and Additional Reading

Bergman R: The Dubai job. *GQ Magazine,* January 2011.

Clancy T: *The Teeth of the Tiger.* New York: G.P. Putnam's Sons, 2003.

Fein RA, Vossekuil B: Assassination in the United States: An operational study of recent assassins, attackers, and near-lethal approachers. *J Forensic Sci,* 44: 321–333, 1999.

Froidevaux P, Bochud F, Baechler S, Castella A, Augsburger M, Bailat C, Michaud K, Straub M, Pecchia M et al.: ^{210}Po poisoning as possible cause of death: Forensic investigations and toxicological analysis of the remains of Yasser Arafat. *Forensic Sci Int,* 259: 1–9, 2016.

Leonard AC: *The Anthrax Letters: A Bioterrorism Expert Investigates the Attack That Shocked America.* New York: Skyhorse Publishing, 2009.

McCormack J, McKinney W: Thallium poisoning in group assassination attempt. *Postgrad Med,* 74: 239–241, 1983.

McFee RB, Leikin JB: Death by Polonium-210: Lessons learned from the murder of former Soviet spy Alexander Litvinenko. *Semin Diagn Pathol,* 26: 61–67, 2009.

McGeough, P: *Kill Khalid: The Failed Mossad Assassintion of Khalid Mishal and the Rise of Hamas.* New York: New Press, 2009.

McGovern G: *Targeted Violence: A Statistical and Tactical Analysis of Assassinations, Contract Killings, and Kidnappings.* Boca Raton, FL: CRC Press, 2010.

Murder-for-Hire: Web hits of a deadly kind, *FBI News,* January 2013.

Musshoff F, Madea B: Ricin poisoning and forensic toxicology. *Drug Test Anal,* 1: 184–191, 2009.

Owen R: The Litvinenko inquiry: Report into the death of Alexander Litvinenko. U.K. House of Commons Papers, UK National Archives, 21, January 2016.

Papaloucas M, Papaloucas C, Stergioulas A: Ricin and the assassination of Georgi Markov. *Pak J Biol Sci,* 11: 2370–2371, 2008.

Sorg O, Zennegg M, Schmid P, Fedosyuk R, Gaide O, Kniazevych V, Saurat JH: 2,3,7,8-tetrachlorodibenzo-p-dioxin (TCDD) poisoning in Victor Yushchenko: Identifcation and measurement of TCDD metabolites. *Lancet,* 374: 1179–1185, 2009.

White RF: Assassination discourse and politician power: The death of Alexander Litvinenko. *Assassination Res,* 5: 1–8, 2008.

Multiple Victim Poisonings

38

38.1 Introduction

Distinct from serial poisonings, multiple victim poisoning refers to incidents in which more than one person is poisoned by the same toxic exposure. Simultaneous illness in groups sharing the same environment or activity has a high probability of being caused by a common toxicant. When individuals disperse after exposure prior to the appearance of symptoms, recognition of a common exposure can be difficult and delayed. Early recognition of multiple victim poisoning exposures is the key to framing an investigative approach, and for initiating measures that address potential public health issues. This chapter highlights some poisoning situations that typically involve multiple victims.

38.2 Exposure Situations and Circumstances

38.2.1 Food Poisoning

Bacterial foodborne agents are the leading cause of food poisoning outbreaks. The most important factors contributing to these poisonings are the contamination of raw foods, inadequate cooking, and improper food storage temperatures. Viral food poisoning is usually related to eating raw fish or food contaminated by infected food-handling personnel. In addition, food poisoning may be due to toxins (e.g., tetrodotoxin from puffer fish), or contamination of food with chemicals. The severity of poisoning as well as the onset of symptoms may vary among individuals in a foodborne poisoning. A further complication in food poisoning investigations is the temporal relationship between exposures and symptom onset. Poisoning may be due to the most recent food ingested, but sometimes the responsible food items may have been consumed days before. Food poisoning is reviewed in more detail in Chapter 22.

38.2.2 Industrial Chemicals

Chemicals used or produced by industrial processes can be a source of acute poisoning in workers, their families, and others. Poisoning incidents are most often prevented or minimized by systems in place within industrial units. However, subtle and unrecognized exposures sometimes occur and produce life-threatening effects in individuals outside the working environment when effects manifest. This could be due to an inherent, delayed biological action, or because toxic substances were somehow transferred to other individuals not associated with the area where the substance originated. For example, an individual working in industries connected with pesticides might appropriate small quantities of a pesticide for home use, or they could indirectly contaminate another environment with material transferred from the workplace by clothing. There are many possible avenues to toxic exposure from industrial chemicals.

38.2.3 Terrorism

Domestic and foreign terrorist groups have an enormous number of toxic substances and delivery methods to choose from for attacks on civilians and structural targets. Toxicants are relatively easy to obtain, or they can be synthesized from materials commonly utilized for legitimate industrial purposes. Some of the known terrorist plots have focused on poisoning food and water supplies and spreading agents on various surfaces to poison individuals who come into contact with those surfaces. Poisons such as cyanide can also be combined with explosive devices to enhance the lethality of the device beyond physical destruction.

38.2.4 Mass Suicide

For a variety of reasons, several individuals might agree to join together in suicide. They could be personally connected or through strangers united by some shared religious, political, or military objectives. Although joint suicides can occur in a particular location, social media can facilitate coordinated suicides by individuals separated by great distances. The motivation for multiple suicide incidents is often obscure, especially when they involve younger individuals.

38.2.5 Recreational Drugs

Illegally produced drugs can have an unexpected toxic potential from contaminants introduced during manufacturing and processing, and from adulterants added by dealers as the drugs move through levels of distribution.

The rapidity of distribution and use of illegal drugs does not always provide a time interval that would allow later users of a particular batch of drugs to benefit from the experience of earlier users. The lifetime of a particular batch of drugs in a distribution area can be a few days, and in some cases only a few hours. Rapid distribution and utilization of drugs are especially evident in large gatherings such as raves and concerts. These gatherings further increase the likely toxicity from illegal drugs because of the increased numbers of first-time users and experimenters, the increased tendency of dealers to misrepresent the identity of drugs to satisfy demands, the increased likelihood of multiple drug use, and the exhausted and dehydrated condition of many drug users.

38.3 Case Studies

Case: Nausea and Vomiting by Restaurant Patrons

In 2004, county, state, and national health agencies were alerted to a possible foodborne illness outbreak associated with a specific restaurant in Lenexa, Kansas. Five patrons became dizzy, began to sweat profusely, and then experienced a bout of vomiting. About 3 weeks later, 28 patrons developed the same symptoms. Authorities closed the restaurant and began an investigation. The patrons and restaurant staff were interviewed, samples of prepared food and their ingredients were collected for analysis, plumbing and water supplies were evaluated, and clinical specimens (including vomitus) were obtained for testing. Initial testing focused on the possible microbial contamination. The individuals who became ill ranged in age from 2 to 79 years. The symptom duration ranged from an hour to several days. The variety of food and the amounts eaten by the affected individuals was determined. The commonalities initially identified were chips, salsa, cheese, rice, and tortillas. Investigators found problems with refrigeration, water lines, and the close proximity of storage areas for potentially toxic substances such as insecticides and cleaning agents. All of these issues were shown to be incidental. The microorganisms identified during microbial testing also proved to be incidental to the event. Chemical analysis of food samples was negative except for the presence of methomyl in samples of salsa (methomyl is a pesticide restricted to use on field crops). Methomyl was also later detected in some urine, plasma, and vomitus samples. It was not detected in the ingredients used to make the salsa, suggesting contamination after preparation at the restaurant. Ultimately, two restaurant employees who were married to one another pled guilty to a charge of conspiracy to tamper with a consumer product. The wife was sentenced to 7 years in prison with a period of probation and ordered to pay restitution. The husband was sentenced to 10 years in prison plus probation and restitution. The poisoning was an act of revenge for the husband's termination by the restaurant a few months prior to the first poisoning incident.

Comments

The motivation for the poisoning was to disrupt or destroy the business of the restaurant. It is likely that the toxicant was selected because it was a well-known poison and was available to the perpetrators rather than based on any specific toxic characteristics of the substance.

Case: Toxic Iced Tea

In 2010, four adults were separately transported by an emergency responder from a restaurant in Dallas, Texas to a hospital emergency department. They were dining at separate times and in different groups over a period of about 4 h. Each individual had similar symptoms later associated with drinking iced tea from a self-serve urn in the restaurant. Symptoms included light-headedness, nausea, and diaphoresis. Two individuals were discharged from the hospital after evaluation and two were admitted for overnight observation. Samples of the iced tea from the restaurant and from containers provided by the patients at the emergency department were obtained for analysis. The initial toxicology screening of the samples was negative for approximately 100 different substances. Ultimately, testing identified sodium azide (sodium azide is an industrial chemical with toxicity similar to cyanide). This incident is currently under investigation and the mechanism by which the tea became contaminated with sodium azide remains unknown.

Comments

Sodium azide is found in research laboratories and has limited agricultural use as a pesticide. For many years, it was a major component of the explosive dispersion device in automobile airbag systems. There are no commercial applications for sodium azide that would explain its presence in a restaurant. The iced tea was accessible to all restaurant workers as well as restaurant patrons.

Case: Election Tampering

In 1981, a religious cult with an international following relocated its commune from India to a rural ranch in Oregon. The ranch was located in a county with a population of about 20,000. The new community was self-contained with its own water supply, sewage system, medical facilities, and small air strip. About 4000 cult members lived at the ranch. However, their expansion activities soon conflicted with the local zoning and planning requirements, and they often became involved in confrontations with the established community leaders. Legal disputes escalated until they reached the level of the State Attorney General. To resolve its political problems, the cult planned to take over the local government by winning the 1984 county elections. This was to be accomplished by causing residents to become ill and unable to vote. A plan was developed to expose the town community to *Salmonella* bacteria. As a test of their methodology prior to the actual election day, cult members contaminated the salad bars of 10 restaurants in the town adjacent to their commune. Unexpectedly, more than 700 of the town's 10,000 residents became ill and triggered a huge response from health officials and other investigative agencies. The *Salmonella* strain utilized by the cult was identified and traced to the clinical laboratory supply company that provided the commune's medical laboratory with supplies for antimicrobial sensitivity testing. From this laboratory testing culture, the cult produced large amounts of *Salmonella* using conventional laboratory equipment. The lengthy investigation culminated with the arrest of the cult senior leaders who were charged with multiple crimes that included poisoning, providing false information, immigration violations, attempted murder, product tampering, and wire tapping. Following the conviction, the leaders served prison sentences and then were deported. Remnants of this cult apparently still exist in India.

Comments

This is the largest act of bioterrorism that has occurred in the United States to date. It is interesting to note that among the most recent terrorist threats identified by the Department of Homeland Security are plans to contaminate salad bars and buffets in restaurants and hotels with lethal material. The toxicants mentioned most often in terrorist threats are ricin and cyanide.

Case: Vegetarian Stew

In 2008, an adult male arrived at a family gathering in a suburb of Maryland about an hour after the family had finished a late dinner. There were six adults at the gathering ranging in age from 38 to 80 years old. The latecomer immediately noticed considerable laughing and confusion within the group. Some members were complaining of dizziness and thirst, and others appeared to be hallucinating. One member was severely nauseated and vomited. The scene prompted a call to emergency medical responders who transported all the six to a hospital emergency department. On arrival, two individuals were unconscious and the others were significantly impaired mentally and unable to provide any useful information relative to the food that they had for dinner. They were all admitted to the hospital with five going to the intensive care unit. The symptoms of the group included tachycardia, mydriasis, aggression, incoherence, and hallucinations. Urine drug screening for commonly abused substances was negative. Eventually, it was determined that the meal consisted of a homemade stew and bread. The stew was primarily potatoes, flavored with garlic, onions, tomato, curry powder, and herbs from the garden. One herb was identified as mint but the identity of another was unknown. Investigators from several agencies visited the home and collected a variety of samples that included the remaining stew, its ingredients, and plant samples from areas around the home. The causative agents in the mass poisoning were determined to be atropine and scopolamine, and the source was jimson weed that was the unidentified garden herb added to the stew.

Comments

The more common poison situation with jimson weed involves adolescents and young adults who intentionally ingest the plant for its hallucinogenic effects. Unintentional ingestion as a food contaminate is uncommon and typically involves its mistaken identity for an edible plant. Jimson weed grows wild and is also used as an ornamental plant throughout the United States.

Case: Train Collision

In 2005, a train delivering chemicals to a textile plant in rural North Carolina stopped near the spur that ran from the main train line to the plant, and a train crew member manually moved a switch that would divert the train onto the side track to travel to the plant. The train then proceeded to the plant. It was late evening when the crew finished unloading and they decided to park the train overnight on the spur and spend the night in a nearby motel. The crew had informed the train dispatcher by radio of their initial departure from the main train line. They also radioed their plans to spend the night. The main track was then cleared for the passage of main line trains. About 7 h later, a train traveling on the main line approached the area of the connecting spur line. This train had two locomotives pulling 42 cars that included three tank cars loaded with 270 tons of liquefied compressed chlorine. This train, traveling at close to 50 miles per hour, was unexpectedly diverted to the spur line and struck the parked train. Eighteen train cars and three engines were derailed, the tank cars were badly damaged and one chlorine tank car was ruptured. Nine people died, more than 500 people were poisoned, and 5400 residents were evacuated. Unbeknownst to the dispatcher, the crew members of the parked train had not returned the switch from the main line to its original position before leaving for their overnight motel stay. Sixty tons of liquefied chlorine spilled from a damaged tanker and rapidly vaporized. Initial notification of local emergency units by local residents occurred within minutes. Fire and rescue responders were en route almost immediately. However, their approach to the crash was delayed for hours by the toxic levels of chlorine gas, which engulfed the crash area.

Comments

Many lessons were learned from this disaster relative to equipment, emergency response to disasters, and railroad operational procedures. The magnitude of this event involved millions of dollars in cleanup and compensation. Chlorine destroyed electrical wiring in all buildings in the vicinity of the crash. All vegetation, insects, and birds were killed. The textile plant eventually closed permanently. The community never recovered. The structures surrounding the crash site were embedded with debris and materials carried in the crashed train cars. The magnitude of the forces involved was exceedingly high. A similar incident of this type had occurred in a rural area of Texas less than a year earlier.

Case: Eight Examples of Poor Judgment

In 2011, eight individuals were poisoned by cyanide liberated from bamboo shoots during processing in an industrial food plant in Thailand. During processing, fresh bamboo shoots are sliced and stored in large vessels for 30 days for pickling before being packaged for sale. The vessels usually contain 20 tons of sliced bamboo shoots. In the plant on the day of this incident, worker 1 accidentally dropped something into a pickling vat and jumped in to retrieve the item. He immediately lost consciousness. Worker 2 then jumped into the vat to rescue him. He also became unconscious. Then workers 3, 4, and 5 jumped into the vat to rescue workers 1 and 2. They too rapidly lost consciousness. Then worker 6 jumped in with the same response. Then workers 7 and 8 joined the group of unconscious workers. The eight workers were soon removed from the vat by rescue workers and transported to the nearest hospital. Workers 4 and 7 died several hours after admission; the others recovered after a few days of hospital care. Only after the surviving patients were stable, was the diagnosis of cyanide poisoning made. Bamboo shoots contain a cyanogenic glycoside that liberates cyanide during processing, and over time cyanide accumulates in the poorly ventilated vats. This particular facility has 10 such vessels.

Comments

Cyanogenic glycosides are present in a number of food plants and seeds. Cyanide is released when fresh plant material is macerated in any fashion that allows plant-hydrolyzing enzymes to come in contact with the plant glycosides and produce cyanide. Cyanogenic glycosides are present in such common fruits as apples, apricots, cherries, peaches, and plums, particularly in the seeds. They are also present in lima beans, cassava, corn, and several nuts. Poisoning from these plant sources is extremely rare, likely due to the fact that they are not processed in such large quantities as are bamboo shoots. This case highlights the presence of cyanogenic glycosides in some plants. Perhaps of greater importance is the dramatic illustration of the potential lethality of poisonous gases and the danger of emotionally driven rescues. Some poisonous gases are lethal after a few breaths. Cyanide is one of these and hydrogen sulfide is another. It is ill advised for anybody to attempt a rescue of an unconscious individual in toxic environment without appropriate self-contained breathing equipment. Individuals commonly feel that they can hold their breath for a time that allows them to make a rescue. These situations can be encountered by first responders investigating suicides or other cases that involve gases in confined spaces such as automobiles.

Case: Poison-Facilitated Space Travel

In 1997, the communications center of the San Diego County Sheriff's Department received an anonymous call regarding a cult whose members had committed suicide a few days earlier in a mansion in a wealthy San Diego suburb. When the call was investigated, deputies found 39 bodies in various stages of decomposition. Most of the bodies were on bunk beds in several rooms. There were 21 females and 18 males ranging in age from 28 to 72 years. The decedents were all dressed in black shirts and tracksuit bottoms, and they had identical new sneakers. Most of the bodies were draped with a purple cloth. The residence was clean and items were arranged in an orderly fashion. The name of the cult was Heaven's Gate. The investigation that followed the discovery revealed that each member had ingested phenobarbital mixed with pudding or applesauce, drank vodka, and then covered their heads with plastic bags before lying down on their beds to die of asphyxiation. The suicides were carried out in three groupings spread over 3 successive days. The intention of the group was to leave their bodies on the Earth, whereas their souls would travel to a spacecraft that was being hidden at the time from Earth's view by the Hale–Bopp Comet. This spacecraft would then transport their souls to an existence beyond human. This plan had been developed over many years since the cult was founded. The Hale–Bopp Comet was only discovered in 1995 and reached its closest point from earth in 1997. The next appearance at this point is expected to be around the year 4385.

Comments

To date, there is no evidence to indicate whether or not the cult members were successful in targeting their souls to a higher level in the universe.

Case: Moscow Theater Siege

In 2002, Chechen terrorists seized a theater in Moscow during a performance attended by more than 800 people. The terrorists placed explosives throughout the theater and these were controlled by individual terrorists who held the detonators for the explosives in their hands. The terrorists demanded that the Russians withdraw from Chechnya or they would blow up the theater with all the audience hostages. The siege ended about 60 h later when the Russian Special Forces pumped an incapacitating gas into the theater through the ventilation system and strategically located holes drilled by the Russian troops. Thirty minutes after the gas was released, the troops stormed the theater. All 33 terrorists were killed, 129 hostages died from the gas, and no Russian troops were lost. About 750 hostages were saved. The exact composition of the gas has not been revealed, but it is known to have contained fentanyl or a derivative of fentanyl. The hostage deaths that occurred were likely due to the emergency medical personnel's lack of knowledge of the composition of the gas. This was the first use of a gas in this type of situation and its availability and tactical use was a military security issue. Moreover, it was employed in a situation identified only 2–3 days prior to its use.

Comments

The availability of the large amount of incapacitating gas and the methods and tactics employed in its use indicates considerable previous research and training with this approach for confronting situations involving large numbers of individuals. Variations of this scenario are likely to be encountered in the future.

Case: Ham and Cheese Sandwiches

In 1986, a 12-year-old girl having lunch at a school in Florida became nauseous and vomited. She indicated that the food she was eating tasted bad. Her meal was a prepackaged unit containing a ham-and-cheese sandwich, diced pears, chocolate milk, and apple juice. Soon more of the children having the same meal in the large dining hall began to have symptoms that included abdominal cramps, nausea, headache, dizziness, malaise, and

Table 38.1   Characteristics of Mass Psychogenic Illness

- Sudden focal onset of symptoms that spreads within a group
- Unusually rapid recovery
- Victims are often young females known to one another
- Usually there is an identifiable triggering stimulus such as a sound, visual observation, taste, or smell that suggests a toxic exposure.
- The illness usually spreads by line of sight or person-to-person communication
- Generally includes extraordinary anxiety
- There is usually an identifiable index case
- Symptoms have no plausible organic basis that can be identified by laboratory or medical evaluations

sore throat. In all, 63 of the 150 children in attendance developed this gastrointestinal illness. The staff suggested to the children that the food might have been contaminated and arranged for their evaluation in local hospital emergency departments. All symptoms subsided within 8 h and almost all the children were discharged from the hospital within 24 h. None of the teachers or other employees of the center had eaten the lunch meal and they did not become ill. Food samples were analyzed for the possible presence of pesticides, heavy metals, and bacterial contamination. The preparation, storage, and distribution of the meals were investigated. On the particular day of the incident, the supplier had prepared 3600 similar meals that were provided to 68 different facilities in the area. No complaints were identified in the other facilities. The conclusion of the extensive investigation carried out by law enforcement, medical, and public health agencies was that the incident was the result of mass sociogenic illness.

Comments

Many incidents similar to the one described have occurred in other regions of the United States, as well as in other countries. Indicators for mass psychogenic illness are listed in Table 38.1.

Case: Extra Strength Heroin

In 2015, more than 70 individuals on Chicago's west side overdosed on heroin during a single weekend in October. Most of these individuals were treated in hospitals and several died. The heroin used in these cases had been fortified with illegally manufactured fentanyl, which is much more potent than heroin. Users expecting to get a product containing 5%–10% heroin unexpectedly received material with a potency equivalent to about 90% heroin. Authorities traced the source of the heroin to two specific distribution areas in Chicago where arrests were made.

Comments

Previous episodes of overdoses and deaths due to fentanyl-laced heroin have occurred in Chicago and in other areas of the country. It seems that the high potency of fentanyl is unappreciated by many distributors who dilute it with other substances and then package it using makeshift utensils in crude facilities.

Case: Arsenic and Insurance Fraud

In 1998, a large number of people attending a small community festival near Osaka, Japan, became severely ill soon after eating a curried beef and rice meal prepared by neighborhood housewives. The most prominent initial symptoms were nausea and vomiting. Almost 70 people were taken to a dozen nearby hospitals. Forty-five people were admitted; 4 died within 24 h. It was determined that the food had been adulterated with arsenic trioxide. One of the housewives was arrested and tried for murder. She was 37 years old and the mother of four children. Her motives were believed to be anger due to alienation by the other housewives, and an insurance scam that would enable her to collect insurance on some of the individuals who died. The woman and her husband were also charged with several other counts of insurance fraud. She had a history of previous arsenic poisoning attempts for insurance. At the time of the curry poisoning, she had access to the arsenic from supplies maintained by her husband who was an exterminator. She was sentenced to death in 2002.

Comments

Group poisonings attract considerable community attention and undergo thorough investigation by the authorities. If the arsenic poisoning had involved one victim from a single food exposure, it could easily have gone unnoticed and the death attributed to natural causes.

Case: Drug Abuse and Infectious Disease

In 2014, an outbreak of HIV infections occurred in a small rural community in Indiana. Previously, there were less than five cases of HIV infections reported per year for this community with a population of about 4000. In a period of a year, more than 180 HIV infections were diagnosed and traced to syringe sharing during intravenous misuse of a commercial extended-release tablet formulation of oxymorphone (Opana ER). By tracing the contacts of the infected individuals, more than 500 others were identified as having a high risk for HIV infection. These included syringe-sharing abusers and sex partners. There was a comprehensive response to this outbreak that involved local, regional, and national law enforcement and public health agencies.

Comments

The community in this case had a long-standing problem with intravenous drug abusers prior to this incident. The outbreak highlights the vulnerability of drug abuse networks for the rapid transmission of HIV and other pathogens. This large outbreak was likely initiated by a single individual with HIV joining the established intravenous drug-abusing network in this small rural community.

References and Additional Reading

Anderson S, DeMent J, Banez Ocfemia C, Hunt DC: Outbreaks of methomyl poisoning caused by the intentional contamination of salsa at the Mi Ranchito Restaurant in Lenexa, KS. Topeka, KS: *Kansas Dept of Health and Environment Report*, April 12, 2011.

Atlas RM: Bioterrorism: From threat to reality. *Ann Rev Microbiol*, 56: 167–185, 2002.

Arcidiacono S, Brand JI, Coppenger W, Calder RA: Epidemiologic notes and reports: Mass sociogenic illness in a day-care center in Florida. *CDC MMWD*, 39: 301–304, 1990.

Bartholomew RE, Goode E: Mass delusions and hysterias: Highlights from the past millennium. *Skeptical Inquirer*, 24: 1–12, 2000.

Brooks M: Knockout gas: Chemical weapon in disguise. *New Scientist*, October 20, 2007.

Buchholz U, Mermin J, Rios R, Casagrande TL, Galey F, Lee M, Quarttrone A, Farrar J, Nagelkerke N, Werner SB: An outbreak of food-borne illness associated with methomyl-contaminated salt. *JAMA*, 288: 604–610, 2002.

Burklow TR, Yu CE, Madson JM: Industrial chemicals: Terrorist weapons of opportunity. *Pediatr Ann*, 32: 230–234, 2003.

Chang S, Lamm SH: Human health effects of sodium azide exposure: A literature review and analysis. *Int J Toxicol*, 22: 175–186, 2003.

Dunning AE, Oswalt JL: Train wreck and chlorine spill in Graniteville, South Carolina: Transportation effects and lessons in small-town capacity for no-notice evacuation. *J Transportation Res Board*, 2009: 130–135, 2007.

Dyson WE: *Terrorism: An Investigator's Handbook*, 4th ed. New York: Routledge, 2015.

Greenberg M, Hamilton R, Phillips S, McCluskey GJ: *Occupational, Industrial, and Environmental Toxicology*, 2nd ed. Maryland Heights, MO: Mosby, 2003.

Harbison RD, Bourgeois MM, Johnson GT: *Hamilton and Hardy's Industrial Toxicology*, 6th ed. Hoboken, NJ: Wiley, 2015.

Jones TF: Mass psychogenic illness: Role of the individual physician. *Am Fam Physician*, 62: 2649–2653, 2000.

Kaushik KS, Kadila K, Praharaj AK: Shooting up: The interface of microbial infections and drug abuse. *J Med Microbial*, 60: 408–422, 2011.

McFee RD, Leikin JB (Eds.): *Toxico-Terrorism: Emergency Response and Clinical Approach to Chemical, Biological, and Radiological Agents.* New York: McGraw-Hill, 2008.

Morgan BW, Skinner CG, Kleiman RJ, Geller RJ, Chang AS: Review of multi-person exposure calls to a regional poison control center. *West J Emerg Med*, 11: 291–293, 2010.

Nesser P: Single actor terrorism: Scope, characteristics and explanations. *PT*, 6: 1–9, 2012.

Nordt SP, Minns A, Carstairs S, Kreshak A, Campbell C, Tomaszweski C, Hayden SR, Clark RL, Joshua A, Ly BT: Mass sociogenic illness initially reported as carbon monoxide poisoning. *J Emerg Med*, 42: 159–161, 2012.

Peters PJ: HIV infection linked to injection use of oxymorphone in Indiana, 2014–2015. *N Engl J Med*, 375: 229–239, 2016.

Prat S, Reolle C, Saint-Martin P: Suicide pacts: Six cases and literature review. *J Forensic Sci*, 58: 1092–1098, 2013.

Riches JR, Read RW, Black RM, Cooper NJ, Timperley CM: Analysis of clothing and urine from Moscow theater siege casualties reveals carfentanil and remifentanil use. *J Anal Toxicol*, 36: 647–656, 2012.

Sang-A-Gad P, Guharat S, Wananukul W: A mass cyanide poisoning from pickling bamboo shoots. *Clin Toxicol*, 49: 834–839, 2011.

Simon JD: *Lone Wolf Terrorism: Understanding the Growing Threat.* Amherst, NY: Prometheus, 2013.

Schwarz ES, Wax PM, Kleinschmidt KC, Sharma K, Chung WM, Cantu G, Spargo E, Todd E: Multiple poisonings with sodium azide at a local restaurant. *J Emerg Med*, 46: 491–494, 2014.

Torok TJ, Tauxe RV, Wise RP, Livengood JR, Sokolow R, Mauvais S, Birkness KA, Skeels MR, Horan JM, Forster LR: A large community outbreak of salmonoellosis caused by internal contamination of restaurant salad bars. *JAMA*, 278: 389–395, 1997.

Tucker JB (Ed.): *Toxic Terror: Assessing Terrorist Use of Chemical and Biological Weapons.* Cambridge, MA: MIT Press, 2000.

Van Sickle D, Wenck MA, Belflower A, Drociuk D, Ferdinands J, Holguin F, Sevendsen E, Bretous L, Jankelevich S, Gibson JJ et al.: Acute health effects after exposure to chlorine gas released after a train derailment. *Am J Emerg Med*, 27: 1–7, 2009.

Appendices

Essential Vocabulary

This list is not a glossary. It is a list of terms that occur frequently in medical descriptions. Familiarity with these terms will be an investigative asset.

Anoxic	lack of oxygen
Anuric	absence of urine
Anticoagulant	prevents blood clotting
Antipyretic	reduces fever
Anxiolytic	controls anxiety (tranquilizer)
Arrhythmia	irregular heart beat
Aspiration	inhalation of secretions or foreign material into the lungs
Ataxia	staggering walk
Bradycardia	slow heartbeat
Cardiac Arrest	heart stops beating
Chronic	happening over a period of time
Cyanosis	blue tinge of nails, face, and toes from lack of oxygen in blood
Delirium	altered mental state (confusion, disorientation, memory problems, hallucinations)
Diaphoresis	sweating
Diuretic	increases urine output
Dyspnea	difficulty breathing
Electrolytes	acids, bases, and salts found in the blood
Emetic	induce vomiting
Fasciculation	twitching of muscles

Gastric Lavage	adding and removing liquids from the stomach in an attempt to remove poisons
Hepatic	refers to liver
Hyperglycemia	high blood sugar
Hypertension	high blood pressure
Hyperthermia	high body temperature
Hyperventilation	rapid breathing
Hypoglycemia	low blood sugar
Hypothermia	low body temperature
Hypotension	low blood pressure
Hypoxia	oxygen deficiency
Miosis	constricted pupils
Mydriasis	dilated pupils
Necrosis	death or decay of tissue
Oliguric	low urine production
Pharmacokinetics	characterize absorption, distribution, metabolism, and excretion of drugs and other potential toxicants
Pharmacology	study of the mechanism of action of drugs
Pneumonia	inflammation of the lungs from infection or aspiration of foreign material
Pulmonary Edema	fluid buildup in lungs
Rhabdomyolysis	breakdown of skeletal muscle tissue
Renal	refers to kidneys
Shock	critical condition caused by a sudden drop in systemic blood flow
Syncope	fainting
Systemic	affecting entire body
Tachycardia	fast heartbeat
Tachypneic	fast rate of respiration
Tinnitus	ringing in the ears
Toxidrome	constellation of signs and symptoms associated with a specific class of poisons
Vasoconstrictor	constricts (reduces diameter) blood vessels
Vasodilator	dilates blood vessels

Index of Case Studies

(*Continued*)

(Continued)

(*Continued*)

(Continued)

(Continued)

(Continued)

Index

Note: Page numbers followed by f and t refer to figures and tables respectively.